OXFORD ENGLISH MONOGRAPHS

General Editors

Irish Modernism and the Politics of Sexual Health

LLOYD (MEADHBH) HOUSTON

OXFORD
UNIVERSITY PRESS

Great Clarendon Street, Oxford, OX2 6DP,
United Kingdom

Oxford University Press is a department of the University of Oxford.
It furthers the University's objective of excellence in research, scholarship,
and education by publishing worldwide. Oxford is a registered trade mark of
Oxford University Press in the UK and in certain other countries

First Edition published in 2023

Impression: 1

Published in the United States of America by Oxford University Press
198 Madison Avenue, New York, NY 10016, United States of America

British Library Cataloguing in Publication Data
Data available

Library of Congress Control Number: 2022944581

ISBN 978–0–19–288949–2

DOI: 10.1093/oso/9780192889492.001.0001

Printed and bound in the UK by
TJ Books Limited

Acknowledgements

I have incurred many debts of gratitude, personal and professional, in the writing of this book and the doctoral thesis from which it grew. There is not enough space to do full justice to them all here.

I could not have undertaken the research which underpins this monograph without the support of the Hertford College Faculty of English DPhil Scholarship in Irish Literature in English and the Clarendon Fund. I wish to thank these bodies for their generosity. I also wish to express my appreciation to the staff of the Bodleian Libraries, Oxford; the British Library; the Wellcome Collection, London; the National Library of Ireland; and the Royal College of Physicians of Ireland for their guidance and assistance.

I could not have begun the doctoral project out of which this book emerged without the input of those with whom I first discussed the ideas it explores. My sincere thanks to Sophie Ratcliffe for taking my incoherent undergraduate thoughts on Joyce, Beckett, and sexual health and wrestling them into order; to Michelle Kelly, for teaching me how to analyse the relationship between literature and the law; and to Jeri Johnson, for her peerless knowledge of all things Joycean and her keen editorial eye. I could not have brought my doctoral project to a conclusion without the input of those who assessed it across its development. My thanks, again, to Sophie and Jeri for their generous feedback during my Transfer of Status, to Sally Shuttleworth and Kate McLoughlin for their insightful comments during my Confirmation of Status, and to Emilie Morin and Kirsten Shepherd-Barr for examining the finished thesis with care and precision, and for supporting and guiding me as I revised it for publication.

Above all, I could not have completed the thesis or this book without the knowledge, insight, and profound generosity of David Dwan. I consider myself truly fortunate to have had such a rigorous, thoughtful, and diligent supervisor, and to have such an exacting and encouraging mentor.

The life of a doctoral student and an early-career researcher can be an isolating one. Many individuals, institutions, and groups have ensured that this has not been the case for me. I am grateful to my DPhil cohort for their companionship and feedback on work in-progress. Oxford's Modern and Contemporary Literature Seminar provided a stimulating and friendly environment in which to engage with my field of study throughout my time at Oxford. I offer my sincere thanks to all those who presented and attended during my tenure as convenor, particularly Lilian and Talitha, whose loyal company greatly enriched our sessions. I am indebted to the Irish Studies community for their personal and professional generosity. Particular thanks to colleagues at the Oxford Seminar in Irish History, the IES Irish Studies Seminar at the University of London, the Vienna Centre for Irish Studies, the Long Room Hub at Trinity College, Dublin, and the British Association for Irish Studies. My thanks also to friends and associates in Joyce Studies, Beckett Studies, and Modernist Studies, and at Goldsmiths, the University of West London, and Fordham University's London Centre for their collegiality, wit, and insight. Hertford College provided a warm and welcoming environment in which to work and relax, and I will cherish the friendships I have made there among its staff and students. I am grateful to Brasenose College HCR for the companionship I have enjoyed there, and to Sos Eltis for her mentorship and enthusiasm. From the moment I arrived in Oxford, Lady Margaret Hall has provided me with support, encouragement, and a sense of belonging. My profound thanks to Helen, Sophie, Christine, Jo, Esther, and Alan for all they have done for me.

Finally, my thanks go to those who have aided me in the process of revising my thesis for publication and seeing the present volume into print. I am grateful to my examiners and the Oxford English Monographs Committee for recommending my thesis for publication, to Ushashi Dasgupta, Emilia Clarke, and Hannah Simpson for their advice on preparing the book proposal, to my readers for their care in reviewing the manuscript, and to Jacqueline Norton, Karen Raith, Ellie Collins, and Emma Varley at Oxford University Press for their editorial oversight and guidance. The manuscript was finalized while I was Banting Postdoctoral Fellow in English at the University of Alberta. I thank the Social Sciences and Humanities Research Council and the Canadian Institute of Health Research for their investment in my work and Robert Brazeau for his advocacy, guidance, and friendship.

I dedicate the present volume to my family, who taught me the value of hard work and a good education; to the chosen family I found while writing it, who taught me about acceptance and belonging; and to Karl for being the most loyal and inspiring friend that anyone could ask for.

Elements of the present monograph first appeared in the following articles and chapters:

'Survival of the Unfittest: Yeats, Synge, and the Rhetoric of Health,' in *Irish Modernisms: Gaps, Conjectures, Possibilities*, edited by Paul Fagan, John Greaney, and Tamara Radak (Bloomsbury Academic, 2021), 115–28.

'"Veni, V.D., Vici": Flann O'Brien, Sexual Health, and the Literature of Exhaustion,' in *Flann O'Brien: Gallows Humour*, edited by Ruben Borg and Paul Fagan (Cork: Cork University Press, 2020), 146–62.

'Beckett in the Dock: Sexuality, Censorship, and the Sinclair Trial,' *Estudios Irlandeses*, 14.2 (October 2019), Samuel Beckett and Biopolitics, Special Issue, edited by Seán Kennedy, 21–37.

'"Sterilization of the mind and apotheosis of the litter": Beckett, Censorship, and Fertility,' *Review of English Studies* 69.290 (June 2018), 546–64.

'A Portrait of the Chief as a General Paralytic: Rhetorics of Sexual Pathology in the Parnell Split,' *Irish Studies Review* 25.4 (2017), 472–92.

I am grateful to my editors and publishers for their permission to reproduce and augment this material here.

Contents

Introduction

Irish Modernism and the Politics of Sexual Health

When W. B. Yeats wished to convey the vitriolic intensity of the 'riots' which greeted the opening run of J. M. Synge's *The Playboy of the Western World* (1907) and signal the perceived hypocrisy of those who incited them, he recounted an anecdote that centred on questions of national identity and sexual health:

> As I stood there watching, knowing well that I saw the dissolution of a school of patriotism that held sway over my youth, Synge came and stood beside me, and said, 'A young doctor has just told me that he can hardly keep himself from jumping on to a seat, and pointing out in that howling mob those whom he is treating for venereal disease.'[1]

The irony Yeats sought to emphasize in his tale is clear enough: while the representatives of Sinn Féin [we ourselves] and Irish Ireland were busy disingenuously excoriating the Abbey for its perceived 'libel' upon the physical and moral purity of 'Irish peasant men' and 'Irish peasant girlhood', the theatre's supporters restrained themselves from revealing an image of Irish sexual life far more damning than anything Synge had brought to the stage.[2] However, the division the anecdote posits between the sober restraint of the Abbey's supporters and the hysterical prudery of the nationalists is not as clear-cut or as sustainable as Yeats would perhaps have hoped. On the one hand, by emphasizing the professional credentials of the young doctor who had provided the damning diagnosis, Yeats appears to align Synge and the Abbey with the amoral, apolitical, and dispassionate rationalism which medicine had made its disciplinary preserve since at least the eighteenth

---

[1] W. B. Yeats, *Early Essays. The Collected Works of W.B. Yeats, Vol. IV*, ed. Richard J. Finneran and George Mills Harper (New York: Scribner, 2007), 227.
[2] 'Abbey Theatre – "The Playboy of the Western World"', *Freeman's Journal and National Press*, 28 January 1907, 10, reproduced in James Kilroy, *The 'Playboy' Riots* (Dublin: Dolmen Press, 1971), 7.

Irish Modernism and the Politics of Sexual Health. Lloyd (Meadhbh) Houston, Oxford University Press.
© Lloyd (Meadhbh) Houston 2023. DOI: 10.1093/oso/9780192889492.003.0001

century, in implied antithesis to the irrational, intemperate, and partisan 'howling' of the nationalist 'mob' he wishes to censure. On the other hand, by using the doctor's diagnosis to present those who opposed the *Playboy* as a sexually incontinent and ethically compromised gaggle of hypocrites, Yeats reveals himself to be, arguably, no less partisan, moralizing, or rhetorically extreme than those whom he sought to critique. Indeed, in deploying a medicalized and politicized conception of sex to attack the rioters, Yeats was, in fact, replicating the very rhetorical strategy the nationalist press had employed to decry the 'extraordinary decadence' and 'neurotic atmosphere' of Synge's play and its 'degenerate' celebration of 'unnatural lust'.[3] For both groups, sexual health provided a notionally extra-moral rhetoric through which to naturalize a normative critique of the other as a threat to the physical and cultural well-being of Ireland and its population. As this example illustrates, Irish culture's engagement with questions of sexual health in the early twentieth century was seldom straightforward, often contentious, and almost always political. The aim of this book is to map this engagement by exploring the politicized role of sexual health as a concept, discourse, and subject of debate within what might be broadly termed Irish modernism.

Whether it be George Moore's caustic depiction of an increasingly 'celibate' and 'empty' Ireland in *The Untilled Field* (1903), James Joyce's playfully self-indicting critique of English 'spyhilisation' in *Ulysses* (1922), or Kate O'Brien's excoriation of those leaders who would tell their populations 'how they are to breed' in *Pray for the Wanderer* (1938), there are few major or minor texts in the Irish modernist canon which do not explicitly or implicitly dramatize debates and dilemmas in the field of sexual health.[4] However, notwithstanding this apparent centrality, no study as yet exists which assesses the significance of these debates for Irish modernism in a systematic manner. *Irish Modernism and the Politics of Sexual Health* addresses this lacuna by exploring the ways in which authors, politicians, and activists in nineteenth- and twentieth-century Ireland harnessed debates over sexual health to envisage competing models of Irish identity, culture, and political community. In doing so, it takes its impetus from three major developments in recent scholarship on modernism, Ireland, and the history

---

[3] 'Avis', 'The Playboys in the Abbey,' *The Leader*, 2 February 1907, 387–8, reproduced in Kilroy, *The "Playboy" Riots*, 70; *Sinn Féin*, 2 February 1907, 2, reproduced in Kilroy, 67.

[4] George Moore, *The Untilled Field*, ed. Richard Allen Cave (Gerrards Cross: Colin Smythe, 2000), 223; James Joyce, *Ulysses*, ed. Hans Gabler (New York: Vintage, 1986), 266; Kate O'Brien, *Pray for the Wanderer* (London: Penguin, 1951), 29.

of sexuality. The first is the emergence of the 'New Modernist Studies' and the increasing attention it has paid to the relationship between modernist culture and the medicalized and politicized models of sex and sexuality which emerged in the late nineteenth and early twentieth centuries. The second is the emergence of Irish Modernist Studies as a vibrant sub-field of Modernist Studies and Irish Studies, and the increasing attention it has paid to the significance of Irish social, cultural, and political history for many major and minor modernist texts. The third is the emergence of a growing body of scholarship on the history of sexuality and the social history of medicine in Ireland, and the pressure it has exerted on exceptionalist narratives of Irish piety, purity, and repression. Bringing together perspectives and insights from these three overlapping areas of scholarly activity, *Irish Modernism and the Politics of Sexual Health* offers not only a fresh and deeply contextualized reading of the emergence and development of Irish modernism but a more nuanced account of the medicalization and politicization of sex in nineteenth- and twentieth-century Irish culture. In order to offer this account and to understand the implications of the three critical developments I have just outlined for this study, it is necessary to answer three overlapping questions: What was 'sexual health' in the late nineteenth and early twentieth centuries? How did it come to be politicized? And what challenges does it present to analysis in the context of both Ireland and modernism?

Sexual Health: Emergence and Politicization

While the term itself was not coined until 1975, the discursive formations and 'styles of reasoning' which rendered the concept of 'sexual health' conceivable and articulable in a European cultural context took shape over a century before.[5] As Yeats's remarks reflect, though both sex and health were, of course, subject to normative regulation long before the nineteenth century, in the course of that century, a rapid proliferation of discourses

---

[5] I derive the term 'styles of reasoning' from Arnold I. Davidson's analysis of the emergence of sexuality, in which he explores the circumstances under which claims about 'sexuality' and 'perversions' became epistemologically viable candidates for the status of 'truth' or 'falsehood'. Arnold I. Davidson, *The Emergence of Sexuality: Historical Epistemology and the Formation of Concepts* (Cambridge, Mass: Harvard University Press, 2001), chaps. 1 and 2; Alain Giami, 'Sexual Health: The Emergence, Development, and Diversity of a Concept,' *Annual Review of Sex Research* 13, no. 1 (2002): 1–35; Anne R. Hanley, 'Histories of "a loathsome disease": Sexual Health in Modern Britain,' *History Compass* 20.3 (March 2022), 1–16.

concerning sex, health, and their interrelation occurred across Europe and the United States, such that it became virtually impossible to conceptualize one without reference to the other.[6] Where once sex had been the subject of moral regulation, typically through institutional religion, in this emergent *scientia sexualis* [science of sex], it came to constitute 'an extremely unstable pathological field' which required categorization, diagnosis, and therapeutic intervention from both the medical profession and the state.[7] In tandem with this transformation, 'health' underwent a similar expansion of its regulatory purview, shifting from a perceived concern with the well-being of individuals, to a focus on statistically calibrated standards of 'normality' and 'abnormality', calculated at the level of 'group', 'population', or 'race'.[8] As Michel Foucault summarizes, under such circumstances:

> Medicine [was no longer] confined to a body of techniques for curing ills and of the knowledge that they require; it […] also embrace[d] a know-ledge of *healthy man*, that is, a study of *non-sick man* and a definition of the *model man*. In the ordering of human existence it assume[d] a normative posture, which authorize[d] it not only to distribute advice as to healthy life, but also to dictate the standards for physical and moral relations of the individual and of the society in which [they live].[9]

In Foucault's view, sex was particularly ripe for this sort of medicalization because, through its combination of intense individual 'corporeality' and its

---

[6] Significant accounts of this shift include Michel Foucault, *The History of Sexuality, 1: The Will to Knowledge* (New York: Pantheon Books, 1978), secs. 2 and 3; Jeffrey Weeks, *Sex, Politics, and Society: The Regulation of Sexuality Since 1800*, Third Edition (London: Pearson, 2012), chap. 8; Davidson, *The Emergence of Sexuality*, chaps. 1–3; Anna Clark, *Desire: A History of European Sexuality*, Second Edition (Abingdon: Routledge, 2019), chaps. 7–9; Chiara Beccalossi, 'Sex, Medicine, Disease: From Reproduction to Sexuality,' in *A Cultural History of Sexuality in the Age of Empire*, ed. Chiara Beccalossi and Ivan Crozier (Oxford: Berg, 2011), 101–22; Alain Giami, 'Sex, Medicine, and Disease,' in *A Cultural History of Sexuality in the Modern Age*, ed. Gert Hekma (Oxford: Berg, 2011), 127–48.

[7] Foucault, *The History of Sexuality, 1: The Will to Knowledge*: 68; 67.

[8] Major statements on this 'medicalization' of European and American culture include Michel Foucault, *The Birth of the Clinic: An Archaeology of Medical Perception*, trans. A. M. Sheridan (London: Routledge, 2003), 33–6; Michel Foucault, Valerio Marchetti, and Graham Burchell, *Abnormal: Lectures at the Collège de France, 1974–1975* (London: Verso, 2003); Thomas Szasz, *The Medicalization of Everyday Life: Selected Essays* (Syracuse, New York: Syracuse University Press, 2007), sec. 1; Peter Conrad and Joseph W. Schneider, *Deviance and Medicalization: From Badness to Sickness*, Expanded ed (Philadelphia: Temple University Press, 1992), chaps. 1, 2, and 9; Peter Conrad, *The Medicalization of Society: On the Transformation of Human Conditions into Treatable Disorders* (Baltimore: Johns Hopkins University Press, 2007), chap. 1.

[9] Foucault, *The Birth of the Clinic: An Archaeology of Medical Perception*, 34.

'procreative effects', it constituted a privileged point of intersection between the 'body'—conceived as a locus of hygiene and discipline—and the 'population'—conceived as a 'multiple unity' subject to broader biological processes which determine its overall 'health'.[10] In such a model, 'undisciplined and irregular' sexual conduct is understood to have effects at two levels: at the level of the body, where it is 'sanctioned by all the individual diseases that the sexual debauchee brings' upon themselves, and, because 'anyone who has been sexually debauched is assumed to have a heredity', also at the level of the population, where both this pathology and the 'debauched' or 'perverted' impulses which brought it about will reiterate themselves for generations.[11] For Foucault, sexuality—the discursive and conceptual formation through which the 'truth' of an individual's identity is held to reside in their sexual preferences and behaviour—comes into being 'at the point where body and population meet' and, as such, becomes a matter not only for 'discipline' but for 'regularization.'[12] As Alain Giami suggests, the concept of 'sexual health'—a further, regulatory extension of 'sexuality'—emerges from this charged point of contact and the medical, social, and political processes of discipline and regularization Foucault envisages.[13] Sexual health thus comprises both an ideal state or condition and a set of strategies of discipline and regulation through which that condition is to be brought about at both the level of the individual and the population.

As Foucault and Giami's remarks indicate, my first two questions are strongly interimplicated. The consolidation of sexual health as a meaningful concept in the late nineteenth and early twentieth centuries coincided with a shift towards an increasingly interventionist conception of the state and a greatly expanded sense of its rights and responsibilities with regards to the well-being of its citizens. In Britain and Ireland, a poor economic climate, under-performance in the Second Anglo-Boer War (1899–1902), and the gloomy findings of the Inter-Departmental Committee on Physical Deterioration (1903–1904) conspired to generate an atmosphere in which greater state welfare provision and more direct government involvement in the private lives of British and Irish citizens were deemed necessary in order to vouchsafe 'national efficiency' and reverse the current of perceived

[10] Michel Foucault et al., *Society Must Be Defended: Lectures at the Collège de France, 1975-1976*, 1st ed (New York: Picador, 2003), 251–2.
[11] Ibid., 252. [12] Ibid., 251–2.
[13] Giami, 'Sexual Health: The Emergence, Development, and Diversity of a Concept,' 3–6; Giami, 'Sex, Medicine, and Disease,' 128–36.

degeneration.[14] This 'new liberal' shift was particularly pronounced in the areas of sex and health.[15] In line with the recommendations of the Royal Commission on Venereal Diseases (1913–1916), Local Government Boards across Britain and Ireland introduced state-funded sexual health clinics, which provided sufferers with confidential diagnosis and treatment, free at the point of delivery.[16] By 1924, some TDs could be found calling for the 'strict segregation' of patients with venereal diseases in Irish public hospitals for both 'moral' and 'health' reasons.[17] In the United States, where popular and medical opinion alike regarded the burgeoning migrant population as a growing threat to the nation's physical and moral integrity, compulsory medical inspections were introduced for all arriving migrants, with the 1891 Immigration Act mandating that all those who were discovered to be 'suffering from a loathsome or dangerous contagious disease' be barred entry.[18] Evidence of gonorrhoea and especially syphilis—perhaps the most

[14] Ina Zweiniger-Bargielowska, *Managing the Body* (Oxford: Oxford University Press, 2010), chap. 2; Martin Pugh, *State and Society: A Social and Political History of Britain Since 1870*, Fifth edition (London: Bloomsbury Academic, 2017), chap. 7.

[15] Diane Paul, 'Eugenics and the Left,' *Journal of the History of Ideas* 45, no. 4 (October 1984): 567–90; Michael Freeden, *The New Liberalism: An Ideology of Social Reform* (Oxford: Oxford University Press, 1986); Leo Lucassen, 'A Brave New World: The Left, Social Engineering, and Eugenics in Twentieth-Century Europe,' *International Review of Social History* 55, no. 2 (August 2010): 265–96.

[16] David Evans, 'Tackling the "Hideous Scourge": The Creation of the Venereal Disease Treatment Centres in Early Twentieth-Century Britain,' *Social History of Medicine* 5, no. 3 (1992): 413–33; Roger Davidson, *Dangerous Liaisons: A Social History of Venereal Diseases in Twentieth-Century Scotland* (Amsterdam: Brill|Rodopi, 2000); Susannah Riordan, 'Venereal Disease in the Irish Free State: The Politics of Public Health,' *Irish Historical Studies* 35, no. 139 (2007): 345–64; Philip Howell, 'The Politics of Prostitution and the Politics of Public Health in the Irish Free State: A Response to Susannah Riordan,' *Irish Historical Studies* 35, no. 140 (November 2007): 541–52; Susannah Riordan, '"Probable Source of Infection": The Limitations of Venereal Disease Policy, 1943–1951,' in *Gender and Medicine in Ireland, 1700–1950*, ed. Margaret H. Preston and Margaret Ó hÓgartaigh (Syracuse, New York: Syracuse University Press, 2012), 203–20; Leanne McCormick, 'Prophylactics and Prejudice: Venereal Diseases in Northern Ireland During the Second World War,' in *Gender and Medicine in Ireland, 1700–1950*, ed. Margaret H. Preston and Margaret Ó hÓgartaigh (Syracuse, New York: Syracuse University Press, 2012), 221–34.

[17] 'Dáil in Committee—Local Government Bill, 1924 (Third Stage) Resumed,' Pub. L. No. 9.13 (1924), https://www.oireachtas.ie/en/debates/debate/dail/1924-11-19/8/.

[18] *Immigration Act of 1891*, 26 Stat. 1084 (Chapter 551) https://govtrackus.s3.amazonaws.com/legislink/pdf/stat/26/STATUTE-26-Pg1084a.pdf. For analyses of United States immigration policy and regimes of social and sexual hygiene, see Alan M. Kraut, *Silent Travelers: Germs, Genes, and the "Immigrant Menace"* (Baltimore: Johns Hopkins University Press, 1995); Amy L. Fairchild, *Science at the Borders: Immigrant Medical Inspection and the Shaping of the Modern Industrial Labor Force* (Baltimore: Johns Hopkins University Press, 2003); Allan M. Brandt, *No Magic Bullet: A Social History of Venereal Disease in the United States Since 1880*, 35th Anniversary Edition (Oxford: Oxford University Press, 2020), chap. 1.

'loathsome' disease of all in the eyes of contemporary public health officials—was grounds for immediate exclusion.[19] Britain's 1905 Aliens Act instituted similar procedures, but, with the class-inflected caveat that only those who travelled in steerage should be subjected to a full medical examination.[20] These measures were supplemented in the United States by explicitly racialized social hygiene programmes such as the infamous 'Tuskegee Study of Untreated Syphilis in the Negro Male' (1932–1972), which saw the United States Public Health Service deliberately neglect to provide adequate advice and treatment to a cohort of 399 syphilitic African American men in order to examine the disease's physiological impact on the country's black population.[21] State-sponsored 'sex education' was advocated as an important preventative adjunct to these measures and, under a variety of euphemistic soubriquets, was introduced to American and European school curricula from the 1910s, often in the face of staunch opposition from parents, the clergy, and social purity groups.[22] Birth control advocates such as Marie Stopes and Margaret Sanger pressured public officials to follow their lead in establishing state-funded centres to provide advice and contraceptives, particularly to working-class women, even as France, Italy, and Ireland passed pro-natalist censorship legislation, implicitly committing

[19] Alison Bateman-House and Amy L. Fairchild, 'Medical Examination of Immigrants at Ellis Island,' *AMA Journal of Ethics* 10, no. 4 (April 2008): 235–41, 235.
[20] The 1905 Act infamously defined 'immigrant' as 'an alien steerage passenger', implicitly exempting those who travelled first- and second-class from its key stipulations, though its scope was greatly expanded in 1920. *Aliens Act, 1905*. 5 Edw. 7. CH. 13. S. 8(1). https://www.legislation.gov.uk/ukpga/1905/13/pdfs/ukpga_19050013_en.pdf; Krista Maglen, *The English System: Quarantine, Immigration and the Making of a Port Sanitary Zone* (Manchester: Manchester University Press, 2014), chap. 5; Becky Taylor, 'Immigration, Statecraft and Public Health: The 1920 Aliens Order, Medical Examinations and the Limitations of the State in England,' *Social History of Medicine* 29, no. 3 (August 2016): 512–33.
[21] The complex circumstances which ultimately resulted in the profoundly unethical Study resist easy summary. For a succinct but nuanced overview of the Study's origins, operation, and aftermath, see James H. Jones, 'The Tuskegee Syphilis Experiment,' in *The Oxford Textbook of Clinical Research Ethics*, ed. Ezekiel J. Emanuel et al. (Oxford: Oxford University Press, 2010), 86–96. For more detailed considerations of the Study and its social, political, and ethical implications, see James H. Jones, *Bad Blood: The Tuskegee Syphilis Experiment*, New and Expanded (New York: Free Press, 1993); Fred D. Gray, *The Tuskegee Syphilis Study: The Real Story and Beyond* (Montgomery: New South Books, 1998); Susan Reverby, ed., *Tuskegee's Truths: Rethinking the Tuskegee Syphilis Study* (Chapel Hill: University of North Carolina Press, 2000); Susan M. Reverby, *Examining Tuskegee: The Infamous Syphilis Study and Its Legacy* (Chapel Hill: University of North Carolina Press, 2013).
[22] Roy Porter and Lesley A. Hall, *The Facts of Life: The Creation of Sexual Knowledge in Britain, 1650–1950* (New Haven: Yale University Press, 1995), chap. 10; Robin E. Jensen, *Dirty Words: The Rhetoric of Public Sex Education, 1870–1924* (Urbana: University of Illinois Press, 2010); Jonathan Zimmerman, *Too Hot to Handle: A Global History of Sex Education* (Princeton: Princeton University Press, 2015), chap. 1.

the state to the cause of raising the flagging birth-rate.[23] At the same time, eugenicists lobbied local and national governments across Europe and North America to introduce measures to segregate, sterilize, and, in extreme cases, exterminate the 'feeble-minded', the 'criminally insane', and other 'social problem' groups whose reproduction was deemed potentially detrimental to the health of the nation.[24] While such legislative efforts were ultimately unsuccessful in Britain, eugenic sterilization policies were introduced in the United States, Canada, Scandinavia, and, most infamously, Nazi Germany.[25] As late as 1946, John Maynard Keynes, one of the intellectual architects of the modern welfare state and a longstanding member of the British Eugenics Society, Malthusian League, and Society for Constructive Birth Control and Racial Progress, could be found lauding eugenics as the 'most important, significant and, [...] *genuine* branch of sociology' in existence.[26] Not everyone was so sanguine. G. K. Chesterton

[23] Angus McLaren, *A History of Contraception: From Antiquity to the Present Day* (Oxford: Blackwell, 1990), chap. 6; Angus McLaren, *Twentieth-Century Sexuality: A History* (Oxford: Blackwell, 1999), chap. 4; John Horgan, 'Saving Us from Ourselves: Contraception, Censorship and the 'Evil Literature' Controversy of 1926,' *Irish Communications Review* 5 (1995): 61–7; Maria Sophia Quine, *Population Politics in Twentieth-Century Europe: Fascist Dictatorships and Liberal Democracies* (London: Routledge, 1996); Richard A. Soloway, *Demography and Degeneration: Eugenics and the Declining Birthrate in Twentieth-Century Britain*, 3rd ed. (Chapel Hill: University of North Carolina Press, 2001), chaps. 5 and 8; Senia Pašeta, 'Censorship and Its Critics in the Irish Free State, 1922–1932,' *Past & Present* 232, no. 1 (2003): 193–218; Diarmaid Ferriter, *Occasions of Sin: Sex and Society in Modern Ireland* (London: Profile Books, 2009), 185–99.

[24] Daniel J. Kevles, *In the Name of Eugenics: Genetics and the Uses of Human Heredity* (New York: Knopf, 1985); Mark B. Adams, ed., *The Wellborn Science: Eugenics in Germany, France, Brazil, and Russia* (New York: Oxford University Press, 1990); Soloway, *Demography and Degeneration*; Marius Turda, *Modernism and Eugenics* (Basingstoke: Palgrave Macmillan, 2010); Alison Bashford and Philippa Levine, eds., *The Oxford Handbook of the History of Eugenics* (Oxford: Oxford University Press, 2010).

[25] John Macnicol, 'Eugenics and the Campaign for Voluntary Sterilization in Britain Between the Wars,' *Social History of Medicine* 2, no. 2 (1989): 147–69; John Macnicol, 'The Voluntary Sterilization Campaign in Britain, 1918-39,' *Journal of the History of Sexuality* 2, no. 3 (January 1992): 422–38; Gunnar Broberg and Nils Roll-Hansen, eds., *Eugenics and the Welfare State: Sterilization Policy in Denmark, Sweden, Norway, and Finland* (East Lansing: Michigan State University Press, 1996); Desmond King, *In the Name of Liberalism: Illiberal Social Policy in the USA and Britain* (Oxford: Oxford University Press, 1999), pt. 2; A. Dirk Moses and Dan Stone, 'Eugenics and Genocide,' in *The Oxford Handbook of the History of Eugenics*, ed. Alison Bashford and Philippa Levine (Oxford: Oxford University Press, 2010), 192–209; Angus McLaren, *Our Own Master Race: Eugenics in Canada, 1885–1945*, Repr. (Toronto: University of Toronto Press, 2014), chaps. 5 and 6.

[26] Emphasis in original. John Maynard Keynes and Alexander Carr-Saunders, 'The Galton Lecture, 1946: Presentation of the Society's Gold Medal,' *Eugenics Review* 38, no. 1 (1946): 40. For accounts of Keynes's engagement with eugenics and its bearing on his social and economic thought, see Thomas C. Leonard, 'Retrospectives: Eugenics and Economics in the Progressive Era,' *Journal of Economic Perspectives* 19, no. 4 (November 2005): 207–24; David Roth Singerman, 'Keynesian Eugenics and the Goodness of the World,' *Journal of British Studies*

was quick to discern in the increasingly interventionist attitude of the emergent welfare state a nascent 'tyranny' in which even the 'sanctuary of sex' would be exposed to the regulatory influence of the 'hygienic logician' and the worst 'extravagances of Eugenics'.[27] In Chesterton's view, as soon as the state declared its intention to 'safeguard the health of the community', its interference in the realm of sex was virtually guaranteed: 'If a man's personal health is a public concern, his most private acts are *more* public than his most public acts.'[28] For good or ill, by the mid-twentieth century the politicization of sex and its relationship to questions of individual and public health was a well-established fact of life in Europe and North America.

As I have indicated, in recent years, the 'New Modernist Studies' has come to position modernism, particularly in its literary manifestations, as especially responsive to this medicalization and politicization of sex.[29] Breaking with traditional conceptions of modernism as a uniformly hostile critique of technical modernity in which scientific concepts were invoked in purely metaphorical form, Tim Armstrong has explored the ways in which modernists eagerly responded to and participated in scientific and medical efforts to 'regulate' and 'clarify' the body.[30] For Armstrong, modernism is 'characterized by a desire to *intervene* in the body' and 'render it part of modernity' inspired by a growing perception that the body comprised an obscure, but ultimately knowable, 'complex of different biomechanical systems'.[31] As a wide range of recent studies have illustrated, sex and sexuality proved a particularly energetic area for such 'intervention'. Indeed, in the view of figures such as Heike Bauer, A. K. Schaffner, and Paul Peppis, the stylistic, discursive, and conceptual exchanges between literary modernism and emergent scientific and medical fields such as sexology were so extensive as to render them mutual participants in the emergence of a 'sexual modernism' in which generic and disciplinary divisions between the 'literary' and

---

55, no. 3 (July 2016): 538–65; Phillip W Magness and Sean J Hernandez, 'The Economic Eugenicism of John Maynard Keynes,' *Journal of Markets and Morality* 20, no. 1 (Spring 2017): 79–100.
[27] G. K. Chesterton, *Eugenics and Other Evils* (London: Cassell and Company, 1922), 151; 152; 148.
[28] Ibid., 153.
[29] For an overview of the 'New Modernist Studies' and the processes of conceptual, chronological, and archival 'expansion' by which it has been characterized, see Douglas Mao and Rebecca L. Walkowitz, 'The New Modernist Studies,' *PMLA* 123, no. 3 (May 2008): 737–48.
[30] Emphasis in original. Tim Armstrong, *Modernism, Technology, and the Body: A Cultural Study* (Cambridge: Cambridge University Press, 1998), 5.
[31] Ibid 6; 2.

'scientific' are often placed under erasure.[32] In such readings, literary modernism emerges as the vibrant interlocutor of a wide range of fields, theories, and specialisms which took the relationship between sex and health as their focus in the late nineteenth and early twentieth centuries, a list which includes venereology (the study, diagnosis, and treatment of venereal diseases);[33] sexology (the study and categorization of human sexuality in both its 'normal' and 'pathological' manifestations);[34] psychiatry and psychology (particularly where they overlap with sexology);[35] ethnography (particularly in its concern with the sexual characteristics, practices, and beliefs of 'primitive' peoples and 'alien' cultures);[36] demography (particularly in its concern with rates of birth and fertility);[37] evolutionary science and degeneration theory (particularly in their concern with natural and artificial

---

[32] Heike Bauer, *English Literary Sexology: Translations of Inversion, 1860–1930* (Basingstoke: Palgrave Macmillan, 2009), 8; Anna Katharina Schaffner, 'Fiction as Evidence: On the Uses of Literature in Nineteenth-Century Sexological Discourse,' *Comparative Literature Studies* 48, no. 2 (2011): 165–99; Anna Katharina Schaffner, *Modernism and Perversion* (Houndmills: Palgrave Macmillan, 2012), 23–9; Paul Peppis, *Sciences of Modernism: Ethnography, Sexology, and Psychology* (Cambridge: Cambridge University Press, 2014), 11; Jana Funke, 'Modernism, Sexuality, and Gender,' in *The Bloomsbury Companion to Modernist Literature*, ed. Ulrika Maude and Mark Nixon (London: Bloomsbury Publishing, 2018), 250. These readings implicitly and explicitly respond to Mark S. Morrisson's calls for a model of 'scientific and technical modernism' which largely places under erasure distinctions between literary and non-literary discourse. Mark S. Morrisson, 'Why Modernist Studies and Science Studies Need Each Other,' *Modernism/Modernity* 9, no. 4 (2002): 675–82; Mark S. Morrisson, *Modernism, Science, and Technology* (London: Bloomsbury Academic, 2017), 7.

[33] Kathleen Ferris, *James Joyce and the Burden of Disease* (Lexington: University Press of Kentucky, 1995).

[34] Lucy Bland and Laura L. Doan, eds., *Sexology in Culture: Labelling Bodies and Desires* (Cambridge: Polity Press, 1998); Bauer, *English Literary Sexology*; Schaffner, *Modernism and Perversion*; Peppis, *Sciences of Modernism*, part 2.

[35] Lyndsey Stonebridge, *The Destructive Element: British Psychoanalysis and Modernism* (New York: Routledge, 1998); Kylie Valentine, *Psychoanalysis, Psychiatry, and Modernist Literature* (Houndmills: Palgrave Macmillan, 2003); Mark S. Micale, ed., *The Mind of Modernism: Medicine, Psychology, and the Cultural Arts in Europe and America, 1880–1940* (Stanford: Stanford University Press, 2004); Maud Ellmann, *The Nets of Modernism: Henry James, Virginia Woolf, James Joyce, and Sigmund Freud* (Cambridge: Cambridge University Press, 2010); Laura Marcus, *Dreams of Modernity: Psychoanalysis, Literature, Cinema* (Cambridge: Cambridge University Press, 2014); Peppis, *Sciences of Modernism*, 5 and 6.

[36] Marc Manganaro, ed., *Modernist Anthropology: From Fieldwork to Text* (Princeton: Princeton University Press, 1990); Elazar Barkan and Ronald Bush, eds., *Prehistories of the Future: The Primitivist Project and the Culture of Modernism* (Stanford: Stanford University Press, 1995); Gregory Castle, *Modernism and the Celtic Revival* (Cambridge: Cambridge University Press, 2001); Sinéad Garrigan-Mattar, *Primitivism, Science, and the Irish Revival* (Oxford: Oxford University Press, 2004); Peppis, *Sciences of Modernism*, part 1.

[37] Mary Lowe-Evans, *Crimes Against Fecundity: Joyce and Population Control* (Syracuse, New York: Syracuse University Press, 1989); Donald J. Childs, *Modernism and Eugenics: Woolf, Eliot, Yeats, and the Culture of Degeneration* (Cambridge: Cambridge University Press, 2001), chaps. 4–6.

selection and various forms of heredity);[38] the eugenics movement (in its desire to 'improve' humanity's physical and intellectual capacities through artificial selection);[39] and the birth control movement (which mobilized eugenic arguments to call for a more woman-centred model of family planning and a more pleasure-centred model of sex).[40] While, for reasons I shall address below, the specificities of social, political, and cultural life in Ireland yielded a version of 'sexual modernism' sometimes quite distinct from the one surveyed in these Anglo-American studies, *Irish Modernism and the Politics of Sexual Health* shares with them an awareness of the vibrant 'two-way' exchanges and moments of 'creative misprision' that took place between literature, science, and medicine concerning questions of sex and its regulation in the late nineteenth and early twentieth centuries.[41]

As the broad conceptual latitude of the phrase 'sexual modernism' suggests, in late nineteenth- and early twentieth-century culture, sex and health came to enjoy a near-infinite explanatory capacity. By 1886, the influential German sexologist, Richard von Krafft-Ebing, could declare sex 'den gewaltigsten Factor im individuellen und im socialen Dasein' [the most powerful factor in individual and social existence].[42] The following year, Friedrich Nietzsche could be found 'waiting for a philosophical *physician*' who would 'pursue the problem of the total health of a people, time, race or of humanity'.[43] By the end of the century, Krafft-Ebing's British counterpart,

---

[38] William Greenslade, *Degeneration, Culture, and the Novel, 1880–1940* (Cambridge: Cambridge University Press, 1994); Childs, *Modernism and Eugenics*, 2001; Jane R. Goodall, *Performance and Evolution in the Age of Darwin: Out of the Natural Order* (London: Routledge, 2002); Tamsen Wolff, *Mendel's Theatre: Heredity, Eugenics, and Early Twentieth-Century American Drama* (Houndmills: Palgrave Macmillan, 2009); Kirsten Shepherd-Barr, *Theatre and Evolution from Ibsen to Beckett* (New York: Columbia University Press, 2015); Václav Paris, *The Evolutions of Modernist Epic* (Oxford: Oxford University Press, 2021).
[39] Childs, *Modernism and Eugenics*, 2001; Daylanne K. English, *Unnatural Selections: Eugenics in American Modernism and the Harlem Renaissance* (Chapel Hill: University of North Carolina Press, 2004); Turda, *Modernism and Eugenics*.
[40] Layne Parish Craig, *When Sex Changed: Birth Control Politics and Literature Between the World Wars* (New Brunswick, New Jersey: Rutgers University Press, 2013); Aimee Armande Wilson, *Conceived in Modernism: The Aesthetics and Politics of Birth Control* (New York: Bloomsbury Academic, 2016).
[41] This model of exchange has most famously been mapped by Gillian Beer in *Darwin's Plots* (1983), from which these frequently cited expressions derive. Gillian Beer, *Darwin's Plots: Evolutionary Narrative in Darwin, George Eliot and Nineteenth-Century Fiction*, 3rd ed. (Cambridge: Cambridge University Press, 2009), 5.
[42] Richard von Krafft-Ebing, *Psychopathia Sexualis: Eine klinisch-forensische Studie* (Stuttgart: Verlag von Ferdinand Enke, 1886), 2.
[43] These remarks are made in the 1886 'Preface' to the Second Edition. Friedrich Wilhelm Nietzsche, *The Gay Science: With a Prelude in German Rhymes and an Appendix of Songs*, ed. Bernard Williams, trans. Josefine Nauckhoff and Adrian Del Caro (Cambridge: Cambridge University Press, [1882] 2001), 6.

Havelock Ellis, would deem sex, in all its 'natural' and 'unnatural' manifestations, the 'central problem of life', which required the attention of
'everyone'.[44] As these remarks suggest, as an analytical category, the concept
of 'sexual health' can seem unserviceably broad, at risk of subsuming any
and every conceivable phenomenon into its explanatory ambit. A challenge
this book faces is thus to analyse the operation of sexual health as a discourse
and category in Irish modernism without simply becoming a second-order
manifestation of a late nineteenth-century tendency to transform everything
into a question of sex or health. To obviate this danger, I will identify and
focus upon four key themes and concerns which dominated social, political,
and cultural debates about sexual health in the period with which I am
concerned: hygiene, autonomy, heredity, and fertility.[45]

Sexual Health: Key Themes

Of all these themes, the relationship between sexual health and hygiene is,
perhaps, the most obvious. To this day, sexual health is intimately associated
with the diagnosis, treatment, and prevention of sexually transmitted infections (or, as such infections were collectively understood and labelled in the
late nineteenth and early twentieth centuries, 'venereal disease').[46] The most
prevalent of these infections in the period with which this book is concerned
were gonorrhoea—a bacterial infection that causes pain, inflammation, and

[44] This remark appears in the 'General Preface' to the *Studies*, dated 'July, 1897'. Havelock
Ellis, *Studies in the Psychology of Sex*, vol. 1 (New York: Random House, [1897] 1942), xxx.

[45] Each of these themes is, of course, closely implicated with other categories, particularly
gender and sexual orientation, whose operation is of central importance to this book, but which
it would be a distortion to analyze as discrete topics in themselves. By exploring the ways in
which, under the rubric of sexual health, ideas of hygiene, competing models of autonomy,
heredity, and fertility interacted with gendered and sexual norms in Irish modernism, I hope to
comment meaningfully on the history of gender and sexuality in Ireland, without artificially
reifying or hypostasizing either category.

[46] As Michael Worboys has noted, though syphilis and gonorrhoea were understood to be
distinct pathological entities by the late nineteenth century, 'venereal disease' remained 'a
singular moral and political construct largely defined by syphilis' and continued to be a widely
used classificatory term, particularly in public discourse, well into the twentieth century.
Michael Worboys, 'Unsexing Gonorrhoea: Bacteriologists, Gynaecologists, and Suffragists in
Britain, 1860–1920,' *Social History of Medicine* 17, no. 1 (April 2004): 45. Though its causative
bacterium, *Chlamydia trachomatis*, was first isolated in 1907, when Ludwig Halberstaedter and
Stanilaus von Prowazek identified it as the source of the eye infection, trachoma, 'chlamydia'
was not diagnostically formulated as an independent, sexually transmitted infection until the
1970s. Michael Worboys, 'Chlamydia: A Disease without a History,' in *The Hidden Affliction:
Sexually Transmitted Infections and Infertility in History*, ed. Simon Szreter (Rochester:
University of Rochester Press, 2019), 153–83.

discharge in affected tissue, and which can lead to infertility, septic arthritis, and endocarditis if left untreated—and syphilis—a relapsing and remitting bacterial infection which, after a brief period of 'primary' and 'secondary' infection (marked by a lesion or chancre at the site of infection and a fever, hair loss, and a widespread rash, respectively), can lie dormant for years at a time before returning in a 'tertiary' form, causing severe neurological damage (neurosyphilis), aortic aneurysm (cardiovascular syphilis), stroke, cranial nerve palsy, and spinal cord inflammation (meningovascular syphilis), or tumour-like growths and inflammations of the skin, bone, and liver (gummatous syphilis).[47] Due to its debilitating and often fatal tertiary symptoms, its resistance to treatment and diagnosis, and its potential for transmission *in utero*—resulting in an extremely high risk of miscarriage and birth defects—syphilis was the more deeply feared and widely discussed of the two conditions, and set the terms for how venereal disease would be depicted and alluded to in fiction, drama, and journalism throughout the late nineteenth and early twentieth centuries.[48]

As developments in the scientific and medical understanding of gonorrhoea and syphilis made physicians and politicians increasingly anxious about the ramifications of both conditions for the well-being of individuals, 'the nation', and 'the race', venereal disease increasingly came to be viewed less as a divinely sanctioned punishment for immoral sexual conduct (the so-called 'wages of sin') than as a public health concern, to be combated though regimes of both personal and social hygiene—though, as Yeats's anecdote suggests, these models of 'hygiene' were often heavily morally freighted.[49] Personal hygiene might take a range of forms, including

[47] Elizabeth A. Martin, ed., *Concise Medical Dictionary*, 8th ed. (Oxford: Oxford University Press, 2010).
[48] For a sense of the place syphilis held in the cultural imaginary of the United Kingdom, Europe, and the United States in the late nineteenth and early twentieth centuries, see Claude Quétel, *History of Syphilis* (Cambridge: Polity Press, 1990), chaps 5–9; Elaine Showalter, 'Syphilis, Sexuality, and the Fiction of the Fin de Siècle,' in *Sex, Politics, and Science in the Nineteenth-Century Novel*, ed. Ruth Bernard Yeazell, Repr. (Baltimore: Johns Hopkins University Press, 1990), 88–115; Elaine Showalter, *Sexual Anarchy: Gender and Culture at the Fin de Siècle* (London: Virago, 1992), chap. 10.
[49] For an account of the ways in which scientific knowledge concerning venereal disease evolved in this period, and its implications for clinical practice in England see Anne R. Hanley, *Medicine, Knowledge and Venereal Diseases in England, 1886–1916* (Basingstoke: Palgrave Macmillan, 2017), particularly the Introduction, and Hanley, 'Sexual Health in Modern Britain,' 1–7. For an overview of the development and operation of this 'medico-moral' model of hygiene in the nineteenth and twentieth centuries, see Frank Mort, *Dangerous Sexualities: Medico-Moral Politics in England Since 1830*. Rev. ed (London: Routledge, 2002), pts. 1 and 4.

abstinence, monogamy, prophylaxis (which encompassed both the use of contraceptives and different modes of chemical disinfection), and sanitary practices such as the regular washing of an individual's body, undergarments, and bedding.[50] Social hygiene typically entailed efforts to monitor and regulate the sexual conduct of perceived 'high-risk' groups—female sex workers, soldiers, immigrants, the urban poor, the physically and mentally 'defective'—often with stigmatizing results and in accordance with a range of gendered and classist double standards.[51] The most infamous manifestation of this drive for social hygiene in Britain and Ireland came in the form of the Contagious Diseases Acts of 1864, 1866, and 1869, which licensed the involuntary inspection, detention, and treatment of women suspected to be engaged in sex work in the vicinity of a range of key British military garrisons, though the sex education programmes, state-funded Venereal Disease Service, and medicalized immigration policies discussed above also shared this hygienic impulse.[52] As the twentieth century progressed, declining birth rates and rising levels of differential fertility—the uneven ways in which this decline was manifesting itself across a range of social groups – combined to generate the impression across Europe and the United States that the most able, intelligent, and affluent were being out-bred by their perceived physical, intellectual, and social inferiors, to the overall detriment of the population's health.[53] As a result, under the growing influence of the eugenics and birth control movements, ideas of sexual and social 'hygiene' increasingly came to encompass not only the regulation of venereal disease but notions of physical and mental 'fitness' and concerns about the size and composition of families.

As Yeats's characterization of the 'mob' who opposed the *Playboy* as an undifferentiated 'howling' mass who lack the capacity for either social or sexual self-restraint suggests, closely bound up with this hygienic ideal was a concern with what I will broadly term autonomy. In virtually all its

[50] Virginia Sarah Smith, *Clean: A History of Personal Hygiene and Purity* (Oxford: Oxford University Press, 2007), chaps. 9 and 10.
[51] Peter Baldwin, *Contagion and the State in Europe, 1830–1930* (Cambridge: Cambridge University Press, 1999), chaps. 5–6; Turda, *Modernism and Eugenics*, chaps. 1–3.
[52] Judith R. Walkowitz, *Prostitution and Victorian Society: Women, Class, and the State* (Cambridge: Cambridge University Press, 1980), pt. 2; Philippa Levine, *Prostitution, Race, and Politics: Policing Venereal Disease in the British Empire* (New York: Routledge, 2003), pt. 1; Maria Luddy, *Prostitution and Irish Society, 1800–1940* (Cambridge: Cambridge University Press, 2007), chap. 4.
[53] For an overview of these anxieties and their roots, see Kevles, *In the Name of Eugenics*, chaps. 5–7; King, *In the Name of Liberalism*, pt. 2; Soloway, *Demography and Degeneration*, chap. 1.

nineteenth- and twentieth-century articulations, good sexual health is staked upon a normative ideal of self-rule, in which the individual possesses the capacity to make rational decisions about their sexual behaviour and to regulate the impulses and desires which inspire it. The individual hygiene practices outlined above were all, to some extent, grounded in the principles of self-regulation, sexual continence, and moral self-possession which comprised this mode of autonomy. While various strands of rationalist and Judeo-Christian thought had long treated sexual desire as a degrading compromise of an individual's autonomy, nineteenth-century medical discourse increasingly presented an incapacity for sexual self-restraint as an index of pathology.[54] In the view of Krafft-Ebing, what distinguished 'Perversität' [perversity]—expressions of the 'Geschlechtstriebes' [sexual instinct] which violated what he presented as its natural procreative function—from 'Perversion'—a pathological deviation of the 'sexual instinct' which compelled the individual to commit these acts—was the involuntary character of the latter state: perverse acts were knowingly committed forms of 'Laster' [vice], which invited moral censure and legal sanction; perversion was a form of 'Krankheit' [illness], which necessitated therapeutic intervention.[55] Diagnoses such as 'spermatorrhoea'—an excessive and involuntary leaking of seminal fluids brought about by excessive masturbation, which was held, in extreme cases, to precipitate potentially fatal interruptions of cerebral activity—literalized such theories, blurring the boundary between a physical and mental incapacity for sexual self-regulation in which cause and effect became increasingly hard to distinguish.[56]

Further complicating the question of whether perceived sexual misconduct contributed to or resulted from a compromised capacity for self-rule was the matter of heredity. As noted above, for Foucault, heredity constituted the conduit through which the pathological effects of individual sexual conduct were understood to inscribe themselves at the level of the

---

[54] For a useful survey of major philosophical positions on desire, see Rockney Jacobsen, 'Desire, Sexual,' in *Sex from Plato to Paglia: A Philosophical Encyclopedia*, ed. Alan Soble, vol. 1, 2 vols. (Westport, Conn: Greenwood Press, 2006), 222–8.

[55] Richard von Krafft-Ebing, *Psychopathia Sexualis: Mit besonderer Berucksichtigung der kontraren Sexualempfindung: Eine medizinisch-gerichtliche Studie fur Arzte und Juriste*, 13. Ausgabe (Stuttgart: Verlag von Ferdinand Enke, 1907), 63. For an account of the emergence of the epistemes and styles of reasoning through which 'perversion' becomes conceivable as a form of 'functional disease', see Davidson, *The Emergence of Sexuality*, 12–25.

[56] E. H. Hare, 'Masturbatory Insanity: The History of an Idea,' *Journal of Mental Science* 108, no. 452 (January 1962): 1–25; Robert Darby, 'Pathologizing Male Sexuality: Lallemand, Spermatorrhea, and the Rise of Circumcision,' *Journal of the History of Medicine and Allied Sciences* 60, no. 3 (1 July 2005): 283–319.

population.[57] Degeneration theory, with its neo-Lamarckian stress on use inheritance—a process whereby regularly employed faculties and traits would grow more pronounced from generation to generation, while their neglected counterparts would atrophy—constituted the clearest and most influential articulation of this logic, transforming a parent's 'vices' into hereditary 'pathologies' that would compromise not only the physical health of their children but their capacity for sexual self-regulation.[58] As Desmond King has noted, this belief was taken up and extended by the eugenics movement, for whom a lack of sexual continence and an incapacity for family planning could be taken as evidence of a lack of 'reason' or 'competence' on the basis of which an individual could be disqualified from full membership of the liberal-democratic *polis* and the rights and protections it afforded.[59] These exclusions and the repressive and illiberal measures such as institutionalization or sterilization they facilitated could then, in turn, be circularly justified as efforts to protect and encourage the good-functioning of the liberal democratic state by maximizing the 'health' and 'reason' of the body politic.[60] As many of the texts surveyed in this study bear out, this tendency to present restrictions on the sexual liberty of certain individuals or social groups as the necessary prerequisite for a higher order of collective liberty and health was to produce an often irresolvable set of ideological tensions and logical contradictions for those who sought to leverage a eugenic conception of sex to militate for social change or political reform.

At the fraught intersection of these anxieties about autonomy and heredity stood the question of fertility and its regulation. On the one hand, if, as many anti-Malthusian demographers and economists argued, a nation's 'health' and 'vitality' were cognate with the size of its population and the rate of its growth, then efforts to limit fertility were tantamount to 'race

---

[57] Foucault, *The History of Sexuality, 1: The Will to Knowledge*: 116–19; Foucault et al., *Society Must Be Defended*, 252.

[58] For an overview of degeneration theory and its cultural ramifications in the nineteenth and twentieth centuries, see J. Edward Chamberlin and Sander L. Gilman, eds. *Degeneration: The Dark Side of Progress* (New York: Columbia University Press, 1985); Sander L. Gilman, *Difference and Pathology: Stereotypes of Sexuality, Race, and Madness* (Ithaca: Cornell University Press, 1985), chap. 9; Daniel Pick, *Faces of Degeneration: A European Disorder, c.1848-c.1918* (Cambridge: Cambridge University Press, 1989), Introduction; Kelly Hurley, 'Hereditary Taint and Cultural Contagion: The Social Etiology of Fin-de-siècle Degeneration Theory,' *Nineteenth-Century Contexts* 14, no. 2 (January 1990): 193–214; Greenslade, *Degeneration, Culture, and the Novel, 1880-1940*, chap. 1; Soloway, *Demography and Degeneration*, chap. 3.

[59] King, *In the Name of Liberalism*, 52–64.   [60] Ibid., 56–7; 62.

suicide'.[61] Furthermore, if as Krafft-Ebing and his contemporaries asserted, sex could only be 'healthy' insofar as it served a reproductive function, then efforts to restrict or control fertility through various forms of contraceptive practice constituted a sanction for perversion and degeneration. Both positions were echoed by religious commentators, particularly Pope Pius XI, whose infamous 1931 encyclical *Casti Conubii* [of chaste marriage] denounced birth control as 'intrinsically evil' and criticized eugenic sterilization policies.[62] On the other hand, if, as degeneration theory and the eugenics movement contended, the most 'unhealthy' and 'unfit' possessed a hereditary incapacity for sexual self-regulation and maintained the highest birth-rates amid an otherwise pervasive demographic slump, then unregulated fertility constituted a substantial threat to public health.[63] For birth control advocates such as Stopes and Sanger, these eugenic anxieties existed alongside a belief that, in obliging women 'to bear and bring forth an infant annually', unregulated fertility 'sap[ped] and divide[d]' their 'vital strength' and 'lower[ed] the vitality' of each succeeding child, with sometimes fatal outcomes.[64] Only safe and reliable contraception, they argued, paired with a medically informed understanding of the mechanics of sex and reproduction, could liberate women from the burden of repeated, unwanted pregnancies and the threat they posed to their well-being and the well-being of their children. In justifying this proposed extension to women's reproductive autonomy, the supporters of birth control aligned themselves with eugenics advocates and neo-Malthusians in stressing the hygienic responsibilities prospective parents bore to the populations to which they would be contributing.[65]

---

[61] Richard A. Soloway, *Birth Control and the Population Question in England, 1877–1930* (Chapel Hill: University of North Carolina Press, 1982), chaps. 1 and 2; Angus McLaren, *Sexuality and Social Order: The Debate over the Fertility of Women and Workers in France, 1770–1920* (New York: Holmes & Meier, 1983), chap. 11; McLaren, *Twentieth-Century Sexuality*, 1999, chap. 4; Soloway, *Demography and Degeneration*, chap. 1; Weeks, *Sex, Politics, and Society*, chap. 7.

[62] 'Lambeth Conference: Resolutions Archive from 1930,' Anglican Community Document Library, 2019, sec. 15, https://www.anglicancommunion.org/media/127734/1930.pdf; Pope Pius XI, '*Casti Connubii*, Encyclical of Pope Pius XI on Christian Marriage to the Venerable Brethren, Patriarchs, Primates, Archbishops, Bishops, and Other Local Ordinaries Enjoying Peace and Communion with the Apostolic See,' The Holy See, February 2016, secs. 61 and 63–71, https://w2.vatican.va/content/pius-xi/en/encyclicals/documents/hf_p-xi_enc_19301231_casti-connubii.html; Craig, *When Sex Changed*, chap. 4.

[63] Soloway, *Demography and Degeneration*, chap. 5.

[64] Marie Carmichael Stopes, *Married Love: A New Contribution to the Solution of Sex Difficulties* (London: A.C. Fifield, 1918), 88–9.

[65] As Richard A. Soloway and others make clear, the eugenics movement did not necessarily welcome this association, with its British old-guard remaining hostile to birth control in general, and Stopes in particular, well into the 1920s. Soloway, *Birth Control and the Population*

In *Radiant Motherhood*, the 1920 sequel to her best-selling *Married Love*, Stopes asserted that the 'power of parenthood ought no longer to be exercised by all, however inferior, as an "individual right",' but should instead be viewed as 'a duty and a privilege' that was 'the concern of the whole community':[66]

> It should be the policy of the community to encourage in every way the parenthood of those whose circumstances and conditions are such that there is a reasonable anticipation that they will give rise to healthy, well-endowed future citizens. It should be the policy of the community to discourage from parenthood all whose circumstances are such as would make probable the introduction of weakened, diseased or debased future citizens. It is the urgent duty of the community to make parenthood impossible for those whose mental and physical conditions are such that there is well-nigh a certainty that their offspring must be physically and mentally tainted, if not utterly permeated by disease.[67]

As Stopes's eugenicist emphasis on the 'community's obligation to vouchsafe its collective well-being against the perceived threat of those whose socio-economic 'circumstances' might predispose them to produce 'diseased or debased future citizens' underscores, by the 1920s the concepts of hygiene, autonomy, heredity, and fertility had become enmeshed in ways that were not simply medical, but decidedly, and often disquietingly, political.

Sexual Health and Irish Culture

As this overview suggests, in the nineteenth and twentieth centuries, the widespread medicalization and politicization of sex combined to render sexual health a conceptual lens through which politicians, activists, and

Question in England, 1877–1930, chaps. 7 and 10; McLaren, *Sexuality and Social Order*, chaps. 9 and 10; June Rose, *Marie Stopes and the Sexual Revolution* (London: Faber and Faber, 1992), chaps. 6–8; Carolyn Burdett, 'The Hidden Romance of Sexual Science: Eugenics, the Nation and the Making of Modern Feminism,' in *Sexology in Culture: Labelling Bodies and Desires*, ed. Lucy Bland and Laura L. Doan (Cambridge: Polity Press, 1998), 44–59; McLaren, *Twentieth-Century Sexuality*, 1999, chap. 4; Soloway, *Demography and Degeneration*, chaps. 6 and 8; Weeks, *Sex, Politics, and Society*, chaps. 7 and 9; Clare Debenham, *Marie Stopes' Sexual Revolution and the Birth Control Movement* (Cham, Switzerland): Palgrave Macmillan, 2018), chaps. 4–9.
[66] Marie Carmichael Stopes, *Radiant Motherhood: A Book for Those Who Are Creating the Future* (New York: G.P. Putnam's Sons, 1920), 211–12.
[67] Ibid., 212.

cultural commentators across Europe and North America could describe, critique, and regulate the sexual conduct of both individuals and the populations they were imagined to constitute. However, notwithstanding the apparently all-pervasive nature of this epistemological revolution concerning sex and health, questions have been raised concerning the extent to which it affected Ireland. As such, a further challenge this book faces concerns the applicability of 'sexual health' as a conceptual paradigm to the history of both sexuality and modernism in Ireland. In a range of influential and theoretically astute monographs and articles, historian and sociologist Tom Inglis has argued that the social, cultural, and political influence of the Catholic Church in Ireland in the late nineteenth and early twentieth centuries was too pervasive for the nation to be greatly affected by *scientia sexualis* and its attendant discourses and disciplines, and has asserted that what was said and written about sex and sexuality in Ireland in this period remained largely confined within 'religious discourse' and a 'thematic of sin'.[68] Yet, as this study will demonstrate, it is clear that many major and minor figures in the cultural life of late nineteenth- and early twentieth-century Ireland actively engaged with precisely those discourses and developments from which the concept of sexual health emerged. Some did so professionally, such as the physician, poet, and first President of the Irish Literary Society, George Sigerson, who published several well-regarded translations of Jean-Martin Charcot's lectures on hysteria, cerebral syphilis, and diseases of the nervous system, which he had attended at the Salpêtrière hospital in Paris throughout the 1870s.[69] Others did so decidedly less professionally, such as Oliver St John Gogarty—the litterateur-cum-ear-nose-and-throat surgeon—who spent much of his time as a medical student composing sexualized doggerel, including a mock epic about a syphilitic sailor called Sinbad, for James Joyce's amusement.[70] Most, like Yeats in his

[68] Tom Inglis, 'Foucault, Bourdieu and the Field of Irish Sexuality,' *Irish Journal of Sociology* 7, no. 1 (1997): 5–28, 5; 12; Inglis, *Moral Monopoly*.

[69] J. B. Lyons, 'Sigerson, George,' in *Dictionary of Irish Biography*, ed. James McGuire and James Quinn (Cambridge: Cambridge University Press, 2009), https://doi.org/10.3318/dib.008072.v1; Jean Martin Charcot, *Lectures on the Diseases of the Nervous System*, trans. George Sigerson (London: New Sydenham Society, 1881); Emilie Morin, 'Theatres and Pathologies of Silence: Symbolism and Irish Drama from Maeterlinck to Beckett,' in *Silence in Modern Irish Literature*, ed. Michael McAteer (Leiden: Brill Rodopi, 2017), 42.

[70] In a letter to Joyce in June 1906, Gogarty jokingly announced that an American edition of *Sinbad* had been published, running to 230 stanzas. Whatever its actual length, only short fragments of the poem survive. A version of its opening is reproduced in Gogarty's 1939 memoir, *Tumbling in the Hay*, when a draft of the poem is discovered by a senior surgeon for whom Gogarty is clerking: 'O what a wondrous paradox! / A sailor who escaped the rocks / Was

censure of the *Playboy* rioters, did so opportunistically, adopting sexual health as a rhetorically expedient normative frame-work through which to advance a favoured political cause or cultural agenda. In each case, the fact that so many figures in Irish public life deemed the discourse of sexual health to be both intelligible and persuasive to an Irish audience attests to the cultural currency which the medicalized and politicized conception of sex upon which the concept rested enjoyed in Irish public life. This impression is borne out even if one looks beyond these, necessarily somewhat rarefied, cultural circles. As Maria Luddy, Greta Jones, and others have shown, the existence of a Dublin branch of the National Association for the Repeal of the Contagious Diseases Acts (active in the 1870s and 1880s), a (relatively short-lived) Belfast Eugenics Society (which operated from 1911–1915), an (admittedly often mis-managed) nation-wide venereal disease treatment service (introduced in 1917), a Northern Ireland Society for Constructive Birth Control, and a Belfast-based Marie Stopes Mother's Clinic (active from 1936–1947) puts pressure on Inglis's claims concerning the uniformly ecclesiastical character of sexual discourse in pre- and post-partition Ireland.[71] As these examples suggest, while far from evenly geographically or socio-economically distributed across the island, a medicalized and politicized conception of sex and its relationship to health undeniably co-existed with (and was often conscripted to bolster) its religious counterpart in late nineteenth- and early twentieth-century Ireland, particularly in the nation's urban centres and among its cultural and political elites.

Nor was a culture of carefully policed knowledge surrounding sex unique to Ireland in this period. While scholarly and polemical material concerning sex, sexual health, and, above all, birth control, was undoubtedly able to circulate more freely in Britain than in Ireland in the first decades of the

---

wrecked by going down the docks / When safe ashore; / And brought to light a hidden pox / And Hunter's sore. // Ah, did he, when he weighed his anchor, / Weigh all the consequence of chancre? / For if he did he would not hanker . . .'. Oliver St John Gogarty, *Tumbling in the Hay* (London: Constable and Company, 1939), 230. Various surviving versions of the poem are reproduced in Oliver St John Gogarty, *The Poems & Plays of Oliver St John Gogarty*, ed. A Norman Jeffares (Gerrards Cross: Colin Smythe, 2001), 441–7.

[71] Luddy, *Prostitution and Irish Society, 1800–1940*, 147–55; Riordan, 'Venereal Disease in the Irish Free State'; Riordan, 'The Limitations of Venereal Disease Policy, 1943–1951'; Susannah Riordan, 'In Search of a Broadminded Saint: The Westmorland Lock Hospital in the Twentieth Century,' *Irish Economic and Social History* 39, no. 1 (1 December 2012): 73–93; McCormick, 'Venereal Diseases in Northern Ireland During the Second World War'; Greta Jones, 'Eugenics in Ireland: The Belfast Eugenics Society, 1911–1915,' *Irish Historical Studies* 28, no. 109 (May 1992): 81–95; Greta Jones, 'Marie Stopes in Ireland: The Mother's Clinic in Belfast, 1936–47,' *Social History of Medicine* 5, no. 2 (April 1992): 255–77.

twentieth century, its readership remained largely confined to a privileged and well-educated minority. As a range of historiography has illustrated, for the majority of Britons in the late nineteenth and early twentieth centuries, a cultivated state of 'innocence' and 'ignorance' concerning sex and sexuality was the (widely lamented) norm, particularly among young women.[72] While practical knowledge of the 'facts of life' was undoubtedly widespread in Britain in this period, it typically circulated through informal networks that varied by region, class, gender, and level of education, and it was not until at least the 1940s that officially sanctioned 'sex education' became sufficiently pervasive to serve as the primary source of sexual knowledge for British young people.[73] Likewise, though less likely to be inflected by overtly religious rhetoric, the stigma surrounding conditions such as venereal disease and the perceived sexual misconduct with which it was cognate was a real and persistent issue across the United Kingdom.[74]

Indeed, in one (admittedly circumscribed) domain, the Irish public sphere was, arguably, better equipped than its British counterpart to facilitate the discussion of sexual health and its attendant social and political ramifications: the theatre. While the creative freedom enjoyed by theatre-makers in Ireland in the late nineteenth and early twentieth centuries can easily be over-stated, the much-vaunted absence of formalized stage censorship in Ireland notionally afforded Irish dramatists and theatre companies greater latitude in their engagement with sex and its evolving relationship to

---

[72] Porter and Hall, *The Facts of Life*, chap. 11; Sally Alexander, 'The Mysteries and Secrets of Women's Bodies: Sexual Knowledge in the First Half of the Twentieth Century,' in *Modern Times: Reflections On a Century of English Modernity*, ed. Mica Nava and Alan O'Shea (London: Routledge, 1996), 161–75; Kate Fisher, *Birth Control, Sex and Marriage in Britain, 1918–1960* (Oxford: Oxford University Press, 2006), chap. 1; Simon Szreter and Kate Fisher, *Sex Before the Sexual Revolution: Intimate Life in England, 1918–1963* (Cambridge: Cambridge University Press, 2010), chap. 2.

[73] For efforts to map these networks and their operation, see Lucinda McCray Beier, ' "We Were Green as Grass": Learning about Sex and Reproduction in Three Working-Class Lancashire Communities, 1900–1970,' *Social History of Medicine* 16, no. 3 (1 December 2003): 461–80; Lucinda McCray Beier, *For Their Own Good: The Transformation of English Working-Class Health Culture, 1880–1970* (Columbus: Ohio State University Press, 2008), chaps. 5 and 6; Hera Cook, *The Long Sexual Revolution: English Women, Sex, and Contraception, 1800–1975* (Oxford: Oxford University Press, 2004), chap. 7.

[74] Susan Lemar, ' "The Liberty to Spread Disaster": Campaigning for Compulsion in the Control of Venereal Diseases in Edinburgh in the 1920s,' *Social History of Medicine* 19, no. 1 (1 April 2006): 73–86; Pamela Cox, 'Compulsion, Voluntarism, and Venereal Disease: Governing Sexual Health in England after the Contagious Diseases Acts,' *The Journal of British Studies* 46, no. 01 (January 2007): 91–115; Samantha Caslin, 'Transience, Class and Gender in Interwar Sexual Health Policy: The Case of the Liverpool VD Scheme,' *Social History of Medicine*, 23 September 2017; McCormick, 'Prophylactics and Prejudice: Venereal Diseases in Northern Ireland During the Second World War.'

health than was technically possible across the Irish Sea.[75] Thus, plays such as Shaw's *Mrs Warren's Profession* (1893) or *The Shewing-Up of Blanco Posnet* (1909), which had both been denied a licence for performance in England by the Lord Chamberlain's office at least in part due to their handling of sex work, could be performed with minimal controversy at venues such as the Abbey and by groups such as the Dublin Repertory Theatre, sometimes decades before comparable English productions were officially countenanced.[76] Of course, as the *Playboy*'s riotous reception attests, the absence of official mechanisms of stage censorship didn't prevent Irish audiences from taking matters into their own hands when the vision of sex being dramatized diverged from their own or its perceived implications for the physical and cultural health of the nation proved unpalatable.[77] But, as shall be seen in Chapter 2, such controversies often served only to illustrate the extent to which a medicalized and politicized conception of

---

[75] The claim that there was 'no stage censorship in Ireland' rests on the fact that, prior to independence, the various theatre licensing acts which established the Lord Chamberlain as the official pre-performance censor for the British stage were never extended to Ireland, and that, post-independence, no equivalent to the 1923 Censorship of Films or 1929 Censorship of Publications Acts was introduced to regulate the activities of Irish theatres. However, as a range of scholarship on theatre and censorship in Ireland has illustrated, the absence of such formalized measures did not mean that other forms of informal regulation were not practised by patrons, funding bodies, and theatre managers, or by those directly involved in productions themselves, especially during moments of heightened political tension such as the Civil War or the Emergency. Donal Ó Drisceoil, *Censorship in Ireland, 1939–1945: Neutrality, Politics, and Society* (Cork: Cork University Press, 1996), 51–4; Joan Fitzpatrick Dean, *Riot and Great Anger: Stage Censorship in Twentieth-Century Ireland* (Madison: University of Wisconsin Press, 2004); Peter Martin, *Censorship in the Two Irelands, 1922–1939* (Dublin: Irish Academic Press, 2006), 111–18; Lauren Arrington, *W.B. Yeats, the Abbey Theatre, Censorship, and the Irish State: Adding the Half-Pence to the Pence* (Oxford: Oxford University Press, 2010).

[76] Despite the best efforts of the Dublin Castle administration to prevent the performance going ahead, the Abbey staged *Blanco Posnet* without incident in the August of 1909. *Mrs Warren's Profession*, which would not receive a licensed performance in England until 1925, was staged by Evelyn Ashley, Flora MacDonnell, and Casmir Markievicz's Dublin Repertory Theatre at the Little Theatre on Upper O'Connell Street in November 1914. For an overview of the circumstances surrounding both productions and the reception they were afforded, see Adrian Frazier, *Behind the Scenes: Yeats, Horniman, and the Struggle for the Abbey Theatre* (Berkeley: University of California Press, 1990), 227–30; Ben Levitas, *The Theatre of Nation* (Oxford: Oxford University Press, 2002), chap. 5; Dean, *Riot and Great Anger*, chap. 4; Leonard W. Conolly, 'Mrs *Warren's Profession* and the Lord Chamberlain,' *Shaw* 24, no. 1 (2004): 46–95; Chris Morash, *A History of Irish Theatre: 1601–2000* (Cambridge: Cambridge University Press, 2004), 143–5; Lucy McDiarmid, *The Irish Art of Controversy* (Ithaca: Cornell University Press, 2005), chap. 3; Nelson O'Ceallaigh Ritschel, 'Shaw and the Dublin Repertory Theatre,' *Shaw* 35, no. 2 (2015): 168–84; Bernard Frank Dukore, *Bernard Shaw and the Censors: Fights and Failures, Stage and Screen* (Cham, Switzerland: Palgrave Macmillan, 2020), chaps. 1 and 2.

[77] For a discussion of this dynamic in operation, see Dean, *Riot and Great Anger*. For a wider discussion of audience and spectatorship in Irish modernism, see Paige Reynolds, *Modernism, Drama, and the Audience for Irish Spectacle* (Cambridge: Cambridge University Press, 2007).

sex was an accepted, if hotly debated, aspect of Irish cultural and intellectual life in the first decades of the twentieth century. Thus, while I take seriously Inglis's reservations about the applicability of a one-size-fits-all Foucauldian model to Irish sexual culture and share his willingness to ask 'what is missing in a Foucauldian analysis' of Irish attitudes to sexual health, I follow figures such as Diarmaid Ferriter and Michael G. Cronin in seeking to challenge the exceptionalist account of Irish sexuality upon which Inglis premises aspects of his work.[78]

It is here that the emergent field of Irish Modernist Studies is particularly significant.[79] Where once Ireland was framed as an insular and regressive back-water which figures such as Joyce and Beckett had been obliged to transcend in order to enter the experimental, cosmopolitan milieu of 'International Modernism', in recent decades Ireland has increasingly been understood as the politically and intellectually heterogeneous crucible of a trans-national, diasporic modernism.[80] Through this reappraisal, a new understanding has emerged of the socio-economically and politically

[78] Inglis, 'Foucault, Bourdieu and the Field of Irish Sexuality,' 16; Tom Inglis, ed., *Are the Irish Different?* (Manchester: Manchester University Press, 2014); Ferriter, *Occasions of Sin*, Introduction; Michael G. Cronin, *Impure Thoughts: Sexuality, Catholicism and Literature in Twentieth-Century Ireland* (Manchester: Manchester University Press, 2012), Introduction.

[79] For a succinct account of what engaging with literary material can add to critical understandings of the history of sexualities in Ireland, in contrast to the 'narrow empiricism' that constrains studies such as Ferriter's *Occasions of Sin*, see the Introduction to Cronin's *Impure Thoughts*. By Cronin's own admission, his perspective on this topic (like my own) is indebted to the deliberately eclectic and inclusive approach adopted by the editors of the fourth and fifth volumes of the *Field Day Anthology of Irish Literature* (1991–2002), and summarized in Siobhán Kilfeather, 'General Introduction: Sexuality, 1685–2001,' *The Field Day Anthology of Irish Writing, Volume IV: Irish Women's Writings and Traditions*, ed. Angela Bourke et al. (Cork: Cork University Press, 2002), 755–60.

[80] Hugh Kenner, *A Colder Eye: The Modern Irish Writers* (London: Allen Lane, 1983), 29. The negative characterization of Ireland outlined above has its roots in the self-fashioning of many Irish modernists themselves. Essays such as Joyce's 'The Day of the Rabblement' (1901), Yeats's *Synge and the Ireland of His Time* (1911), Beckett's 'Recent Irish Poetry,' and Seán Ó Faoláin's 'Irish Poetry Since the War' all offer some version of this thesis. It was most influentially articulated by Richard Ellmann, in his monumental *James Joyce* (1959, rev. 1982), and Hugh Kenner, particularly in *The Pound Era* (1971) and *A Colder Eye* (1983). The version of Irish modernism outlined above is derived from Joe Cleary, 'Introduction: Ireland and Modernity,' in *The Cambridge Companion to Modern Irish Culture*, ed. Joe Cleary and Claire Connolly (Cambridge: Cambridge University Press, 2005), 1–21; Edwina Keown and Carol Taaffe, 'Introduction: Ireland and Modernism,' in *Irish Modernism: Origins, Contexts, Publics*, ed. Edwina Keown and Carol Taaffe (Oxford: Peter Lang, 2010), 1–6; Carol Taaffe, 'Irish Modernism,' in *The Oxford Handbook of Modernisms*, ed. Peter Brooker et al. (Oxford: Oxford University Press, 2010), 782–96; Joe Cleary, 'Introduction,' in *The Cambridge Companion to Irish Modernism*, ed. Joe Cleary (Cambridge: Cambridge University Press, 2014), 1–18; Jean-Michel Rabaté, 'Intellectual and Aesthetic Influences,' in *The Cambridge Companion to Irish Modernism*, ed. Joe Cleary (Cambridge: Cambridge University Press, 2014), 21–34; Lauren Arrington, 'Irish Modernism and Its Legacies,' in *The Princeton History*

debilitating but culturally and aesthetically energizing character of late nineteenth- and early twentieth-century Ireland's fraught relationship with modernity. Terry Eagleton has influentially argued that, unlike many of its European peers, Ireland did not leap 'at a bound' from 'tradition' to 'modernity', but instead represented 'an exemplary case of what Marxism has dubbed combined and uneven development'.[81] In Eagleton's view this resulted in the emergence of an 'archaic avant-garde', whose modernism was seldom an uncomplicated celebration or manifestation of modernity, but often its querulous and sceptical interlocutor, 'hostile to that stately march of secular reason' which was, for many nationalists, revivalists, and modernists, precisely where 'a soulless Britain had washed up'.[82] This 'uneven development' hypothesis has been taken up and extended by a range of critics—most notably those associated with the Field Day enterprise—who approach the emergence of Irish modernism through a post-colonial lens.[83] For Joe Cleary, while the received narrative of European modernization—'an inventory of inaugural ruptures' ranging from the Protestant Reformation to the emergence of capitalism (or, indeed, 'sexuality')—would cast Ireland as a peripheral and reactive consumer of a modernity being fashioned and theorized elsewhere, a post-colonial perspective might note that 'colonies' such as Ireland were, in fact, 'the first to endure the accelerated processes of social transformation and cultural hybridization' that characterize modernity.[84] As the work of Philippa Levine, Alison Bashford, and Angus

of Modern Ireland, ed. Richard Bourke and Ian McBride (Princeton: Princeton University Press, 2016), 236–52; Lauren Arrington, 'Irish Modernism,' Oxford Research Encyclopedia of Literature, February 2017, http://literature.oxfordre.com/view/10.1093/acrefore/9780190201098.001.0001/acrefore-9780190201098-e-237; Gregory Castle and Patrick Bixby, 'Introduction: Irish Modernism, from Emergence to Emergency,' in *A History of Irish Modernism*, ed. Gregory Castle and Patrick Bixby (Cambridge: Cambridge University Press, 2019), 1–22; Paul Fagan, John Greaney, and Tamara Radak, 'Introduction: Irish Modernisms in the Plural,' in *Irish Modernisms: Gaps, Conjectures, Possibilities*, ed. Paul Fagan, John Greaney, and Tamara Radak (London: Bloomsbury, 2021), 1–7.

[81] Terry Eagleton, *Heathcliff and the Great Hunger: Studies in Irish Culture* (London: Verso, 1995), 274.

[82] Ibid., 280.

[83] Ibid., chap. 7; Seamus Deane, *Strange Country: Modernity and Nationhood in Irish Writing Since 1790*, 1995 (Oxford: Oxford University Press, 1997); Seamus Deane, 'Dead Ends: Joyce's Finest Moments,' in *Semicolonial Joyce*, ed. Derek Attridge and Marjorie Elizabeth Howes (Cambridge: Cambridge University Press, 2000), 21–36; Conor McCarthy, *Modernisation, Crisis and Culture in Ireland, 1969–1992* (Dublin: Four Courts Press, 2000), Introduction; Castle, *Modernism and the Celtic Revival*, 2001, Introduction; Joe Cleary, 'Toward a Materialist-Formalist History of Twentieth-Century Irish Literature,' *Boundary 2* 31, no. 1 (1 March 2004): 207–41; Cleary, 'Introduction: Ireland and Modernity'; Cleary, 'Introduction'; Castle and Bixby, 'Introduction.'

[84] Cleary, 'Introduction: Ireland and Modernity,' 3; 6.

McLaren makes clear, this fast-tracked encounter with modernity often included a particularly intense and repressive experience of imperial regimes of sexual hygiene, such as the Contagious Diseases Acts, which were pioneered in Britain's Asian colonies, or the voluntary and compulsory sterilization schemes which succeeded in gaining and maintaining legislative support in Canada, even as their putative British counterparts were decisively defeated in Westminster.[85] In such a reading, Ireland becomes not a belated and recalcitrant site of deficient and partial modernization, but a locus of 'alternative enlightenment' in which modernity received some of its earliest and most stringent critiques from figures as aesthetically and politically diverse as Yeats and Brian O'Nolan (Flann O'Brien).[86]

Irish Modernism and the Politics of Sexual Health maintains a more circumspect view of Ireland's colonial status, following Stephen Howe, Linda Connolly, and others in asserting that understanding Ireland as an 'imperial' culture better explains the varied ways in which different segments of Ireland's population could be both victims of and willing participants in an unbalanced process of modernization which was variously embraced and resisted.[87] Nevertheless, it shares with Eagleton and Cleary a sensitivity to Ireland's status as a cultural field that unevenly combined modern, pre-modern, and anti-modern currents, and charts the ways this 'uneven development' rendered the emergence of 'sexual modernism' in Ireland a more politically charged, culturally urgent, and less comfortably reciprocal exchange between literature and medical science than that

---

[85] Levine, *Prostitution, Race, and Politics*, part 1; Alison Bashford, *Imperial Hygiene: A Critical History of Colonialism, Nationalism, and Public Health* (Houndmills: Palgrave Macmillan, 2004), chap. 7; McLaren, *Our Own Master Race*. The role of eugenics in shaping the social and public health policy of British colonial administrations in Canada, Australia, New Zealand, South Africa, Hong Kong, and China and a range of other European and American colonies is surveyed in relevant chapters of Bashford and Levine, eds. *The Oxford Handbook of the History of Eugenics*.

[86] Cleary, 'Introduction: Ireland and Modernity,' 3; 6.

[87] Stephen Howe, *Ireland and Empire: Colonial Legacies in Irish History and Culture* (Oxford: Oxford University Press, 2000), chap. 1; Stephen Howe, 'Questioning the (Bad) Question: "Was Ireland a Colony?",' *Irish Historical Studies* 36, no. 142 (November 2008): 138–52; Linda Connolly, 'The Limits of "Irish Studies": Historicism, Culturalism, Paternalism,' in *Enemies of Empire: New Perspectives on Imperialism, Literature, and Historiography*, ed. Eóin Flannery and Angus Mitchell (Dublin: Four Courts Press, 2007), 189–210; Terence Brown, *The Literature of Ireland: Culture and Criticism* (Cambridge: Cambridge University Press, 2010), chaps. 1 and 7. A recent systematic articulation of this position is offered in *The Princeton History of Modern Ireland* (2016). Of particular relevance in the present context are Richard Bourke, 'Introduction,' in *The Princeton History of Modern Ireland*, ed. Richard Bourke and Ian McBride (Princeton: Princeton University Press, 2016), 15 and Arrington, 'Irish Modernism and Its Legacies,' 236.

charted by Bauer, Schaffner, and Peppis in an Anglo-American context. To register the complexities of this process, I follow Emer Nolan, Paige Reynolds, and others in embracing an understanding of Irish modernism that encompasses both the forces of what has traditionally been dubbed 'revivalism' (in its Gaelic and literary guises) and the wider currents of Anglo-American and European avant-garde cultural experimentation commonly referred to as 'modernism', eschewing the binary opposition which has often been taken to exist between them.[88] This focus allows me to maintain a sensitivity to the particularities of Irish culture and politics, especially in the domain of sex, while at the same time highlighting the ways in which different factions within Ireland responded to wider British, European, and trans-Atlantic events and trends. As a result, I focus both on literary figures who maintained close ties to Ireland (Yeats, Synge, Gogarty, Brian O'Nolan), and those who addressed Ireland from a greater geographical or cultural remove (Joyce, Beckett, Kate O'Brien, Shaw). I also attend to the array of politicians, journalists, and cultural commentators with whom these authors variously collaborated, socialized, and quarrelled, including both major figures such as Maud Gonne, Arthur Griffith, and D. P. Moran, and less often surveyed individuals such as Hanna Sheehy-Skeffington, Signe Toksvig, and Ethel Mannin. In doing so, I offer an account the emergence and development of Irish modernism that balances the canonical and the

[88] P. J. Mathews, *Revival: The Abbey Theatre, Sinn Féin, the Gaelic League and the Co-Operative Movement* (Cork: Cork University Press in Association with Field Day, 2004); Emer Nolan, 'Modernism and the Irish Revival,' in *The Cambridge Companion to Modern Irish Culture*, ed. Joe Cleary and Connolly, Claire (Cambridge: Cambridge University Press, 2005), 157–72; Paige Reynolds, *Modernism, Drama, and the Audience for Irish Spectacle* (Cambridge: Cambridge University Press, 2007), Introduction; Rónán McDonald, 'The Irish Revival and Modernism,' in *The Cambridge Companion to Irish Modernism*, ed. Joe Cleary (Cambridge: Cambridge University Press, 2014), 51–62. 'Modernism' is infamously difficult to define. In this study, I broadly follow figures such as Michael Whitworth in construing modernism as a 'fragile unity' which encompasses a 'set of responses to problems posed by the conditions of modernity' (Michael H. Whitworth, ed., 'Introduction,' in *Modernism: A Guide to Criticism* (Oxford: Wiley-Blackwell, 2007), 3. For a useful recent survey of the emergence and development of modernism as a cultural phenomenon and critical concept, and the debates to which it has given rise, see Sean Latham and Gayle Rogers, *Modernism: Evolution of an Idea* (London: Bloomsbury Academic, 2015). For overviews of recent criticism in Modernist Studies, see Whitworth, ed., *Modernism*; Peter Brooker et al., eds., *The Oxford Handbook of Modernisms* (Oxford: Oxford University Press, 2010); Mark A. Wollaeger and Matt Eatough, eds., *The Oxford Handbook of Global Modernisms* (Oxford: Oxford University Press, 2012); Jean-Michel Rabaté, ed., *A Handbook of Modernism Studies* (Oxford: Wiley-Blackwell, 2013); Ulrika Maude and Mark Nixon, eds. *The Bloomsbury Companion to Modernist Literature* (London: Bloomsbury Publishing, 2018). Other foundational studies to which my thinking on the subject is indebted are included in the Bibliography.

over-looked across a range of genres and forms to reveal the ways in which key events in Irish cultural and political history—the fall of Charles Stewart Parnell, the *Playboy* riots, the passage of the 1929 Censorship of Publications Act—contributed to and were shaped by ongoing local, national, and international debates and dilemmas in the field of sexual health.

Structure and Scope

As this outline indicates, *Irish Modernism and the Politics of Sexual Health* charts Irish culture's engagement with the medicalization and politicization of sex across a roughly eighty-year period, from the foundational vigour of Charles Stewart Parnell in the 1880s—whose public persona (the 'Parnell myth') was to offer an exemplary paradigm of hygienic virility to figures such as Yeats and Joyce in the first decades of the twentieth century—to the self-conscious weariness concerning sexual health and its regulation which permeates Brian O'Nolan's prose in the early 1960s. In book-ending my account of Irish modernism in this way, I seek to illustrate both the extent to which Irish modernism derived its aesthetic force and cultural relevance from its deliberately provocative deployment of a medicalized and politicized conception of sex, and the ways in which the increasing normalization of this model of sexual health in the nation's political and cultural life eventually served to rob Irish modernism of much of its experimental impetus and iconoclastic charge.

In line with my historicizing approach and the schematized analysis of sexual health offered above, I develop my thesis across six chronologically sequenced chapters, clustered into four thematically organized parts. In Part I, I address the themes of autonomy and heredity by examining the role of sexual health discourse in two of the most significant controversies in the cultural and political history of modern Ireland: the split in the Irish Parliamentary Party precipitated by Parnell's involvement in the O'Shea divorce scandal (the 'Parnell Split'), surveyed in Chapter 1, and the *Playboy* riots, explored in Chapter 2. Both scandals have traditionally been characterized (and were strategically framed by their participants) as exemplary manifestations of Irish nationalism's repressed and repressive attitude towards sex and sexuality, in which constitutional nationalists, Sinn Féin republicans, and Irish Ireland revivalists are cast as the prudish and censorious opponents of a more frank and progressive literary avant-garde. In both instances, I argue that this overlooks the extent to which nationalists and modernists alike employed rhetorics of sexual health and sexual pathology to diagnose what they perceived to be the ills of contemporary Irish political and cultural life (by which they usually meant each other), and to envisage and articulate their (often no less conflicting) models of personal, cultural, and political autonomy. Rather than viewing 'nationalism' and 'modernism' as uncomplicatedly distinct and conflicting forces in these debates, neatly divided by their opposing conceptions of sex and its relationship to health, I suggest that it is more productive to view the responses generated by these scandals as, admittedly ideologically heterogeneous, instantiations of an emerging 'sexual modernism' in Ireland.

In the case of the Split, I offer a fresh reading of the much-discussed Parnell myth as a symbolic edifice within which a range of anxieties concerning the relationship between Irishness and sexual health could be foregrounded and negotiated. Surveying a selection of journalistic, biographical, and more overtly literary writing about Parnell, I demonstrate how the images of restraint, continence, and carefully regulated passion that were used to characterize the Chief by his allies before the Split and by modernist authors in its aftermath bequeathed to Irish modernism a pointedly sexualized model of artistry rooted in an ideal of self-siring masculine autonomy. I also chart how, in the hands of Parnell's enemies and detractors, the tropes of the myth could be used to present Parnell as a degenerative and sexually pathological threat to the physical and intellectual integrity of the Irish people.

This discussion is continued in my second chapter, in which I explore the role that both this image of hyper-masculine autonomy and the rhetoric of sexual pathology through which it was challenged play in the oeuvre of J. M. Synge and the controversies it provoked. Calling into question received accounts of the *Playboy* riots, which pit a sexually progressive Abbey Theatre against a rebarbative nationalist rabble, I contend that Synge, his supporters, and his opponents were in fact united in their use of a 'rhetoric of health': an over-determined discourse in which the lexicons of evolution, ethnography, eugenics, and degeneration are combined for political ends. Through this re-reading of the riots and an examination of Synge's critical, autobiographical, and ethnographic prose, I illustrate the ways in which the explanatory mechanisms of biology and sexual health could be harnessed to naturalize divergent political positions in debates over Ireland's future. I also highlight how Yeats, in his hyper-sexualized posthumous defence of Synge, sought to position his friend as the true inheritor of Parnell's virility, nobility, and hygienic autonomy, in contrast to the mob of syphilitic 'Eunuchs' who had opposed him.[89] In doing so, I illustrate the ways in which both the Split and the 'riots' lent a political urgency and an aesthetic potency to questions of sexual pathology and sexual health that was to inform Irish cultural and political debate for decades to come.

In Part II, I address the theme of hygiene by examining how figurations of venereal disease, accounts of its aetiology, and campaigns for its regulation were used by politicians, activists, and authors to construct and contest models of Irish identity in the first decades of the twentieth century. Building on Chapter 1's discussion of rhetorics of sexual pathology in the Split, in Chapter 3, I trace the ways in which references to venereal disease were employed in the anti-enlisting campaigns of the Irish Transvaal Committee, *Inghinidhe na hÉireann* [daughters of Ireland], and Sinn Féin to offer an explanatory metaphor for the malign impact of British imperial rule in Ireland. At the same time, I explore the ways in which figures such as Oliver St John Gogarty and James Joyce echoed and endorsed these positions, using venereal disease and its impact on the Irish population to critique British militarism. However, in doing so, I also acknowledge the ways in which Joyce was to distance himself from the more chauvinistic deployments of this rhetoric, particularly where they concerned Ireland's Jewish population. Finally, I trace the contours of an emerging weariness in Joyce's rendering of the entire question of sexual health as the grounds for conceptualizing Irish national identity, a topic that will be taken up and explored in greater depth in Part IV.

In Part III, I explore the relationship between fertility and autonomy. In doing so, I address arguably the most significant (and fraught) point of intersection between debates over sexual health and modernism in Ireland: the 1929 Censorship of Publications Act and its infamous prohibition of printed material relating to contraception, birth control, and abortion. Where conventional accounts of the Act's passage and operation have framed the responses of Irish modernists such as Yeats, Beckett, and Kate O'Brien as ethically valorous and politically subversive rejections of sexual repression and state-mandated philistinism, I explore the ideological tensions and contradictions that could attend such opposition.

On the one hand, in Chapter 4, by situating Samuel Beckett's personal, journalistic, and literary responses to the Act in relation to the comments of both other modernists (Yeats, Gogarty, Shaw) and a range of public and

---

[89] W. B. Yeats, *The Poems*, ed. Daniel Albright (London: Everyman, 2000), 162.

political figures, I demonstrate the ways in which, through the Act, wider European debates over fertility, population control, and eugenics became bound up with a broader competition for political influence and cultural capital between intellectual, governmental, and confessional factions within the emergent Free State. In doing so, I complicate the traditional picture of Beckett's heroic opposition to the 'filthy censor' and their 'filthy synecdoche' by outlining the debts which Beckett's infamous anti-natalism owes to a strand of Irish sectarian eugenicism which both contributed to and was intensified by the drafting and passage of the Act, before exploring how Beckett subjected this tendency to self-critical scrutiny in his later work.[90]

On the other hand, in Chapter 5, I move beyond this more traditional and male-centred framing of the Censorship Act as a matter of sectarian and demographic concern, to explore the responses of women such as Hannah Sheehy-Skeffington, Signe Toksvig, and, in particular, Kate O'Brien to its passage and operation. In doing so, I chart the ways in which O'Brien's model of an ideal relationship—one compacted between two intelligent, capable, and 'beautiful' individuals, in which sex is the mutually fulfilling realization of shared desire, and where children are the products of active choice rather than unavoidable necessity—reflects and responds to ongoing debates concerning birth control and eugenics in European, British, and Irish culture. In the process, I demonstrate the contradictions and paradoxes that could arise for those, like O'Brien, who sought to marry a eugenic conception of sex and sexuality with an investment in individual liberty and social equality.

Finally, in Part IV, I bring together all four key themes to investigate the legacy of sexual health as a focus of social and cultural debate in 1960s Ireland, and to highlight the increasing exhaustion of Irish modernism's iconoclastic engagement with the topic. To do so, I examine Flann O'Brien's much maligned final novel, *The Hard Life* (1961)—a *Bildungsroman* set in turn-of-the-century Dublin in which a lexicon of weariness and fatigue predominates—and its consistent thematic concern with issues of sexual health and public welfare. The 1960s marked a period of relative liberaliza-tion, modernization, and prosperity for the Republic of Ireland. I explore why, under such circumstances, O'Nolan felt compelled to retreat from an increasingly confident present into what he constructs as the sexually squalid and politically paralysed culture of turn-of-the-century Dublin.

[90] Samuel Beckett, *Murphy*, ed. J. C. C. Mays (London: Faber, 2009), 50.

Moving beyond *The Hard Life*, I identify how, in O'Nolan's late fiction and *Cruiskeen Lawn* columns, the key themes and debates addressed in *Irish Modernism and the Politics of Sexual Health* re-emerge in a performatively exhausted or 'used-up' manner. At the same time, by examining O'Nolan's thwarted efforts to stage a Syngean confrontation with Dublin audiences and a Joycean confrontation with the censorship board, I illustrate the ways in which Irish modernist provocations in the domain of sexual health had come to be surpassed by their context, even as the issues which animated them remained both socially divisive and culturally urgent. In doing so, I suggest the ways in which the politicization of sexual health in Ireland could remain a nightmare from which modernists were increasingly ill-equipped to help the nation to awake.

PART I
SCANDALOUS AUTONOMY

1

'Bred out of the contagion of the throng': Irish Modernism, Sexual Health, and the Parnell Myth

I believe opinion is divided between the people who regard me
as a saint or a statue, and those who suspect me of being an Irish
Don Juan who will eventually compromise Socialism by some
outrageous scandal of the Parnell sort.

George Bernard Shaw to Jules Magny (16 December 1890)

If we have to refer to this subject we do it in the same way as a
surgeon is obliged at times to cut up a corpse.

Timothy Healy discussing Katharine O'Shea,
National Press (29 June 1891)

— That bitch, that English whore, did for him, the shebeen
proprietor commented. She put the first nail in his coffin.

— Fine lump of a woman all the same, the soi-disant townclerk
Henry Campbell remarked, and plenty of her. She loosened
many a man's thighs.

James Joyce, *Ulysses* (1922)

Few figures loom as large in the political, cultural, and sexual history of
Ireland as Charles Stewart Parnell. Politically, he galvanized the Irish
Parliamentary Party into a disciplined electoral force, articulated a flexible
agenda that spoke to the interests of traditionally antagonistic sections of
Irish society, and brought the nation to the verge of Home Rule. Culturally,
he fashioned a public persona premised upon intense self-possession, radical
strength of will, and a seemingly total disregard for popular opinion, which
confounded Arnoldian stereotypes of the turbulent Celt and provided Irish
authors and playwrights with an enduring paradigm of artistic autonomy.
Sexually, the divorce scandal which brought an end to his leadership of the

Irish Modernism and the Politics of Sexual Health. Lloyd (Meadhbh) Houston, Oxford University Press.

IPP, split the nation along Parnellite and anti-Parnellite lines, and, in the eyes of many, drove the 'Uncrowned King of Ireland' into an early grave, became the focal point for a vituperative and sensationalist debate over sexual morality that would set the terms of Irish public discourse concerning sex well into the twentieth century.

The personal, political, and aesthetic ideals that Irish modernists found embodied in the figure of Parnell—chief among them independence, self-mastery, and a capacity for radical self-fashioning—have been well documented.[1] What has been less often noted is the centrality of sexual health to their conception, articulation, and emulation of those virtues. In his caustic 1934 poem 'Parnell's Funeral', W. B. Yeats contrasts the hygienic isolation of the deceased parliamentarian with what he presents as the pathological profusion of those who brought him low:

> Come, fix upon me the accusing eye.
> I thirst for accusation. All that was sung,
> All that was said in Ireland is a lie
> Bred out of the contagion of the throng,
> Saving the rhyme rats hear before they die.[2]

Unlike those contemporary populist worthies ('de Valera', 'Cosgrave', 'O'Duffy') who answer to the 'crowd', in Yeats's eulogy, Parnell acknowledges only one 'master': the 'solitude' that guarantees his antiseptic autonomy.[3] As the thinly veiled sexual ring of 'Bred' insinuates, for Yeats, Parnell's heroic self-rule entailed not simply an eschewal of the 'throng' and its 'contagion', but the intimate acts by which both were propagated. Such celebrations of Parnell's salubrious independence were far from confined to Yeats. Defending Parnell in an open letter published at the height of the O'Shea divorce scandal, George Bernard Shaw lauded the beleaguered

---

[1] Dominic Manganiello, *Joyce's Politics* (London: Routledge, 1980), chap. 1; Michael Steinman, *Yeats's Heroic Figures: Wilde, Parnell, Swift, Casement* (Albany: State University of New York Press, 1983), chap. 4; John Kelly, 'Parnell in Irish Literature,' in *Parnell in Perspective*, ed. David George Boyce and Alan O'Day (London: Routledge, 1991), 251–8; Andrew Gibson, *James Joyce* (London: Reaktion Books, 2006), 44; David Dwan, *The Great Community: Culture and Nationalism in Ireland* (Dublin: Field Day, 2008), 188–99; Joseph Valente, *The Myth of Manliness in Irish National Culture, 1880–1922* (Urbana, Ill: University of Illinois Press, 2011), chap. 2; James Alexander Fraser, *Joyce & Betrayal* (London: Routledge, 2016), 14–19; Edna Longley, "The Rhythm of Beauty': Joyce, Yeats, and the 1890s', in *Parnell and His Times*, ed. Joep Leerssen (Cambridge: Cambridge University Press, 2020), 185–98.

[2] W. B. Yeats, *The Poems*, ed. Daniel Albright (London: Everyman, 2000), 330.   [3] Ibid.

parliamentarian's 'inflexible indifference to the unsympathetic and unintelligent clamours which rise every now and then from the nurseries of English prejudice' and urged him to hold firm in his defiance of those 'morbidly sexual members of the community' who sought to persecute him.[4] Indeed, as Timothy Healy's remarks to an anti-Parnellite rally in June 1891 make clear, even those most vociferously engaged in such persecution were eager to invoke the model of sanitary self-rule Parnell emblematized, if only to damn him for failing to uphold it:

> I believe no more wholesome and no more chastening step will be taken [...] than when Ireland, erect and in its strength, casts from the body politic the ulcer which these men endeavour to graft upon it (loud applause). We must purge Ireland of this corrupt humour with which they have endeavoured to inoculate our blood (applause).[5]

In each of these examples, the figure of Parnell is closely tied (positively or negatively) to a form of health in which sex is treated with extreme ambivalence. The thinly veiled phallic undertones of Healy's image of a virile and tumescent Ireland purging itself of contagion appear to present masculine sexual potency as a key component of the nation's physical and cultural well-being. Yet, the comment itself was made to excoriate Parnell for having displayed an apparent excess of the same virility. Bernard Shaw's letter indicts those who would chastise Parnell for his sexual conduct, even as it insinuates that the impulse to do so was itself 'morbidly sexual'. 'Parnell's Funeral' presents the fecundity of the anti-Parnellite 'throng' as a pestilent affront to the Chief's autonomy, yet, within two years of completing it, Yeats would undergo the Steinach 'rejuvenation' operation in the hope of restoring not only his poetic potency but his capacity for just such apparently degrading sexual activity.[6] If, as the snatch of conversation from *Ulysses* which serves as one of the epigraphs to this chapter illustrates, James Joyce felt that

---

[4] George Bernard Shaw, 'The Other Side. Bernard Shaw Repeats His Sticking Tight Advice,' in *The Matter with Ireland*, ed. Dan H. Laurence and David H. Greene, 2nd ed. (Gainesville: University Press of Florida, 2001), 33; 31. The letter was originally published in *The Star*, 27 November 1890, 1.

[5] *National Press*, 6 June 1891 quoted in Frank Callanan, *T.M. Healy* (Cork: Cork University Press, 1996), 296. This chapter is indebted throughout to Callanan's study of Healy's life, which extensively reproduces much of his polemical commentary during the Split.

[6] For the Steinach operation and its relationship to Yeats's writing and politics in this period, see Virginia D. Pruitt, 'Yeats and the Steinach Operation,' *American Imago* 34, no. 3 (Fall 1977), 287–96; Richard Ellmann, *W.B. Yeats's Second Puberty: A Lecture Delivered at the Library of Congress on April 2, 1984* (Washington: Library of Congress, 1985); Tim Armstrong,

Parnell's legacy revealed the hypocrisy and moral cowardice of a nationalist population unwilling to confront the realities of their own desires, it could leave modernists appearing just as conflicted in their attitudes to sex, particularly in its relationship to health.

As this overview indicates, the Parnell myth—the carefully curated cult of personality which surrounded the parliamentarian before, during, and after his fall from grace—bequeathed to Irish modernism an ideal of heroic autonomy firmly rooted in a medicalized and politicized conception of sex. In doing so, it brought that model of autonomy into potential conflict with the other facets of sexual health I identified in my Introduction. In what follows, I trace the tensions and contradictions to which this could give rise and what they can reveal about the political and aesthetic self-fashioning of a range of Irish modernists. Perhaps counter-intuitively in the context of such an account, this interrogation of the politics of sexual health in Irish modernist responses to the Parnell myth must begin with a discussion of celibacy.

Hygienic Autonomy: Celibacy and the 'Parnell Myth'

Parnell's reserve, froideur, and stoicism have long been commonplaces of Irish literary and political historiography.[7] In virtually every piece of bio-graphical, journalistic, or literary writing devoted to Parnell, particularly

Modernism, Technology, and the Body: A Cultural Study (Cambridge: Cambridge University Press), 1998, chap. 5; Donald J. Childs, *Modernism and Eugenics: Woolf, Eliot, Yeats, and the Culture of Degeneration* (Cambridge: Cambridge University Press), 2001, chap. 7; R. F. Foster, *W.B. Yeats: A Life, The Arch-Poet, 1915–1939*, vol. 2 (Oxford: Oxford University Press, 2003), chap. 13; Joseph M. Hassett, *W.B. Yeats and the Muses* (Oxford: Oxford University Press, 2010), chap. 7.

[7] Major surveys of the Parnell myth which stress these features include Herbert Howarth, *The Irish Writers, 1880–1940: Literature Under Parnell's Star* (London: Rockcliff, 1958); F. S. L. Lyons, 'The Parnell Theme in Literature,' in *Place, Personality, and the Irish Writer,* ed. Andrew Carpenter (Gerrards Cross: Colin Smythe, 1977), 69–96; F. S. L. Lyons, *Ireland Since the Famine,* Repr. (London: Fontana Press, 1992), pt. 2, chap. 3; F. S. L. Lyons, *Charles Stewart Parnell,* New ed. (Dublin: Gill & Macmillan, 2005); Conor Cruise O'Brien, *Parnell and His Party, 1880–90,* Corrected Impression (Oxford: Oxford University Press, 1978), chap. Epilogue; William Michael Murphy, *The Parnell Myth and Irish Politics, 1891–1956* (New York: Peter Lang, 1986); David George Boyce and Alan O'Day, eds., *Parnell in Perspective* (London: Routledge, 1991); Kelly, 'Parnell in Irish Literature'; Frank Callanan, *The Parnell Split: 1890–91* (Cork: Cork University Press, 1992); Callanan, *T.M. Healy,* pt. 2; Dwan, *The Great Community,* 188–99; R. F. Foster, *Modern Ireland: 1600–1972,* Repr. (London: Penguin Books, 2011), chap. 17; Valente, *The Myth of Manliness,* chaps. 1–2; Paul Bew, *Enigma: A New Life of Charles Stewart Parnell* (Dublin: Gill & Macmillan, 2012); Elizabeth Mannion, 'Staging Parnell: Biodrama at the Early Abbey Theatre,' *New Hibernia Review* 22, no. 2 (2018), 146–58.

those addressing his character prior to the Split, the same semantic field is consistently deployed to describe his demeanour and bearing. Parnell is variously: 'impassive, rock-like'; 'calm, silent, and restrained'; 'le moins agité des agiteurs' [the least agitated of agitators]; 'the lock-mouthed master of loose-lipped men'; 'encased in steel'; the embodiment of an imperturbable 'serenity', 'iron resolution', and 'impenetrable reserve'.[8] In many of these texts, this unprecedented continence in word and deed found its tacitly (and, sometimes, explicitly) sexual correlative in an ideal of hygienic autonomy rooted in a curiously virile mode of celibacy. Prior to the revelations of the O'Shea divorce case, Parnell's apparently preternatural restraint was frequently figured as a form of abstinence rooted in a symbolic marriage between Parnell and Ireland itself. An article in the London *Leader* in 1888 is typical in offering an almost hagiographic account of Parnell in which his chaste devotion to the nationalist cause is fetishized in an insistently nuptial register:

> The Irish people [...] know that under that cold face beats a heart which throbs with love for Ireland. [...] He is, indeed, the 'Uncrowned King of Ireland', loved with a love and followed with a fidelity which no leader has commanded since the days of Hugh Roe O'Donnell. There is a kind of shadowy tradition that in his early manhood 'Charlie Parnell' was crossed in love. He certainly has not been crossed in love since he 'took off his coat' to fight the battle of Ireland [...] she has been his queen, his mistress, the only love of his heart, his Dark Rosaleen.[9]

The Mangan-tinged characterization of Ireland as a loyal and long-suffering mistress was a well-worn one, as was the trope of the nationalist hero forgoing a consummated romantic relationship on the terrestrial plane to pledge himself to Erin's service on a spiritual one.[10] The invocation of an

[8] T. C. Luby, R. F. Walsh, and J. C. Curtin, *The Story of Ireland's Struggle for Self-Government* (New York: Gay Brothers & Company, 1893), 743; *Freeman's Journal*, 18 February 1881; J. L. Garvin, 'Parnell and His Power,' *Fortnightly Review* 64 (1 December 1891), 880; R. Barry O'Brien, *The Life of Charles Stewart Parnell, 1846–1891*, vol. 1 (London: Smith, Elder, 1898), 145; James Joyce, *Occasional, Critical, and Political Writing*, ed. Kevin Barry, trans. Conor Deane (Oxford: Oxford University Press, 2008), 194; Garvin, 'Parnell and His Power,' 880; T. P. O'Connor, *Charles Stewart Parnell: A Memory* (London: Ward, Lock, Bowden & Co., 1891), 213.
[9] J. Connellan, 'Life of Charles Stewart Parnell, Esq., M.P.' (London, 1888), reprinted from *The Leader*, quoted in Callanan, *T.M. Healy*, 284.
[10] Examples of this trope in Irish culture are too numerous to permit a comprehensive summary. As Connellan's comments suggest, one influential example was Mangan's famous

anecdotal early heart-break rehearses this narrative to suggest that Parnell's service to Ireland leaves no room for another, more tangible female presence in his life. The over-wording of terms of 'fidelity', loyalty, and commitment offer some sense of just how disastrous the revelations of the O'Shea trial were ultimately to prove for Parnell's public image and the mythic celibacy upon which it was staked. Parnell's perceived complicity in this rhetoric is suggested in an account of a (probably apocryphal) exchange between Parnell and the solicitor W. H. Duignan, who asked the Irish leader why he did not marry. According to Duignan, Parnell replied 'I am married—to my country, and can best serve as I am'.[11] Whether or not the remark emanated from Parnell himself, the fact that it was attributed to him, and the stress it lays on the politically beneficial character of his celibacy (he can 'best serve' as a bachelor) emphasize the centrality of sexual continence to the Parnell myth.

In a context where parish priests were playing an increasingly central role in shaping the moral and political investments of their flock, the ways in which Parnell's chaste devotion to his political vocation echoed the under-lying logic of clerical celibacy are unlikely to have escaped the notice of the Irish public.[12] Certainly, as Frank Callanan has documented, the British political elite were quick to give Parnell's apparently celibate reserve an ecclesiastical cast, with figures from Mary Gladstone to Margot Asquith commenting on his 'spiritual' appearance, 'saint-like face', and 'almost Christ-like countenance', often in the same breath as they testified to the

---

1847 lyric, in which the speaker pledges to rear 'Again in golden sheen' the throne of the eponymous Rosaleen who shall enjoy sovereignty over both his heart and the nation. James Clarence Mangan, *The Collected Works of James Clarence Mangan, Vol. 3: Poems, 1845–1847*, ed. Jacques Chuto (Blackrock: Irish Academic Press, 1996), 168–9. For a discussion of other influential renderings of this convention, see Marjorie Elizabeth Howes, *Yeats's Nations: Gender, Class, and Irishness* (Cambridge: Cambridge University Press), 1996, 74–6; Susan Cannon Harris, *Gender and Modern Irish Drama* (Bloomington: Indiana University Press, 2002), chap. 1; Gerardine Meaney, *Gender, Ireland and Cultural Change: Race, Sex and Nation* (New York: Routledge, 2010), chap. 1; Valente, *The Myth of Manliness*, chap. 3.

[11] *The Nation*, 2 January 1886.

[12] For an account of the growing influence of the Catholic clergy on the social, political, and sexual life of nineteenth-century Irish parishioners, see Tom Inglis, *Moral Monopoly: The Rise and Fall of the Catholic Church in Modern Ireland*, 2nd ed (Dublin: University College Dublin Press, 1998), chaps. 6–8, especially 137–57 and 166–9. For broader accounts of the relationship between Parnell and the Catholic Church in Ireland, see Emmet Larkin, *The Roman Catholic Church in Ireland and the Fall of Parnell, 1888–1891* (Liverpool: Liverpool University Press, 1979), especially chaps. 1–4; C. J. Woods, 'Parnell and the Catholic Church,' in *Parnell in Perspective*, ed. David George Boyce and Alan O'Day (London: Routledge, 1991), 9–37; Frank Callanan, *The Parnell Split: 1890–91* (Cork: Cork University Press, 1992), 260–7.

sexual fascination he inspired among their intimate circle.[13] However, as the *Leader*'s image of Parnell's 'throbbing' heart suggests, and the breathless testimony of more than a few female English Liberals attests, the consistent emphasis laid on Parnell's steely reserve, and the celibacy with which it was cognate, should not be read as an indication that contemporary commentators believed him to lack passion (or desire).[14] Indeed, as a range of critics have noted, his placid exterior is most often presented as a façade, masking and regulating intense inner turmoil.[15] The sense of a constant struggle between powerful drives within Parnell is suggested by the antithetical imagery which Standish O'Grady employed to characterize his temperament, in which an 'ice clear, ice cold intellect, work[ed] as if in the midst of fire'.[16] This vein of imagery was also taken up by the Parnellite *United Ireland* to describe the frenzy of his final campaign and the fascination it afforded the English press: '[It] is the man himself that conquered them, the Titan as he flamed out in the last struggle, like an unsuspected volcano breaking in red devastation through its accumulated ice.'[17] Decades after his death, Katharine Parnell was to reprise the theme in her intimate biography of her husband, stating that 'few knew of the volcanic force and fire that burned beneath his icy exterior'—the not-so-subtle implication of course being that, if anyone was in a position to know, it was the woman who had shared his bed for over a decade.[18] In the Parnell myth, the intense self-mastery of celibacy thus co-existed with a no less strongly stressed sexual potency, which it served to hold in check. For Parnell's brother, this dynamic

---

[13] Mary Gladstone, *Her Diaries and Letters*, ed. Lucy Masterman (London: E. P. Dutton, 1930), 408–11, quoted in Callanan, *T.M. Healy*, 679, n. 57; Margot Oxford, *More Memories* (London: Cassell, 1933), 55, quoted in Callanan, *T.M. Healy*, 679, n. 57. In the same note, Callanan also quotes an unpublished 1899 diary entry in which Mary Gladstone describes how, upon meeting Parnell during a visit to Hawarden, her friend Kathleen Clive found herself 'counting the moments till he [would] look at her again'.

[14] Profiling Parnell in his 1916 memoir, *Portraits of the Seventies*, the Liberal politician G. W. E. Russell quotes an 'Englishwoman of Liberal sympathies' (possibly Kathleen Clive) who, having met Parnell at a dinner in 1899, reported that she had 'never before felt such power and force, in any man': '[I]f he looks at you, you can't look away, and if he doesn't you are wondering how soon he will look at you again. I am afraid that I have very little trust in his goodness; I should think it's a very minus quality; but I believe absolutely in his strength and his power of influence. I should be sorry if he were my enemy; I think he would stop at nothing.' G. W. E. Russell, *Portraits of the Seventies* (London: T. Fisher Unwin, 1916), 214, quoted in Frank Callanan, *T.M. Healy* (Cork: Cork University Press, 1996), 679 n. 57.

[15] The most relevant discussions in the present context are Dwan, *The Great Community*, 2008, 188–99 and Valente, *The Myth of Manliness*, chap. 1.

[16] Standish O'Grady, *The Story of Ireland* (London: Methuen & Co., 1894), 210–11.

[17] 'Parnell and Our Policy,' *United Ireland*, 12 October 1895.

[18] Katharine Parnell, *Charles Stewart Parnell, His Love Story and Political Life*, vol. 2 (London: London & Co, 1914), 248–9.

was at the heart of Parnell's courtship of the Irish people, serving as both an aphrodisiac and a prophylactic: 'a robe that attracted the loyalty' and excited the 'wild enthusiasm' of his countrymen, 'while at the same time repelling their intimacy'.[19]

What was at stake in this paradoxical image of radical chastity and intense virility for Parnell and his supporters, and what was its relationship to sexual health?[20] As the case of Parnell vividly illustrates, Irish attitudes to sexual health in the late nineteenth century were profoundly ambivalent, if not actively contradictory. On the one hand, as Tom Inglis and others have argued, the growing 'moral monopoly' of the Catholic Church in Irish public life could make it seem like there was no such thing as healthy sex at all, rendering the topic an apparently undiscussable locus of anxiety which necessitated firm social regulation.[21] British stereotypes of the Irish as 'undisciplinable, anarchical, and turbulent' exemplars of a politically disabling mode of Celtic femininity reinforced this impression, encouraging advocates of independence to stress the purity and restraint of the Irish, particularly in sexual matters.[22] Underpinning both positions was a well-worn

---

[19] John Howard Parnell, *Charles Stewart Parnell: A Memoir* (New York: Henry Holt, 1914), 127.

[20] For a survey of critical literature on the social and cultural significance of celibacy in the late nineteenth and early twentieth centuries, see Benjamin Kahan, *Celibacies: American Modernism and Sexual Life* (Durham: Duke University Press, 2013), Introduction. Parnell's virile celibacy differs significantly from the queerer and more subversive forms of celibacy mapped by Kahan in his study, and is more closely aligned with the modes of masculine self-possession charted in Valente, *The Myth of Manliness*, Introduction and chaps. 1–2. The fact that late marriage and permanent celibacy were an increasingly widespread norm in late nineteenth-century Ireland may well have served to render Parnell's celibate persona less unusual than it might have appeared in other national contexts, even as it may also have served to make its undertones of barely contained sexual potency more legible. For a discussion of the factors underpinning Irish demographic patterns in this period, see Robert E. Kennedy, Jr, *The Irish: Emigration, Marriage, and Fertility* (Berkeley: University of California Press, 1973), chap. 7; Timothy Guinnane, *The Vanishing Irish: Households, Migration, and the Rural Economy in Ireland, 1850–1914* (Princeton, N.J: Princeton University Press, 1997), chap. 7.

[21] Tom Inglis, 'Foucault, Bourdieu and the Field of Irish Sexuality,' *Irish Journal of Sociology* 7, no. 1 (1997), 5–28; Inglis, *Moral Monopoly*, chaps. 6–8; Tom Inglis, 'Origins and Legacies of Irish Prudery: Sexuality and Social Control in Modern Ireland,' *Éire-Ireland* 40, no. 3 (2005), 9–37; Tom Inglis, 'The Irish Body,' in *Are the Irish Different?*, ed. Tom Inglis (Manchester: Manchester University Press, 2014), 88–98; Chrystel Hug, *The Politics of Sexual Morality in Ireland* (Basingstoke: Palgrave Macmillan, 1998); James M. Smith, *Ireland's Magdalen Laundries and the Nation's Architecture of Containment* (Manchester: Manchester University Press, 2008).

[22] Quoting Henri Martin, Matthew Arnold influentially presented the Celt as 'Sentimental—*always ready to react against the despotism of fact*' and argued that the rational, masculine Anglo-Saxon had failed his feminized neighbour in neglecting to cultivate a 'vital union' between the two races and cultures. Matthew Arnold, *On the Study of Celtic Literature* (London: Smith, Elder, & Co., 1867), 109; 102; xii. For a discussion of the gendered and ethnic

rationalist conception of sexual desire as a degrading compromise to a subject's autonomy which impaired their capacity for reasoned thought and self-mastery.[23] The gendered dynamics of this ideal of rational self-rule, particularly in its Enlightenment manifestations, have been well-canvassed, with numerous commentators noting the ways in which figures such as Descartes and Rousseau coded rationality as a signally masculine trait in contrast to the apparent unreason of feminine corporeality.[24] In late nineteenth-century Europe, this framing of well-regulated masculine desire as a component of 'reason' was both bolstered and brought into the domain of health through the proliferation of discourses and diagnostic taxonomies concerning perceived sexual perversions to which sexology gave rise.[25]

politics of this model of Celtic identity, see Howes, *Yeats's Nations*, chap. 1; Susan Cannon Harris, *Gender and Modern Irish Drama* (Bloomington: Indiana University Press, 2002), chap. 2; Valente, *The Myth of Manliness*, chap. 1.

[23] In 'Cratylus', Plato has Socrates liken desire to a chain whose heaviness increased in direct proportion to its strength, while in the *Republic* he has Socrates liken the loss of libido in old age to the experience of a slave who has escaped from long bondage to a savage and unstable master. For Kant, sexual desire famously constituted an extreme form of objectification which violated the subjectivity not only of the desired other but of the desiring individual themselves. Plato, *The Dialogues of Plato Translated into English with Analyses and Introductions*, trans. Benjamin Jowett, 3rd: Revised and Updated (Oxford: Oxford University Press, 1892), 346–7; Plato, *Republic*, trans. Robin Waterfield, Reissued [1993] (Oxford: Oxford University Press, 1998), sec. 329c; Immanuel Kant, *Lectures on Ethics*, trans. Louis Infield (New York: Harper and Row, 1963), 163. For an overview of philosophical positions on desire, see Rockney Jacobsen, 'Desire, Sexual,' in *Sex from Plato to Paglia: A Philosophical Encyclopedia*, ed. Alan Soble, vol. 1, 2 vols. (Westport, Conn: Greenwood Press, 2006), 222–8.

[24] The Cartesian mind-body distinction has long been understood in gendered terms, with masculinity elevated to a state of transcendent reason and femininity reduced to an inescapable biological facticity. Likewise, while Rousseau argued that sex in the state of nature had been a mutually desired and mutually fulfilling exchange between two equally matched (heterosexual) partners, in *Émile* (1762), he argued that men were far more likely to transcend their embodied situation and its attendant desires: 'Le mâle n'est mâle qu'en certains instants, la femelle est femelle toute sa vie, ou du moins toute sa jeunesse.' [The male is only male at certain moments, the female is female all her life, or, at least, all her youth.] Jean Jacques Rousseau, *Œuvres complètes de J.-J. Rousseau*, vol. tome II: *La nouvelle Héloïse. Émile. Lettre à M. de Beaumont* (Paris: Alexandre Houssiaux, 1852), 634. For a representative overview of this phenomenon and the commentary it has generated, see Victor J Siedler, 'Reason, Desire, and Male Sexuality,' in *The Cultural Construction of Sexuality*, ed. Pat Caplan, Repr [1987] (London: Routledge, 1996), 82–112. For a version of this critique in the context of Modernist Studies, see Rita Felski, *The Gender of Modernity* (Cambridge, Mass: Harvard University Press, 1995), Introduction.

[25] Numerous accounts have been offered of this phenomenon across a range of disciplines. Significant statements in the present context include Michel Foucault, *The History of Sexuality, 1: The Will to Knowledge* (New York: Pantheon Books, 1978), pts. 3 and 4; Jeffrey Weeks, *Sex, Politics, and Society: The Regulation of Sexuality Since 1800*, Third Edition [1981] (London: Pearson, 2012), chap. 8; Jeffrey Weeks, *Sexuality and Its Discontents: Meanings, Myths, and Modern Sexualities*, Reprinted (London: Routledge, 1985), chap. 4; Lucy Bland and Laura L. Doan, eds., *Sexology in Culture: Labelling Bodies and Desires* (Cambridge: Polity Press, 1998); Heike Bauer, *English Literary Sexology: Translations of Inversion, 1860–1930*

As I suggested in my Introduction, in texts such as Richard von Krafft-Ebing's voluminous *Psychopathia Sexualis* (1886), which comprised 238 case studies by its twelfth edition (1902), irresistible sexual urges came to be treated as evidence not merely of irrationality, but of physical and mental pathology.[26] In late nineteenth-century Ireland, to be sexually incontinent was thus not only to offend against Catholic social teaching but to conform to a model of Irish identity increasingly synonymous with a mode of pathological irrationality and a perceived incapacity for personal and national self-governance.

On the other hand, for men at least, the absence of sex (or sexual desire) could be just as 'unhealthy' as its excessive presence. While the oft-invoked 'crisis of masculinity' which beset *fin de siècle* Europe can be over-stressed, the medical literature surrounding 'male hysteria' in the 1880s and 1890s undoubtedly reflects an abiding concern with the pathological effects of impotence and diminished or repressed libido in men.[27] As Mark S. Micale has shown, 'anaphrodesia' (the absence of sexual desire), 'testicular anaesthesia', and 'genital asthenia' (a progressive loss of sex drive) were all identified as symptomatic of the malady, which, in a cruel irony, was most commonly held to manifest itself in impotent episodes of hyper-eroticized involuntary bodily convulsion.[28] This perspective was not merely confined to the world of clinical science. In his 1887 novel *A Mere Accident*, George Moore offers a medically inflected study of the queer-coded Anglo-Catholic ascetic John Norton, whose celibacy and religious devotion are figured as, at

(Basingstoke: Palgrave Macmillan, 2009); Heike Bauer, ed., *Sexology and Translation: Cultural and Scientific Encounters Across the Modern World* (Philadelphia: Temple University Press, 2015).

[26] Richard von Krafft-Ebing, *Psychopathia Sexualis: Mit besonderer Berucksichtigung der kontraren Sexualempfindung: Eine medizinisch-gerichtliche Studie fur Arzte und Juriste*, 12. Ausgabe (Stuttgart: Verlag von Ferdinand Enke, 1902).

[27] For the origins of this historiographical turn, see Roger Horrocks and Jo Campling, *Masculinity in Crisis: Myths, Fantasies, and Realities* (New York: St. Martin's Press, 1994); John Tosh, 'What Should Historians Do with Masculinity? Reflections on Nineteenth-Century Britain,' *History Workshop* 38 (1994), 179–202. For an account of cultural attitudes to impotence in this period, see Angus McLaren, *Impotence: A Cultural History* (Chicago: University of Chicago Press, 2007), chaps. 5 and 6.

[28] Moty, 'Hystérie Chez l'homme,' *Gazette Des Hôpitaux* 30 (12 March 1885), 235–6; Elisé-Samuel Maricourt, *Contribution à l'Étude de l'hystérie Chez l'homme* (Paris: Medical Dissertation, 1877), 42; Joseph Grasset and Sidoine Jeannet, *Quelques Cas d'hystérie Mâle et de Neurasthénie* (Montpellier: C Coulet, 1892), 9–11, quoted in Mark S Micale, *Hysterical Men: The Hidden History of Male Nervous Illness* (Cambridge, Mass: Harvard University Press, 2008), 187.

best, a psychologically distorting fig-leaf for repressed same-sex desire, and, at worst, an incipient mode of violent sexual pathology.[29] For Friedrich Nietzsche, whose thought was to influence many Irish modernist appropriations of the Parnell myth, asceticism and abstinence, the 'morbid' by-products of a Christian 'misunderstanding of the body', made a virtue of 'poor nutrition' by rejecting true 'health' as a species of 'enemy', 'devil', or 'temptation'.[30] The *great* health' of the mature 'free spirit', Nietzsche argued, embraced rather than eschewed the imperatives of sexual desire, which he considered the basis for all evolutionary progress:[31]

'Perfection': in those states (especially in sexual love, etc.) there is naively revealed what the deepest instinct acknowledges to be the higher, more desirable, more valuable in general, the upward movement of its type; likewise, *which* status it's really *striving for*. Perfection: that is the extraordinary expansion of its feeling of power; it is wealth; it is the necessary bubbling and brimming over all limits...[32]

[29] Challenged concerning his desire to lead a cloistered existence instead of perpetuating his aristocratic line, Norton, who expresses his appreciation for the '[h]andsome lads of sixteen' who serve as altar boys at the ecclesiastical college where he is training, asserts that he finds something 'very degrading' and 'very gross' in the prospect of life with a woman, preferring to remain 'unspotted' and 'free from all befouling touch'. This desire for purity is compromised when Norton becomes involved with a young woman called Kitty, who takes her own life after being sexually assaulted, possibly by Norton himself. George Moore, *A Mere Accident* (London: Vizetelly & Co, 1887), 62; 103. In 1895 Moore revised and condensed *A Mere Accident* into a novella entitled 'John Norton', which he included as one of the three case studies that comprise the collection *Celibates*. George Moore, 'John Norton,' *Celibates* (London: Walter Scott, 1895), 315–452. Moore's depiction of Norton in both iterations echoes his handling of the character of Cecelia Cullen in *A Drama in Muslin* (1885), whose ardent celibacy is presented as a by-product of her physical disability, thinly veiled queer attachment to the novel's protagonist, Alice Barton, violent horror of men and reproductive sexuality, and growing religious vocation. George Moore, *A Drama in Muslin: A Realistic Novel*, ed. Alexander Norman Jeffares (Gerrards Cross: Colin Smythe, 1981), 58–63; 97; 103; 184–8; 226–33; 297–309.
[30] Friedrich Wilhelm Nietzsche, *The Anti-Christ, Ecce Homo, Twilight of the Idols, and Other Writings*, ed. Aaron Ridley and Judith Norman, trans. Judith Norman (Cambridge: Cambridge University Press, 2005), 50. Emphases Nietzsche's. Commentary on Nietzsche's conception of health and its role in his philosophy is voluminous. For a useful discussion of Nietzsche's idiosyncratic interpretation of evolutionary theory and its relationship to sex, desire, and health, see Gregory Moore, *Nietzsche, Biology, and Metaphor* (Cambridge: Cambridge University Press, 2002), chap. 3.
[31] Emphasis in the original. Friedrich Wilhelm Nietzsche, *Human, All Too Human: A Book for Free Spirits*, trans. R. J. Hollingdale (Cambridge: Cambridge University Press, 1996), 8.
[32] Friedrich Wilhelm Nietzsche, *Writings from the Late Notebooks*, ed. Rüdiger Bittner, trans. Kate Sturge (Cambridge: Cambridge University Press, 2003), 160. Emphasis and ellipsis Nietzsche's.

The echoes of these lines of thought in Yeats's denunciation of the '*Hysterica passio*' of the 'throng' he believed had brought down Parnell, or the 'eunuch-like tone and temper' of those who opposed what he identified as the sexual potency of J. M. Synge's dramatic oeuvre are not far to seek.[33] They are also legible in the coda to the 1903 edition of Moore's *The Untilled Field*, in which a trio of iconoclastic émigrés discuss how nothing 'thrives in Ireland but the celibate, the priest, the nun, and the ox', and decry the nation's culture of clerical sexual surveillance in a decidedly Nietzschean key: 'That which tends to weaken life is the only evil, that which strengthens life the only good, and the result of this puritanical Catholicism will be an empty Ireland.'[34] In such a context, as Joseph Valente has suggested, the same Celticist scheme which obliged nationalists to stress Irish purity, also made it necessary for them to emphasize the virile potency of the nation and its political and cultural avatars or risk being deemed too passive to be worthy of self-rule at all.[35]

Parnell's public persona was carefully calibrated to balance these conflicting imperatives and the anxieties to which they gave rise, serving as a sort of sexual golden mean in which neither continence nor virility was compromised or allowed to compromise the perceived '*great* health' of the autonomous leader. Though Parnell did not coin the term, as both a project and a slogan, 'Home Rule', with its overtones of regulated domesticity, patriarchal autocracy, and intimate self-mastery, performed a very similar balancing act. Joyce draws attention to both sides of this sexualized ideal of autonomy and the strain involved in balancing them in *Ulysses* through the ironic juxtaposition of the two advertisements which follow Bloom throughout the novel: the 'HOUSE OF KEY(E)S' (*U* 7.141) circular, with its 'innuendo of home rule' (*U* 7.150), which Bloom is trying to have placed in the *Daily Telegraph*, and the notice for '*Plumtree's Potted Meat*' (*U* 5.145), with its oft-highlighted suggestion of phallic penetration and its painful reminder of Molly's infidelity, which confronts him in his morning copy of the

---

[33] In 'On Those That Hated *The Playboy of the Western World*, 1907', Yeats famously presents a midnight encounter between crowds of 'Eunuchs' who throng the streets to look upon the 'sinewy thigh' of Synge, whom Yeats figures as Don Juan on horse-back. Yeats, *The Poems*, 2000, 329; 162; W. B. Yeats, *Memoirs*, ed. Denis Donoghue (London: Papermac, 1988), 177.

[34] George Moore, *The Untilled Field*, ed. Richard Allen Cave (Gerrards Cross: Colin Smythe, 2000), 223. An inveterate reviser of his own writing, Moore excised 'The Way Back' from the collection in its 1914 and 1931 editions.

[35] Valente, *The Myth of Manliness*, Introduction.

Freeman's Journal.[36] In Joyce's view, while the advocates of Home Rule stressed an ideal of hygienic autonomy and self-regulation, they did so in conversation with a model of masculine virility in which no home could be complete without regularly 'potted meat'. Parnell's political and cultural appeal lay in his capacity to suggest both tendencies at once. His political and personal ruin stemmed from the collapse of this carefully calibrated dialectic and the revelations of the O'Shea divorce case which precipitated it.

Succumbing to Heredity: Portraits of Parnell as a General Paralytic

When Parnell was named as a co-respondent in Captain William O'Shea's divorce proceedings against his wife, Katharine, in December 1889, the reputation for superhuman reserve upon which Parnell's public persona had been constructed, combined with the pointedly sexual nature of his perceived transgressions, lent an added potency and urgency to sexual health rhetoric which anti-Parnellites were quick to exploit. They did so by staging a protracted assault on the claims to hygienic autonomy upon which the Parnell myth had hitherto been so conspicuously staked. Their most consistent target was Parnell's mental health. Their preferred rhetorical strategy centred on questions of heredity.

In the outpouring of vituperation which followed the Split, Parnell's failure to uphold in the arena of his sexual life the heroic reserve and ardent restraint upon which his public persona rested, and the protracted deceit the affair was perceived to have required of him, were presented as having precipitated (or, in more charitable accounts, stemmed from) a descent into congenital insanity. At the centre of this recharacterization of the Chief was his former deputy, Timothy Healy, a former member of *United Ireland* staff who broke away to found the *National Press* in the March of 1891 in response to what he presented as 'a situation which had become not only a scandal, but a source of public danger'.[37] Introducing the paper, Healy promised that the *National Press* would reunify Irish nationalism behind 'principle' not 'personality'.[38] A key manoeuvre in sponsoring this shift away from the fetish of Parnellism was to insinuate that the 'personality' in

---

[36] James Joyce, *Ulysses*, ed. Hans Gabler (New York: Vintage, 1986). Cited parenthetically by episode and line number.
[37] 'At the Outset,' *National Press*, 7 March 1891, 4.   [38] Ibid., 4.

question was pathologically unstable. An early manifestation of this rhetoric, and the fissures within the Irish party which it reflected, came in an article in the *New York Times* of 13 July 1890 by Harold Frederic, a friend and collaborator of Healy. Amid an increasingly visible disagreement between Parnell and Healy on the question of peasant proprietorship, Frederic presented Parnell's unexpected intervention in the debate over Balfour's 'Purchase of Land and Congested Districts (Ireland) Bill' as evidence of his increasingly fragile mental state:

> There has all along been the difficulty of seeing how he could maintain this post once the O'Shea case had come to trial, and last night a number of Irish members were disposed to fear that brooding upon this trouble had brought on the mental disturbance to which he is hereditarily predisposed. It is the only way in which they are able to account for his astonishing and contemptuous act of treachery to them.[39]

Healy was rapidly identified as the inspiration for (if not the author of) Frederic's article, and, though he denied responsibility for its contents, he did not disavow its sentiments or intervene to curtail its circulation. Instead, Frederic's attacks only grew more explicit and ferocious, with one article, on the basis of Parnell's 'strong hereditary predispositions towards mental disturbance', claiming in its headline that 'lunacy' was 'a charitable construction to put upon his conduct' and baldly inquiring 'is Parnell a crazy man?'.[40] These trans-Atlantic salvos did not escape the notice of Parnell, who, in the midst of the Split, angrily claimed that Healy had cabled to America 'to consign [him] to the lunatic asylum'.[41] This perception became so widespread that the *National Press* felt compelled to defend itself by disparaging what it dubbed the *United Ireland*'s 'drive him into an-asylum--or-the-grave yarns'.[42] Whatever their origin, the immediate import of Frederic's remarks was clear enough: the strain of the O'Shea case had precipitated Parnell's lapse into a politically disastrous form of inherited madness which his lieutenants could no longer afford to ignore. However, their implications did not stop there. More significantly, by linking a suggestion of hereditary mental illness to the sexual impropriety for which

---

[39] *New York Times*, 13 July 1890.
[40] Harold Frederic, 'Is Parnell a Crazy Man: His Foul Betrayal of the Cause of Ireland. Lunacy a Charitable Construction to Put Upon His Conduct—What His Colleagues Bear—Beginning of the O'Shea Scandal,' *New York Times*, 7 December 1890, 12.
[41] Callanan, *The Parnell Split*, 283.   [42] *National Press*, 13 October 1891.

the O'Shea trial was a byword, Frederic presented Parnell as both a victim of and locus for degeneration through what would have been legible to many readers as a tacit diagnosis of congenital syphilis and incipient General Paralysis of the Insane (GPI).[43]

In a late nineteenth-century cultural context where, as Sander L. Gilman and others have illustrated, the concepts of 'perversion' and 'degeneration' functioned as virtual synonyms, the birth defects, developmental delays, and learning difficulties caused by congenital syphilis appeared to offer tangible evidence of the hereditary ramifications of perceived sexual deviancy for the individual and the population to which they belonged.[44] Alfred Fournier, one of Europe's foremost authorities on syphilis and its treatment in the late nineteenth and early twentieth centuries, presented the illness as an eschatological threat to the fabric of European society. According to Fournier, congenital syphilis threatened the state with citizens incapable of work, soldiers incapable of combat, increased rates of separation and divorce— 'avec toutes les calamités sociales qui en dérivent' [with all the social calamities which derive from them]—sterile marriages, 'abâtardissement et dégénération de la race' [bastardization and degeneration of the race], polymortality of the young, and eventual depopulation.[45] In offering this prognosis, Fournier drew on the work of Bénédict Augustin Morel, whose account of 'des dégénérescences physiques, intellectuelles, et morales de l'espèce humaine' [the physical, intellectual, and moral degeneration of the

[43] In making this assertion I am both drawing on and extending Callanan's detailed and probing analysis of anti-Parnellite efforts to pathologize the Chief's public image in the aftermath of the O'Shea divorce. While Callanan's study of the Split acknowledges that 'Parnell's physical aspect and demeanour became [in the wake of the O'Shea trial] a political issue' and traces the ways in which his deteriorating health and dishevelled appearance were presented as indices of his moral decline, it does not highlight the role suggestions of sexual pathology played in such a campaign. Likewise, despite offering a thoroughgoing and perceptive account of Healy's 'sexual rhetoric' against Parnell in chapter 14 of his biography of Parnell's lieutenant to which the present discussion is indebted, Callanan does not identify or unpack the references to venereal disease and degeneration with which it was encoded. Callanan, *The Parnell Split*, 162; Callanan, *T.M. Healy*, chaps. 10–14.

[44] In an overview of degeneration theory's relationship to sexology and psychoanalysis, Gilman asserts that '[n]o realm of human experience is as closely tied to the concept of degeneration as that of sexuality [. . .] The concepts of human sexuality and degeneracy are inseparable within nineteenth-century thought. Both evolved together and provided complementary paradigms for understanding human development.' As a result, Gilman notes, the 'hidden decay of syphilis,' with 'its mythic relationship to sexuality' and 'its ability to destroy across generations,' saw it become 'one of the late nineteenth-century paradigms for degenerative sexuality.' Sander L. Gilman, 'Sexology, Psychoanalysis, and Degeneration: From a Theory of Race to a Race to Theory,' in *Degeneration: The Dark Side of Progress*, ed. J. Edward Chamberlin and Sander L. Gilman (New York: Columbia University Press, 1985), 72; 85.

[45] Alfred Fournier, *Prophylaxie de la Syphilis* (Paris: J. Rueff, 1903), 4.

human species] became a commonplace of late-nineteenth century scientific and cultural commentary. Morel famously defined 'dégénérescence' as 'une déviation maladive d'un type primitif' [a morbid deviation from an original type], in a neo-Lamarckian narrative of environmentally determined progressive decline soon extended to account for cultural as well as biological decay.[46] British psychologist Henry Maudsley, in his influential *The Physiology and Pathology of the Mind* (1867), cites a case study from Morel's *Traité* to illustrate this trend:

> *First generation.* – Immorality. Alcoholic excess. Brutal degradation.
>
> *Second generation.* – Hereditary drunkenness. Maniacal attacks. General Paralysis.
>
> *Third generation.* – Sobriety. Hypochondria. Lypemania. Systematic mania. Homicidal tendencies.
>
> *Fourth generation.* – Feeble intelligence. Stupidity. First attack of mania at sixteen. Transition to complete idiocy, and probable extinction of the family.[47]

The degenerative slide from 'Immorality' to 'extinction' via a succession of ever-intensifying psychological and physiological pathologies charts a medico-moral narrative of progressive corruption that furnished contemporary cultural and political commentators with an uncommonly flexible vehicle for social critique. As Morel's genealogy suggests, 'General Paralysis'—a terminal state of spastic muscular weakness, violent personality changes, and dementia whose roots in syphilitic infection were strongly suspected, but, as yet, unproven in contemporary medicine—offered both the ideal metaphor for and exemplification of this process.[48] Decried as the 'apotheosis

---

[46] The best-known and most influential application of degeneration theory to the realm of culture is the Hungarian social critic Max Nordau's 1892 polemic, *Entartung* [degeneration]. In a dedication to the Italian criminologist Caesar Lombroso, Nordau famously asserted that degenerates 'sind nicht immer Verbrecher, Prostituierte, Anarchisten und erklärte Wahnsinnige. Sie sind manchaml Schriftsteller und Künstler' [are not always criminals, prostitutes, anarchists, and pronounced lunatics; they are often authors and artists]. Bénédict Augustin Morel, *Traité des Dégénérescences Physiques, Intellectuelles et Morales de l'Espèce Humaine et des Causes qui Produisent ces Variétés Maladives* (Paris: J. B. Ballière, 1857), 5; Max Nordau, *Entartung*, vol. 1 (Berlin: Carl Dunder, 1893), vii.

[47] Henry Maudsley, *The Physiology and Pathology of the Mind* (London: Macmillan, 1867), 215–16.

[48] Prior its being definitively identified as a form of tertiary syphilis in 1913, GPI was taken to stem from a broader confluence of immoral and improvident behaviours, including over-work, alcoholism, and sexual excess. This is not to say that syphilis and GPI were not strongly

of selfishness', and a condition whose 'opening chapter' was 'moral decadence' and whose conclusion was 'inevitable premature extinction', in the nineteenth century GPI became a byword for a corrupt and corrupting contemporary culture.[49] In the hands of Healy and his allies it afforded a valuable opportunity to naturalize a moral critique of Parnellism through a diagnostic register that productively hovered between the literal and the metaphorical, allowing them to present Parnell's continued influence in Irish politics as a demoralizing contagious disease.

Unfortunately for the Chief and his supporters, it was a narrative that modernism was on-hand to reinforce. In a fortuitous coincidence for the anti-Parnellite lobby, just a week after the *National Press* was founded the effects of GPI and congenital syphilis were given infamous visibility on the British stage by the London début of Henrik Ibsen's *Ghosts* (1881), which was presented in a private performance on 13 March 1891 by the subscription-only Independent Theatre Society (ITS).[50] At the climax of the play, the young artist Oswald Alving reveals to his mother that his 'mind' has been 'broken down' by an attack of neurosyphilis.[51] Oswald, who has been informed by a Parisian doctor that the 'sins of the fathers are visited upon the children' and that his 'worm-eaten' condition has its origins in paternal dissipation, asks his mother to help him take his own life should a final episode of cerebral softening leave him incapable of doing so himself.[52] The scandal provoked by the production became legendary (and somewhat laughable) even in its own day, with William Archer—the play's translator and a founding member of the ITS—offering an amusing compendium of the deluge of abuse it received:

associated throughout the nineteenth century (its status as a form of sexual pathology was widely agreed upon by at least mid-century), but to suggest the variety of social problems the illness could be invoked to address in the period. Jennifer Wallis, ' "Atrophied", "Engorged", "Debauched": Muscle Wastage, Degenerate Mass and Moral Worth in the General Paralytic Patient,' in *Insanity and the Lunatic Asylum in the Nineteenth Century*, ed. Thomas Knowles and Serena Trowbridge (London: Pickering & Chatto, 2015), 100.

[49] R. S. Stewart, 'The Increase of General Paralysis in England and Wales: Its Causation and Significance,' *Journal of Medical Science* 42 (October 1896), 776.

[50] For an account of this performance and its position within the broader rise of 'Ibsenism', see Tracy C. Davis, 'The Independent Theatre Society's Revolutionary Scheme for an Uncommercial Theater,' *Theatre Journal* 42, no. 4 (December 1990), 447; Katherine E. Kelly, 'Pandemic and Performance: Ibsen and the Outbreak of Modernism,' *South Central Review* 25, no. 1 (2008), 12–35.

[51] Henrik Ibsen, *Ghosts; An Enemy of the People; The Wild Duck*, Authorized English Edition, trans. William Archer (London: Walter Scott, 1904), 67.

[52] Ibid., 69.

'Ibsen's positively abominable play entitled *Ghosts*...This disgusting
representation...Reprobation due to such as aim at infecting the modern
theatre with poison after desperately inoculating themselves and others...
An open drain; a loathsome sore unbandaged; a dirty act done publicly; a
lazar-house with all the doors and windows open...Candid foulness...
Ibsen's melancholy and malodorous world...Absolutely loathsome and
fetid...Gross, almost putrid indecorum...Literary carrion...Crapulous
stuff...Novel and perilous nuisance.' *Daily Telegraph* (leading article).
'This mass of vulgarity, egotism, coarseness, and absurdity.' *Daily
Telegraph* (criticism). [...] 'Morbid, unhealthy, unwholesome and disgusting story...A piece to bring the stage into disrepute and dishonour every
right-thinking man and woman.' *Lloyd's*.[53]

While the analogy can be over-stressed, as both Ben Levitas and Irina Ruppo
Malone have noted, the Ibsenic qualities of Parnell's fall from grace and the
Parnellian qualities of the controversy surrounding the London premiere of
Ghosts would not have been far to seek for Irish cultural and political
commentators.[54] They were certainly detected by the young Bernard Shaw,
who, in *The Quintessence of Ibsenism*—published in the October of 1891—
presented the play as 'an uncompromising and outspoken attack on marriage as a useless sacrifice of human beings to an ideal'—a comment which
might have served equally well to characterize Shaw's journalistic position
on the O'Shea scandal.[55] Responding to an attack on Parnell by the Baptist
minister John Clifford in a letter in the Liberal Party-financed *Star*, Shaw
remarked that 'the relation between Mr Parnell and Mrs O'Shea was a
perfectly natural and right one' and that the 'whole mischief in the matter
lay in the law that tied the husband and wife together and forced Mr Parnell
to play the part of clandestine intriguer, instead of enabling them to dissolve
the marriage by mutual consent, without disgrace to either party'.[56] In line
with his Fabian eugenicist principles and his defence of *Ghosts*, Shaw
concluded that to oblige Parnell to resign over his role in the divorce

[53] William Archer, 'Ghosts and Gibberings,' *Pall Mall Gazette*, no. 8127 (8 April 1891), 3.
[54] Ben Levitas, *The Theatre of Nation* (Oxford University Press, 2002), 10–11; Irina Ruppo
Malone, *Ibsen and the Irish Revival* (Basingstoke: Palgrave Macmillan, 2010), 12–18.
[55] George Bernard Shaw, *The Quintessence of Ibsenism* (London: Walter Scott, 1891), 82. For
a discussion of Shaw's response to the O'Shea scandal and the Split, see Nelson O'Ceallaigh
Ritschel, *Bernard Shaw, W.T. Stead, and the New Journalism: Whitechapel, Parnell, Titanic, and
the Great War* (Cham, Switzerland: Palgrave Macmillan, 2018), chap. 3.
[56] George Bernard Shaw, 'Shall Parnell Go?,' in *The Matter with Ireland*, ed. Dan H. Laurence
and David H. Greene, 2nd ed. (Gainesville: University Press of Florida, 2001), 30.

would be to sacrifice him in the name of a marriage law that favoured a mode of spurious moral 'purity' over true public 'health':

> Until marriage laws are remodelled to suit men and women and to further the happiness and health of the community, instead of to conform to an ideal of 'purity,' no verdict in a divorce case will force any man to retire from public life if it appears that he behaved no worse than the law forced him to. Mr. Parnell's business is simply to sit tight and let the pure people talk.[57]

As the events of the Split were to show, Shaw fatally underestimated not only the power of this purity rhetoric but also its capacity to assimilate precisely the eugenic conception of public health through which he sought to defend Parnell. While Frederic and Healy's deployment of the suggested taint of congenital syphilis was undertaken in the service of a radically different social agenda to that of Ibsen or Shaw, the capacity for the illness to signify an inheritable form of social corruption remained the same, as did the sense that the health of the individual could serve as a metonym for the health of the community or nation.[58] If, as it was for Clement Scott at the *Daily Telegraph*, Ibsen's play was an 'essay on heredity and contagious disease [...] cut into lengths', in the hands of the anti-Parnellite press, the fallen parliamentarian's life became something very similar: a lurid script in which the sins of the leader were visited upon the party (and the nation), leaving its Parnellite wing prostrated, worm-eaten, and waiting to be put out of its misery.[59] Whether or not they bore a direct connection to the *Ghosts* controversy, images of toxic 'inoculation', open 'sores', and sexual infection and accusations of 'egotism', 'morbid' brooding, and 'dirty acts done publicly' were to be consistently marshalled in the reportage and invective surrounding Parnell after the Split, and were to remain features of nationalist rhetoric for decades after its apparent resolution.

Healy was to exploit this rich seam of imagery to the full in his attacks on Parnell's political strategy and his refusal to concede the leadership of the Irish Party, through articles and speeches in which echoes of contemporary

---

[57] Ibid., 30–1.

[58] For an account of Ibsen's medically engaged depiction of syphilis, his nuanced deployment of the illness as a vehicle for social critique in his work, and its broader influence in modernism, see Alexis Soloski, '"The Great Imitator": Staging Syphilis in *A Doll's House* and *Ghosts*,' *Modern Drama* 56, no. 3 (2013), 287–305.

[59] Clement Scott, 'Royalty Theatre,' *The Daily Telegraph*, 14 March 1891.

medical conceptions of neurosyphilis, degeneration, and their psychopathological effects abound. Discussing the 'Rise and Fall' of Parnell in a March
1891 article for the *New Review*, Healy presents the primary defect of his
former leader as a propensity for megalomania which eluded the notice of
his allies, but which chimed with the hereditary disposition towards madness so regularly evoked by his biographers: 'The chief mischief no one
exactly divined—the deterioration which unchecked power seems to produce in the mind of its possessor.'[60] While at one level this remark seems to be
staked upon a clichéd assertion of the corrupting effects of absolute power,
the pseudo-medical ring of 'deterioration' and the image of mental pathology it evokes, combined with the deliberately tautologous pun of 'chief
mischief' (linking Parnell's leadership to his perceived misconduct), con-
spire to present Parnell's egomaniacal supremacy as a distinctly morbid
psychiatric phenomenon, born of sexual excess. This image of megalomaniacal insanity and diseased ambition had its parallels in contemporary medical thought, particularly in psychiatric accounts of GPI. In a study of the
relationship between mental illness and the nervous system, Henry
Maudsley identifies the dominant psychological characteristic of the 'general
paralytic' to be a predisposition towards 'extraordinary delusions of grand-
eur', wildly incommensurate with the status or abilities of the individual in
question.[61] In his exhaustive 1880 study of the illness, William Julius Mickle
emphasizes the 'expansive egoism' of the sufferer in the early stages of the
illness, and the 'inflated view' the patient will entertain of their own 'position, power, and aptitudes'.[62] Healy was repeatedly to characterize Parnell
in precisely these terms during the latter's post-Split leadership campaign,
claiming that he had 'gone politically raving mad', denouncing his 'insane
pretensions', and asserting in the wake of his death that he must not be
judged 'by the deeds of the days of mad ambition, when for his sin, God took
away his understanding'.[63] This tendency may even be detected in Healy's
infamous (and most likely apocryphal) declaration that he would hound
Parnell into a lunatic asylum or the grave, a narrative trajectory suggestive of
the accepted nineteenth-century aetiology of GPI (and syphilis more

[60] T. M. Healy, 'The Rise and Fall of Mr Parnell,' *New Review* IV, no. 22 (March 1891), 196.
[61] Maudsley, *The Physiology and Pathology of the Mind*, 177. Healy's image of Parnell as psychotically self-centred also resonates with Max Nordau's diagnosis of Oscar Wilde's pathologically self-regarding aestheticism as an exemplary manifestation of the 'Ich-Sucht' [ego-mania] of contemporary decadence. Max Nordau, *Entartung*, vol. 2 (Berlin: Carl Dunder, 1893), 137–8.
[62] William Julius Mickle, *General Paralysis of the Insane* (London: H. K. Lewis, 1880), 10.
[63] *The Nation*, 29 June 1891; *The Nation*, July 24, 1891; *The Nation*, 8 October 1891.

broadly), in which immorality and sexual 'excess' precipitated a physical and mental decline into insanity, death, or both.[64] This pathological metaphorical frame could likewise be deployed to account for the continued loyalty of the Parnellite wing of the party following the Split, allowing Healy to elide physical corruption, moral improbity, and political calumny to present Parnellism as a degenerative contagion: '[M]inds are attacked by disease like the body: the germs are there, the development is at first scarcely to be remarked—after a certain point it is difficult if not impossible to prevent destructive growth.'[65] While the 'disease' remains unnamed, the sexually pathological resonances of this image of a mind beset by destructive bacterial growth would have not been far to seek for a contemporary audience. Indeed, even if they had been, Healy was on hand to clarify them: 'For ten years we did not know where Parnell lived. The Irish leader was living in caves and holes where nobody could find him. We are told that Mr Parnell was all the time in bad health. He was and I will tell you what was the matter with him—he had *Kitty on the brain*.'[66] In this decidedly suggestive piece of pseudo-diagnosis, Healy neatly presents Parnell's desire for Katharine O'Shea as both a symptom and the cause of a quasi-metaphorical sexual malady which simultaneously emanated from and drew him inexorably back to the decidedly yonic 'caves and holes' which their relationship had made his abode. Through this strategically circular rhetorical manoeuvre, Healy characterizes Katharine O'Shea as the source of a contagion which compromised Parnell's capacity to fulfil his parliamentary duties, even as he suggests that the desire which drew Parnell to her revealed him to have been constitutionally unfit to lead from the outset. In his post-Split rhetoric Healy thus exploited the very ambivalences concerning sexual health and healthy sexuality which had made the Parnell myth so politically effective and culturally compelling to recast its central figure as both the victim of an acquired sexual pathology and the pathologically sexual emblem of desire at its most compromising and irrational. As the *Ghosts* controversy suggests, this rhetoric, with its elision of personal and public health and its images of acquired and inherited sexual pathology more closely resembled the

[64] Whatever the provenance of the remarks, the asylum-or-the-grave telos of Parnell's last campaign became an ingrained part of the 'Parnell myth' and its tragic structure in both its Parnellite and anti-Parnellite renderings. Stewart, 'The Increase of General Paralysis in England and Wales: Its Causation and Significance,' 773; Callanan, *T.M. Healy*, 290.
[65] Healy quoted in a letter from Alfred Webb to John Dillon, 7 February 1897, Dillon Paper, TCD MS 6760.
[66] Emphasis in original. *National Press*, 6 July 1891.

discursive strategies and thematic concerns of an emerging literary modernism than either its Irish exponents, such as Shaw, or many of its subsequent critics might have been willing to admit. As Frank Callanan has pointed out, this rhetoric was not intended to remain confined to the world of politics but was 'calculated to pass directly into popular usage, as well as to provide primers for parish orators, lay and clerical'.[67] As such, its impact was destined to outlast the Split and, in Callanan's view, ultimately came to 'set the themes of modern Irish nationalism'.[68] In setting the discursive terms of engagement for the increasingly fractious relationship between Irish nationalism and an emerging Irish modernism, it was also to prove significant in shaping the artistic self-fashioning of many Irish modernists.

Overcoming Heredity: Parnellites of the Western World

As John Kelly and Elizabeth Mannion have noted, the earliest and most sustained efforts to recuperate and exploit the 'Parnell myth' in the decades following the Split were undertaken by the founders of the Irish Literary Theatre, and its spiritual successor, the Abbey.[69] In Kelly's view, plays such as Yeats's *The Countess Cathleen* (1899), Edward Martyn's *The Heather Field* (1899), and George Moore's *The Bending of the Bough* (1900)—an extensive reworking of Martyn's *The Tale of a Town* (written 1899 and published 1902) undertaken in collaboration with Yeats—share a common Ascendancy longing for a figure of Parnell's stature, magnetism, and class background to unify the vituperative factions of contemporary nationalism through a combination of autocratic force of will and aristocratic *nobelesse oblige*.[70] Mannion concurs, tracing this tendency through two successive 'waves' of biographical drama concerning Parnell at the Abbey in the 1910s and the 1930s.[71] However, notwithstanding the comprehensive scope of these surveys, neither addresses the Abbey's equally prevalent, and, arguably, more influential tendency to bring to the stage avatars of the dead leader who emblematized the same virile autonomy with which he had been synonymous before the Split. Nowhere is this tendency more visible than in one of the most infamous recuperations of the Parnell myth and its

---

[67] Callanan, *T.M. Healy*, 258.   [68] Ibid., 259.
[69] Kelly, 'Parnell in Irish Literature,' 259–65; Mannion, 'Staging Parnell,' 146–55.
[70] Kelly, 'Parnell in Irish Literature,' 259–61.   [71] Mannion, 'Staging Parnell.'

politicized model of sexual health to be staged in Ireland in the twentieth century: J. M. Synge's *Playboy of the Western World* (1907).

The complex politics of heredity, degeneration, and eugenics in the *Playboy* and the riots which its first production precipitated will be analysed in greater detail in Chapter 2; however, even a brief survey reveals multiple levels on which Synge's play engages directly with the Parnell myth and the politicization of sexual health to which it gave rise. The surface similarities between Parnell and Christy are plain enough. Like Parnell, Christy hails from a privileged background in which he takes a haughty pride:

> CHRISTY [*With a flash of family pride*] And I the son of a strong famer [*with a sudden qualm*], God rest his soul, could have bought up the whole of your old house a while since, from the butt of his tail-pocket, and not have missed the weight of it gone.
>
> MICHAEL [*Impressed*] If it's not stealing, it's maybe something big.
>
> CHRISTY [*Flattered*] Aye; it's maybe something big.[72]

Like Parnell, Christy finds that his high birth and aristocratic hauteur inspire the, often sexualized, admiration of an appreciative public:

> PEGEEN [*Standing beside him, watching him with delight*] You should have had great people in your family, I'm thinking, with the little, small feet you have, and you with a kind of quality name, the like of what you'd find on the great powers and potentates of France and Spain.
>
> CHRISTY [*With pride*] We were great, surely, with wide and windy acres of rich Munster land.
>
> PEGEEN Wasn't I telling you, and you a fine, handsome young fellow with a noble brow?
>
> CHRISTY [*With a flash of delighted surprise*] Is it me?[73]

Like Parnell, Christy becomes the subject of intense speculation concerning his possible involvement in political violence ('Maybe he was fighting for the Boers'), land agitation ('Maybe the land was grabbed from him, and he did what any decent man would do'), and sexual misconduct ('Did you marry

---

[72] J. M. Synge, *Collected Works, 4: Plays, Book 2*, ed. Ann Saddlemyer (Gerrards Cross: Colin Smythe, 1982), 69.

[73] Ibid., 79.

three wives maybe?').[74] Like Parnell, Christy woos a woman (Pegeen-Mike) who is already pledged to another, less prepossessing man (Shawn Keogh) whose principal interest in their union is financial rather than romantic ('Aren't we after making a good bargain'), and ultimately wins her through a combination of dynamism, vigour, and self-assertion.[75] Like Parnell, Christy overcomes a poor constitution and meagre intellect ('that dribbling idiot') to attain an apparently self-willed condition of hyper-masculine virility ('the champion playboy of the western world').[76] Like Parnell, having had his crimes and deceptions exposed publicly, Christy has a woman's undergarments flung at him and is instructed to flee from the site of his intrigues in disguise:[77]

> CHRISTY It's Pegeen I'm seeking only, and what'd I care if you brought me a drift of chosen females, standing in their shifts itself, maybe, from this place to the Eastern World?
>
> SARA [*runs in, pulling off one of her petticoats*] They're going to hang him. [*Holding out petticoat and shawl.*] Fit these upon him and let him run off to the east.[78]

And, most obviously, like Parnell, Christy finds himself the victim of what Synge presents as a self-lacerating spasm of mob violence, justified through a

---

[74] Ibid., 69; 70. On 18 April 1887, the *Times* circulated what it presented as a facsimile of a letter in which Parnell endorsed the 1882 Phoenix Park murders. Parnell denied the accusations with characteristic reserve and the letters were ultimately proven to be a forgery by a parliamentary Special Commission and Parnell and the IPP were completely exonerated. Bew, *Enigma: A New Life of Charles Stewart Parnell*, 149–64.

[75] Synge, *Collected Works*, 4: 59. In the aftermath of the scandal, it became clear that the principal reason that William O'Shea had delayed initiating divorce proceedings against his wife and Parnell for so long was because he anticipated that Katharine's nonagenarian Aunt Ben would leave her niece a substantial sum of money, and he hoped to share in the windfall. When, following Aunt Ben's death on 19 May 1889, it became clear that that he would not be entitled to a share and that her will would be the subject of probate proceedings for at least the next three years, he filed for divorce. Bew, *Enigma: A New Life of Charles Stewart Parnell*, 166.

[76] Synge, *Collected Works*, 4: 143; 139.

[77] Parnell's elaborate disguises and aliases ('Fox', 'Preston') were revealed in the divorce proceedings and offered as evidence that William O'Shea had not connived in his wife's infidelity (which he, in fact, had), and were widely discussed in the British and Irish press. *The Guardian*, 19 November 1890, 6; *The Times*, 18 November 1891. Synge's biographer, W. J. McCormack, cites two apparently widespread stories concerning Parnel's post-Split public reception in which a 'shift had been 'thrown in his face' or in which he had been 'discovered with a lady's shift in his cab'. However, McCormack does not cite a source for either tale, so their provenance is hard to ascertain. W. J. McCormack, *Fool of the Family: A Life of J.M. Synge* (London: Weidenfeld & Nicolson, 2000), 312.

[78] Synge, *Collected Works*, 4: 169.

blend of hypocritical moralism and a craven regard for British judicial authority:

SHAWN [*Triumphantly, as they pull the rope tight on his arms*] Come on to the peelers, till they stretch you now.

CHRISTY Me!

MICHAEL If we took pity on you, the Lord God would, maybe, bring us ruin from the law today, so you'd best come easy, for hanging is an easy and a speedy end.[79]

On the basis of such parallels, Synge's biographer, W. J. McCormack, is undoubtedly justified in claiming that, in the *Playboy*, the playwright had 'disinterred Parnell'.[80] However, such an assertion raises the question, to what end had Synge exhumed his former Wicklow neighbour?

A hint is given in the title of a pseudonymous article Synge penned, but ultimately declined to publish, in the aftermath of the *Playboy* debacle: 'Can We Go Back into Our Mother's Womb? A Letter to the Gaelic League' (1907). Leaving aside, for the moment, the degenerationist and Oedipal implications of the letter's image of Irish Ireland retreating up the maternal birth canal (addressed in Chapter 2), in the present context, the most significant feature of the letter's title is the ways in which it presents the Gaelic League and its political proponents as an affront to the principles of aesthetic and sexual autonomy with which Synge felt Parnell to embody. As Emilie Morin has noted, Synge shared with many late nineteenth- and early twentieth-century dramatists a fascination with psychiatric asylums and their inmates, particularly the 'hysterical' patients exhibited by lecturers at the famous Salpêtrière hospital in Paris, and made ready use of this knowledge to cultivate a decidedly medicalized rhetoric of public vituperation in his confrontations with the Irish Ireland movement.[81] Adopting an attitude that was to become common among the male Irish modernists who took

---

[79] Ibid., 169.   [80] Mc Cormack, *Fool of the Family*, 2000, 426.

[81] Synge's interest in mental illness and institutionalization is apparent throughout his drama (particularly *In the Shadow of the Glen* (1903) and *The Playboy*) and prose (particularly 'Étude Morbide' (written *c.* 1897–1898, revised 1907), 'The Oppression of the Hills' (written *c.*1898–1902, published 1905), 'The People of the Glens' (1907).) His awareness of the work of the Salpêtrière is reflected in an 1897 letter from his Parisian friend, the journalist and translator Stephen McKenna, who offered to send him a book on magnetism and hypnotism by '[Alfred] Binet and [Charles] Féré' (presumably their 1887 co-authored monograph, *Le magnetisme animal* [animal magnetism]), both of whom had been recruited to the hospital's staff by

Parnell as their political and artistic ideal, Synge's ventriloquized 'Hedge Schoolmaster' emphasizes his revulsion at the Gaelic League for premising their schemes of national revival on an ardent (and, in Synge's view, spurious) fetishization of a point of cultural 'origin' which he figures as feminized, hysterical, and incontinent—a 'gushing, cowardly, and maudlin' doctrine exemplified by the 'hysteria of old woman's talk'.[82] Crucially, in Synge's view, in pursuing this policy, the League is betraying an Irish nationalist tradition vouchsafed by a succession of hyper-masculine Ascendancy autocrats, at whose head is, of course, Parnell:

> I believe in Ireland. I believe the nation that has made a place in history by seventeen centuries of manhood, a nation that has begotten Grattan and Emmet and Parnell will not be brought to complete insanity in these last days by what is senile and slobbering in the doctrine of the Gaelic League.[83]

As this image of an Ireland reduced in its 'last days' from a position of virile and self-actualizing 'manhood' to a 'senile and slobbering' condition of 'complete insanity' makes clear, in both the article and the play it was written to defend, Synge inverts the rhetoric of the Healyite press to restage the fall of Parnell as a national tragedy in which the representatives of an insular, petty-bourgeois cultural nationalism, not the Chief, are presented as the true degenerative threat to the nation's physical and mental integrity. Where once Healy had constructed Parnell as a figure who had emerged from the womb compromised by infection and instability, Synge now figures Healy's successors returning to the womb, bringing infection and instability in their wake. In such a context, Synge figures the revivifying promise of his own artistic project, as implicitly realized in the figure of Christy, in pointedly Parnellian terms:

> The delirium will not last always. It will not be long—we will make it our first hope—till some young man with blood in his veins, logic in his wits

---

Charcot and published extensively on hysteria, heredity, and degeneration (David M. Kiely, *John Millington Synge: A Biography* (Dublin: Gill & Macmillan, 1994), 21.) For a discussion of the impact of late nineteenth-century medical accounts of hysteria on the dramaturgy of Yeats and Synge, see Emilie Morin, 'Theatres and Pathologies of Silence: Symbolism and Irish Drama from Maeterlinck to Beckett,' in *Silence in Modern Irish Literature*, ed. Michael McAteer (Leiden: Brill Rodopi, 2017), 40–3.

[82] J. M. Synge, *Collected Works, 2: Prose*, ed. Alan Price (Gerrards Cross: Colin Smythe, 1982), 399–400.
[83] Ibid., 399.

and courage in his heart, will sweep over the backside of the world to the uttermost limbo this credo of mouthing gibberish [...] This young man will teach Ireland again that she is part of Europe, and teach Irishmen that they have wits to think, imagination to work miracles, and souls to possess with sanity. He will teach them that there is more in heaven and earth than the weekly bellow of the Brazen Bull-calf and all his sweaty gobs, or the snivelling booklets that are going through Ireland weekly like the scab on sheep, and yet he'll give the pity that is due to the poor stammerers who mean so well though they are stripping the nakedness of Ireland in the face of her own sons.[84]

Synge's idealized artist-politician will not sow the seeds of congenital madness as Parnell was alleged to have done, but restore 'sanity' to the people; he will not expose Ireland to shame through sexual controversy as Parnell was charged with doing, but will put an end to the flouting of the nation's cultural 'nakedness'; perhaps most crucially, he will not succumb, as Parnell eventually had, to the pathological influence of contemporary journalism, but, Moses-like, will free the people from their thraldom to the 'Brazen Bull-calf' of the British and Unionist press—an image which combines an ancient Greek torture device (the Brazen Bull), a false idol (the Golden Calf), and an avatar of English cultural hegemony (John Bull)—and the infectious influence of its Irish nationalist equivalent ('the snivelling booklets' of the Gaelic League and Irish Ireland). In short, he will lead the nation into the implied Promised Land of political and cultural self-determination and physical and cultural health as Parnell would have done had he not been brought low by conventional morality, mass-media sensationalism, and factional squabbling. In his own artistic self-fashioning, and in his construction of the figure of Christy Mahon in the *Playboy*, Synge thus reconfigures the Parnell myth to sponsor a hyper-sexualized image of the ideal Irish modernist as a figure who combined virile masculinity, aristocratic hauteur, and a hygienic form of intellectual and political autonomy. However, as Christy's consistently thwarted efforts to overcome and negate his own heredity through parricide and self-reinvention make clear, Synge retained a painful awareness of the ways notions of physical and intellectual inheritance threatened to undermine that ideal.

[84] Ibid., 400.

Rejecting Fertility: Irish Modernism's Self-Siring Heroes

Synge was far from unique in framing his sense of modernist artistic vocation in this manner, or in conscripting the shade of Parnell to do so. Nor was he alone in maintaining an anxious relationship to ideas of heredity. Indeed, in the hands of figures such as Yeats and Joyce, Parnell's virile celibacy came to serve as the basis for a model of masculine artistry so strongly rooted in an ideal of hygienic sexual autonomy that it repudiated any suggestion of external biological origin or issue. An early example of this trend comes in Yeats's *On Baile's Strand* (1903), one of the three plays chosen to form part of the Abbey's opening-night statement of aesthetic and ideological intent in December 1904.[85] The parallels between the radically heterodox and fiercely autonomous Nietzschean poet-hero Cuchulain and Parnell are well-established, having been confirmed by Yeats in comments made to Joseph Holloway in 1905.[86] Like one of Nietzsche's 'free spirits', Cuchulain embodies a '*great* health' which combines self-mastery, self-overcoming, and a potent fusion of violence and libido that pointedly offends against the norms of bourgeois romance:

CUCHULAIN [...] I have never known love but as a kiss

In the mid-battle, and a difficult truce

Of oil and water, candles and dark night,

[...]

A brief forgiveness between opposites

That have been hatreds for three times the age

Of this long-'stablished ground.[87]

---

[85] For an account of the practical, aesthetic, and political circumstances surrounding the opening of the Abbey Theatre, see Adrian Frazier, *Behind the Scenes: Yeats, Horniman, and the Struggle for the Abbey Theatre* (Berkeley: University of California Press, 1990), chaps. 4 and 5; Levitas, *The Theatre of Nation*, chap. 3.

[86] Robert Goode Hogan and Michael J. O'Neill, eds., *Joseph Holloway's Abbey Theatre: A Selection from His Unpublished Journal: Impressions of a Dublin Playgoer* (Carbondale: Southern Illinois University Press, 2009), 58; Michael Steinman, *Yeats's Heroic Figures: Wilde, Parnell, Swift, Casement* (Albany: State University of New York Press, 1983), 70–1. For the Nietzschean dimensions of Cuchulain's characterization in the play, see Otto Bohlmann, *Yeats and Nietzsche: An Exploration of Major Nietzschean Echoes in the Writings of William Butler Yeats* (London: Macmillan, 1982), 25; 145; Frances Nesbitt Oppel, *Mask and Tragedy: Yeats and Nietzsche, 1902–10* (Charlottesville: University Press of Virginia, 1987), 147–58; Levitas, *The Theatre of Nation*, 81–3; Michael Valdez Moses, 'The Rebirth of Tragedy: Yeats, Nietzsche, the Irish National Theatre, and the Anti-Modern Cult of Cuchulain,' *Modernism/Modernity* 11, no. 3 (2004), 561–79.

[87] W. B. Yeats, *The Variorum Edition of the Plays of W.B. Yeats*, ed. Russell K. Alspach and Catherine C. Alspach (London: Macmillan, 1966), 489.

Like Parnell at his most mythic, Cuchulain explicitly and implicitly repudi-
ates the degrading compromises of modern, bourgeois politics and the
negative modes of dependency it entails in pointedly sexual terms. Asked
to curb the 'wildness of [his] blood' and swear an oath of loyalty to the High
King, Conchubar, and '[w]hatever child' he may 'set upon the throne',
Cuchulain defiantly refuses:[88]

> CUCHULAIN [. . .] I'll not be bound.
>
> I'll dance or hunt, or quarrel or make love,
>
> Wherever and whenever I've a mind to.
>
> If time had not put water in your blood,
>
> You never would have thought it.
>
> CONCHUBAR   I would leave
>
> A strong and settled country to my children.[89]

As these remarks make clear, what distinguishes the self-mastery and
independence of the libidinous Cuchulain from the prosaic conformity of
the once virile Conchubar is not merely attitude, but progeny. Where
Conchubar is beholden to (and, implicitly, vitiated by) his children—a
'soft' and unprepossessing brood, who lack the 'pith' and 'marrow' of their
elders—Cuchulain refuses to subject himself to what he presents as the
'mockery' of childbearing.[90] Indeed, so keen is Yeats to stress the apparent
biological independence of his hyper-masculine protagonist, that he rewrites
Cuchulain's origin story to present him as the product of a supernatural
union between a human woman and a bird of prey:[91]

> CUCHULAIN   For you thought
>
> That I should be as biddable as others
>
> Had I their reason for it; but that's not true;
>
> For I would need a weightier argument

---

[88] Ibid., 481.

[89] Ibid., 477–9. Joseph Valente rightly emphasizes that, as Cuchulain's remarks make clear,
Conchubar was once as dynamic and turbulent as his insubordinate vassal, and has only
recently renounced these values in favour of his present condition of settled domesticity.
Valente, *The Myth of Manliness*, 170–1.

[90] W. B. Yeats, *The Variorum Edition of the Plays of W.B. Yeats*, ed. Russell K. Alspach and
Catherine C. Alspach. London: Macmillan, 1966, 481; 483.

[91] W. B. Yeats, *The Plays. The Collected Works of W.B. Yeats, Vol. II*, ed. David R Clark and
Rosalind E Clark (Houndmills: Palgrave Macmillan, 2001), 852, n. 251.

Than one that marred me in the copying,

As I have that clean hawk out of the air

That, as men say, begot this body of mine

Upon a mortal woman.[92]

The ways in which the passage champions a highly sexualized ideal of autonomy, nobility, and hygiene ('that clean hawk out of the air') over the perceived dependency, compromise, and corruption of reproductive sexuality ('one that marred me in the copying') are clear enough. However, like the Parnell myth, the arrestingly surreal anecdote stages a seemingly irreconcilable dialectic between virility and celibacy. On the one hand, the image of the bird of prey swooping down upon Cuchulain's mother, appears to present Yeats's hero as the product of a feat of violent and predatory masculine potency in a manner that anticipates 'Leda and the Swan' (1923). On the other hand, the suggestion of spontaneous generation in the almost *ex nihilo* appearance of the hawk, which is variously described as having come 'out of the sun' and 'clean [...] out of the air', works to present Cuchulain as the result of a sort of pagan immaculate conception.[93] This uncertainty is reinforced through the ambiguity of the formation 'begot [...] Upon', which leaves it unclear precisely how the 'begetting' occurred and whether its having taken place *upon* Cuchulain's mother is meant to signal that it did not take place *within* her.

An almost comically extreme rendering of the same impulse is offered in the second chapter of Joyce's *A Portrait of the Artist as a Young Man* (1916), in which an adolescent Stephen Dedalus visits an anatomy theatre at his father's *alma mater* in Cork. As Simon Dedalus searches for the initials he carved into his desk as a student, Stephen is suddenly confronted with 'the word *Foetus* cut several times in the dark stained wood' and experiences a moment of vertiginous disorientation:[94]

The sudden legend startled his blood: he seemed to feel the absent students of the college about him and to shrink from their company. A vision of their life, which his father's words had been powerless to evoke, sprang up

[92] Yeats, *Variorum Plays*, 483–5.   [93] Ibid., 481.
[94] James Joyce, *A Portrait of the Artist as a Young Man: Authoritative Text, Backgrounds and Contexts, Criticism*, ed. John Paul Riquelme, Hans Walter Gabler, and Walter Hettche (New York: W. W. Norton, 2007), 78.

before him out of the word cut in the desk [...] the word and the vision capered before his eyes as he walked back across the quadrangle and towards the college gate.[95]

While the intensity of Stephen's reaction is undoubtedly a reflection of the shock he feels at finding 'in the outer world' an emanation of the 'monstrous reveries' which 'he had deemed till then a brutish and individual malady of his own mind', it also reflects a profound discomfort at being confronted with a suggestion of his own contingency and dependence upon a prior biological cause.[96] Like Conchubar's children or the 'mockery' Cuchulain imagines his own progeny would make of him, the word 'Foetus', with its connotations of gestation and maternal dependence, affronts the myths of autonomy and radical self-fashioning so central to the rhetorics of both modernism and Parnellism. As if in direct rebellion against this unwelcome reminder, the idiosyncratic 'esthetic [sic] theory' which Stephen articulates to Lynch in the novel's fifth chapter envisages a mode of 'artistic conception, artistic gestation, and artistic reproduction' in which conventional, fleshly maternity is displaced, so that in the 'virgin womb of the imagination' the word may be 'made flesh'.[97] As Stephen himself stresses, this scheme represents his attempt to rescue an autonomous conception of 'beauty' from the degrading compromises of a narrowly utilitarian evolutionary model in which 'every physical quality admired by men in women is in direct connexion with the manifold functions of women for the propagation of the species' and 'eugenics' replaces the 'esthetic' [sic].[98] This scheme is extended (and lampooned) in the 'Scylla and Charybdis' episode of Ulysses, in which Buck Mulligan playfully glosses Stephen's semi-serious account of Shakespeare's self-siring art: 'Himself his own father, Sonmulligan told himself. Wait. I am big with child. I have an unborn child in my brain. Pallas Athena! A play! The play's the thing! Let me parturiate!' (U, 9.875–77). As David Weir rightly notes, this sort of masculine 'womb envy' was hardly a novelty, with a heritage reaching back to Eve's birth out of Adam's body in the Book of Genesis.[99] The Parnell myth and the Irish cultural anxieties surrounding purity and impotence it sought to address help to explain why this model of 'patriarchal parturition', with its undertones of virile chastity

---

[95] Ibid., 78–9.   [96] Ibid., 79.   [97] Ibid., 184; 191.   [98] Ibid., 183.
[99] David Weir, 'A Womb of His Own: Joyce's Sexual Aesthetics,' James Joyce Quarterly 31, no. 3 (Spring 1994), 208.

and hygienic sexual autonomy, was to prove such an urgently stressed part of many Irish modernist's conception of artistic vocation.[100]

However, no matter how ardently they may sponsor it, it is important to note that neither Yeats nor Joyce presents this vision of total sexual autonomy as uncomplicatedly positive or sustainable. Simultaneously bearing out Stephen's theory of 'artistic reproduction' and bathetically undermining its lofty aspirations, Joyce heralds his young protagonist's principal feat of 'artistic conception' in the novel—the writing of the 'Villanelle of the Temptress'—with a moment of 'tremulous morning knowledge' strongly evocative of a nocturnal emission, from which Stephen awakens to find his 'soul all dewy and wet'.[101] While not necessarily a repudiation of his young protagonist's pretensions to aesthetic and sexual autonomy, this moment does seem to register Joyce's awareness that such aspirations risked reducing artistic production to a feat of empty onanism. He appears to have Stephen concede as much when his young protagonist admits that, in order to account properly for his model of 'artistic reproduction' he will 'require' not only a 'new terminology' but a 'new personal experience'.[102] The conclusion of On Baile's Strand, in which Cuchulain unknowingly confronts his equally noble, potent, and self-willed son, only to be goaded into murdering him, and, upon realizing what he has done, drowning himself in futile combat with the ocean waves, registers more serious reservations about the value and viability of a Parnellian model of radical sexual health. As this tragic dénouement seems intended to suggest, the line between Cuchulain's fiercely guarded independence and a fatal form of traumatic isolation was far from clear-cut. However, whatever its tragic implications, Cuchulain's unwitting filicide serves only to intensify his identification with a Parnellian model of sexual health, offering a final, hyperbolic literalization of the Chief's radical sexual hygiene and virile autonomy. On the one hand, as this Parnellian peripeteia makes clear, the tragedy of the play is not that Cuchulain fails to replicate the radical sexual health of the Parnell myth, but rather that he inhabits it too fully to survive amid a compromised and compromising political present. On the other hand, as the play's concluding feat of murder-suicide anxiously suggests, Yeats clearly struggled to see how such a model could perpetuate itself without violating its own principles in the process.

---

[100] Ibid., 208.   [101] Joyce, A Portrait of the Artist as a Young Man, 191.
[102] Ibid., 184.

As Brian O'Nolan (in his 'Flann O'Brien' persona) makes clear in 1939's *At Swim-Two-Birds*, another, arguably greater, threat to the sustainability of this Parnellian ideal was a changing sense of what constituted sexual health in an increasingly modern and bureaucratized world. In a characteristic act of simultaneous reverence and subversion, the novel's student narrator has his creation, the puritanical author and moral philosopher Dermot Trellis, mutate Stephen's dream of radical aesthetic autonomy and 'artistic reproduction' into precisely the sort of 'eugenic' scheme it was intended to repudiate. In Trellis's hands, 'artistic reproduction' becomes 'aestho-autogamy', a fully fledged system of postmodern 'psycho-eugenics' in which, through the act of writing, the male author becomes able to conceive, gestate, and deliver a population 'already matured, teethed, reared, educated, and ready to essay those competitive plums which make the Civil Service and the Banks so attractive to the younger breadwinners of today' without recourse to the 'monotonous and unimaginative process by which all children are invariably born young'.[103] In this tongue-in-cheek model of aesthetic bio-power, progenitive sex is reduced to an act of reproduction no less mechanical than any documented by Walter Benjamin, while, like Stephen's 'dewy' spasms of artistic onanism in *A Portrait*, the novel becomes a masturbatory form to be 'self-administered in private' (*CN*, 21). However, the apparently total artistic and sexual autonomy offered by aestho-autogamy is almost immediately undermined when Trellis is so 'blinded by the beauty' of one of his creations, the virtuous Sheila Lamont, 'that he so far forgets himself as to assault her' (*CN*, 58), in the process siring Orlick, the counter-author who will eventually attempt to have him executed. While the ways in which Trellis's theory parodies the proscriptions of the 1929 Censorship of Publications Act and its infamous prohibition of all printed matter relating to birth control or abortion have been emphasized by a range of scholars, its debts to a sexualized model of artistic autonomy catalysed by the Parnell myth and its violent dismantling in the Split have received less attention.[104] In such a context, the novel's climax, in which Trellis is put on trial by his own creations for an act of sexual misconduct which violates the

[103] 'Flann O'Brien' (Brian O'Nolan), *The Complete Novels* (New York: Alfred A. Knopf, 2007), 37. Hereafter cited parenthetically as *CN*.

[104] Keith Hopper, *Flann O'Brien: A Portrait of the Artist as a Young Post-Modernist* (Cork, Ireland: Cork University Press, 1995), 76–88; Keith Hopper, 'The Dismemberment of Orpheus: Flann O'Brien and the Irish Censorship Code,' in *Literature and Ethics: Questions of Responsibility in Literary Studies*, ed. Daniel K. Jernigan et al. (Amherst, N.Y: Cambria Press, 2009), 125–8; Maebh Long, *Assembling Flann O'Brien* (London: Bloomsbury Academic, 2014), 32–8.

sanctity of his public persona, becomes a scenario pregnant with Parnellian resonances. Moreover, by stressing the utilitarian and eugenicist dimensions of Trellis's appropriation of Stephen's 'esthetic theory', O'Nolan subtly undermines the model of autonomy with which 'artistic reproduction' is cognate for Joyce's young protagonist by consciously conscripting 'aestho-autogamy' into the service of a bureaucratically administered, capitalist state, emblematized through the 'Civil Service' and the 'Banks'. Where Joyce's Stephen aspires to the boundary-transgressing and fiercely independent *'great* health' of a Parnell or a Cuchulain, Trellis's creations exemplify the homogenous and utilitarian 'public health' of the modern welfare state. By 1939, O'Nolan seems to imply, though sexual health remained decidedly politicized in Ireland, the ideological vision it was being conscripted to sponsor and the nature of the 'health' it denoted had changed considerably.

Conclusion

The Parnell myth constituted an unusually flexible cultural formation through which anxieties over the relationship between Irish identity and sexual conduct and debates over the physical and cultural well-being of the nation could be mediated. In the hands of Parnell's allies and followers, the myth could be used to envisage not only a model of national and cultural self-rule but a highly sexualized form of modernist aesthetic practice premised upon a self-siring masculine ideal of 'artistic reproduction' and an aggressive rejection of all forms of biological origin or issue. In the hands of his enemies and detractors, its tropes could be used to present Parnell as a degenerative and sexually pathological threat to the physical and intellectual integrity of the Irish people in a manner indebted less to Catholic moralism than to Ibsenite modernism. As both examples illustrate, the O'Shea divorce scandal and the ensuing Split gave to this sexual health rhetoric a new urgency and sharpened political edge in late nineteenth and early twentieth-century Irish culture that was to resurface consistently in the, often vexed, relationship between modernists and nationalists. Above all, as the next chapter will show, the debates over degeneration, sexual health, and masculinity which the Parnell myth had crystalized and the Split had intensified would go on to form the basis for arguably the most notorious confrontation between these two groups in Irish cultural history: the *Playboy* riots.

2

'Survival of the unfittest': Synge, Yeats, and the Rhetoric of Health

> I restored the sex-element to its natural place, and the people were so surprised they saw the sex only [...] I think squeamishness is a disease and that Ireland will gain if Irish writers deal manfully, directly, and decently with the entire reality of life.
>
> J. M. Synge to Stephen McKenna (28 January 1904)

> Synge is the evil genius of the Abbey and Yeats his able lieutenant. Both dabble in the unhealthy.
>
> Joseph Holloway's diary (26 January 1907)

> But life became sweet again when I had learnt all I had not learnt in shaping words, in defending Synge against his enemies, and knew that rich energies, fine, turbulent or gracious thoughts, whether in life or letters, are but love-children.
>
> W. B. Yeats, *Synge and the Ireland of His Time* (1911)

Of all the responses to the controversies surrounding the first run of J. M. Synge's *The Playboy of the Western World* (1907), perhaps the most caustic was to come from the playwright himself. In a journal entry written following his friend's death in March 1909, Yeats quotes a piece of verse Synge had dedicated 'To a Sister of an Enemy of the Author's, who disapproved of *The Playboy*':

> Lord confound this surly sister,
> Blight her brow with blotch and blister,
> Cramp her larynx, lung, and liver,
> In her guts a galling give her.
> Let her live to earn her dinners
> In Mountjoy with seedy sinners:

Irish Modernism and the Politics of Sexual Health. Lloyd (Meadhbh) Houston, Oxford University Press.
© Lloyd (Meadhbh) Houston 2023. DOI: 10.1093/oso/9780192889492.003.0003

Lord, this judgment swiftly bring,
And I'm your servant,—J.M. Synge.[1]

Synge's alliterative taxonomy of physical ailments apparently had the desired effect, for, in the same journal entry, Yeats records how Synge had explained 'with mirthful eyes' that, since he had written the poem, its subject's husband had 'got drunk, gone with a harlot, got syphilis, and given it to his wife'.[2] While this vituperative account of a woman unwittingly contracting a painful and stigmatizing illness as a result of her partner's infidelity is unlikely to inspire the same mirth in contemporary readers that it did in its author, it is nevertheless instructive in its (admittedly glib) deployment of a narrative of sexual pathology to position those members of the audience who vocally disrupted Synge's play in the name of an apparently scandalized sense of national purity among the 'seedy sinners' whose degenerate condition it was intended to diagnose and critique.[3] For, in hyperbolically appropriating a medicalized conception of sex for agonistic ends, 'The Curse' (as it came to be titled), and the anecdote that accompanies it, bear witness to the widespread cultural currency in post-Split Ireland of what may be termed the 'rhetoric of health': an over-determined pseudo-scientific discourse in which the lexicons of evolutionary theory, degeneration, and eugenics were combined for strategic political ends.[4] The appeal

---

[1] W. B. Yeats, *Memoirs*, ed. Denis Donoghue (London: Papermac, 1988), 202.   [2] Ibid.
[3] Even Yeats seems to have been somewhat taken aback by his friend's capacity for rancour in this instance, admiringly introducing the poem as evidence that Synge 'knew how to hate'. Ibid., 201. However, as shall be seen in Chapter 3, Synge was far from alone in deploying politicized references to venereal disease and sex work in this manner.
[4] For discussions of individual elements of this rhetoric, the scientific and medical sources from which they were derived, and their influence on the revival, see David Bradshaw, 'The Eugenics Movement in the 1930s and the Emergence of *On the Boiler*,' in *Yeats Annual No. 9* (London: Macmillan, 1992), 189–215; Donald J. Childs, *Modernism and Eugenics: Woolf, Eliot, Yeats, and the Culture of Degeneration* (Cambridge: Cambridge University Press, 2001), 7–9; Rónán McDonald, '"Accidental Variations": Darwinian Traces in Yeats's Poetry,' in *Science and Modern Poetry: New Approaches*, ed. John Holmes (Liverpool: Liverpool University Press, 2012), 152–67; Rónán McDonald, 'The "Fascination of What I Loathed": Science and Self in W.B. Yeats's *Autobiographies*,' in *Modernism and Autobiography*, ed. Maria DiBattista and Emily O. Wittman (Cambridge: Cambridge University Press, 2014), 18–30; Gregory Castle, *Modernism and the Celtic Revival* (Cambridge: Cambridge University Press, 2001), chaps. 1–4; Susan Cannon Harris, *Gender and Modern Irish Drama* (Bloomington: Indiana University Press, 2002), chaps. 1 and 2; Sinéad Garrigan Mattar, *Primitivism, Science, and the Irish Revival* (Oxford: Oxford University Press, 2004), chaps. 2–4; Alan Graham, 'Sassenachs and Their Syphilization: The Irish Revival, Deanglicization, and Eugenics,' in *Science, Technology, and Irish Modernism*, ed. Kathryn Conrad, Cóilín Parsons, and Julie McCormick Weng (Syracuse, New York Syracuse University Press, 2019), 203–14; Seán Hewitt, *J.M. Synge: Nature, Politics, Modernism* (Oxford: Oxford University Press, 2021), chaps. 5 and 6.

of this medicalized and medicalizing rhetoric for figures across the Irish political spectrum was its capacity to naturalize a wide range of ideological positions through the explanatory mechanisms of biology and the truth-claims of empiricism. The contradictions to which this could give rise inscribe themselves in Synge's invocation of venereal disease as a form of divine retribution against those who criticized his work for its perceived blasphemy and degenerate sexuality, a rhetorical manoeuvre which, ironically, replicates the basic assumptions of the very value system it was intended to repudiate.

The aim of this chapter is to explore how this rhetoric was wielded by figures on all sides of the *Playboy* debacle, before, during, and after the riots that would secure Synge's place in Irish cultural and sexual history, and to identify the competing political ends it was conscripted to serve. Rather than treating 'modernism' and 'nationalism' as uncomplicatedly distinct or antithetical forces in these exchanges, neatly divided by their respectively pragmatic and moralistic conceptions of sex, this chapter argues that Synge's play and the responses it generated are best viewed as part of a nascent 'sexual modernism' in Ireland, to which various strands of revivalism exuberantly (and vituperatively) contributed. To make this case, it is first necessary to explore how degeneration theory, which provided the rhetoric of health with much of its conceptual vocabulary, shaped the thinking of Synge's most vocal critics and consistent targets throughout his career: the supporters of Sinn Féin and 'Irish Ireland'.

Degeneration Theory and the Philosophy of Irish Ireland

Of all the practitioners of the rhetoric of health in the first decades of the twentieth century, one of the most prominent and persistent was the editor and polemicist, D. P. Moran, the chief exponent of what he influentially dubbed the 'philosophy of Irish Ireland'.[5] Conceived as a practical response to Douglas Hyde's influential call to de-Anglicize Ireland, the movement's programme of social, cultural, and economic autarchy was summarized in 1919 by Arthur Clery in the image of 'the star of Irish Ireland' whose five points were 'language, industries, music, dancing and games'.[6] The followers of Irish Ireland were urged to learn Irish, to read Irish literature, to buy Irish

---

[5] Moran employed this phrase as the title for his most influential collection of essays in 1905.

[6] Arthur Clery, *Dublin Essays* (Dublin: Maunsel, 1919), 131.

goods, to wear Irish clothing, to sing Irish songs, to dance Irish steps, to play Irish sports, and—as Gabriel Conroy discovers to his embarrassment in Joyce's 'The Dead'—to holiday in their beloved homeland. In Book V of *The Trembling of the Veil* (1922), Yeats recalls his own comically thwarted attempts to comply with the sartorial dicta of Irish Ireland, believing that he would soon be 'dressed according to public opinion' until he received a letter of apology from his tailor explaining that the delivery of his 'Conemarra cloth' suit would be delayed, as it had to come 'all the way from Scotland'.[7] While Moran distinguished himself from Arthur Griffith in asserting that separatism was an impracticable dream, both Irish Ireland and Sinn Féin shared an investment in a model of self-reliance rooted in which a return to Gaelic culture was insistently sponsored and fetishized. As the movement's seemingly tautologous moniker suggests, this push to revive a culturally and economically Irish Ireland often risked lapsing into a xenophobic drive to establish an ethnically *Irish* Ireland. A prominent advertisement for furniture retailer 'John S. Kelly' in Moran's daily newspaper, *The Leader*, demonstrates how the logic of economic revival and ethnic exclusion could operate hand-in-hand, claiming that his 'Sinn Féin' shop offered discounts to Gaelic League members, supported 'Home Manufacture', and had '[n]o connection with the Jews'.[8]

The rhetorical underpinning of Moran's programme was a lexicon of quasi-metaphoric terminology drawn from contemporary science, which owed its most prominent debts to discourses of degeneration. As suggested in the previous chapter, the concept of 'degeneration' brought together a range of nineteenth-century psychopathological theories of biological decline, in which environmentally acquired physiological deficiencies became transmissible from generation to generation. By the time of Max Nordau, this model had been extended to offer an account of social and cultural decline as a whole, in which the 'social organism' became as susceptible to contamination and decay as the individual.[9] The utility of these theories for an advocate of cultural de-Anglicization such as Moran was clear, enabling him to contrast the 'degenerate' present with the physical

[7] W. B. Yeats, *Autobiographies. The Collected Works of W.B. Yeats, Vol. III*, ed. William H. O'Donnell and Douglas N. Archibald (New York: Scribner, 1999), 272.

[8] Quoted in Deirdre Toomey, 'Moran's Collar: Yeats and Irish Ireland,' in *Yeats Annual No. 12*, ed. Warwick Gould and Edna Longley (London: Macmillan, 1996), 77.

[9] For an overview of Nordau's thought and influence in this regard, see Hans-Peter Söder, 'Disease and Health as Contexts of Modernity: Max Nordau as a Critic of Fin-de-Siècle Modernism,' *German Studies Review* 14, no. 3 (October 1991), 473.

and cultural 'purity' of a pre-imperial past. Moran's deployment of a degeneration-inflected rhetoric of health is particularly evident in the essays which comprise *The Philosophy of Irish Ireland* (1905), first published serially in the *New Irish Review* between 1898 and 1900. The title of the collection's first essay sets the tone: 'Is the Irish Nation Dying?'[10] Moran's answer is staked upon the belief that the most distinctive and distinguishing of the 'several collections of human energies' that compose a nation is its language.[11] On this basis Moran presents Ireland with a damning diagnosis, noting with dismay that both 'the language [the Irish] speak and the literature [they] read, are borrowed from another country'.[12] For Moran, thanks to this linguistic dispossession, the most distinctive racial features of the Irish have become their deterioration and regression: 'There are certainly some traits to be found in Ireland which stamp the people as a distinct race even yet; but they characterize her torpor and decay rather than her development'.[13] In Moran's view, the fatal moment of cultural contamination in Irish history was the establishment of Grattan's Parliament in 1782, which Moran figures in terms of a dangerous hybridization of Irish identity in which 'the Gael' was replaced with 'an English-speaking, English-imitating mongrel'.[14] Moran's use of the term 'mongrel' echoes the logic of degeneration in its metaphorical alignment of notions of cultural and racial purity, through which he seeks to figure Anglo-Irish culture as a dysgenic threat to Irish bodily well-being. Moran thus appropriates the fundamental tenet of Morelian theory, which identifies degeneration as 'une déviation maladive d'un type primitif' [a morbid deviation from an original type], to support his sectarian reconfiguration of the ecumenical nationalism of Young Ireland.[15] While Moran felt it foolhardy to 'fall out' with Thomas Davis's 'comprehensive idea of the Irish people as a composite race', he insisted that the 'foundation of Ireland must be the Gael, and the Gael must be the element that absorbs'.[16] This rhetoric recurs in Moran's vehement rejection of the cultural legacy of Young Ireland, whose greatest crime was to bring 'into life a mongrel thing which they called Irish literature, in the

---

[10] David Patrick Moran, *The Philosophy of Irish Ireland*, ed. Patrick Maume (Dublin: University College Dublin Press, 2006), 1.
[11] Ibid., 2.   [12] Ibid., 2.   [13] Ibid., 2.   [14] Ibid., 35.
[15] Bénédict Augustin Morel, *Traité des Dégénérescences Physiques, Intellectuelles et Morales de l'Espèce Humaine et des Causes qui Produisent ces Variétés Maladives* (Paris: J.B. Ballière, 1857), 5. For a discussion of the sectarianism of Irish Ireland, see Conor Cruise O'Brien, *Ancestral Voices: Religion and Nationalism in Ireland* (Chicago: University of Chicago Press, 1995), 32–43.
[16] Moran, *The Philosophy of Irish Ireland*, 37.

English language'.[17] Unsurprisingly, Moran was to anathemize the work of W. B. Yeats as the epitome of this unhealthy cultural miscegenation, which he argued could only be rendered palatable to the public through the smokescreen of Arnoldian Celticism.[18]

Both Moran's disdain for Yeats and his use of degeneration rhetoric feature prominently in his response to *Diarmuid and Grania*, written by Yeats in collaboration with George Moore and first performed in October 1901. From the outset the play was described by *The Leader* as 'degenerate and unwholesome' and fundamentally 'un-Irish'.[19] These criticisms were undoubtedly exacerbated by its billing alongside Douglas Hyde's Irish-language short *Casadh an tSugáin* [turning the jug], performed by Hyde himself with an amateur troupe of Gaelic League enthusiasts, in stark contrast with the professional company of English actors who performed Yeats and Moore's work to the accompaniment of Elgar.[20] As *The Leader*'s choice of adjectives indicates, Moran clearly collocates the cultural fusion of an Irish legend, Ascendancy authors, and English performers, with a dysgenic dilution of the Irish blood. A fortnight later the pseudonymous 'Mac an Cuill' [son of the pole] was to intensify this argument by figuring the perceived anglicization of *Diarmuid and Grania* as a form of violent sexual assault:

> Diarmuid and Grania [...] is an Irish legend. The Irish mind made it, and the Irish mind preserved it, pure and fresh and wholesome and clean. And now the English mind takes it by force, drags it through the mire of the London streets, brings it back to us bedraggled, besmirched, and befouled, and asks us to admire it in its new dress![21]

The gendered personification of the myth, the over-wording of sanitary adjectives with sexual connotations ('pure', 'fresh', 'wholesome', 'clean'), and the barely concealed insinuation of English sexual violence ('takes it by force'), exemplify *The Leader*'s tendency to figure Anglo-Irish literature as a degenerate sexual aberration which threatens the cultural and physical integrity of the Irish population.

---

[17] Ibid., 43.   [18] Ibid., 104.   [19] *The Leader*, 2 November 1901, 158.
[20] R. F. Foster, *W.B. Yeats: A Life, The Apprentice Mage, 1865–1914*, vol. 1 (Oxford: Oxford University Press, 1997), 252.
[21] *The Leader*, 16 November 1901, 188–9.

As mentioned in Chapter 1, in the logic of Irish Ireland, the necessary corollary of this degeneration is the feminization of the once virile and masculine 'Gael' into the feeble and hysterical 'Celt', most influentially theorized by Ernest Renan and Matthew Arnold.[22] In the age of Charcot and Freud, such accusations of irrational femininity took on both a degree of scientific legitimacy and a pointed pathological bite, with the 'hysterical woman' (and her even more troubling male counterpart) serving as an increasing locus of medical and social concern throughout the *fin de siècle*.[23] The mutually reinforcing operation of the gendered logics of Arnoldian Celticism and hysteria in an Irish context are reflected in Moran's review of a 1905 revival of *Cathleen ni Houlihan* (1902), in which he aligns Yeats and Lady Gregory's play and its protagonist with the kinds of pathologically feminized Celticism which his hypermasculine vision of Irish Ireland was intended to counter:

> The 'poor old woman' symbol for Ireland is too greenly sentimental for us. Vigorous Ireland has told the old weeping, wailing creature to move out of its way; but the 'poor old woman' has gained admittance to the scented drawing-rooms where they take a little green sentimentality with the coffee and gossip.[24]

Moran extends the senescent hysteria with which he characterizes the *Sean-Bhean bhocht* [poor old woman] to the effete femininity of the 'scented drawing-rooms' in which the Anglo-Irish literati take their 'coffee and gossip', all of which is to be shouldered aside by the robust and dynamic figure of 'Vigorous Ireland'. Moran presents this femininity as a contagious threat to audiences who 'simper and sigh' over Yeats Gregory's Cathleen, urging Irish Irelanders to demand instead 'a modern man with a heart and a

---

[22] Ernest Renan, 'De la poésie des races celtiques,' *Revue des deux mondes* 5 (1854), 473–506; Matthew Arnold, *On the Study of Celtic Literature* (London: Smith, Elder, & Co., 1867).

[23] Accounts of the gendered politics of hysteria and its cultural currency in the late nineteenth and early twentieth century are legion. Some of the more influential include Michel Foucault, *Madness and Civilization: A History of Insanity in the Age of Reason*, ed. David Cooper, trans. Richard Howard (London: Routledge, 2007), chap. 5; Henri F. Ellenberger, *The Discovery of the Unconscious: The History and Evolution of Dynamic Psychiatry* (New York: Basic Books, 1970), chap. 7; Mark S Micale, *Hysterical Men: The Hidden History of Male Nervous Illness* (Cambridge, Mass: Harvard University Press, 2008); Elaine Showalter, *The Female Malady: Women, Madness, and English Culture, 1830–1980*, Reprinted (London: Virago, 2009); Andrew Scull, *Hysteria: The Disturbing History* (Oxford: Oxford University Press, 2011).

[24] *The Leader*, 17 January 1905, 330.

head and a strong hand'.[25] Thus, argued Irish Ireland, if the Celt was an archetype of pathologized femininity—hysterical, weak, and a locus of infection—then the Gael must be a paradigm of masculine strength, virility, and robust health.

The debts this model of virile masculinity owed to English notions of 'muscular Christianity' and an imperial discourse in which Celtic femininity necessitated and legitimized British rule in Ireland are not far to seek.[26] However, less commonly examined are the anxieties which Moran's collocation of cultural revival and a resurgence of Irish machismo reflected over the gendered implications of Irish Ireland's pointedly non-political and non-violent agenda. If, as David Dwan has argued, the implicit logic of Young Ireland's diffuse and relatively unsystematic political programme was a form of classical republicanism rooted in the cultivation of civic virtue, martial valour, and masculine self-possession then Moran's insistence that nationalism should concern itself largely with questions of domestic economy could be seen as a worrying emasculation.[27] While Davis and others had espoused the need for a form of economic protectionism responsive to the specificities of Ireland's social and historical situation, this desire to reshape the traditionally feminized sphere of *oikos* coexisted with a belief in the purifying power of war and the need to cultivate an engaged *polis*.[28] In comparison with the citizen-soldier sponsored (however anachronistically) by the *Nation*, the *Leader*'s image of an Irishman who asserted his national identity not on the battlefield or in the political arena, but in the corner shop and the haberdashery, was apt to seem more than a little limp. Equally unflattering comparisons were likely when such a figure was measured against the fabled virility and stoic reserve of Parnell in his parliamentary and legal confrontations with the British establishment. In such a context, the rhetoric of hypermasculinity articulated in phallically titled organs such as *An Claidheamh Soluis* [the sword of light] and its reports on the 'visible and palpable proof' of the Gael's 'sudden reaccession to manhood', was

---

[25] Ibid., 330.

[26] For accounts of the influence of English muscular Christianity on turn-of-the-century efforts to cultivate Irish masculinity, see Susan Cannon Harris, *Gender and Modern Irish Drama* (Bloomington: Indiana University Press, 2002), 31–2; Joseph Valente, *The Myth of Manliness in Irish National Culture, 1880–1922* (Urbana, Ill: University of Illinois Press, 2011), Introduction.

[27] David Dwan, 'Cultural Development: Young Ireland to Yeats,' in *The Princeton History of Modern Ireland*, ed. Ian McBride and Richard Bourke (Princeton, NJ: Princeton University Press, 2016), 217–35.

[28] Thomas Davis, 'The Morality of War,' *The Nation*, 10 June 1843; John Mitchel, *Jail Journal* (New York: Press of the Citizen, 1854), 109.

necessary not only to confound British stereotypes of Celtic effeminacy but to paper over the cracks of an increasingly strained republican tradition.[29] For both Griffith and Moran, the basis for this resurgent masculinity was a return to the 'protoplasm' of Irish-language culture, as sponsored by the Gaelic League and organizations such as Michael Cusack's Gaelic Athletic Association, which, Cusack claimed, had been founded in response to a childhood fascination with the Taliteann Games and a desire to realize the linked dreams of national independence, Gaelic revival, and masculine self-actualization: 'Having a mind to make up, I made it up. I resolved to be a Fenian. To be a Fenian I should be a hurler. I became a hurler and a Fenian. This was the beginning of my manhood.'[30] Underpinning Cusack's syllogistic model of personal and national *Bildung*, and facilitating its performative assertion of blunt masculine self-assurance, was a conviction that 'Nature' and 'heredity' had vouchsafed to the Irish all the 'workable elements, necessary and sufficient to resist and resent the insolent claims of a hostile gang to rule Ireland'.[31] As Cusack's remarks suggest, Irish Ireland consistently deployed a gendered rhetoric of health, rooted in degeneration theory, to sponsor a conscious withdrawal from a modern 'mongrel' state of physical and cultural heterogeneity to a former state of 'wholesome' unity.

'Can We Go Back into Our Mother's Womb?': Incest and Isolationism

Synge's growing opposition to the kinds of middle-class Catholic cultural isolationism favoured by Irish Ireland is evident in 'Can We Go Back into Our Mother's Womb?', the pseudonymous 1907 open letter to the Gaelic League discussed in the previous chapter. In the letter, Synge presents the Irish as trapped within a political and cultural binary of their own fashioning in which Ireland is opposed to England to the exclusion of the potentially revivifying aesthetic energies of his own 'European' art: 'Was there ever a sight so piteous as an old and respectable people setting up the ideals of Fee-Gee because, with their eyes glued to the navel of John Bull, they dare not be

---

[29] 'The Third Oireachtas,' *An Claidheamh Soluis*, 10 June 1899, 200.
[30] *United Irishman*, 20 May 1899, 1; 'Míceál' (Michael Cusack), 'The Gaelic Athletic Association – What Does It Mean?,' *United Irishman*, 18 March 1899, 3.
[31] 'Míceál' (Michael Cusack), 'The Gaelic Athletic Association,' *United Irishman*, 25 March 1899, 3.

Europeans for fear the huckster across the street might call them English.'[32] In Synge's view, the epitome of this paradoxically Anglo-centric navel-gazing is the 'gushing, cowardly, and maudlin' doctrine of reviving the Irish language, a regressive endeavour which he alleges will reduce Ireland from a 'place in history' secured by 'seventeen centuries of manhood' to a 'slobbering and senile' state of 'complete insanity' and senescent 'hysteria'.[33] As the letter's references to hysteria, senility, and uncontrolled salivation make clear, in mounting this critique, Synge appropriates Irish Ireland's gendered rhetoric of health to present the movement as the pathological antithesis of a conspicuously Anglo-Irish tradition of Cuchulainoid heroism exemplified by 'Grattan', 'Emmett', and 'Parnell' (all of whom Moran had discounted as 'mongrel' members of the 'Pale ascendancy').[34] More than simply a formulaic evocation of the Ascendancy's greatest hits, this roll-call (composed of two parliamentarians and a physical force nationalist) specifically lays claim to the linked fora of republican virtue which Moran's petty-bourgeois cultural nationalism had apparently ceded (parliament and the battlefield) and the masculine self-determination with which they were cognate. Just as Moran deployed a pseudo-evolutionary model of 'hereditary influences' to present the impact of Anglo-Irish politics and culture as fundamentally degenerative, so Synge now figures Irish Ireland's fantasies of cultural autarchy as a wilfully atavistic attempt to resist the inevitable currents of biological and social change. The title of Synge's letter offers a particularly graphic rendering of the insular mindset which he feels is emblematic of those who opposed the *Playboy*, whom he figures attempting to retreat up the maternal birth canal.

Alongside the regressive impulse this image so grotesquely evokes, and the imputations of hysteria coded by its reference to maternal wombs, its thinly veiled Oedipal undertones serve to align the chauvinism of the Gaelic League and the *Playboy*'s critics with an impulse towards endogamy and incest. While such a suggestion plays upon the well-worn comic trope of Ireland's rural population as a gaggle of inbred bumpkins, it also evokes a long-running and often politicized debate in Victorian and Edwardian society over the propriety and physiological ramifications of

[32] J. M. Synge, *Collected Works, 2: Prose*, ed. Alan Price (Gerrards Cross: Colin Smythe, 1982), 399–400.
[33] Ibid., 399–400.
[34] Moran, *The Philosophy of Irish Ireland*, 46. Yeats positions himself atop a similarly composed Anglo-Irish 'ancestral stair' in section II of 'Blood and the Moon'. W. B. Yeats, *The Poems*, ed. Daniel Albright (London: Everyman, 2000), 287.

consanguineous marriage. From the middle of the nineteenth century, the public health impact of endogamous unions became a matter of increasingly vocal dispute within the medical and political establishment.[35] The dominant positions which were to emerge in this debate are show-cased in a pair of articles published in the *Lancet* in the early 1860s. The first, an editorial on 'The Degeneration of Race', presented the causal relationship between inbreeding and congenital defects as an established fact, affirmed by physicians, historians, and ethnologists alike. In the view of such authorities, marriage between family members led inevitably to 'the intellectual and physical degeneration of the offspring of such unions'.[36] The article's author claimed that, despite the 'rapid extinction' of 'exclusive aristocratic families', such unions remained alarmingly common, giving rise to 'a large proportion of the idiots, the epileptics, the scrofulous, the rachitic, the enfeebled, and the incapable' who presently afflicted the nation.[37] Without further investigation into the causes of these 'hereditary scourges', the article concluded, Britain risked finding itself possessed of a population worthy of 'the imagination of Dante' at his most infernal.[38] The dissenting opinion was offered by Dr S. Anderson Smith, a Fellow of the Royal College of Surgeons, who wrote to the *Lancet* in 1861 to question this apparent consensus. For Smith, consanguineous marriage was both divinely ordained—how else, he reasoned, was the human race supposed to have proliferated beyond Adam and Eve, or replenished its stocks after the Noahic flood?—and an instinctual reflection of an innate antipathy between and among different social groups. Exemplary for Smith in this regard were the Celts, who, 'rather than intermarry with the Saxon invaders', contracted increasingly close-knit endogamous unions, and 'colonists', who prefer to 'annihilate' those whom they subjugate, rather than marry 'aborigines'.[39] In Smith's account, consanguineous marriage thus constituted an ecclesiastically sanctioned means of cultural and political consolidation rooted in the chauvinistic logic of not only colonial nationalism but also anti-colonial resistance, an irony Synge was to exploit in his critiques of Irish Ireland.

---

[35] For an overview of these debates, to which my own discussion is indebted, see Nancy Fix Anderson, 'Cousin Marriage in Victorian England,' *Journal of Family History* 11, no. 3 (1986), 285–301.

[36] 'The Degeneration of Race,' *The Lancet* 76, no. 1947 (22 December 1860): 619–20.

[37] Ibid., 620.   [38] Ibid.

[39] S. Anderson Smith, 'The Degeneration of Race,' *The Lancet* 77, no. 1956 (23 February 1861), 202.

Both positions attracted stringent advocates throughout the late nineteenth century. Despite having wedded his own first cousin, Emma Wedgwood, in 1839, Charles Darwin concluded his 1862 study of fertilization in orchids with a denunciation of consanguineous marriage, remarking that, given the effort required to achieve cross pollination, it may be inferred that there is 'something injurious in the process [of self-fertilization]':[40]

Nature thus tells us, in the most emphatic manner, that she abhors perpetual self-fertilization. For may we not further infer as probable, in accordance with the belief of the vast majority of the breeders of our domestic productions, that marriage between near relatives is likewise in some way injurious,—that some unknown great good is derived from the union of individuals which have been kept distinct for many generations?[41]

This image of the incest taboo as an instinctual reaction to the apparently degenerative outcomes of endogamy was challenged by the ethnologist Alfred Henry Huth in his 1875 study, *On the Marriage of Near Kin*. On the basis of a comparative examination of marriage practices among ancient and contemporary societies, Huth argued that the human aversion to incest was not innate, but socially determined, and had no grounding in an observable increase in the frequency or severity of congenital defects among the offspring of consanguineous unions.[42] Huth's findings were in turn questioned by the Finnish anthropologist Edward Westermarck, who influentially hypothesized that the incest taboo arose from an aversion to sexual intercourse with near kin born of natural selection—the so-called 'Westermarck effect'. Westermarck contended that, rather than reflecting a conscious awareness of the negative effects of inbreeding on the part of early human societies, the high rates of sterility in the offspring of consanguineous unions rendered the prohibition of incest evolutionarily advantageous.[43] Hopes for a definitive statistical answer to the question in the United

---

[40] Charles Darwin, *On the Various Contrivances by Which British and Foreign Orchids Are Fertilised, and on the Good Effects of Intercrossing* (London: John Murray, 1862), 360.

[41] Ibid., 360–1.

[42] Alfred Henry Huth, *The Marriage of Near Kin Considered with Respect to the Laws of Nations: The Results of Experience and the Teachings of Biology* (Longmans, Green, and Company, 1887), 353–4.

[43] Edward Westermarck, *The History of Human Marriage* (London: Macmillan, 1891), 352–3.

Kingdom were dashed when an amendment to include a question relating to cousin marriage in the 1870 Census Bill was defeated by a substantial margin in the Commons.[44] Nevertheless, the debate remained live well into the first decades of the twentieth century, drawing medical, psychological, and anthropological commentary from figures such as Charcot, Krafft-Ebing, Havelock Ellis, and Ernest Crawley.[45]

Whether the scientifically literate Synge encountered these widely diffused lines of argument directly or at second-hand, both sides of the debate were grist to his polemic mill, and significantly inflected the rhetoric of health he was to adopt in his rejection of Irish Ireland and Sinn Féin isolationism.[46] On the one hand, in line with the biological and psychological arguments of Darwin and Krafft-Ebing, the degenerate impulse towards and degenerative impact of incest could be presented as the evolutionarily mandated correlative of the social, cultural, and economic chauvinism of Irish Ireland and Sinn Féin. On the other hand, from an anthropological standpoint, this stymying nativism could in turn be presented as a misreading of the traditions of the pre-imperial Gaelic culture which Irish Ireland and its advocates so fetishized. Furthermore, in the context of the *Playboy* and the controversy to which it gave rise, it could be positioned as a betrayal of the frank and pragmatic sexuality which ethnologists and anthropologists claimed was exemplary of these 'primitive' cultures, and what Synge held to be their final foothold in modern Europe, the Aran Islands.[47]

[44] 'Census Bill—[Bill 211]—Second Reading,' *House of Commons Debates*, no. 203 (22 July 1870), cc805–13.

[45] Jean Martin Charcot, *Leçons du Mardi à la Salpêtrière: Policliniques, 1888–1889* (Paris: Progrés Médical, 1889), 11–12; Richard von Krafft-Ebing, *Psychopathia Sexualis: Mit besonderer Berucksichtigung der kontraren Sexualempfindung: Eine medizinisch-gerichtliche Studie fur Arzte und Juriste*, 13. Ausgabe (Stuttgart: Verlag von Ferdinand Enke, 1907), 447–9; Havelock Ellis, *Sexual Selection in Man: Touch. Smell. Hearing. Vision* (Philadelphia: FA Davis Company, 1905), 204–9; Alfred Ernest Crawley, *The Mystic Rose: A Study of Primitive Marriage* (London: Macmillan, 1902).

[46] W. J. McCormack, for example, traces Synge's discussions of nerve decay in 'Étude Morbide' (which I examine in greater depth later in this chapter) to debates over the relationship between insanity and heredity which played out in the *Westminster Review* and *Fortnightly Review* throughout the 1890s. W. J. McCormack, *Fool of the Family: A Life of J.M. Synge* (London: Weidenfeld & Nicolson, 2000), 455. For an overview of the sources and extent of Synge's scientific knowledge and its impact on his writing, see Garrigan Mattar, *Primitivism, Science, and the Irish Revival* (Oxford: Oxford University Press, 2004), chap. 4.

[47] In section I of *The Aran Islands* (1907), Synge describes life on Inishmaan as 'perhaps the most primitive that is left in Europe'. Synge, *Collected Works*, 2: 53.

'We were always primitive': Primitivism and Inbreeding

Synge's sensitivity to these possibilities is clearly inscribed in the surviving fragments of his uncompleted autobiography, composed sporadically between 1896 and 1898 and revised in 1907.[48] The lion's share of the text is given over to an account of a nascent romance between the young Synge and an unnamed 'girl of [his] own age', whom he presents as a 'neighbour'.[49] The ten-year-old Synge and his playmate are first presented responding with almost eroticized delight to the natural world in a wood close to Synge's home following the death of an aunt, an incident which Synge explains in explicitly primitivist terms. Far from provoking grief in the young couple, the 'sense of death seems to have been only strong enough to evoke the full luxury of the woods'—a feeling which Synge supposes 'makes all primitive people inclined to merry making at a funeral'.[50] This innocent response to death is paralleled by the naturally decorous sexuality the two young people apparently share: 'We were always primitive. We both understood all the facts of life and spoke of them without much hesitation but a certain propriety that was decidedly wholesome. We talked of sexual matters with an indifferent and sometimes amused frankness that was identical with the attitude of folk-tales.'[51] Throughout both the fragmentary autobiography, and Synge's prose at large, 'primitive' and its cognates operate almost synonymously with this 'amused frankness' in the sphere of sexual desire. As the 1904 letter to Stephen McKenna which provides the epigraph to this chapter makes clear, Synge came to regard this effort to restore the 'sex-element' to its 'natural place' in cultural discourse as a key feature of his work.[52] However, as the tension between 'propriety' and 'frankness' in his heavily qualified account of his younger self's 'decidedly wholesome' attitude to sex makes clear, Synge's sense of the relationship of an unselfconscious and instinctual 'primitive' sexuality to contemporary social mores was often more strained than he might have wished to admit.

The same ambivalence can be detected in an introductory fragment of the autobiography, in which Synge expounds a model of life-writing and selfhood in which primitivism, evolutionary theory, psychology, and an occult sense of *anima mundi* are fused: 'If by the study of an adult who is before his time we can preconstruct [sic] the tendency of life and if—as I believe—we

---

[48] Ibid., 3.   [49] Ibid., 6.   [50] Ibid., 7.   [51] Ibid.
[52] J. M. Synge, *The Collected Letters of John Millington Synge*, ed. Ann Saddlemyer, vol. 1 (Oxford: Clarendon Press, 1983), 75.

find in childhood perfect traces of the savage, the expression of a personality will reveal evolution from before history to beyond the science of our epoque [sic].'[53] Underpinning this over-determined model of personal, cultural, and biological development is the belief that childhood is marked with 'savage' vestiges of humanity's social (and, by extension, sexual) past. As Sander L. Gilman has illustrated, the conviction that personal, cultural, and biological development were but micro- and macrocosmic manifestations of the same underlying evolutionary process, and might, thus, be used to illustrate and illuminate one another, was a common feature of early sexology.[54] For figures such as Heinrich Kaan, whose *Psychopathia Sexualis* (1844) shaped much subsequent thinking on the topic, forms of childhood sexual 'deviancy' (particularly masturbation) and the sexual conduct of 'primitive' cultures were analogous, insofar as both constituted a degenerate and degenerative mode of sexual disinhibition, in which the libido remained unconstrained by humanity's more highly 'evolved' faculties (reason) and more highly 'developed' social codes (shame).[55] This analogy was extended at the biological level by Morel, for whom the perceived degenerative effects of such erotic atavism, particularly forms of cognitive disability which limited a subject's capacity for sexual self-regulation, constituted an inheritable form of evolutionary arrest that risked stranding the degenerate individual (and their offspring) in an earlier phase of human development.[56] However, what Kaan and Morel present as an uncomplicatedly negative form

[53] Synge, *Collected Works*, 2: 3.
[54] Sander L. Gilman, 'Sexology, Psychoanalysis, and Degeneration: From a Theory of Race to a Race to Theory,' in *Degeneration: The Dark Side of Progress*, ed. J. Edward Chamberlin and Sander L. Gilman (New York: Columbia University Press, 1985), 72–9.
[55] Heinrich Kaan, *Psychopathia Sexualis* (Leipzig: Leopold Voss, 1844), pt. 1. As Gilman notes, this teleological conception of human social and sexual development was taken up and extended by Richard von Krafft-Ebing in the first chapter of his own, better known, 1886 study of the same name, in which he charted the parallel development of human social organization and sexual conduct from what he presents as the shameless promiscuity of 'primitive' cultures, past and present, to the morally and legally regulated monogamy of modern Europe. Richard von Krafft-Ebing, *Psychopathia Sexualis: Eine Klinisch-Forensische Studie* (Stuttgart: Verlag von Ferdinand Enke, 1886), chap. 1.
[56] In a representative case study, Morel describes a twenty-three-year-old woman from an isolated French village who has the appearance and intellectual capacity of a ten-year-old, the genital development of a seven-year-old, lacks any physiological signs of puberty, and still possesses a full set of milk teeth. He notes that '[l]e sentiment de la pudeur ne semble pas encore s'être éveillée chez cette fille' [the feeling of shame did not yet seem to have been awakened in this girl] and records that the examination of her body and genitals by her family doctor in Morel's presence 'n'a, en effet, paru lui causer aucun embarras' [did not, in effect, seem to cause her any embarrassment]. Morel, *Traité*, 22. As Gilman summarizes in an analysis of this case study, the figure of the 'cretin here is the child and the primitive. The cretin's physiognomy is that of the child, her sexual attitude that of the child and the primitive.' For Morel, Gilman

of social and sexual regression, Synge handles more ambiguously, engaging in an act of unstable mutual redefinition in which it is unclear whether childhood has taken on the more brutal and asocial characteristics of the 'primitive', or whether the perceived savagery of 'primitive' cultures is being justified as a form of naïve innocence. This instability is further intensified by Synge's implicit self-presentation as an 'adult who is before his time', a phrase which insinuates both a sense of social and cultural anachronism (and, presumably, open-mindedness) and a suggestion of early-blooming sexual precocity. As if to underscore this double entendre, Synge offers as an example of his accelerated development a childhood visit to a 'ladies' bathing place' which was interrupted by a sudden downpour.[57] Reflecting on the experience of being hastily bundled into an occupied bathing-box, Synge remarks that, though little boys 'are rightly considered inoffensive', thanks to such experiences 'some of them grow up with souvenirs that illustrate a celebrated line in Dante' (presumably the description of the sorceress Manto's pubic hair in Canto 20 of the *Inferno*).[58] After such an eyeful, Synge's assertion that he and his young playmate were 'always primitive' becomes less uncomplicatedly 'wholesome' than his account of their child-hood antics would seem to insist. The potential disjunction between this unmediated sexual impulse and norms of civilized conduct is all the more pointed when read in the light of a fact Synge crucially elides: the model for this young woman was in fact his cousin, Florence Ross.[59]

In such a context, the account Synge offers in the abortive autobiography of his first exposure to Darwin, and the diabolical consequences he imagined would ensue, take on a greater medical and scientific significance than their tone of self-ironizing hyperbole might suggest. Following a well-worn trope of Edwardian autobiography, Synge describes his first reading of 'a book of Darwin' at the age of fourteen as an experience which robbed 'the sky [of] its blue and the grass its green' and left him writhing in an 'agony of doubt'.[60] In contrast to the young Yeats, who derived from his reading of evolutionary

---

argues, the 'unrestrained sexuality of the cretin, the cretin's childlike appearance, the geograph-ical and familial isolation of the cretin' thus provided 'the ideal cases upon which to base the portrayal of retrogressive sexuality'. Gilman, 'Sexology, Psychoanalysis, and Degeneration,' 74.

[57]   Synge, *Collected Works*, 2: 4.

[58]   Ibid. 'E quella che ricuopre le mammelle, / che tu non vedi, con le trecce sciolte, / e ha di là ogne pilosa pelle, // Manto fu, che cercò per terre molte[.]' [And the one there who covers her breasts, which you do not see, with her loosened tresses, and on that side has such hairy skin, was Manto, who quested through many lands] (*Inferno*, Canto 20, 52–5).

[59]   W. J. Mc Cormack, *Fool of the Family: A Life of J.M. Synge* (London: Weidenfeld & Nicolson, 2000), 43.

[60]   Synge, *Collected Works*, 2: 10.

theory a pugnacious desire to refute the pious, in the midst of this early paroxysm of inchoate atheism, Synge imagines himself to have become the 'playfellow of Judas': 'Incest and parricide were but consequences of the idea that possessed me.'[61] Read in the light of Synge's partially elided involvement with his cousin, the links this passage, and the autobiographical fragments more generally, forge between an ambivalently conceived 'primitive' sexuality, evolutionary theory, and the spectre of inbreeding are striking. This is not to engage in a pseudo-Freudian attempt to place sublimated incestuous desire at the core of the Syngean oeuvre, but instead to acknowledge that the anxiety with which Synge's efforts to imagine a utopian 'primitive' sexuality are so often marked is bound up with a concern for the potentially degenerative outcomes such unbridled libido might entail. Such anxieties find their fullest expression in a fragment of the putative autobiography in which Synge recounts his adolescent resolution never to marry because of his persistent illness:

> This ill health led to a curious resolution which has explained in some measure all my subsequent evolution. Without knowing, or, as far as I can remember, hearing anything about doctrines of heredity I surmised that unhealthy parents should have unhealthy children. Therefore, I said, I am unhealthy, and if I marry I will have unhealthy children. But I will never create beings to suffer as I am suffering, so I will never marry.[62]

While predicated upon a disavowal of a theorized understanding of Lamarckian inheritance, Synge's emphasis that this realization shaped 'all [his] subsequent *evolution*' seems intended to link this conviction to his wider response to Darwin. Likewise, the suggestion that this insight presented itself to him spontaneously situates it within the same terrain of innate knowledge occupied by 'the facts of life' in his account of his flirtations with his cousin.[63] In both cases, a 'primitive' drive to free-love appears to contain within it the seeds of the Dantean catalogue of 'the idiots, the epileptics, the scrofulous, the rachitic, the enfeebled, and the incapable' enumerated in the *Lancet*. The 'primitive' thus comes to occupy a fraught and ambiguous semantic valence within Synge's rhetoric of health, valourizing a pre- or asocial sexual licence even as it evokes the spectre of degeneration with which such licence was cognate.

---

[61] Yeats, *Collected Works*, 3: 77; Synge, *Collected Works*, 2: 11.
[62] Synge, *Collected Works*, 2: 9.   [63] Emphasis mine.

In this regard, these autobiographical fragments anticipate Synge's curiously ambivalent account of sexuality on the Aran Islands, which he presents as being unselfconscious and instinctual, while at the same time emphasizing that it does not transgress the norms of 'civilized' conduct. This is particularly clear in a passage in a which an equally precocious young woman—'not yet half way through her teens', yet 'in some ways more consciously developed' than anyone else on Aran—expresses her delight at Synge's photography: 'The complete absence of shyness or self-consciousness in most of these people gives them a peculiar charm, and when this young and beautiful woman leaned across my knees to look nearer at some photograph that pleased her, I felt more than ever the strange simplicity of the island life.'[64] On the surface, Synge offers an apparently innocent vignette of 'primitive' fascination with modern technology. However, if one bears in mind the implied position of the kneeling young woman's chest as she strains across Synge's lap, it becomes clear that, in this moment, both parties must have been able to feel far more than just the 'simplicity' of life on Aran. The obliquely signalled sexual licence of primitive life on the islands takes on a more sinister character in the Nietzschean reverie with which Part One of the travelogue concludes. Recounting a dream in which the 'luring excitement' of a piece of supernatural music possesses his 'nerves and blood' with the irresistible urge to dance, Synge emphasizes how he struggles to 'remain quiet' by 'holding [his] knees together with [his] hands', lending a decidedly erotic character to the 'agony' and 'ecstasy' of the Dionysiac frenzy to which he rapidly succumbs.[65] Significantly, Synge attributes this self-annihilating 'vortex' of 'passion' to an atavistic resurgence of the 'psychic memory' of the 'neighbourhood' and the primitivism with which it is cognate.[66] Synge addresses the topic of the islanders' sexuality most explicitly in Part Three of *The Aran Islands*, in which he again strains to present the desires of the islanders as

---

[64] Ibid., 114; 106.

[65] Ibid., 100; 99. In the 'Preface' to the revised edition of *The Birth of Tragedy* (1872, revised 1886), Nietzsche famously outlines the simultaneous 'horror' and 'blissful ecstasy' which arise from the 'breakdown of the *principium individuationis*' [principle of individuation], 'complete self-forgetting', and '*intoxication*' that characterize the '*Dionysiac*'. To illustrate his point, Nietzsche cites the example of 'St John's and St Vitus' dancers' who 'roamed from place to place, impelled by the same Dionysiac power, singing and dancing as they went'. Friedrich Wilhelm Nietzsche, *The Birth of Tragedy and Other Writings*, ed. Raymond Geuss and Ronald Speirs, trans. Ronald Speirs (Cambridge: Cambridge University Press, 1999), 17. Emphases Nietzsche's.

[66] Synge, *Collected Works*, 2: 99.

simultaneously socially unmediated and beyond the reproach of mainland morality:

> The direct sexual instincts are not weak on the island, but they are so subordinated to the instincts of the family that they rarely lead to irregularity. The life here is still at an almost patriarchal stage, and the people are nearly as far from the romantic moods of love as they are from the impulsive life of the savage.[67]

The ambiguity of the term 'irregularity'—it is unclear to which of a plethora of perversions it might refer—is somewhat clarified by the telling, if no less obscure phrase 'the instincts of the family'. More than the legally governed structure of the marital home, Synge's use of the term 'instincts' suggests the web of social, cultural, and evolutionary forces which figures such as Huth and Westermarck had held composed the incest taboo. As such, one of the unspoken 'irregularities' of which Synge seems eager to absolve the islanders, is the same endogamous tendency for which he so castigated the advocates of Irish Ireland, and its most obvious sexual correlate, inbreeding.

The contortions of logic which this absolution required of Synge are most visible in his account of the islanders' signature footwear, the 'pampootie'—a soft shoe made from raw animal hide—and the evolutionary benefits such primitive attire has conferred on them. Finding that Synge's shoes have been torn to pieces by the 'sharp-edged fossils' which abound on Aran, his hosts fashion him a pair of island boots to ease his passage along the rocky coast of Inishmaan.[68] Newly equipped to navigate this pointedly ancient terrain, Synge records that he 'learned the natural walk of man' and discovered the 'natural use' of his toes.[69] In theorizing the evolutionary legacy to which he has just been granted access, Synge presents the potentially bestial characteristics of the islanders which the pampootie has allowed them to retain as a revivifying counterpart to, and constituent component of, their inherently aristocratic nature:

> The absence of the heavy boot of Europe has preserved to these people the agile walk of the wild animal, while the general simplicity of their lives has given them many other points of physical perfection. Their way of life has never been acted on by anything much more artificial than the nests and

---

[67] Ibid., 144.   [68] Ibid., 65.   [69] Ibid., 65; 66.

burrows of the creatures that live round them, and they seem, in a certain sense, to approach more nearly to the finer types of our aristocracies—who are bred artificially to a natural ideal—than to the labourer or citizen, as the wild horse resembles the thoroughbred rather than the hack or cart-horse. Tribes of the same natural development are, perhaps, frequent in half-civilised countries, but here a touch of the refinement of old societies is blended, with singular effect, among the qualities of the wild animal.[70]

Some critics have sought to present Synge's Aran writings as an attempt to isolate the islanders in a pre-Darwinian Eden.[71] However, such a reading overlooks the ways in which passages such as these deploy an evolutionarily inflected primitivism to engage in a delicate balancing act in which a range of apparently incompatible value systems are used to redeem one another. The atavistic threat of the islanders' physical proximity to 'the wild animal' is rendered a virtue through Synge's invocation of the 'finer types' of European aristocracy as a point of comparison which transforms the absence of economic and technical modernity on Aran from a potentially degenerative social delay into the catalyst for a process of natural 'refinement'. This analogy in turn reciprocally redeems the aristocratic features of the island-ers, which are presented not as the inauthentic product of the eugenics (or incest) necessary to engineer an 'artificially' bred European aristocracy, but as their rightful evolutionary bounty. The islanders are thus elevated from a subhuman state to the level of 'physical perfection', while at the same time being insulated from the socio-economic inequalities attendant upon a genuine aristocracy. The metaphorical invocation of horse-breeding serves to reinforce this manoeuvre, naturalizing Synge's potentially classist com-mitment to the elevation of the 'thoroughbred' islanders above the 'cart-horse' of the mainland labouring classes through the explanatory mechan-ism of evolutionary biology. The centrality of evolutionary rhetoric to the articulation of this argument is underscored when this passage is compared with an earlier account of the same experience published in *The Gael* in 1901, in which references to horse-breeding and aristocracy are absent.[72] Rather than seeking to insulate the inhabitants of Inishmaan from

[70] Ibid., 66.
[71] Mary Burke, 'Evolutionary Theory and the Search for Lost Innocence in the Writings of J. M. Synge,' *The Canadian Journal of Irish Studies* 30, no. 1 (2004), 50.
[72] J. M. Synge, 'The Last Fortress of the Celt,' in *Travelling Ireland: Essays, 1898–1908*, ed. Nicholas Grene (Dublin: Lilliput Press, 2009), 15.

Darwinian scrutiny, Synge revised his Aran writings precisely in order to apply such an optic to consolidate and redeem their 'Edenic' isolation.

This gymnastic evolutionary approach to the islanders not only underpins Synge's account of their physiological features but colours his account of the socio-economic condition of the islands as a whole. Synge frames his account of life on the Aran Islands within a binary in which socio-economic 'modernity' is collocated with a degenerate form of complexity which consistently threatens the robust simplicity of life on Aran. This narrative is plotted in miniature in the 'Preface' to *The Aran Islands*, in which Synge unfavourably contrasts the encroachment of the fishing industry on Aranmor with the other 'more primitive' islands, which are nevertheless subject to equally unwelcome 'changes'.[73] Underpinning this short passage, and Synge's account of complexity as a whole, is the work of the biologist, sociologist, and political theorist, Herbert Spencer. Spencer's model of evolution fused the biological and the social in a totalizing narrative in which in which the 'law of all progress', whether it be in the realms of 'Earth', 'Life', 'Society', 'Government', 'Manufactures', 'Commerce', 'Language', 'Literature', 'Science', or 'Art', was the development 'of the simple into the complex'.[74] Spencer read these processes of biological and social evolution as mutually reinforcing and fundamentally beneficial, commenting in his influential *Principles of Biology* (1864, revised 1898) that '[s]lowly, but surely, evolution brings about an increasing amount of happiness'.[75] This model of progressive development from savage darkness to civilized *eudaimonia* posed problems for those who sought to present a return to the 'primitive' as a revivifying cultural and political endeavour. As David Dwan has noted, one solution was to accept the basic trajectory Spencer had outlined, but transvalue its poles of orientation.[76] This approach was adopted by Yeats in his 1893 lecture 'Nationality and Literature', in which he analogized the development of a national literature to the growth of a tree 'from a simple seed' to 'innumerable and intricate leaves, and flowers, and fruits', emphasizing (in transparently Spencerian terms) their shared movement 'from unity to multiplicity, from simplicity to

---

[73] Synge, *Collected Works*, 2: 47.
[74] Herbert Spencer, 'Progress: Its Law and Cause,' in *Essays: Scientific, Political, and Speculative*, Library, vol. 1 (London: Williams & Norgate, 1891), 10; 14.
[75] Herbert Spencer, *The Principles of Biology*, Revised and Enlarged, vol. 1 (London: Williams & Norgate, 1898), 438.
[76] David Dwan, *The Great Community: Culture and Nationalism in Ireland* (Dublin: Field Day, 2008), 86–7.

complexity'.[77] However, for Yeats, this growing complexity was not conducive to happiness but to abstraction and senescence, with the 'old nations [...] forgetting in a trance of subtlety the flaming heart of man'.[78] A similar trajectory is plotted in 'The Celtic Element in Literature' (1898), in which Yeats recasts the 'natural magic' of the Arnoldian Celt as 'the ancient religion of the world', whose unity has been compromised by an increasingly 'crowded and complicated world'.[79] Sinéad Garrigan Mattar emphasizes the ways in which Yeats's modification of Arnold in this essay is indebted to a selective reading of the work of Celtologist Andrew Lang, accepting Lang's thesis of a unified 'early human' spiritual animism, while tacitly disregarding its implications of 'savage' backwardness.[80] Thus, as Dwan and Garrigan Mattar demonstrate, by reading scientific discourses against themselves, Yeats was able simultaneously to appropriate and repudiate Spencerian theory, advocating a return to a primitivist mythopoesis whose apparent homogeneity in fact served only to render it all the more cosmopolitan.

A similar strategy of inverted Spencerianism is evident throughout Synge's Aran writings, in which he consistently decries the homogenizing effects of socio-economic modernization. In one early example, Synge castigates the Congested District Boards for encouraging a mode of increasing industrial specialization on Aranmor which has served only to render the island more blandly uniform than ever before. In Synge's view, thanks to these misguided social enterprise schemes there now remains 'very little [...] to distinguish it from any fishing village on the west coast of Ireland'.[81] Synge's resistance to this increasing specialization is reflected in his characterization of the inhabitants of Inishmaan as omnicompetent, free from the depersonalizing influence of 'the division of labour', whose absence results in the 'correspondingly wide development of each individual' on the island. Synge notes that each male islander is bilingual, 'a skilled fisherman', able to 'manage a curragh', 'farm simply, burn kelp, cut out pampooties, mend nets, build and thatch a house, and make a cradle or a coffin'.[82] Spencer had identified this absence of specialization as characteristic of 'barbarous tribes', noting that 'society in its first and lowest form is a homogeneous aggregation of individuals having like powers and like

[77]   W. B. Yeats, *Uncollected Prose*, ed. John P. Frayne, vol. 1 (London: Macmillan, 1970), 268.
[78]   Ibid., 1:272–3.
[79]   W. B. Yeats, *Early Essays. The Collected Works of W.B. Yeats, Vol. IV*, ed. Richard J. Finneran and George Mills Harper (New York: Scribner, 2007), 129–30.
[80]   Garrigan Mattar, *Primitivism, Science, and the Irish Revival*, 75–6.
[81]   Synge, *Collected Works*, 2: 47.   [82]   Ibid., 132.

functions' where '[e]very man is warrior, hunter, fisherman, tool-maker, [and] builder'.[83] However, what serves for Spencer as an index of 'barbarous' simplicity becomes for Synge the source of the islanders' physical and mental vitality, granting them 'the alertness of the primitive hunter' and necessitating 'considerable activity of mind'.[84] Synge's deployment of this evolutionist rhetoric of health thus permits him to follow Yeats in transvaluing simplicity as a richer and more unified species of complexity, while at the same time holding at bay the impression of degenerate insularity with which he associated Gaelic revivalism.

An unintended irony of Synge's construction of the islanders as robustly self-reliant is its resemblance to D. P. Moran's image of 'Vigorous Ireland' and the autarchic philosophy for which it was the vehicle. Indeed, Moran himself had noted the 'curious versatility of the Irishman', arguing that: 'We all have a bit of everything in us, and none of us have any specialised characteristic stamped upon us, by a long line of hereditary influences, except the almost universal inclination to cringe and crawl which over a century of Pale ascendancy has driven into our souls.'[85] As often occurs in Moran's writing, a Lamarckian vocabulary of 'hereditary influences' is invoked to suggest the degenerative impact of the Anglo-Irish 'ascendancy' on an otherwise formless section of the Irish population who remain pregnant with political possibility. Moran's response to this protean nature is highly instrumentalist, figuring Ireland's 'ignorant peasants' as so much 'raw material' in the shaping hands of a Catholic professional class brought to self-determining political awareness by Irish Ireland.[86] However, in Moran's view this project to sculpt the peasant is fraught with danger, because upward social mobility is concomitant with a downward evolutionary movement towards 'an aristocracy and society, more or less alien in blood'.[87] As his account of the naturally aristocratic islanders makes clear, for Synge, whom Yeats believed to be 'almost as proud of his [Ascendancy] blood as of his genius', the evolutionarily insulated inhabitants of Inishmaan offered a wholly different horizon of political opportunity.[88] For both Synge and Moran, the rhetoric of health serves as the vehicle for the articulation of normative socio-political commitments which can be disguised as the products of apparently irresistible natural forces. Nevertheless, despite their shared investment in the Irish peasant as an evolutionarily sheltered

[83] Spencer, 'Progress: Its Law and Cause,' 19.   [84] Synge, *Collected Works*, 2: 132.
[85] Moran, *The Philosophy of Irish Ireland*, 46.   [86] Ibid., 4.   [87] Ibid., 7.
[88] Yeats, *Memoirs*, 1988, 201.

wellspring of cultural and physical regeneration, the political ends to which Moran and Synge enlist this figure remain diametrically opposed. The extent of this difference, and the centrality of the rhetoric of health to its articulation, are given prominent expression in Synge's most infamous, and controversial work, *The Playboy of the Western World*.

The Degeneration of the Western World: Degeneration Theory and the *Playboy*

More than any other dramatic work by Synge, *Playboy* embraces a degenerationist rhetoric of health as the vehicle through which to confront the autarchic nationalist programmes of Irish Ireland and Sinn Féin in their own terms. Throughout the play, Synge consistently presents insularity as the predominant feature of contemporary Irish political life, ascribing to it a range of regressive physiological effects. This tendency finds its most emphatic expressions in the engagement of cousins Shawn Keogh and Pegeen Mike, established at the play's opening. Synge positions the proposed union between Shawn and Pegeen as an example of a threefold form of insularity, in which ecclesiastically endorsed incest is to be undertaken to consolidate the family's property and livestock holdings:

> SHAWN Aren't we after making a good bargain, the way we're only waiting these days on Father Reilly's dispensation from the bishops or the Court of Rome?[89]

Shawn's reference to a Papal dispensation offers a pointed cue to Catholic members of the play's audience that the proposed union violates the prohibition against marriages within the 'fourth degree of kinship' (first cousins) which had been a feature of Canon Law since the Middle Ages.[90] In such a context, Shawn's framing of their engagement as a 'good bargain' offers the first of many indications that the marriage is being dictated by economic imperatives, rather than a concern for the health and vitality of the offspring it may yield. In part, this reflects the generally accepted account

---

[89] J. M. Synge, *Collected Works, 4: Plays, Book 2*, ed. Ann Saddlemyer (Gerrards Cross: Colin Smythe, 1982), 59.
[90] R. Burstel, 'Consanguinity (in Canon Law),' in *The Catholic Encyclopaedia* (New York: Robert Appleton Company, 1908), http://www.newadvent.org/cathen/04264a.htm.

of consanguineous marriage as a means to retain property and direct its inheritance.[91] Indeed, Alfred Henry Huth went so far as to posit that the incest taboo had arisen in large part to prevent precisely this monopolizing tendency from determining the course of human sexual and social relations.[92] However, in an Irish setting this phenomenon was not merely an anthropological curio, but a pressing demographic reality. The disappearance of subsistence farming in the aftermath of the Famine had resulted in an increasing unwillingness on the part of Irish men and women to marry unless both parties possessed sufficient holdings of farm land.[93] Griffith regularly offered graphic accounts of the Famine as part of a British 'plan for the extermination of the Nationalist population' of Ireland.[94] One of the primary motives for Sinn Féin's vocal advocacy for economic autarchy (exemplified in a range of 'Buy Irish' campaigns) was to insulate Ireland against this perceived genocidal threat. Thus, for Synge to suggest that Irish reproductive behaviour remained contingent upon a socio-economic crisis orchestrated by Britain was a radical assault on the claims to autonomy that were fundamental to both Sinn Féin and Irish Ireland. Even the hapless Keogh's soubriquet, 'Shaneen', seems intended to underscore this uncomfortable British influence, homophonically evoking Moran's favoured epithet for Anglophile toadies, 'Shoneen'.[95] For Synge, this intrusion of contemporary economic reality into the sexual practices of the Mayoites is figured as contributing directly to the degenerate stock Pegeen lists when questioning the interest of the Pope in Ireland:

PEGEEN [I]f I was him, I wouldn't bother with this place where you'll meet none but Red Linahan, has a squint in his eye, and Patcheen is lame in his heel, or the mad Mulrannies were driven from California and they lost in their wits.[96]

Tellingly, this catalogue of the stymied, the lame, and the deranged is composed almost exclusively of men, who, like Shawn, offer an obvious

[91] Anderson, 'Cousin Marriage in Victorian England,' 285.
[92] Huth, *The Marriage of Near Kin Considered with Respect to the Laws of Nations*, 24.
[93] Robert E. Kennedy, *The Irish: Emigration, Marriage, and Fertility* (Berkeley: University of California Press, 1973), 142–55.
[94] Arthur Griffith, 'The Economics of the Irish Famine,' *United Irishman*, 6 December 1902, 5.
[95] For a compendium of disparaging Moranite epithets, see Toomey, 'Moran's Collar: Yeats and Irish Ireland,' 45.
[96] Synge, *Collected Works*, 4: 59.

contrast with the vitality of the play's female cast. In this sense, Synge's appropriation of Moran's rhetoric of degeneration is doubly subversive of the radically autonomous and hypermasculine image of 'Vigorous Ireland' presented in the pages of *The Leader*, implying that Irish Ireland's phallo-centric isolationism renders its supporters complicit in the weakening of the already debilitated 'Gael'. This is particularly clear in the case of the 'mad Mulrannies', whose return from Californian émigré life stems not from Irish patriotic fervour, but from an American drive to return to degenerate Erin her damaged goods.

Synge further emphasizes this tendency when he has Pegeen present the Widow Quin as a locus of insularity so intense as to allow the passage of her breast milk to be traced through the mouth of a sheep to the stomach of a visiting Bishop:

> PEGEEN [...] Doesn't the world know you reared a black lamb at your own breast, so that the Lord Bishop of Connaught felt the elements of a Christian, and he eating it after in a kidney stew?[97]

Pegeen here presents the Widow as the apotheosis of a community so close-knit as to be engaged in a pseudo-eroticized form of cannibalism, position-ing the Bishop of Connaught in suggestive proximity to the Widow's breast. However, this attempt by Pegeen to render the Widow Quin unappealing to Christy comes laden with an unpleasant irony of its own, serving as a reminder of the clergy's role in abetting her own incestuous engagement to Shawn. This irony is further emphasized by Synge only a few lines later, when the Widow Quin warns Christy of the dangers of wooing Pegeen, who is 'waiting only [...] on a sheepskin parchment to wed with Shawn Keogh of Killakeen'.[98] Synge suggests that the permission for Pegeen's consanguin-eous marriage will be given on a document written on the skin of an animal that has been eaten by a local Bishop, and suckled at the teat of the Widow Quin herself. In doing so, Synge deploys Irish Ireland's preferred rhetoric of health, and his own counter-discourse of incest and inbreeding, to position the Catholic Church—the religious underpinning of Moran's sectarian philosophy—as an institutional sanction for the ongoing degeneration of the population. As much as any other aspect of Synge's drama, it was this characterization of the Irish as evolutionarily compromised inbreds that was

---

[97] Ibid., 89.   [98] Ibid., 91.

to incense the portions of its first audience most closely aligned with Moran and Griffith, and which was to inflect the infamous riots it precipitated.

Shifting the Blame: Reconsidering the *Playboy* Riots

The incident which apparently sparked the *Playboy* riots has become a cliché of Irish literary historiography, neatly encapsulated in Lady Gregory's opening-night telegram to the absent Yeats: 'Audience broke up in disorder at the word shift.'[99] In Gregory's vignette, and the myth to which it gave rise, a prudish and narrow-minded coterie of nativists, incensed by the scandalously frank sexual lexicon of Synge's play, erupt in violent opposition to a perceived slander on Irish femininity. However, a closer examination of contemporary press coverage and eyewitness testimony suggests that behind the disturbances which beset the play's premiere lurked the airing of a very different kind of dirty laundry. More than a suggestion of sexual impurity on the part of Ireland's women, it is the degenerate state of the nation's male population, and the parricidal pseudo-poet Synge sponsors as their antithesis, which appear to have most animated the play's earliest audiences. The *Freeman's Journal*, the Abbey's most persistent and bitter critic throughout the *Playboy*'s initial run, emphasized this fact in their summary of the play's action. Central to the *Freeman*'s account of the play is the opposition between Shawn Keogh, who 'is making sheep's eyes at Margaret' (Pegeen), and 'the tramp' (Christy), compared to whom 'the worst specimen of stage Irishman' is a 'refined, acceptable fellow'.[100] Intentionally or otherwise, the review's account of Shawn's ovine love-making links his meek sexual demeanour (his 'sheep's eyes') to the intensely insular network of sexual and social bonds within which the Widow Quin's black lamb circulates. At the same time, the review condemns Christy by positioning him as the malign apotheosis of the 'stage Irishman', a loquacious and unscrupulous mainstay of British theatre since at least the time of Boucicault. As far as the *Freeman* was concerned, Synge had maligned the present condition of Irish masculinity as pathologically compromised, only to sponsor a 'hideous

---

[99] Isabella Augusta Persse Gregory, *Our Irish Theatre: A Chapter of Autobiography* (New York: Capricorn Books, 1965), 112.
[100] 'The Abbey Theatre, "The Playboy of the Western World,"' *Freeman's Journal*, 28 January 1907, 10, reproduced in James Kilroy, *The "Playboy" Riots* (Dublin: Doleman Press, 1971), 7; 9.

caricature' culled from an alien and Hibernophobic cultural tradition in its stead.[101]

This sensitivity to the play's caustic rendering of the degenerate condition of Irish manhood was not confined to its opponents. Praising the play in the *Irish Times* for its unsettling realism and 'moral courage', Patrick Kenny discussed the relationship between the 'half idiot' Shawn and the vivacious Pegeen in explicitly Spencerian terms:

> Why is 'Pegeen' prepared to marry him? 'God made him; therefore, let him pass for a man', and in all his unfitness, he is the fittest available! Why? Because the fit ones have fled. He remains because of his cowardice and his idiocy in a region where fear is the first of the virtues, and where the survival of the unfittest is the established law of life.[102]

For Kenny, Synge's message was clear: Ireland's insistently dysgenic breeding patterns—in which the 'human specimens most calculated to bring the race lower' were 'select[ed] for continuance' while the most able were left to emigrate—were not only violently at odds with the laws of natural selection but also tantamount to race suicide.[103] Synge endorsed Kenny's reading in an *Irish Times* piece the following day, praising it as a rare moment of critical clear-sightedness.[104] Yeats was so taken with Kenny's review that, when formulating strategies to mitigate the risks the riots posed to the reception of a mooted American edition of the play with John Quin in the February of 1907, he suggested that 'Pat' be invited to provide an introduction.[105] As these remarks suggest, at least as much as its fidelity to peasant life in the West, it was the play's evolutionist interrogation of the operation of natural and artificial selection in Ireland that the Abbey and its allies were most keen to foreground in their defence of the *Playboy*.

Nor were Darwinian readings of the play solely the preserve of the Protestant intelligentsia. During the debate Yeats organized to capitalize on the play's notoriety, Mr D. Sheehan, who identified himself as both a 'medical student' and a 'peasant who knew peasants', claimed he 'had never

---

[101]   Kilroy, 9.
[102]   'Pat' (Patrick Kenny), 'That Dreadful Play', *Irish Times*, 30 January 1907, 9, reproduced in Kilroy, 38.
[103]   Ibid.   [104]   Ibid., 41.
[105]   John Kelly et al., eds., *The Collected Letters of W. B. Yeats*, InteLex Electronic Edition (Oxford University Press, 2002), sec. 566.

seen the doctrine of the survival of the fittest treated with such living force' as in the *Playboy*.[106] For Sheehan, the true object of Synge's satire was the 'form of marriage law' which underwrote the pathological union of a 'fine woman like Pegeen Mike' and 'a tubercule Koch's disease man like Shaun [sic] Keogh'.[107] Like Kenny, Sheehan saw in Synge's play an image of the west of Ireland, not as the untainted wellspring of Gaelic culture, but as an anti-Darwinian incubator for a pathologically compromised masculine population, doomed to a state of terminal atrophy akin to the muscular wastage of tuberculosis. In a breeding pool so shallow and contaminated, Sheehan argued, it should come as no surprise that, 'when the artist appears in Ireland who was not afraid of life' and 'his nature', the 'women of Ireland would receive him'.[108] In a telling echo of the infamous 'riots' themselves, the remainder of Sheehan's comments were rendered inaudible by the 'disorder' of the audience, many of whom left the auditorium in 'astonishment' and disgust.[109] As in the case of the play itself, the resistance of Irish Ireland had been provoked not so much by a reference to the undergarments of Irish women, as by the suggestion that the degenerate state of Irish manhood would leave such women disinclined to remove their undergarments at all.

Disinfecting Don Juan: Yeats's Construction of Synge

The same slippage between a pseudo-scientific model of biological fitness and a performative mode of self-fashioning underpins the image of Synge as a virile and dynamic revivifying cultural force that Yeats was to propagate in the aftermath of the playwright's death in 1909. Yeats's construction of Synge as his 'anti-self' or as a sort of 'Übermensch of the Western World' has been well-documented.[110] However, the pervasive role medical discourses, and particularly discourses of sexual health, played in that construction, and, by extension, the importance of Synge to Yeats's eugenic thinking have received relatively scant critical attention. In the 1905 'Preface' to the first edition of *The Well of the Saints*, Yeats emphasizes the paucity and pathological character of the work the younger writer showed him:

---

[106] 'Parricide and Public. Discussion at the Abbey Theatre,' *Freeman's Journal*, 5 February, 1907, 6–7, reproduced in Kilroy, *The 'Playboy' Riots*, 1971, 86.
[107] Ibid.   [108] Ibid.   [109] Ibid.   [110] Dwan, *The Great Community*, 2008, 178.

He had, however, nothing to show but one or two poems and impression-
istic essays, full of that kind of morbidity that has its root in too much
brooding over methods of expression, and ways of looking upon life, which
come, not out of life, but out of literature, images reflected from mirror to
mirror.[111]

While this is not an unfair assessment of the rather self-conscious 'Étude
Morbide' (written c. 1899) and 'Vita Vecchia' (written c. 1895–97), it is
nevertheless significant that, for Yeats, the 'morbidity' of Synge's work
derives from an excess of literary influence and meta-literary introspection
which reduces it to an exercise in stylistic *mise en abyme*. In this sense, the
'morbidity' Yeats diagnoses would appear to constitute a kind of aesthetic
sterility born of the sort of cultural inbreeding and intellectual incest which
Synge had so excoriated in Irish Ireland and comparable to the impotent
ressentiment which Yeats was to identify as the key-note of the movement's
politicized aesthetic. In establishing the myth of Synge's aesthetic origins,
Yeats emphasizes that he was determined not to allow Synge to suffer a
similar fate, deploying a gendered rhetoric of health to present his as the
crucial transformative influence in the impressionable young author's
development.

Yeats's criticisms of Synge's 'morbid' early prose seem to have been
inflected by the work itself, particularly the 'Étude Morbide', in which the
narrator-diarist fears his 'brain by some horrible decadence is grown a
register for appalling things', finding the newspapers full of lurid stories
of 'men who have gone mad and slain their kindred' and reading 'in reviews
[. . .] analysis of nerve decay'.[112] Synge's self-reflexive account of the texts
that beset him seems to figure the unnameable decadence he detects growing
in his mind (which the reference to nerve decay allusively links to the later
stages of syphilitic infection) as a contagious product of this journalistic
reading matter. It is worth comparing this earlier account of a Synge infected
with meta-stylistic concerns—implicitly borne of an excessive regard for
other authors—with Yeats's later figuration of Synge in both his journal and
Synge and the Ireland of His Time as a figure naturally impervious to the
'contagious opinions of poorer minds', possessed of a literary immune
system sufficiently robust 'to reject from life and thought all that would
mar [his] work'.[113] Read in this light, the infamous exhortation to 'Give up

---

[111] Yeats, *Collected Works*, 4: 216.   [112] Synge, *Collected Works*, 2: 29.
[113] Yeats, *Memoirs*, 154; Yeats, *Collected Works*, 4, 238.

Paris' for the Aran Islands in order to 'express a life that has never found expression' is inflected with a concern for health and purity that is only partially metaphorical.[114]

Underpinning this push to purge Synge's oeuvre of all that was 'morbid' and 'decadent' was a desire to position the playwright as the antithesis of what Yeats perceived to be the degenerate state of contemporary nationalist politics. At times, this critique was very close to Synge's own, in both its tone and execution. As I noted in my Introduction, when describing a disrupted performance of the *Playboy* in *Synge and the Ireland of His Time*, Yeats would follow his friend in presenting the play's opponents as a pack of syphilitic hypocrites, 'howling' at Synge's frank handling of sex and sexuality even as a doctor in the audience restrained himself from pointing out those audience members he was 'treating for venereal disease'.[115] Beyond the broad insinuation of sexual impropriety and moral lassitude, Yeats's positioning of this anecdote in the essay undertakes a more specific critique of Sinn Féin and Irish Ireland. Yeats locates this image of the venereally corrupted rioters in the paragraph immediately following his account of Griffith's ongoing accusations of plagiarism against Synge's *In the Shadow of the Glen* (1903), which had been a bugbear of the *Sinn Féin* editor since its début. Yeats specifically (mis)quotes Griffith's claim that Synge derived his plot not from an authentic Aran folk-tale, but 'from a writer of Roman decadence'.[116] In doing so, he is most likely referring to an editorial concerning a 1905 revival of Synge's play in which Griffith had claimed that:

> Mr. Synge's Nora Burke is not an Irish Norah Burke—his play is not a work of genius—Irish or otherwise—it is a foul echo from degenerate Greece [...] She is a Greek—a Greek of Greece's most debased period and to dress her in an Irish costume and call her Irish is not only not art, but it is an insult to the women of Ireland.[117]

Just as in his selective retelling of the origins of Synge's first voyage to Aran, Yeats positions what he presents as Synge's engagement with the authentic culture of the west of Ireland in opposition to the morbid tendencies of decadent aesthetics. Furthermore, Yeats seems to imply through the proximity of Griffith's and Synge's remarks that the real reason Griffith is so keen to displace the geographical and cultural origins of Synge's 'degenerate' tale

---

[114] Yeats, *Collected Works*, 4: 216–17. [115] Ibid., 227. [116] Ibid.
[117] *United Irishman*, 28 February 1905.

is that it offers an uncomfortable reminder of the degenerate stock from which he draws his followers.

More common, however, than these explicitly medicalized salvoes, were comments rooted in a rhetoric of health whose origins were decidedly Nietzschean. In a journal entry written in the weeks before Synge's death, Yeats described the exponents of Irish Ireland as having 'suffered through the cultivation of hatred as the one energy of their movement a deprivation which is the intellectual equivalent of the removal of the genitals'.[118] In Yeats's view, Moranite agon constituted a mode of *Untermenschlich* nay-saying that, because of its parasitic dependence upon the positions which it sought to oppose, was necessarily incapable of producing original thought.[119] Early issues of *Samhain*, the journal of the Irish Literary Theatre, consistently pitted 'Drama' against 'those enemies of life, the chimera of the Pulpit and the Press'.[120] As the journal entry implies, for Yeats the sexual correlate of this *ressentiment* was castration. However, such imputations of impotence were not merely metaphorical. In a later journal entry, Yeats revisits and extends this Nietzschean premise, explicitly linking the intellectual sterility of contemporary nationalism to what he presents as the endemic celibacy of the Irish population:

Hatred as a basis of imagination [...] helps to dry up the nature and makes the sexual abstinence, so common among young men and women in Ireland, possible. This abstinence reacts in turn on the imagination, so that we get at last that strange eunuch-like tone and temper. For the last ten

---

[118] Yeats, *Memoirs*, 1988, 176.

[119] In the 'First Essay' of *On the Genealogy of Morality* (1887), Nietzsche identifies negation (saying 'no' to everything that is 'outside', 'other', or 'non-self') as the principle 'creative deed' of slave morality. Because of this impotent *ressentiment*, slave morality is analogous to an organism that requires 'external stimuli in order to act at all'. The degenerative impact of such herd morality is outlined in section five of *Beyond Good and Evil* (1886). Friedrich Wilhelm Nietzsche, *On the Genealogy of Morality*, ed. Keith Ansell-Pearson, trans. Carol Diethe, rev. student ed. (Cambridge: Cambridge University Press, 2007), 20; 91–2. For an overview of Yeats's engagement with Nietzschean thought, see Otto Bohlmann, *Yeats and Nietzsche: An Exploration of Major Nietzschean Echoes in the Writings of William Butler Yeats* (London: Macmillan, 1982); Frances Nesbitt Oppel, *Mask and Tragedy: Yeats and Nietzsche, 1902–10* (Charlottesville: University Press of Virginia, 1987). For Nietzsche's conception of degeneration, see Gregory Moore, *Nietzsche, Biology, and Metaphor* (Cambridge: Cambridge University Press, 2002), pt. 2; C. Heike Schotten, *Nietzsche's Revolution: Décadence, Politics, and Sexuality* (New York: Palgrave Macmillan, 2009), chaps 1–3.

[120] W. B. Yeats, *The Irish Dramatic Movement. The Collected Works of W.B. Yeats, Vol. VIII*, ed. Mary Fitzgerald and Richard J. Finneran (Houndmills: Palgrave Macmillan, 2003), 36.

or twenty years there has been a perpetual drying of the Irish mind, with the resultant dust-cloud.[121]

Much like Patrick Kenny, who had seen in the *Playboy* an indictment of Ireland's dysgenic marriage patterns, Yeats detects in Griffithite opposition to the play both the result and root of the emasculation which its rhetoric of Cuchulainoid machismo had been intended to remedy. The strategy of sexually pathologized othering which underpinned these private reflections was ultimately to find public expression in the short poem 'On Those that Hated *The Playboy of the Western World*, 1907', in which Griffith and his supporters are again figured as 'Eunuchs' running through Hell to 'stare / Upon great Juan riding by' and 'rail and sweat' while 'Staring upon his sinewy thigh'.[122] In contrast to the shrill, hysterical, and emasculated followers of Sinn Féin and Irish Ireland, Yeats presents an intimidatingly sexual and hypermasculine image of Synge, virtually identical to Moran's 'Vigorous Ireland', and all the more strikingly paradoxical for being applied to a figure whose fragile constitution he had praised as vouchsafing his art.

Conclusion

As Yeats's construction of Synge as a mirthfully antagonistic Don Juan suggests, a sensitivity to the rhetoric of health not only emphasizes the prominent role which contemporary medical and scientific thought played in shaping the foundational mythology of the revival but reveals striking parallels between the ways in which the revival's exponents and contemporary advanced nationalists harnessed the explanatory mechanisms of biology to naturalize their visions of Irish identity. For Moran and his allies, degeneration theory provided a compelling metaphorical corelative to the malign effects of British cultural and political influence in Ireland and allowed an (often wishful) image of a unified, pre-imperial Gaelic past to be contrasted with a physically and intellectually compromised 'mongrel' present. It likewise allowed an increasingly insular focus on domestic economy to be presented as the key to a resurgence of virile masculinity, rather than an emasculating betrayal of a republican tradition rooted in ideals of civic virtue and martial valour. For Synge, evolutionary and anthropological

---

[121] Yeats, *Memoirs*, 1988, 176–7.   [122] Yeats, *The Poems*, 2000, 162.

accounts of consanguineous marriage provided a vocabulary through which to present this nativist commitment to autarchy as a form of cultural incest alien to the very 'primitive' culture Irish Ireland so fetishized. While such rhetorical similarities should not be taken to suggest that the political investments of Irish Ireland or the Abbey were proximate, or even similar, they do indicate the permeable nature of the apparently clear boundary between a sexually conservative nationalism and a sexually frank modernism which the *Playboy* riots have traditionally been held to reflect. Rather than treating 'modernism' and 'nationalism' as uncomplicatedly distinct or antithetical forces, neatly divided by their respectively pragmatic and moralistic conceptions of sex, this chapter has argued that Synge's play and the responses it generated are best viewed as part of a nascent 'sexual modernism' in Ireland, to which various strands of revivalism exuberantly (and vituperatively) contributed. Like the Parnell Split before them, the *Playboy* riots reveal turn-of-the-century Irish modernism to comprise a heterogenous and increasingly medicalized cultural field in which competing strands of advanced nationalist and revivalist opinion vied to conscript the ideal of sexual health to sanction their vision of social, political, and aesthetic independence. As Part II shall demonstrate, in this emergent sexual modernism, hygiene was to prove no less mutable or divisive an ideal than autonomy.

PART II

HYGIENE AND ITS DISCONTENTS

3

'Their syphilisation you mean': Irish Modernism and the Politics of Venereal Disease

In the February of 1924, Dr Thomas Percy Kirkpatrick, Ireland's foremost venereal disease specialist, received a disquieting letter, written in a disordered hand and composed in an obvious state of distress. It was addressed to the 'Dr of the Lock Up Hospital, Dublin' and had been sent from Coolbanagher in Portalington by an English-born sex worker, concerned about her health and by the treatment she had received at the hands of the local medical authorities. In it, she offered not only an outline of her present condition but a harrowing account of her experiences of plying her trade in Dublin at the height of the War of Independence (1919–1921):

Dear Sir,

I am writing to beg you to give consideration to what I am here stateing [*sic*] I am suspected to be deceased [*sic*] at least it is so stated by Country Doctors who have tried to disease [. . .] by putting Writings on me and daily fumeings [*sic*] I was in the City of Dublin about 3 years ago as followed through the city by fumeing [*sic*] of gas and wirings were held on my head to keep me distinct from the rest[.] the English military were there at the time and I being English thought they would favour me but not so[.] death head was burned on to me as a deased [*sic*] case death head is still burnt on to me and stink and I cant [*sic*] make it out[.] they told me I was Clock [*sic*] a mocked [*sic*] that is my head was a phone for the wiring to be burned too and the reason I am writing to get you to either Examine or see into my case[.] I am poor only for that I would gone to the City and got my self Examined [*sic*] I was in the Coombe Hospital and 7 years ago and was treated for slight rupture of the wound[.] I wrote there and got no answer to my letter[.] when in Dublin I stayed Mrs [C] 27 Rialto Cottages second Avinue [*sic*] I have not been fast so I cant [*sic*] make it out[.] the Dr [D] of

Irish Modernism and the Politics of Sexual Health. Lloyd (Meadhbh) Houston, Oxford University Press.

Emo Dispencery [sic] has not made a statement to myself that I was deceased [sic] but I have heard it through the wiring burnt to my head[.] If they wish to prove me a case for asylums then I must go to an English asylum were [sic] I was born of an English mother which they never cease to remind me I must by [sic] begging you to excuse the liberty I have taken[.] I remain Dear Sir[,]

Sincerely Yours [T.F.][1]

The author's low level of literacy, the traumatic nature of the events described, and her self-professed inability to make sense of what has happened to her make aspects of her account difficult to interpret or corroborate. The narrative the letter articulates, however, is clear enough: upon entering Dublin, its author sought to engage in sex work with British troops. Having been born to an English mother, she expected to receive favourable treatment at their hands. However, upon discovering that she was infected, they used a heated wire to brand her with a 'death's head'—a skull and cross-bones—to distinguish her from other women who took the soldiers as their clients. While doing so, they appear to have mocked her about the nature of the branding. The scars from this incident persisted and may have become infected (she notes that they 'stink'). The local medical authorities have made her feel further stigmatized by 'putting writings' on her and subjecting her to what she describes as daily 'fumeings' [sic]. She has unsuccessfully attempted to communicate with the Coombe Hospital, where she had previously been treated, and has been informed that, if she wishes to enter an asylum (presumably a Magdalene laundry, though potentially a psychiatric hospital), she will have to return to England. At the level of personal experience, the woman's letter illustrates the often violent stigma attached to venereal disease, especially among sex workers, in times of armed conflict. At a political level, her letter reveals the complex network of sectarian assumptions which governed the treatment of both sex workers

---

[1] 'T.F. to T.P.C. Kirkpatrick,' 6 February 1924, TPCK/3/5: Kirkpatrick Collection, Patient Letters (1 of 2), Royal College of Physicians of Ireland. The material contained within the Royal College of Physicians of Ireland's Kirkpatrick collection is subject to the one-hundred-year rule, and, as such, the letter has been anonymized. For a full account of the Kirkpatrick collection, its contents, and their implications for the history of sexual health in Ireland, see Lloyd (Meadhbh) Houston, '"Dear Dr Kirkpatrick": Recovering Irish Experiences of VD, 1924–47,' in *Patient Voices in Modern Britain*, ed. Anne R. Hanley and Jessica Meyer (Manchester: Manchester University Press, 2021), 255–98.

and venereal disease sufferers during and after the War of Independence. Moreover, it highlights the role sexual health played in both defining and undermining the boundaries of national identity in a period of political turbulence. The woman believes that her English heritage will secure her the 'favour' (custom and preferential treatment) of the soldiers. However, her diseased state undermines this identification and sees her treated in a brutal manner. It is only when the woman seeks treatment for her infection and the abuse to which it gave rise that her English identity is invoked, this time to exclude her from care.

Whatever the veracity of the woman's account, the noxious fusion of sexual stigma, sectarianism, and militarism it highlights was a very real facet of Irish social and political life, and one that was to inscribe itself thoroughly in the work of Irish modernists. As Chapter 1's discussion of rhetorics of sexual pathology in the Parnell Split suggests, the use of venereal disease— particularly syphilis—as an index of 'immorality' and cultural and ethnic alterity in Irish political life long pre-dated the War of Independence. In what follows, I examine how figurations of venereal disease, accounts of its aetiology, and campaigns for its regulation were used by politicians, activists, and authors to construct and contest models of Irish identity in the first decades of the twentieth century. I will begin by exploring perhaps the most often noted and least thoroughly explored depiction of venereal disease in the Irish literary canon: James Joyce's 'The Sisters'.

'When children see things like that...': The Priesthood, the Pox, and Precarious Masculinity

A passing reference to the potentially syphilitic origins of Reverend Flynn's *'paralysis'* (D 1.10) in 'The Sisters' has long been a commonplace in critical discussions of *Dubliners*.[2] Since the appearance of Burton A. Waisbren and Florence L. Walzl's 'Paresis and the Priest' in 1974, a footnote or introductory remark has attended Joyce's description of Flynn's paralytic condition in most editions of the collection, suggesting its resemblance to advanced neurosyphilis.[3] However, despite this pseudo-consensus, Flynn's condition

---

[2] James Joyce, *Dubliners: A Norton Critical Edition*, ed. Margot Norris, Hans Walter Gabler, and Walter Hetcche (New York: W.W. Norton, 2006). Cited parenthetically by story and line number.
[3] Burton A. Waisbren and Florence L. Walzl, 'Paresis and the Priest: James Joyce's Symbolic Use of Syphilis in "The Sisters,"' *Annals of Internal Medicine* 80, no. 6 (1 June 1974), 758.

and its role within the story or the collection as a whole are seldom the subject of further discussion. In his seminal biography, Richard Ellmann offers a starting point for critical inquiry by identifying Flynn's paralysis as a 'symptom of the "general paralysis of an insane society" with which Ireland was afflicted'.[4] As Ellmann's reference to the 1904 pseudo-manifesto 'A Portrait of the Artist' suggests, it is possible to read the details of Flynn's expiration as part of a nationalist parable of encroaching imperial paralysis, smuggled into the story via the symbolic resonances of those items of naturalist clutter which appear most innocuously constitutive of its *effet de réel*. In such a reading, the 'green faded look' (*D* 1.110–11) of Flynn's garments serves to identify him as the shabby embodiment of a waning Ireland, whose 'little house' occupies a geographically and politically subordinate position on 'Great Britain Street' (*D* 1.85). This gnomonic figure (*D* 1.11), whom imperial oppression has left as incomplete as a Euclidian parallelogram and as spiritually bankrupt as a simoniac (*D* 1.12), has been reduced to a state of paralytic senility by a syphilitic infection which finds an obvious analogue in the British occupation of Ireland.[5]

Valid as this reading and the anti-imperial resonances it detects in the story are, they form only part of the political critique with which Joyce opens *Dubliners*. As in so much of his work, in 'The Sisters' and its narrative siblings ('An Encounter' and 'Araby'), Joyce seeks to interrogate the intersecting influence of those three masters (English, Italian, and Irish) against whom Stephen Dedalus directs his infamous *non serviam*. In order to identify the dominant cultural formations which Joyce problematizes in 'The Sisters', it is necessary to explore the story's evolution from its initial appearance in John Eglinton's farming-journal-cum-literary-review, *The Irish Homestead*, in August 1904 to its positioning as the opening of *Dubliners* in 1914. Doing so, it becomes clear that, in rewriting 'The Sisters', Joyce introduces the protean spectre of syphilis into the story in order to position the Catholic Church as a degenerative threat to precisely the sorts of resurgent masculinity that Irish Ireland nationalists sought to champion and which Yeats and Synge had endeavoured to conscript to their own cultural and political ends.

---

[4] Richard Ellmann, *James Joyce*, Revised Edition (Oxford: Oxford University Press, 1984), 163–4. Hereafter cited parenthetically as *JJII*.
[5] Walzl reads the incomplete Euclidian '*gnomon*' (*D* 1.11) as a symbol of the stunted development of the Irish character under British rule. See Florence L. Walzl, 'Joyce's "The Sisters": A Development,' *James Joyce Quarterly* 10, no. 4 (1973), 387.

As has been outlined in Chapter 2, Irish Ireland rooted its policies of linguistic, cultural, and economic de-Anglicization in a model of Cuchulainoid hyper-masculinity designed to resist the dominance of Arnoldian Celticism and the pathologically feminized image of Irish identity it offered. In the 1914 version of 'The Sisters', such rugged masculinity is espoused by Old Cotter and the narrator's uncle, both of whom are concerned by the influence of Flynn's 'Education' (D 1.58) on the boy's development. Old Cotter's misgivings prompt him to advocate outdoor play 'with young lads his own age' (D 1.52–53), in implied contrast with the less salubrious forms of indoor 'play' with which he associates Flynn. The boy's uncle reinforces this position, teasing the narrator for his 'rosicrucian' esotericism (D 1.55) before instructing him to 'take exercise' (D 1.56), 'box his corner' (D 1.54–55), and have 'a cold bath' every morning (D 1.57). The Cusackian ring of this self-consciously hackneyed litany of macho truisms is plain, echoing the Gaelic Athletic Association [GAA] and its supporters in its endorsement of masculine self-discipline and physical culture in contrast to the emasculating Yeatsian mysticism of the Celtic revival (the 'New Patriotism') and the 'Young Degeneracy' with which the organization held it to be cognate:

> [The New Patriotism] tells us we are but blind bats, that Nationality is not a thing of right, arms, freedom, franchises, brotherhood, duties, manliness, and memory, but a thing of loud singing and lute-playing, of mystic prose and thrice-mystic poesy [...] I suspect this New Patriotism is, after all, a relative of Young Degeneracy. Ever I see it strutting about mouthing its shibboleth of 'No Politics'—which means in its jargon no reference to the fact that that fine fellow the Gael is famishing to death.[6]

As was suggested in the previous chapter, such espousals of republican martial virtue ('arms', 'franchises', 'manliness') and denunciations of the decadent aestheticism ('Young Degeneracy') of Yeats and his circle were offered at least in part to counterbalance the implicit threat of feminization which attended Irish Ireland's investment in domestic economy. However, where the GAA and its supporters held Anglo-Irish occultism to be the source of the Gael's famished state, the macho duologue between Old Cotter and the narrator's uncle comes much closer to the position of

---

[6] 'Nationalist,' 'The New Patriotism,' *United Irishman*, 11 March 1899, 3.

Yeats and Synge in ascribing responsibility for such degeneracy to the Catholic Church.

Tellingly, Old Cotter's rubric for masculine personal development is absent from 'The Sisters' in its 1904 *Irish Homestead* guise and was added by Joyce in parallel with the revised symptoms of Flynn's illness and the references to 'paralysis' which insinuate its syphilitic cause. In its *Irish Homestead* form, 'The Sisters' presents Flynn as the sufferer of a mental illness ('Upper storey ... gone') whose effects were exacerbated by his 'scrupulousness' and brought to a head by the shattering of a chalice.[7] While this incident is undoubtedly replete with sexual connotations, these remain relatively oblique, the cause of Flynn's death is elided, and the word 'paralysis' remains absent from the story. By contrast, when revising 'The Sisters' to open *Dubliners* in the summer of 1906, Joyce was to introduce three instances of 'paralysis' and its cognates into the narrative, in each case having the young narrator collocate the malady with references to 'sin' (*D* 1.83) and Flynn's pathological need to confess.[8] As Joyce would have been aware from his own attempts at medical study, in contemporary clinical discourse 'paralysis' served as a metonym for syphilis in its most infamous and debilitating manifestation, general paralysis of the insane.[9] Joyce's revisions reinforce the venereal connotations of Flynn's 'paralysis' through the introduction of a range of physical details which closely resemble the symptoms of neurosyphilis. The young narrator notes Flynn's trembling hands (*D* I.105), grotesque smile (*D* 1.80), involuntary drooling (*D* 1.81), and mumbled speech (*D* 1.76), all of which indicate a failure of muscular co-ordination consistent with advanced tertiary syphilis. Eliza's description of regularly discovering Flynn 'with his breviary fallen on the floor, lying back in the chair with his mouth open' (*D* 1.255–56) suggests that the priest suffered from seizures caused by cerebral syphilitic lesions. This pathologized image stands in stark contrast to the endearing description of the somnolent priest's 'make believe' attempts to read his 'Prayer Book' offered by the narrator in the story's 1904 iteration.[10] In the *Irish Homestead* version this moment offers a benign example of the narrator's

---

[7] 'Stephen Daedalus' (James Joyce), 'The Sisters,' *The Irish Homestead*, 13 August 1904, 676; 677.

[8] Hans Walter Gabler contends that Joyce's most substantial revisions to 'The Sisters' took place between 23 June and 9 July 1906.Hans Walter Gabler et al., eds., *The James Joyce Archive*, vol. 4 (New York: Garland, 1977), xxix.

[9] Joyce abortively attempted to study medicine in Dublin and Paris in October and December 1902 (*JJII*, 104; 109).

[10] 'Stephen Daedalus' (James Joyce), 'The Sisters,' 676.

mischievous precocity, in its revised form it links the 'Divine Office'—a priest's duties as outlined in their breviary—with a morbid tableau of syphilitic paralysis. Read in the light of this fusion of Catholic doctrine and the apparent ravages of venereal disease, Old Cotter's anxiety as to the 'effect' (D 1.68) such a sight may have on a young mind seems to position Irish Ireland's hypermasculine ideal of brotherhood, duties, and manliness in conscious opposition to the movement's sectarian investments.

This tension between Irish Ireland's masculinism and its perceived deference to the priesthood is heavily inscribed in the revisions Joyce makes to the ways in which Flynn's influence on the young narrator is registered in the text. In its 1904 form, this evidence is confined to the ecclesiastical diction ('as if by Providence') and pious register ('in whose light the Christian must take his last sleep') with which Joyce inflects the story.[11] What is conspicuously absent in this iteration is not only any mention of *paralysis* itself but the almost voyeuristic fascination which this 'maleficent and sinful being' (D 1.13) evokes in the young narrator, filling him 'with fear' even as he longs 'to be nearer to it and to look upon its deadly work' (D 1.14–15). One of the most substantial revisions to the story in this regard is the addition of the narrator's dream, which serves as a troubling expression of a nascent sexuality whose focal point has become Flynn and his symptoms. Despite his efforts to anchor himself in the naive comforts of 'Christmas' and the womb-like security of his blankets (D 1.75–76), the narrator feels himself drawn into 'some pleasant and vicious region' (D 1.88) in which he is pursued by the 'heavy grey face of the paralytic' (D 1.74–75). This image of Flynn's pathological and seemingly inescapable influence takes on an even more worrying complexion when read in conversation with the following story, 'An Encounter'. The narrator's fascination with the word *paralysis*, which he repeats to himself during his nightly vigil at the priest's window, anticipates the circular discourse of the 'queer old josser' (D 2.248) in the succeeding story. Like the queer old josser, the narrator's fixation with Flynn's paralysis threatens to leave him 'magnetised by some words of his own speech, his mind [...] slowly circling round and round in the same orbit' (D 2.230–31). Likewise, the juxtaposition of the 'pleasant' and the 'vicious' in the narrator's dream suggests a sadomasochistic fusion of pleasure and pain which adumbrates the josser's erotically charged fantasies of punitive flagellation. Through these parallels and lexical echoes

---

[11] Ibid., 676.

Joyce implies that Irish Ireland's insistent collocation of authentic Irishness with Catholicism in the present threatens to afflict future generations with precisely the kinds of perceived sexual degeneracy against which the movement purported to insulate the country. Thus, even as Irish Ireland sought to position the resurgent Gael as the embodiment of muscular Catholicism, Joyce uses the physical and moral taint of syphilitic infection to undermine the linked ideals of impregnable masculine corporeality and Catholic moral purity upon which this model of identity was founded.

The tacit erotic freight of the narrator's recollections of Flynn manifests itself more directly when his recollection of the priest's unsettling habit of letting 'his tongue lie upon his lower lip' (D 1.147) prompts him to resume articulating the previous night's reverie. The narrator presents a scene decked in the trappings of Orientalist fantasy, where 'long velvet curtains and a swinging lamp of antique fashion' (D 1.152–53) evoke a 'Persia' (D 1.155) identified in terms of its apparent distance from the social mores of contemporary Ireland. The seemingly unspeakable sexual implications of this dream and its conclusion are suggested by Joyce's use of ellipses—'. . . . But I could not remember the end of the dream' (D 1.155–56)—to position the reader in knowing proximity to the 'puzzled' narrator, who has earlier attempted in vain 'to extract meaning from [Old Cotter's] unfinished sentences' (D 1.72–73) regarding Flynn. Vincent Cheng reads this narratorial fantasy of licentious alterity as a manifestation of the young boy's desire to escape the culturally and politically torpid 'labyrinth' of contemporary Ireland.[12] However, in doing so, he elides the ways in which Joyce uses the lingering memory of the syphilitic clergyman who provided the dream's imaginative catalyst to thwart this escape by psychologically rooting the threatening sexual licence for which this landscape is a shorthand in the narrator's experience of Ireland and its priesthood.

This Orientalized landscape and its implied syphilitic threat recur in 'Araby', which, as its title suggests, contains a string of uncanny doublings, parallels, and lexical echoes with 'The Sisters'. Its narrator, another young boy, resides in a house in the 'back drawingroom' of which a priest has recently died (D 3.7–8). Joyce's decision to distinguish this house, fittingly located at a literal dead end on 'North Richmond Street' (D 3.1), from Flynn's Great Britain Street abode suggests the endemic nature of the diseased ministry he epitomizes. The narrator characterizes his infatuation

---

[12] Vincent Cheng, *Joyce, Race, and Empire* (Cambridge: Cambridge University Press, 1995), 79–82.

with Mangan's sister as a 'chalice' to be borne 'safely through a throng of foes' (D 3.63–64), recalling both the shattered chalice which marked 'the beginning' (D 1.282) of Rev. Flynn's syphilitic decline and the 'idle chalice' (D 1.303) which signifies its fatal end. Like the young narrator of 'The Sisters' and the queer old josser of 'An Encounter', the protagonist of 'Araby' is subject to a lexical fixation whose repetition casts 'an Eastern enchantment' (D 3.107) over him which evokes the earlier narrator's dream. While the web of geographical parallels and recurring diction through which Joyce links the opening triptych of Dubliners are in part the product of a retrospective attempt to confer coherence to a diverse group of self-contained narratives, the points at which Joyce establishes liaisons between the stories are both specific and symbolically resonant. Through his Orientalized fantasies of Mangan's sister (D 3.103–07) the narrator of 'Araby' attempts to escape from a physical space haunted by a diseased priestly presence into a mental space which 'The Sisters' has already linked to a pathologized image of paralysis. Through these echoes Joyce suggests that Irish Ireland's deference to the priesthood would subvert and frustrate not only the symbolic union of a young male patriot and a feminine avatar of Irish nationality upon which so many nationalist narratives were staked but precisely the kinds of normative heterosexual union between two Irish young people which the movement sought to encourage.

The impact of these revisions, is, of course, not merely a matter of content, but of style. The eroticized Orientalist tropology Joyce deploys to underscore Flynn's syphilitic symptoms in 'The Sisters' inflects the story with psycho-sexual Gothic overtones whose strongest generic debts are not to the 'scrupulous meanness' of realism, but to the polyvocal stylistic profusion of decadence.[13] Most obviously, in an Irish context, the imbuing of Catholic ritual with a seductive complexity and licentious theatricality chimes with Dorian Gray's reflections on the 'subtle fascination' of the Roman Mass.[14] Suggestively, Wilde's description of Dorian's pointedly aesthetic appreciation of the 'jewelled, lantern-shaped monstrance', 'the chalice', and the 'fuming censers' wielded by altar boys during Communion is precipitated by a discussion of dreams which offer a pleasant and vicious fusion of 'horror and misshapen joy' in which 'black fantastic

---

[13] Richard Ellmann, ed., Letters of James Joyce, vol. 2 (London: Faber and Faber, 1966), 134. Hereafter cited parenthetically as LII.

[14] Oscar Wilde, The Picture of Dorian Gray: A Norton Critical Edition, ed. Michael Patrick Gillespie, 2nd ed (New York: W. W. Norton & Co, 2007), 264.

shapes' and 'dumb shadows crawl into the corners of the room and crouch there', and is followed by an account of Dorian's interest in the 'burning odorous gums of the East' and their sensuous effects.[15] Moreover, this fusion of Gothic dreamscape, Catholic ritual, and Orientalist hedonism, is framed in relation to Dorian's investment in the materialist neurology of the *Darwinismus* [Darwinism] movement and his insistence on 'the absolute dependence of the spirit on certain physical conditions, morbid or healthy, normal or diseased'.[16] Reading *The Picture of Dorian Gray* (1890) in Italian in the summer of 1906—just as he was undertaking revisions to 'The Sisters'—it was by these features (its 'catalogued atrocities, lists of perfumes and instruments', and resemblance to Huysmans) that Joyce found himself most struck.[17] Without wishing to position Wilde's novel as the sole or even the primary influence on Joyce's revisions to 'The Sisters'—the salient features are common to any number of decadent texts, major and minor— the similarities between the cocktail of Catholicism, Orientalism, and psychopathology which inflect the reveries of the protagonists of both texts underscore the extent to which Joyce aligns the priesthood with decadence and a predatory queerness in 'The Sisters'.[18] Where the GAA and its advocates located the 'Young Degeneracy' and its threat to Irish masculinity outside their ranks, through the tropes of decadent fiction and the suggestion of syphilitic infection Joyce undermines this divide, situating the physiological taint of degeneration, the perceived moral threat of same-sex desire, and the very real physical and psychological threat of child abuse firmly within the institutional apparatus of the Catholic Church.

As has been often noted, throughout *Dubliners* Joyce seeks 'to convert or pervert stories of imagined adventure, escape, heroism or fame into studies in a cultural pathology'.[19] For Joyce, syphilis provides a means by which

---

[15] Ibid., 264; 263; 265.

[16] Ibid., 264. For an account of the *Darwinismus* movement—a German strain of evolutionary thought, exemplified by the work of Ernst Haeckel, and eschewing Darwinian natural selection in favour of a neo-Lamarckian model of use-inheritance—see Paul Weindling, 'Ernst Haeckel, *Darwinismus*, and the Secularization of Nature,' in *History, Humanity, and Evolution: Essays for John C. Greene*, ed. John C. Greene and James R. Moore (Cambridge: Cambridge University Press, 1989), 311–27.

[17] Richard Ellmann, ed., *Selected Letters of James Joyce* (London: Faber and Faber, 1975), 96. Hereafter cited parenthetically as *SL*.

[18] For accounts of Joyce's debts to and deployment of Wilde in his handling of gender and queer desire, see Joseph Valente, ed., *Quare Joyce* (Ann Arbor: University of Michigan Press, 1998), chaps. 2, 3, 4, and 7.

[19] Seamus Deane, 'Dead Ends: Joyce's Finest Moments,' in *Semicolonial Joyce*, ed. Derek Attridge and Marjorie Howes (Cambridge: Cambridge University Press, 2000), 21.

both to effect this subversion and to reify this pathology, allowing him to present the complex and mutually reinforcing effects of British occupation and the models of Irish identity which nationalists constructed in response. However, as the tale's uncomfortable collocation of syphilis with same-sex desire, and same-sex desire with child abuse makes clear, a subversive appropriation and inversion of the gendered rhetoric of health through which cultural nationalists sought to justify and naturalize their programmes of social and political reform was by no means guaranteed to yield a progressive or liberal politics of gender or sexuality. Indeed, for all that Joyce was to critique Irish Ireland's cult of masculinity for its deforming effect on Irish youth, he was equally convinced in public and private that Wilde's queerness—though Joyce studiously avoided any direct allusion to it—was ultimately 'the logical and inevitable product of the Anglo-Saxon college and university system' and the 'seclusion and secrecy' they enforced.[20] Notwithstanding, then, the desire of Joyce Studies to find in the author a reflection of contemporary identity politics or an anticipation of deconstructive critiques of gender, sexuality, and colonialism, attention must be paid to the ways in which the normative assumptions which undergirded the rhetoric of sexual pathology upon which Joyce drew to critique Irish Ireland and their allies were apt to reinscribe themselves in the critiques that rhetoric facilitated. In this sense, as will be seen in the cases of Samuel Beckett and Flann O'Brien, modernist efforts to reject the constraints of Irish Catholic sexual mores could, and often did, lapse into a no less conservative strain of iconoclasm. Both this rhetorical strategy and this dynamic were to recur in Joyce's interrogation of the impact of British militarism in Ireland in *Ulysses* (1922).

An 'army rotten with venereal disease': *Ulysses*, Syphilis, and Militarism

As he stops to collect an erotic epistle at the Westland Row post office in the 'Lotus Eaters' episode of *Ulysses*, Leopold Bloom's eye is caught by a British 'recruiting poster' depicting 'soldiers of all arms on parade' (*U* 5.57).[21]

---

[20] James Joyce, *Occasional, Critical, and Political Writing*, ed. Kevin Barry, trans. Conor Deane (Oxford: Oxford University Press, 2008), 150.
[21] James Joyce, *Ulysses*, ed. Hans Gabler (New York: Vintage, 1986). Cited parenthetically by episode and line number.

The 'showy' appearance (*U* 5.69) and concomitant sexual appeal of these troops brings to his mind contemporary nationalist anti-enlisting propaganda: 'Maud Gonne's letter about taking them off O'Connell street at night: disgrace to our Irish capital. Griffith's paper is on the same tack now: an army rotten with venereal disease: overseas or halfseasover empire' (*U* 5.70–72). Bloom's collocation of militarism and sexually transmitted disease chimes with a prominent strain of nationalist discourse which figured the occupying British forces as a constant threat to the physical and moral well-being of the Irish. As Bloom's reflections indicate, the most vociferous exponents of this position were Maud Gonne and Arthur Griffith, who had overseen the anti-enlisting activities of the Irish Transvaal Committee.[22] The 'letter' to which Bloom refers was addressed to the *Freeman's Journal* on 6 June 1904. In it, Gonne recounts the difficulties facing children who wished to attend Irish language classes in Dublin, decrying 'the condition of the streets' brought about by 'the disgraceful conduct of the British military'.[23] Gonne shares her experiences of a journey to the General Post Office made at 10 p.m., during which she was 'jostled against by soldiers and screamed at by poor unfortunate girls, whom the soldiers seem to incite to insult any respectable woman who ventures, on what they consider [...] their side of the street'.[24] Gonne's implied fear that it is becoming impossible to visit the GPO without contracting GPI prompts her to dub this spectacle 'one of the most humiliating evidences of foreign rule' and its 'demoralising effect on men's characters' she has ever experienced.[25] The letter's petition for the nocturnal removal of British troops from O'Connell Street was reiterated in pamphlets published and circulated by Gonne's feminist-nationalist organization, *Inghinidhe na hÉireann*. The group's publications targeted 'Irish Girls', emphasizing their patriotic duty to forego the company of enlisted Irishmen, whose complicity in the country's occupation rendered them 'traitors'.[26] These pamphlets used degenerationist rhetoric to link the soldiers' perceived ideological infidelity with a physiological descent into disease and debility. In these publications, membership of the 'most degraded and immoral army in Europe' renders the servicemen 'unfit to be the companion of any girl',

---

[22] Donal P. McCracken, *Forgotten Protest: Ireland and the Anglo-Boer War*, Updated and Revised (Belfast: Ulster Historical Foundation, 2003), 158.

[23] Maud Gonne-MacBride, 'To the Editor of the Freeman's Journal,' *Freeman's Journal*, 6 June (1904), 6.

[24] Ibid.   [25] Ibid.

[26] Inghinidhe na hÉireann, *Irish Girls!* (Dublin: Inghinidhe na hÉireann, 1914).

aligning them with the 'lowest and most depraved characters' drawn from 'the slums of English cities'.[27] In line with contemporary theories of degeneration, the rhetoric of Gonne and *Inghinidhe na hÉireann* presents venereal disease, poverty, and moral degradation as the interimplicated symptoms of a debilitating decline from a state of physical and cultural 'purity' with which the British armed forces threaten Ireland.

Griffith's publications of this period were, indeed, firmly 'on the same tack'. The week before Gonne's letter appeared in the *Freeman*, Griffith's *United Irishman* devoted several columns to a meeting of the South Dublin Union Board intended to address the conduct of the 'most licentious soldiery in Europe' on Dublin's streets.[28] As the decade progressed, Griffith's campaign intensified, with *Sinn Féin* featuring twelve articles on the subject of venereal disease in the British Army between May 1906 and February 1907.[29] The topic was a propaganda windfall for Sinn Féin, with venereal disease offering a statistical index of English 'immorality', against which the Irish could be constructed as physically and culturally 'pure'. At the rhetorical level, venereal disease provided Griffith with a persuasive explanatory metaphor through which to replicate Sinn Féin's call for linguistic, cultural, and economic autarchy at the microcosmic level of the individual Irish body. One such article reports the remarks of Dr Ridgeway, Dean of Carlisle, to a meeting of the Christian Social Union, in which he declared that: 'Seventy per cent of [British] soldiers, not during war, but in England, during peace, were on the sick list in the course of the year, large numbers through the sin of impurity.'[30] Ridgeway concluded that if this venereal 'evil were not destroyed by the people it would destroy the people'.[31] The author notes that, while the English population is empowered to remedy this problem by Act of Parliament, the Irish must 'accept the sin of impurity quartered in their midst in that dutiful submission which becomes a people who have no Constitution other than that derived from the clean, pure hearts God and their mothers gave them'.[32] The play on 'Constitution' in both its legal and medical senses juxtaposes the political disempowerment of the Irish with their apparently innate bodily well-being, the origins of which it locates in a union between feminine purity and dutiful piety.

---

[27] Ibid.   [28] *United Irishman*, 28 May 1904, 5.
[29] *Sinn Fein*, 6 May 1906; 7 July 1906; 8 September 1906; 15 September 1906; 10 November 1906; 17 November 1906; 24 November 1906; 1 December 1906; 22 December 1906; 19 January 1907; 9 February 1907; 22 February 1907.
[30] 'The British Army,' *Sinn Féin*, 6 May 1906, 2.   [31] Ibid.   [32] Ibid.

While this social purity rhetoric certainly did not go unchallenged in nationalist circles—Pádraic Pearse, for one, had little patience for those who conflated patriotism with an exaggerated sense of national cleanliness—it was widespread in the first decades of the twentieth century.[33] The most prominent example of this tendency with which Joyce was to engage directly was a series of articles published by Oliver Gogarty in *Sinn Féin* between September and December 1906 under the heading 'Ugly England'. Of all the authors surveyed in this study, Gogarty possessed by far the most detailed and extensive medical knowledge: studying anatomy at the Royal University and Trinity College, Dublin, and completing his clinical training at the Richmond Hospital, he qualified as an MD in 1909, and became a Fellow of the Royal College of Surgeons of Ireland the following year, specializing in Ear, Nose, and Throat surgery.[34] By all accounts an able diagnostician, he correctly identified that J. M. Synge was suffering from Hodgkin's disease rather than the tuberculosis with which the ailing playwright's doctor had erroneously diagnosed him, and referred Joyce to a colleague for treatment when the young author suspected he had contracted an unspecified sexually transmitted infection:

> Congratulations that our holy mother has judged you worthy of the stigmata [...] As it would be absurd and pernicious for me to prescribe for a penis in a poke[,] so to speak[,] I enclose a letter for you to hand to my old friend[,] Dr. Walsh[:] one of the best. He will see you right for me and [,] if you can be repaired[,] repair you. [...] If I would venture an opinion—you have got a slight gleet from a recurrence of original sin. But you'll be all right.[35]

[33] In a 1912 article for *An Barr Buadh* [the trumpet of victory], Pearse presents the parable of 'an fear meathta' [the degenerate man]: a figure so obsessed with 'ghlaine' [cleanliness] that he cannot bring himself to utter the word 'bríste' [trousers] aloud for fear that 'd'fhéidir go mbeadh bean ag éisteacht' [a woman might be listening]. Eventually, the titular figure becomes so monomaniacally focused upon scouring books for possible 'salachair' [dirt] that his mind is permanently 'truaillígheadh' [polluted] and it becomes impossible for him to think or speak of anything else. Pádraig Mac Piarais, 'Fabhal-Scéalta: Sliocht Leabhair Bhuidhe Bhaile i bhFad Síos Annso: VII. An Fear Meatha,' *An Barr Buadh* I, no. 7 (Aibreán 1912), 2. I am indebted to Aidan Beatty for providing me with access to this resource.
[34] For an overview of Gogarty's medical career, see Ulick O'Connor, *Oliver St John Gogarty: A Poet and His Times* (Dublin: O'Brien Press, 2000), chap. 10 and J. B. Lyons, *James Joyce and Medicine* (Dublin: Dolmen Press, 1973), chap. 4.
[35] Reproduced in Lyons, *James Joyce and Medicine*, 59–60. Gogarty sent the letter in early March from Worcester College, Oxford, where he was spending a sabbatical in the hopes of

As the tone of this correspondence indicates, at least where his friends (and, as his life-writing reveals, patients) were concerned, Gogarty's attitude to venereal disease was at once playful and pragmatic, combining clinical insight with a bawdy rhetorical exuberance and a good-natured sympathy for the unfortunate sufferer.[36] As the scathingly diagnostic register of the articles which comprise the 'Ugly England' series makes clear, such sympathy evidently did not extend to the British.

The first of these articles positions itself as a blend of travel writing and anthropology, offering its readers a scathing typology of the 'English common man' in his natural habitat.[37] From the outset Gogarty constructs a pathologized caricature of English identity, in which simply 'to touch' this 'human dredger' threatens to render the Irish equally 'despicable'.[38] This tendency inscribes itself onomastically, with Gogarty refusing to refer to his archetypal Englishman as 'John Bull', preferring instead the soubriquet 'Sludge'.[39] Through this cloacal epithet Gogarty presents Englishness as a corrupting tide of effluent against which the Irish must construct a cultural and political levee. The greatest marker of this corruption for Gogarty is, of course, venereal disease. He notes that though this 'English monster' lauds the 'virtuous forbearance' of his military, he has nevertheless published 'a book—too sordid and lost to see his own hypocrisy—wherein are statistics to prove [...] that his own army is rottener and more immoral than any or all the armies in Europe'.[40] The 'book' in question was Dr Frederick F. MacCabe's *War with Disease* (1906), which *Sinn Féin* had 'reviewed' on 7 July 1906.[41] It consisted of a collection of lectures on preventative medicine originally delivered to the 'officers, NCOs, and men of the Cavalry Brigade at

winning the Newdigate Prize. In the letter of introduction to Walsh, he jokingly explained that his friend had been unsuccessfully 'seeking employment as a water-clock' and would be 'glad if he could reconvert his urethra to periodic and voluntary functions', noting that 'Mr. Joyce is the name of the tissues surrounding the infected part' (Ibid., 60). For speculations concerning the nature and impact of this infection on Joyce's life and work, see Kathleen Ferris, *James Joyce and the Burden of Disease* (Lexington: University Press of Kentucky, 1995); Erik Holmes Schneider, *Zois in Nighttown: Prostitution and Syphilis in the Trieste of James Joyce and Italo Svevo (1880–1920)* (London: Ashgrove Publishing, 2014); Kevin Birmingham, *The Most Dangerous Book: The Battle for James Joyce's Ulysses* (London: Head of Zeus, 2014), chap. 24.

[36] Describing his time as a student at the Richmond Hospital in his 1939 memoir, *Tumbling in the Hay*, Gogarty discusses his efforts to combat the stigma facing venereal disease sufferers under his care, and offers an amusing and compassionate account of the ways in which the eminent surgeon Sir Thomas Myles, to whom Gogarty had been assigned as a clinical clerk, used his knowledge of Shakespeare's life and works to reassure and support a patient with tertiary syphilis who had been mocked by his ward-mates for his condition. Gogarty, *Tumbling in the Hay*, chap. 20.

[37] Oliver St John Gogarty, 'Ugly England (I),' *Sinn Féin*, 15 September 1906, 3.   [38] Ibid.
[39] Ibid.   [40] Ibid.   [41] 'The British Army,' *Sinn Féin*, 7 July 1906, 3.

the Curragh' in Kildare.[42] As part of his lecture on the prevention of venereal disease MacCabe had noted that infection rates among British troops in India ran as high as '517 per 1,000' men admitted to hospital and recommended the nightly disinfection of all servicemen returning from duty in Irish cities.[43] On this basis Gogarty was able to claim that the British Army constituted 'a body of men who, as their own statistics show, are already more than half leprous with venereal excess'.[44] It was a thesis that Gogarty was to pursue not only in the columns of *Sinn Féin* but in his creative practice, above all, in his influential tenement drama, *Blight, the Tragedy of Dublin*, which premiered in December 1917.

'The wages of sin is a month in the Locke': *Blight*, Blighty, and British Militarism

Lauren Arrington has identified a decisive 'shift to politics' in the programme of the nearly bankrupt Abbey Theatre in the wake of the Easter Rising. She locates the first instance of this shift in a series of debates organized by W. B. Yeats in the autumn of 1918 to publicize a revival of his 1903 hunger strike drama, *The King's Threshold*.[45] However, I would argue that Gogarty's *Blight*, which opened almost a year earlier and was revived three times in 1918, might productively be considered an early participant in (and financial success story of) this politicizing turn.[46] I would further contend that it is Gogarty's depiction of venereal disease and the medico-legal apparatus through which it was regulated which cements *Blight*'s status as agitprop theatre.

In the play's opening scene, Lily Foley, a young sex worker whose father has sought employment as a British serviceman, and Miss Maxwell-Knox, a District Visitor for a local Protestant social purity movement, engage in a tensely comic bout of verbal sparring in which allusions to venereal disease play a central role. Spotting Lily in make-up and a provocative fur coat, the

---

[42] Frederick F. MacCabe, *War with Disease*, Second (London: Baillière, Tindall, and Cox, 1907), ix.

[43] Ibid., 39; 37–8.   [44] Gogarty, 'Ugly England (I),' 3.

[45] Lauren Arrington, *W.B. Yeats, the Abbey Theatre, Censorship, and the Irish State: Adding the Half-Pence to the Pence* (Oxford: Oxford University Press, 2010), 20–1.

[46] 'Blight—The Tragedy of Dublin by Oliver St. John Gogarty as Gideon Ousley,' The Abbey Archive, 2017, https://www.abbeytheatre.ie/archives/play_detail/10218/.

zealous reformer loudly proclaims that the 'wages of sin is death'.[47] Lily greets this remark with an obscene '*gesture to Miss MK with her fingers and thumb*' and a rendition of the chorus of the popular 1916 music hall number 'Take Me Back to Dear Old Blighty': '*Hi tiddy li-i-ti, Carry me back to Blighty*'.[48] Undeterred, Miss Maxwell-Knox reiterates her pious platitude with renewed emphasis, prompting the adolescent streetwalker to declare that the 'wages of sin' are not 'death', but 'a month in the Locke' [*sic*].[49] The 'Locke' in question was Dublin's Westmoreland Lock Hospital. Located at 21 Townsend Street, since 1792 it had served as one of the capital's dedicated institutions for the treatment of venereal disease. Significantly, it is an institution the interior of which is apparently known to both women. For the biblical tag which the District Visitor so chidingly cites and which the young streetwalker so bitterly subverts served as the institution's semi-official motto, inscribed above its chapel door in red lettering as a morbid warning to patients and patrons alike.[50] As the exchange continues, its caustic political implications become increasingly apparent. Asked by Miss Maxwell-Knox why she is not at a Magdalene laundry 'doing *honest* work', Lily retorts that it is because, when she was, she 'didn't get *honest* wages'.[51] This materialist account of sex work in Ireland is underscored and explicitly linked to the debilitating socio-economic impact of British militarism when Mrs Larissey, the Foleys' neighbour, sharply reminds Miss Maxwell-Knox that, if Lily has been driven to seek financial sustenance through commercial sex, it is only because her father has been forced to serve the British war effort by the meagre employment prospects of Dublin under British rule:

MRS L If ye can't mind yer own business, ye can interview her father when he comes back from the fighting [...] If it's good yer after maybe ye'll explain to [the landlord] how Mrs Foley is to pay him 4/6 a week and keep her six children and the baby that's coming on the pay of her husband who got a job at the Front?[52]

---

[47] 'Alpha and Omega' (Oliver St John Gogarty), *Blight, the Tragedy of Dublin: An Exposition in Three Acts* (Dublin: Talbot Press, 1917), 15.

[48] Ibid.   [49] Ibid.

[50] The tag is derived from Romans, 6.19–23. Laurence M. Geary, '"The Wages of Sin Is Death": Lock Hospitals, Venereal Disease, and Gender in Pre-Famine Ireland,' in *Gender and Medicine in Ireland, 1700–1950*, ed. Margaret H. Preston and Margaret Ó hÓgartaigh (Syracuse, New York: Syracuse University Press, 2012), 167.

[51] 'Alpha and Omega' (Oliver St John Gogarty), *Blight*, 15. Emphasis Gogarty's.

[52] Ibid., 16–18.

Miss Maxwell-Knox rebuffs Mrs Larissey's analysis of Lily's position, instructing her not to refer to Mr Foley's position as 'a job', but to view him as 'fighting for humanity and civilization, as every able-bodied man should'—a claim certain to invite derision from a sizeable portion of any Dublin audience only a year after the execution of the Easter rebels. However, the irony of Miss Maxwell-Knox's remarks runs deeper than a simple condemnation of British barbarity. For, in praising the civilizing humanitarian virtues and 'able' bodies of the British Army, Miss Maxwell-Knox is venerating both the single largest client-base of the sex industry in Ireland and the nation's most prominent vector for venereal disease.

The pathological co-dependence of British garrisons and commercial sex in Ireland was acknowledged by contemporary commentators of every political stripe. An 1854 Select Committee on Dublin Hospitals reported that, of the 6,550 unmarried women admitted to medical institutions in the city with venereal disease in 1850, at least half were believed to have been infected by soldiers.[53] Gogarty himself drew playful attention to the issue in what is perhaps his most frequently quoted piece of doggerel, 'The Irish Yeoman's Return', published under the suggestive pseudonym 'J.R.S. of Knocklong' in the staunchly Unionist *Irish Society* in June 1901. What at first blush appears to be a straight-faced ode of welcome for an Irish regiment returning from the Boer War proves, on closer inspection, to be an acrostic in which the first letters of each line combine to declare that 'THE WHORES WILL BE BUSY'.[54] A 'Public Health Circular' issued by the Sinn Féin Public Health Department in February 1918, shortly after the premiere of Gogarty's play, addressed the perceived threat posed by the '100,000 Irishmen serving in the British army' who would return to Ireland following the cessation of hostilities in Europe, 15,000 of whom—'at the very lowest estimate'—it predicted would be syphilitic.[55] Penned by Kathleen Lynn, a physician, activist, and founder of St Ultan's Children's Hospital, and Richard Hayes, a Sinn Féin MP and eventual director of the Abbey Theatre, the pamphlet outlines what it presents as the devastating impact of the 'the great black plague' on Ireland's 'living children and her yet unborn children' and on the as yet untainted blood of the 'rural districts':

---

[53] *Report of the Select Committee on Dublin Hospitals*, 1854, Q. 39.

[54] 'J.R.S. of Knocklong' (Oliver St John Gogarty), 'The Irish Yeoman's Return, or Love Is Lord of All,' *Irish Society*, June 1901.

[55] Kathleen Lynn and Richard Hayes, 'Public Health Circulars, No. 1' (Sinn Féin Public Health Department, Dublin, February 1918), 1.

If from some imaginable cause thousands of Consumptives were to be dumped down en masse on our shores and scattered among our people, we would hear a loud outcry of its criminality from many quarters, and it would be incumbent on any Government having a sense of its responsibilities to devise a scheme to cope with such an evil. Here is a greater danger threatening us and State and Sanitary Authorities are quite inactive.[56]

In this context Lily's wry recitation of 'Take Me Back to Dear Old Blighty'— which narrates the fate of three homesick British soldiers on the Western Front—offers, through its tacit echo of the venereal *Blight* of the play's title, a bleak adumbration of her syphilitic fate, revealed in the play's third act. For Gogarty then, venereal disease and the Lock hospitals through which the British state inadequately endeavoured to contain its spread are the necessarily pathological corollaries of Ireland's occupied status. The syphilitic blight which afflicts Dublin's tenement dwellers is the result of the physically and morally corrupt military administration of Ireland. Indeed, Gogarty goes so far as to argue that the decorous squeamishness which causes the Irish to 'mix morals even in [their] medicine' and blinds the Dublin Corporation to the realization that 'prevention is better than cure' is itself a form of 'imported hypocrisy' alien to an implicitly pure Irish outlook.[57]

'The "venereal excess" cry' and the 'old pap of racial hatred': Sinn Féin, Sex, and Anti-Semitism

It is perhaps unsurprising to state that Joyce balked at Gogarty's position, particularly in the 'purity' which it tendentiously afforded Ireland. For Joyce, if any one was 'too sordid and lost to see his own hypocrisy', it was Gogarty. In a letter to his brother Stanislaus, dated 4 October 1906, he wishes that 'some unkind person would publish a book about the venereal condition of the Irish; since they pride themselves so much on their immunity' (*LII*, 170–71). Joyce insists that syphilis is 'a disease like any other disease', caused by 'anti-hygienic conditions' (*LII*, 170) and 'venereal ill-luck' (*LII*, 171), rather than the 'excess' which Gogarty had sought to censure. The source of Joyce's frustration was not simply Gogarty's hypocrisy, but his

---

[56] Ibid., 2.
[57] 'Alpha and Omega' (Oliver St John Gogarty). *Blight, the Tragedy of Dublin: An Exposition in Three Acts* (Dublin: Talbot Press, 1917), 43–4.

sense that these articles revealed an ugly strain of bigotry in Sinn Féin's rhetoric. In particular, Joyce sensed that 'the "venereal excess" cry', and the degenerationist anxieties it engaged, were being deployed to '[educate] the people of Ireland on the old pap of racial hatred' (*LII*, 167) and replicate in inverted form the strategies of othering which underpinned Britain's imperial public health and social hygiene policy. This tendency is exemplified by Gogarty's second 'Ugly England' article, which characterizes the degenerate 'Sludge' through a range of dehumanizing epithets as 'an ogre', a 'no more than human animal', 'a slave', and 'a sewer'.[58] In a sectarian manoeuvre sure to please a *Sinn Féin* readership, Gogarty positions Oliver Cromwell's ascent to power as the originary moment of this 'devolution' in the 'Anglo-Saxon' race, which he associates with the rise of evangelical Protestantism.[59] By an act of gymnastic chauvinism, Gogarty proceeds to argue that this 'Puritanism' has inscribed itself in 'the physiognomy and physique of the people' in the 'distinctly Jewish' features of their 'race-type'.[60] In an anthropometric register Gogarty describes the 'anaemic face and aquiline nose' of a nearby shop-girl, whose poor teeth, 'narrow' palate, and inability to 'breathe well' he presents as defects common in 'half-breeds'.[61] As in his first article, Gogarty implies that the clearest manifestation of this degenerative threat in Ireland is the venereally diseased British Army, whose officials fear that the 'hot-blooded Irish may become too educated [...] to bring upon themselves the moral ruin and physical decay which joining the English mercenary forces certainly involves'.[62]

The debts such anti-Semitic rhetoric owes to the Dreyfus affair and the Limerick pogrom are not far to seek, with both scandals being afforded consistent and often inflammatory coverage by Griffith's *United Irishman*. The Limerick pogrom—a three-month sequence of boycotts and attacks against Jewish traders, many of whom had fled Russia following anti-Jewish purges in Kishnev—was incited by a sermon delivered by the Redemptorist preacher Father John Creagh on 13 January 1904, in which he instructed his flock to cast from their community 'a viper that might at any moment slay its benefactor'.[63] The common tropology of anti-Semitic slander—the crucifixion, Christian martyrology, the blood libel—which Creagh drew upon to figure the Jewish population of Limerick as a parasitic threat ('leeches [who]

[58] Oliver St John Gogarty, 'Ugly England (II),' *Sinn Féin*, 24 November 1906, 3.
[59] Ibid.   [60] Ibid.   [61] Ibid.   [62] Ibid.
[63] Fr John Creagh, 'Jewish Trading, Its Growth in Limerick, Address to the Confraternity,' *Munster News*, 13 January 1904, reproduced in Dermot Keogh and Andrew McCarthy, *Limerick Boycott 1904: Anti-Semitism in Ireland* (Douglas Village, Cork: Mercier Press, 2005), 35–6; 35.

draw our blood') to the city's Catholic community has been well documented by critics and historians.[64] Less often noted are the ways in which Creagh, and the anti-Semitic tradition upon which he drew, figured Jews as a degenerate and degenerative sexual threat to the nation's physical and cultural integrity. Since the mid-nineteenth century, Jewishness, mental illness, and nervous disease had been virtually synonymous in European medical and popular discourse. Charcot spoke for many during one of his hugely influential Tuesday lessons at the Salpêtrière in 1888 when he stressed 'combien, dans la race, les accidents nerveux de tout genre [...] se montrent incomparablement beaucoup plus fréquents qu'ailleurs' [how incomparably more frequent nervous accidents of all types are among the [Jewish] race than elsewhere].[65] This predisposition to neurological illness was attributed to the sexual alterity of the Jewish, who were held by popular opinion and sexology alike to be both pathologically endogamous and dangerously licentious.[66] In the case of Creagh's polemic, a particular focal point was the seductive danger Jewish traders posed to 'the women of a house' and the sanctity of the marital home: 'The Jew has got a sweet tongue when he wishes—he passes off his miserable goods upon her.'[67] Creagh invoked the sexually vulnerable figure of the 'servant girl' as an example of the kind of woman too easily tempted by 'the designing Jew' and his 'cheap, gaudy jewellery, [and] showy dresses'.[68] Under such an influence, Creagh warned, Ireland's young women would squander their 'scanty earnings' in pursuit of a debauched and implicitly sexualized aesthetic.[69] Turning to the figure of the housewife, Creagh sketched a narrative of furtive meetings and spousal deceit fitted with all the trappings of an extra-marital affair:

She has to spare and stint to get the money to pay off the Jew without her husband knowing it, and then follow misery, sorrow, and deceit. The wife is afraid lest her husband should find out that she has been dealing with the Jews. The Jew makes his appearance while the husband is in the

---

[64] Ibid. For an overview of the pogrom and its relationship to anti-Semitism in Ireland more broadly, see Keogh and McCarthy, *Limerick Boycott 1904: Anti-Semitism in Ireland* and Cormac Ó Gráda, *Jewish Ireland in the Age of Joyce: A Socioeconomic History* (Princeton: Princeton University Press, 2006), chap. 9.

[65] Jean-Martin Charcot, *Leçons du Mardi à la Salpêtrière: Policliniques, 1888–1889* (Paris: Progrés Médical, 1889), 11.

[66] Sander L. Gilman, *Difference and Pathology: Stereotypes of Sexuality, Race, and Madness* (Ithaca: Cornell University Press, 1985), 153–6.

[67] Creagh, 'Jewish Trading,' in Keogh and McCarthy, *Limerick Boycott 1904*, 35.

[68] Ibid., 36.   [69] Ibid.

house. [...] The wife, too, will beg the Jew not to come to her house—she does not want him coming, and then stealthy visits must be paid at night, in the darkness, lest the dealings be found out. Stand at a prominent Jew's house at night, and you will be surprised to see the number and the class of people who are going in and out, under cover of shawls, to pay the Jew his usury.[70]

Tellingly, the nature of the 'payment' exacted in such an encounter is left elliptically vague, tacitly aligning Limerick's Jewish pedlars with sex work and the diverse physical and social maladies with which it was cognate. Creagh underscored this image of Limerick's Jewish community as a sexually corrupting influence on the local population when, drawing on the cultural isolationist rhetoric of Irish Ireland, he accused the city's Jewish pedlars of 'distributing to innocent country people indecent pictures, impure books, and aiding [in the] corruption of morals in other ways'.[71] Even before Creagh's sermon, concerns about Ireland's Jewish community, particularly in Dublin and Limerick, had prompted a number of investigations by the RIC under the direction of Dublin Castle. A common allegation concerned Jewish tea dealers, who were alleged to be in the habit of 'collecting from hotels and other large establishments of the sort, used tea leaves, drying them, mixing with them deleterious drugs, and selling the compound to the poorer classes as tea'.[72] These contaminated preparations were presented as a concern to public health, 'producing nervous disease and insanity' in the unwitting consumer, symptoms heavily inflected by contemporary anxieties around degeneration and venereal disease.[73] As these examples suggest, in both Creagh's sermon and the broader terrain of contemporary Irish anti-Semitism, Sinn Féin and Irish Ireland's investments in domestic economy took on a pointedly sexual dimension, in which conducting business with an outsider constituted a sexually corrupting violation of the *oikos* that threatened not only 'local trade and industry' but the purity of the Irish population.[74]

As has often been noted, the most obvious mouthpiece for Gogarty's fusion of Anglophobia and anti-Semitism within the world of *Ulysses* is 'the citizen' (*U* 12.58), whose monomaniacal conception of Irish national identity is deliberately indebted to the worst excesses of both Creagh's sermon and Sinn Féin rhetoric:

[70] Ibid.   [71] Ibid.
[72] Sir Anthony MacDonnell to Sir John Ross, 2 February 1903, reproduced in Keogh and McCarthy, *Limerick Boycott 1904*, 22.
[73] Ibid., 23.
[74] Creagh, 'Jewish Trading,' in Keogh and McCarthy, *Limerick Boycott 1904*, 36.

– Those are nice things, says the citizen, coming over here to Ireland filling the country with bugs.

[...]

– Swindling the peasants, says the citizen, and the poor of Ireland. We want no more strangers in our house.   (*U* 12.1141–51)

In this regard, it is perhaps unsurprising that the citizen's most programmatic endorsement of Irish cultural and economic autarchy is initiated by a venereally inflected pun. After a discussion of the Irish language movement prompts J. J. O'Molloy and Bloom to speak in defence of English 'moderation and botheration and their colonies and their civilisation' (*U* 12.1195–96) the citizen rounds on the colonial apologists, exclaiming: 'Their syphilisation, you mean... To hell with them! [...] No music and no art and no literature worthy of the name. Any civilisation they have they stole from us' (*U* 12.1197–1200). While hardly an inspired exercise in linguistic gymnastics, Joyce's wordplay nevertheless succeeds in neatly encapsulating Sinn Féin's tendency to figure English culture as a pathological and parasitical threat to Irish socio-economic integrity. The citizen reprises this theme when the conversation turns to 'Edward the peacemaker' (*U* 12.1399), remarking that he finds 'a bloody sight more pox than pax about that boyo' (*U* 12.1400–01), a reflection that prompts Alf Bergen to compare Edward's stable of racehorses to 'all the women he rode' (*U* 12.1406). The citizen's characterization of the English monarch as a syphilitic womanizer is predicated on an implicit contrast with the sexual purity of the Irish, whose bodily integrity is intended to mirror the integrity of the nation as a whole. However, the limits of this virginal conception of Irish identity have in fact already been suggested through another venereal allusion made earlier in the episode while the citizen decries the Anglicization of the once Parnellite *Irish Independent*:

Listen to the births and deaths in the *Irish all for Ireland Independent* [...]
And he starts reading them out:

[...] Deaths. Bristow, at Whitehall lane, London: Carr, Stoke Newington of gastritis and heart disease: Cockburn, at the Moat house, Chepstow...

– I know that fellow, says Joe, from bitter experience.

– Cockburn [...] How's that for a national press, eh, my brown son!

(*U* 12.221–34)

Here the corruption of the '*Irish all for Ireland Independent*' by English death notices is ironically paralleled and undercut by Joe's bawdy allusion to a personal brush with venereal disease (Cock-burn), which places under tacit erasure the innate Gaelic purity the citizen strives to defend. Indeed, the very structure of the pun is predicated on an Irish mispronunciation of the surname (the citizen's repetition suggests that he only gets it right on his second attempt) which seems to align the infection it encodes with the citizen rather than the deceased inhabitant of Chepstow.

Joyce's problematization of Sinn Féin's attempts to construct a model of national identity predicated on an illusory sexual purity finds its fullest expression in the 'Circe' episode of *Ulysses*, which contains the novel's highest concentration of references to syphilis and its treatment. This satirical project manifests itself in Joyce's characterization of 'THE FIGURE' (*U* 15.217) Bloom encounters at the episode's opening: '*A sinister figure leans on plaited legs against O'Beirne's wall, a visage unknown, injected with dark mercury. From under a wideleaved sombrero the figure regards him with evil eye*' (*U* 15.212–14). This individual, who accosts Bloom upon his entrance to Nighttown, seems to serve simultaneously as a gatekeeper to its brothels—demanding that Bloom utter a 'Password' before entry (*U* 15.219)—and a member of their staff. This paradox is reflected in its vexed identity as an embodiment of syphilitic infection and an example of the measures taken to police its transmission and mitigate effects. The figure's '*plaited legs*' may be the product of 'Locomotor ataxy' (*U* 15.2591), a failure of muscular co-ordination caused by neurosyphilis, while its '*evil eye*' suggests iritis, a symptom of tertiary infection with which Joyce may have been painfully familiar.[75] Most tellingly, the figure has been 'injected with dark mercury', a common treatment for the illness prior to the development of Salvarsan in 1909.

Amalgamated in 'THE DARK MERCURY' (*U* 15.749) are the desire to police the perceived vice of Dublin's brothels and a depiction of the dehumanizing effects such vice can produce, registered in its unstable role as both a preventative and a sufferer of syphilitic infection. Bloom addresses the figure, assuming it to be a sex worker: '*Bueños noches, señorita Blanca, que calle es esta?*' (*U* 15.218). Its response, '*Sraid Mabbot*', marks it out as a 'Gaelic league spy' (*U* 15.220), a member of the organization whose policies of Irish language revival and cultural de-Anglicization stood at the heart of

---

[75] '(locomotor ataxia) a form of neurosyphilis [...]. Severe stabbing pains in the legs [and] unsteady gait [...] are common. Some patients have blurred vision caused by damage to the optic nerves'. Elizabeth A. Martin, ed., *Concise Medical Dictionary*, 8th ed. (Oxford: Oxford University Press, 2010), 716.

Sinn Féin's political agenda. The manifest evidence of the figure's diseased condition thus jostles uncomfortably against its alignment with a model of Irish identity predicated on a physical purity which it fails to embody. Like Joe's 'Cockburn', this figure illustrates Joyce's desire to use venereal disease to permeate the apparently immutable physical boundaries within which Sinn Féin sought to locate Irishness.

Part of what Joyce highlights in his efforts to drown out 'the "venereal excess" cry' in *Ulysses* are what he perceives to be the reductive debts which Sinn Féin's 'purity' rhetoric owed to Catholic sexual politics. For Joyce, these threatened to undermine Griffith's commitment to 'secular liberty' (*LII*, 187) and an ecumenical nationalism whose roots lay in Young Ireland. Gogarty's contributions to *Sinn Féin* are clear examples of this shift towards a model of sexually constructed Irish identity in which nationalism and Catholicism are treated as synonyms. In their colloquial tone, sectarian outlook, and heavy use of disparaging epithets ('Sludge', 'Snudge', 'Snuck'), Gogarty's articles self-consciously emulate the idiosyncratic style and polemical content of Moran's *Leader* editorials.[76] In *Ulysses*, Joyce problematizes this investment in bodily 'purity' and the 'racial hatred' it facilitated through his satirical deployment of Bloom's potato as an unstable emblem of blighted Irish identity. During the composition and revision of 'Circe' Joyce emphasized the role of the prophylactic herb *moly*, given to Odysseus by Hermes. He outlined its function in a letter to Frank Budgen in September 1920: '[*Moly* is] the gift of Hermes...the invisible influence (prayer, chance, agility, *presence of mind*, power of recuperation) which saves in case of accident. This would cover immunity from syphilis ($\sigma \acute{u}$ $\varphi \iota \lambda o \varsigma$ = swine-love?)'[77] Bloom's potato offers a clear parallel to this gift in 'Circe', apparently embodying precisely the kinds of 'immunity' upon which Gogarty and his readership had so spuriously prided themselves in 1906.[78] Time and again in 'Circe' the potato is invoked as the questionable talisman of a 'pure' Ireland, protected from illness by its emblematic tuber. The folk-lore associations between the potato and immunity are sceptically expressed in 'Oxen of the Sun': 'Spud again the rheumatiz? All poppycock you'll scuse me saying'

---

[76] For an account of the *Leader*'s house-style and Moran's agonistic political philosophy, see Deirdre Toomey, 'Moran's Collar: Yeats and Irish Ireland,' in *Yeats Annual No. 12*, ed. Warwick Gould and Edna Longley, 45–83 (London: Macmillan, 1996).

[77] Stuart Gilbert, ed., *Letters of James Joyce*, vol. 1, 3 vols. (London: Faber and Faber, 1957), 147–8. Hereafter cited parenthetically as *LI*. Emphases Joyce's.

[78] Budgen identifies this parallel in Frank Budgen, *James Joyce and the Making of* Ulysses (Bloomington: Indiana University Press, 1973), 230.

(*U* 14.1480–81). However, by the time Bloom enters Nighttown these curative properties have expanded exponentially, as Bloom notes: 'The Providential... Poor mamma's panacea' (*U* 15.201–02). The 'invisible influence' (*LI*, 148) of the potato here imbues Bloom's Irish heritage with an explicitly religious ('Providential') dimension, just as the Sinn Féin discourse of 'purity' which Joyce satirizes was founded upon an implicitly Catholic sexual politics.

The hypocrisy Joyce detects in this union manifests itself in the conclusion of the blasphemous bidding prayer made by 'THE DAUGHTERS OF ERIN' (*U* 15.1940)—Joyce's rendering of *Inghinidhe na hÉireann*—to Bloom during his martyrdom: 'Potato Preservative against Plague and Pestilence, pray for us' (*U* 15.1952). The prophylactic connotations of the Francophone pun 'Preservative' have already been underscored in 'Oxen of the Sun', where 'Preservative had given [the clients of the sex worker "Bird in the Hand"] a stout shield of oxengut' (*U* 14.465) as protection from the 'foul plague Allpox' (*U* 14.464). The biblically inflected 'Plague and Pestilence' thus take on decidedly venereal resonances, just as the 'Providential' (prophylactic) role of Erin's 'Potato Preservative' is shown to be irreconcilable with the Catholic dogma which Joyce detected in Sinn Féin's conception of Irish identity. Joyce's decision to have a pious parody of *Inghinidhe na hÉireann*, staunch allies of Griffith, perform their devotion to a sexualized symbol of Ireland emphasizes the moment's subversive political content. Undertaken in concert with their anti-enlisting activities, theatrical performances were central to *Inghinidhe na hÉireann*'s programme of nationalist consciousness-raising, with the group regularly organizing elaborate multi-night cycles of 'Gaelic Tableaux'. These stylized sequences combined scenes from Gaelic mythology ('The Faerie Changeling') and Irish history ('The Story of King Brian'), with conceptual pieces depicting images such as 'Ireland Fettered' and 'Ireland Free'.[79] By having the Daughters of Erin enact a blasphemous tableau in celebration of a sexually suspect emblem of Irish national identity, Joyce thus subverts a prominent nationalist attempt to stage a culturally and politically unified Ireland founded upon a dubious claim to sexual purity. The ultimate expression of this ambivalence comes when the English sex worker Zoe runs her hand over Bloom's crotch and makes an unsettling discovery:

---

[79] 'The Gaelic Tableaux,' *United Irishman*, 13 April 1901, 4–5.

ZOE

(*in sudden alarm*) You've a hard chancre.

[…]

(*Her hand slides into his left trouser pocket and brings out a hard black shrivelled potato. She regards it and Bloom with dumb moist lips.*)

BLOOM

A talisman. Heirloom.

ZOE

For Zoe? For keeps? For being so nice, eh?   (*U* 15.1303–15)

Zoe believes Bloom to have a syphilitic 'chancre' (an indication of primary infection), which is revealed to be the '*black shriveled potato*' that has acted as Bloom's protective 'talisman' throughout the episode. However, in the context of this substitution, the potato now serves as an ominous symbol of corrupted Irish nationhood through which Joyce imbues the suggestion of syphilitic infection with resonances of the Great Famine of the 1840s and '50s.[80] Rather than raising the spectre of the Famine to advance a nationalist agenda, a common trope in Griffith's writing, Joyce figures this emblem of Irish nationalism as an infectious and corrupting influence in itself.[81] Bloom's description of his chancre-tuber as an 'heirloom' evokes contemporary syphilology's image of the illness as an inherited and incurable dysgenic threat, explaining why Zoe will take possession of it 'For keeps' (with no hope of cure) as her reward for 'being so nice' (sexually willing). In this moment Joyce brings together Bloom—the Irish-born son of a Jewish Hungarian immigrant, baptized in both the Protestant and Catholic Churches—and Zoe—an English-born Jewish sex worker, resident in Dublin—through an emblem of Irish identity which hovers unstably between its irreducibly dual roles as 'a killer of pestilence by absorption' (*U* 15.1357–58) and an apparent propagator of syphilitic infection. Through the suitably universal spectre of the 'foul plague Allpox' (*U* 14.464), Joyce thus constructs a scene which resists both the politicized binary of Irish

---

[80] A link possibly suggested by Gogarty's *Blight*, which Ellmann lists among the contents of Joyce's Trieste library. Richard Ellmann, *The Consciousness of Joyce* (London: Faber and Faber, 1977), 98.

[81] For a discussion of Joyce's responses to this discourse and to the Famine more generally, see Mary Lowe-Evans, *Crimes Against Fecundity: Joyce and Population Control* (Syracuse, New York: Syracuse University Press, 1989), chap. 1.

purity and English corruption which Sinn Féin sponsored, and the racialized opposition between the muscular Gael and the degenerate Anglicized Jew which it entailed.

'Mary Shortall was in the lock with the pox': Joyce's Syphilitic Acts of Union

Notwithstanding the satirical force of this critique, neither the nature nor the cause of Joyce's rebuttal of Gogarty's articles and *Sinn Féin's* broader position on sexual health in Ireland should be misconstrued. While Joyce is undeniably 'nauseated' (*LII*, 191) by Gogarty's hypocrisy, he is also palpably amused by it, and draws his brother's attention to it as a source of entertainment, and, more importantly, as part of a broader attempt to defend Sinn Féin's policies and political approach. Thus, though Joyce rejects *Sinn Féin's* purity rhetoric—'their lying drivel about pure men and pure women and spiritual love and love forever' (*LII*, 191–92)—it is important to bear in mind that, in doing so, he does not reject their platform or broader ideology. The young Joyce's commitment to a Griffithite policy of economic separatism following his departure from Ireland is well documented, taking tangible form in his attempt to establish himself as an agent for Foxford tweeds in Trieste in 1909 (*JJII*, 269; 303). This investment manifests itself in his letters to Stanislaus in Joyce's increasingly strained attempts to isolate Griffith and his political philosophy from the apparently malign influence of *Sinn Féin's* regular contributors, whom Joyce characterizes as mercenary hacks. In a letter written just after the publication of 'Ugly England', Joyce unfavourably contrasts Gogarty's article with 'Griffith's speech at the meeting of the National Council', whose insights he believes sufficiently profound to 'justif[y] the existence of his paper' (*LII*, 167) on their own. Joyce claims that, in order to make up space, '[Griffith], probably, has to lease out his columns to scribblers like Gogarty and Colm, and virgin martyrs like his sub-editor' (*LII*, 167). Following the publication of Gogarty's second article, Joyce addresses his brother's objections to *Sinn Féin* with a similar appeal to editorial pragmatics: 'You complain of Griffith's using Gogarty & Co. How do you expect him to fill his paper: he can't write it all himself' (*LII*, 187). In a final bid to insulate Griffith, Joyce prophesies that, should Sinn Féin's policies succeed, Gogarty will 'play the part of [Leonard] MacNally and [Thomas] Reynolds' (*Ibid*) and betray the movement. Far from rejecting Sinn Féin outright, in these letters Joyce shows a willingness, if not to endorse, then, at least, frustratedly accept sexual health rhetoric as a necessary evil in order to achieve the movement's political aims and fill the pages of its flagship periodical.

Indeed, Joyce's writing in this period sometimes seems not simply tolerant of, but actively indebted to Griffithite thinking and 'the "venereal excess" cry' (*LII*, 191) to which it gave rise. References to syphilitic infection are a regular rhetorical feature of Joyce's artistic self-fashioning and cultural critique of Ireland under British rule throughout the first decades of the twentieth century. As has been noted above, the 1904 pseudo-manifesto 'A Portrait of the Artist' concludes with an image of revolution in which 'the competitive order is employed against itself, the aristocracies are supplanted; and amid the general paralysis of an insane society, the confederate will issues in action'.[82] In a diary entry written on 13 August the same year, Stanislaus Joyce records how:

> Jim [...] boasts of his power to live, and says, in his pseudo-medical phraseology, that it comes from his highly specialized central nervous system. He talks much of the syphilitic contagion in Europe, is at present writing a series of studies in it in Dublin, tracing practically everything to it. The drift of his talk seems to be that the contagion is congenital and incurable and responsible for all manias and being so, that it is useless to try to avoid it.[83]

However, when Joyce turns specifically to the question of syphilis in Ireland, socialist prophecies and decadent images of universal 'syphilisation' give place to a decidedly *Sinn Féin* inflected aetiology of the illness, in which responsibility for the presence of the illness in Ireland resides firmly with the British. In a discussion prompt for Berlitz students in Trieste composed *circa* 1905, Joyce claims that: 'Ireland is a great country. It is called the Emerald Isle. The metropolitan government, after centuries of strangling it, has laid it waste. It's now an untilled field. The government sowed hunger, syphilis, superstition, and alcoholism there; puritans, Jesuits, and bigots have sprung up' (*JJII*: 217). Though Joyce's tongue is seldom far from his cheek, especially in such moments of adolescent provocation, the statement bears

---

[82] James Joyce, *Poems and Shorter Writings: Including Epiphanies, Giacomo Joyce, and 'A Portrait of the Artist,'* ed. Richard Ellmann, A. Walton Litz, and John Whittier-Ferguson (London: Faber and Faber, 1991), 218.

[83] Stanislaus Joyce, *The Complete Dublin Diary of Stanislaus Joyce*, ed. George H. Healy (Ithaca: Cornell University Press, 1971), 51.

close attention for the political and cultural co-ordinates within which it situates its characterization of contemporary Ireland. Most obviously, it ascribes responsibility for the contemporary cultural and economic under-development of Ireland to the 'metropolitan', which is to say, British, government. Furthermore, it presents the presence of syphilis in Ireland not simply as a by-product of British imperial governance, but as a con-scious technique for the oppression of the Irish comparable to the Famine ('hunger') or the brewing industry ('alcoholism')—a rhetorical and historio-graphical manoeuvre lifted straight from the playbook of Sinn Féin and Irish Ireland. Nor is this pragmatic sensibility or political affiliation confined to his letters and personal writing of the early 1900s. However much he may have critiqued Sinn Féin's use of venereal disease as a means to police the boundary of Irish identity, in both *Dubliners* and *Ulysses*, syphilis and its metastases are deployed to oppose and critique British rule in Ireland. Such a critique would appear to be offered in 'Circe' when, in the midst of the psycho-sexual phantasmagoria of Bloom and Stephen's visit to Bella Cohen's Mecklenburg Street brothel, the sex worker Kitty breathlessly relates how: 'Mary Shortall was in the lock with the pox she got from Jimmy Pidgeon in the blue caps had a child off him that couldn't swallow and was smothered with convulsions in the mattress' (*U* 15.2578–80). Kitty's reference to 'the blue caps' identifies the pox-ridden Pidgeon as a member of the Royal Dublin Fusiliers, the predominately Irish regiment which Bloom identifies as being 'rotten with venereal disease' in 'Lotus Eaters'.[84] While Joyce is more often held up by critics as a vocal opponent of the artificial binary of Irish purity and English corruption upon which much contem-porary advanced nationalist propaganda was predicated, in this moment, he highlights, in affectingly stark terms, the very real role British militarism played in the transmission of venereal disease in Ireland.

Contained within this indictment of British militarism is a repudiation of the models of ethnic and sexual difference through which British rule in Ireland was rationalized and justified in the late nineteenth and early twentieth centuries. As I emphasized in Part I, the Arnoldian image of the Celt as 'feminine', 'sentimental', and fundamentally 'undisciplinable' con-structed Irishness as a state of hysterical and self-destructive femininity which could only be redeemed through 'vital union' with the rational,

[84] Major Arthur Mainwaring, *Crown and Country: The Historical Records of the 2nd Batt. Royal Dublin Fusiliers, formerly the 1st Bombay European Regiment, 1662–1911* (London: Arthur L. Humphreys, 1911), 294.

masculine 'Anglo-Saxon'.[85] As my reading of Healy's post-Split character-izations of Parnell in Chapter 1 has already suggested, in the masculinist logic of contemporary degeneration theory and the discourses of social hygiene to which it gave rise, such pathologized femininity was closely allied to the dysgenic impact of syphilis and its hereditary manifestations. The illness and its inherited degenerative effects were an abiding concern for British colonial administrators and medical specialists alike. In an 1891 letter to the Secretary of State, Lord Landsdowne, Viceroy of India, expressed his concern that 'infected men' would return home from overseas service 'to spread the contagion among the civil population of Great Britain' and 'transmit a heritage of misery to posterity'.[86] British and European venerealogists offered an alarming image of this heritage, outlining the still births, birth defects, and life-long health problems to which congenital syphilis gave rise.[87] As discussed in Chapter 1, for Alfred Fournier, the effects of congenital syphilis constituted, for both the individual and the species, a litany of 'déchéance' [decay], 'abâtardissement' [bastardization], 'infériorisation' [inferiority], and 'dégénéresence' [degeneration].[88] Similar, if less shrill, characterizations were offered by respected British sexologists well into the twentieth century. In Havelock Ellis's *Essays in War Time* (1916), a polemic on 'The Conquest of Venereal Disease' appears alongside discussions of 'War and Eugenics', 'Eugenics and Genius', and 'The Production of Ability', in which syphilis is presented as 'the most dangerous of all racial poisons'.[89] As Joyce's description of the new-born's dysphagia, 'convulsions', and suffocation makes clear, Mary Shortall's child is the victim of congenital syphilis, and, as such, an apparent manifestation of the degenerative process which Fournier, Ellis, and Landsdowne outline. However, by having Kitty insist that it is Jimmy Pidgeon who has infected Mary Shortall with syphilis, and not the reverse, Joyce subverts a dominant

---

[85] Matthew Arnold, *On the Study of Celtic Literature* (London: Smith, Elder & Co, 1867), 108–9, xii; Marjorie Howes, *Yeats's Nations: Gender, Class, and Irishness* (Cambridge: Cambridge University Press, 1996), chap. 1; Susan Cannon Harris, *Gender and Modern Irish Drama* (Bloomington: Indiana University Press, 2002), chap. 1.

[86] Lord Landsdowne (Viceroy of India) to India Secretary, Lord Cross, 4 February 1891, quoted in Philippa Levine, *Prostitution, Race, and Politics: Policing Venereal Disease in the British Empire* (New York: Routledge, 2003), 44.

[87] For an overview of British medical thought surrounding congenital syphilis in the early twentieth century, see D'Arcy Power and J. Keogh Murphy, eds., *A System of Syphilis, with an Introduction by Sir Jonathan Hutchinson* (London: Frowde, 1908), chaps. 22–25.

[88] Alfred Fournier, *Prophylaxie de la Syphilis* (Paris: J. Rueff, 1903), 383.

[89] Havelock Ellis, *Essays in War Time: Further Studies in Social Hygiene* (London: Constable and Company, 1916), 33.

narrative of British social hygiene policy which positioned subaltern women as a pathological threat to the administrators of colonial rule. Far from offering salvation from a hereditary state of sexually pathologized irrationality, in Joyce's rendering the 'vital union' of an archetype of Irish femininity with an avatar of British martial authority serves only to deprive the Irishwoman of her health, her liberty, and her child, whose death may be read as a symbol of Ireland's thwarted political futurity.

Conclusion

Notwithstanding the strong nationalist resonances of such an image, it would be naive, on the basis of moments such as these, to offer an uncomplicated portrait of the artist as a young Shinner, or to lose sight of the ambivalence which often inflects Joyce's critiques of British imperialism or his deployment of nationalist arguments. Returning to the Triestene pedagogical gambit, it is clear that, for Joyce, the corollary of the British campaign of sexual germ-warfare he identifies is not merely the frustration of Ireland's socio-economic potential, but religious zealotry, sectarianism, and xenophobia—an indictment of precisely the culturally Catholic and ethnically Irish image of Ireland which Sinn Féin's anti-imperial rhetoric was intended to sponsor. Complicating matters yet further, Joyce intertextually frames this image of Irish inanition, inebriation, and infection through a reference to George Moore's 1903 short story collection, *The Untilled Field*. Opening with 'In the Clay', a story in which an Irish sculptor is driven from his native village because the clergyman who has commissioned an altarpiece from him realizes its model is a local girl, and progressing through tales of emigration ('Home Sickness'), frustrated sexual desire ('Some Parishioners'), and a thwarted scheme for clerical marriage ('A Letter to Rome'), Moore's collection insistently presents a meddlesome Catholic priesthood as the single greatest barrier to the cultivation of social and sexual modernity in Ireland. Fused, then, within Joyce's deliberately scandalous image of an infected Ireland full of unfulfilled promise is a revivalist critique of the nation's Church-abetted socio-economic and intellectual underdevelopment and an aetiology of British imperialism and Irish sexual disease in which the Irish Ireland movement is presented as a symptomatic manifestation of the very cultural pathology it sought to remedy.

Indeed, at times in *Ulysses*, Joyce seems less concerned with highlighting either the culpability of Ireland's British military authorities or the hypocrisies of Sinn Féin in their handling of venereal disease, than with emphasizing how threadbare the entire question of ascribing blame for the presence of sexually transmitted infection in Ireland had become. A hint of this exhaustion is caught in the 'Eumaeus' episode of the novel, in which redundancy, dead metaphors, and a general air of performative lassitude are the dominant stylistic features. Sitting in the cabman's shelter with a worse-for-wear Stephen Dedalus, Bloom is confronted with the 'glazed' face (*U* 16.704) of a 'frowsy whore' (*U* 11.1252) he had earlier encountered when leaving the Ormond Hotel bar in 'Sirens'. Joyce's emphasis on the sex worker's 'demented glassy grin' (*U* 16.724) and Bloom's sense that she is 'not exactly all there' (*U* 16.724–25) suggest that she is suffering from the early stages of neurosyphilis. Bloom, adopting the haughty tone of a '*paterfamilias*' (*U* 16.744), expresses to Stephen his disbelief that 'a wretched creature', fresh from 'the Lock hospital reeking with disease', should be 'barefaced enough to solicit' openly on the streets of Dublin (*U* 16.729–30). The indignant Bloom insists that 'women of that stamp' (*U* 16.741) ought to be 'licensed and medically inspected by the proper authorities' (*U* 16.743).

The Joycean ironies one would expect from such a moment are all present and correct, the most obvious being that Bloom, who questions how 'any man in his sober senses' (*U* 16.730) could endanger his health through sexual contact with what he perceives to be a syphilitic woman, has himself previously engaged her for an, albeit abortive, 'Appointment' (*U* 11.1257) while she was working at a Magdalene laundry ('any chance of your wash': *U* 11.1255–56). A greater irony is articulated by Stephen, who reflects that in Ireland 'people sell much more than she ever had and do a roaring trade' (*U* 16.736–37). Stephen's wry remark emphasizes the paradox of punishing Irish sex workers for fraternizing with British troops when other forms of political, cultural, and economic complicity in the operation of British imperialism were richly rewarded. As Stephen argues, by the logic of Ireland's subaltern position, the sex worker is merely 'a bad merchant. She buys dear and sells cheap' (*U* 16.738). Here syphilis is apparently figured as the basis for an uncomplicated nationalist indictment of British occupation, consistent in both tone and content with contemporary Sinn Féin and *Inghinidhe na hÉireann* anti-enlisting propaganda.

However, perhaps the greatest irony of all is that the scheme Bloom proposes is neither novel nor innovative, but instead deliberately evokes a long-abandoned body of British social hygiene policy: the Contagious Diseases Acts. Introduced to the United Kingdom in 1864, in their domestic manifestation these Acts established 'subjected districts' in which any woman suspected to be engaged in sex work within a five-mile radius of a British military encampment could be subjected to an involuntary and invasive medical examination. If a woman refused, she faced a month's imprisonment, and, if found to be infected with venereal disease, could be forcibly hospitalized for up to three months (a period extended to six months in 1866 and nine months in 1869).[90] Following a protracted campaign by a coalition of first-wave feminists and social purity advocates, the Acts were repealed in 1886. The Acts have most commonly been understood as manifestations of a gendered double-standard in which male promiscuity was licenced at the expense of women's bodily and personal autonomy, demonizing female sex workers, while leaving their clients unmolested.[91] Less often remarked upon, however, are the colonial origins of these Acts, which were first introduced not in Britain or Ireland, but in Hong Kong in 1857.[92] As Philippa Levine has demonstrated, in Britain's Asian, Caribbean, and Australian colonies, the inability of mid-nineteenth-century diagnostic medicine to distinguish between venereal and non-venereal treponemal infections dovetailed all too easily with imperialist narratives of British cultural and racial supremacy to allow conditions such as yaws, pinta, and bejel to be misdiagnosed as syphilis and taken as proof of the degenerate and immoral condition of the indigenous population.[93] As a result, colonial Contagious Disease policies were introduced earlier and repealed later than their domestic counterparts.

Viewed in the light of this martial heritage, Bloom's tone of apparently disinterested empiricism ('medically I am speaking', U 16.728) and his desire to regulate only female sex workers position him as a mouthpiece for an outmoded British social hygiene policy intended to serve the interests of Ireland's military administration. Joyce sartorially reinforces the imperial undertones of this moment through the sex worker's 'black straw sailor hat' (U 11.1252), ironically costuming her in the uniform of the 'gunboat' (U 16.727) whose crew seemingly constitutes her clientele. However, Joyce's decision to have an Irishman, Bloom—however overdetermined his national identity may be—rather than a figure of British military authority, serve as the sexually compromised mouthpiece for a punitive and

---

[90] Peter Baldwin, Contagion and the State in Europe 1830–1930 (Cambridge: Cambridge University Press, 1999), 372–3.
[91] Judith R. Walkowitz, Prostitution and Victorian Society: Women, Class, and the State (Cambridge: Cambridge University Press, 1980), pt. 2; Maria Luddy, Prostitution and Irish Society, 1800–1940 (Cambridge: Cambridge University Press, 2007), chap. 4.
[92] Levine, Prostitution, Race, and Politics, 40.   [93] Ibid., 65.

superannuated colonial social hygiene policy frustrates the polemical potential of this scene in favour of a more ambivalent image of mutual Anglo-Irish
infection. Moreover, in framing Bloom and Stephen's conversation—the
longest in the novel concerning the regulation of syphilis—in relation to
the long-defunct Contagious Diseases Acts, and by positioning that conversation in the novel's most pointedly weary episode, Joyce seems to suggest
that attempts to arbitrate Irish identity in relation to sexual health were
already past their sell-by date. As the concluding chapters of this book will
illustrate, this sense that nationalist claims concerning the exemplary sexual
purity of the Irish had ossified into empty cliché was to be deepened and
extended in the emergent Free State by Samuel Beckett, Kate O'Brien, and
Flann O'Brien.

PART III
HEREDITY AND FERTILITY

4

'Sterilization of the mind and apotheosis of the litter': Beckett, Censorship, and Fertility

An Act to make provision for the prohibition of the sale and distribution of unwholesome literature and for that purpose to provide for the establishment of a censorship of books and periodical publications, and to restrict the publication of reports of certain classes of judicial proceedings and for other purposes incidental to the matters aforesaid.

Censorship of Publications Act, 1929: Preamble

I believe that birth control [...] will inevitably lead to race suicide, and the book which advocates that, no matter what the arguments it puts forward may be, no matter how it is treated, will equally come under this ban[.]

James FitzGerald-Kenney addressing the Dáil
(19 February 1929)

Hitherto we have been concerned mainly with hygiene in the physical world: the cleaning of milk, the cleaning of butter, of farmsteads, and so on [...] We are embarking on an attempt by the State into the region of the hygiene of the mind.

Sir John Keane addressing the Seanad (11 April 1929)

To claim that Samuel Beckett was opposed to censorship is unlikely to raise many eyebrows. From the goading of the 'filthy censors' in *Murphy*, to the withdrawal of *All that Fall* (1956) and *Endgame* (1956) from the 1958 Dublin International Theatre Festival following the suppression of a proposed stage adaptation of *Ulysses* (1922), Beckett's distaste for publications control was forthright and thoroughgoing.[1] As the deliberate 'care' with

---

[1] Samuel Beckett, *Murphy*, ed. J. C. C. Mays (London: Faber, 2009), 50; James Knowlson, *Damned to Fame: The Life of Samuel Beckett* (London: Bloomsbury, 1997), 447–8.

Irish Modernism and the Politics of Sexual Health. Lloyd (Meadhbh) Houston, Oxford University Press.

which the narrator of *Murphy* seeks to provoke the censor and 'debauch the cultivated reader' suggests, Beckett's prose repeatedly engages with and responds to the implicit and explicit threat of suppression.[2] The recent historicizing and Hibernicizing turn in Beckett Studies, and the growing interest in Beckett within Irish Studies more broadly, has done much to root this opposition in an Irish context.[3] Central to such accounts has been the Free State's 1929 Censorship of Publications Act, which, in an effort to combat the circulation of 'evil literature' in the young nation, infamously prohibited all printed matter which advocated 'the unnatural prevention of conception or the procurement of abortion or miscarriage'.[4] John P. Harrington has shown how 'Che Sciagura' [what a misfortune] (1929), one of Beckett's earliest pieces of published prose, and 'Censorship in the Saorstat' (written *c.*1934–1936, published 1983) seek to satirize and scandalize what he presents as Ireland's 'agenda for *cultural exclusivism*'.[5] Patrick Bixby argues that this climate of censoriousness and the coercive collocation of Catholicism, fertility, and Irish identity which he claims the Act legally mandated were key catalysts for Beckett's antagonistic rendering of post-independence Irish political and cultural self-fashioning.[6] More recently, Seán Kennedy has offered a reading of the short story *Premier amour/First Love* (written *c.* 1946, published in French in 1970 and in an English self-translation in 1973) which emphasizes Beckett's opposition to what he presents as the Catholic pro-natalism of the Censorship Act, a thesis reinforced and extended in Paul Stewart's study, *Sex and Aesthetics in Samuel Beckett's Work* (2011), in which resistance to reproductive sexual activity is

[2] Beckett, *Murphy*, 75.

[3] Monographs and collections devoted to uncovering an 'Irish' Beckett include John P. Harrington, *The Irish Beckett* (Syracuse, New York: Syracuse University Press, 1991); Mary Junker, *Beckett: The Irish Dimension* (Dublin: Wolfhound Press, 1995); Emilie Morin, *Samuel Beckett and the Problem of Irishness* (Basingstoke: Palgrave Macmillan, 2009); Patrick Bixby, *Samuel Beckett and the Postcolonial Novel* (Cambridge: Cambridge University Press, 2009); Jennifer M. Jeffers, *Beckett's Masculinity* (New York: Palgrave Macmillan, 2009); Seán Kennedy, ed., *Beckett and Ireland* (Cambridge: Cambridge University Press, 2010); Andrew Gibson, *Samuel Beckett*, Critical Lives (London: Reaktion Books, 2010); Rina Kim, *Women and Ireland as Beckett's Lost Others: Beyond Mourning and Melancholia* (Basingstoke: Palgrave Macmillan, 2010); Alan Graham and Scott Eric Hamilton, eds., *Samuel Beckett and the 'State' of Ireland* (Newcastle upon Tyne: Cambridge Scholars Publishing, 2017).

[4] Dáil Éireann, 'Censorship of Publications Act, 1929,' Irish Statute Book, July 2014, http://www.irishstatutebook.ie/1929/en/act/pub/0021/print.html.

[5] Harrington, *The Irish Beckett*, 21–7; 35–9; 22. For a similar reading, see David A. Hatch, 'Samuel Beckett's "Che Sciagura" and the Subversion of Irish Moral Convention,' *Samuel Beckett Today/Aujourd'hui* 18 (2007), 241–55.

[6] Bixby, *Samuel Beckett and the Postcolonial Novel*, 9–14.

identified as central to the Beckettian aesthetic.[7] In each case, Beckett is presented as an uncomplicatedly valiant defender of the linked modernist ideals of intellectual and sexual autonomy outlined in Part I, in the face of the culture of state-mandated philistinism and fertility represented by the Censorship Act.

While these critics are undoubtedly correct to assert that the Censorship Act and the fertility cult it seemed to represent were 'problems of Irishness' with which Beckett grappled throughout his career, the accounts they offer of the nature of that problem and the manner of Beckett's responses to it are often limited and selective.[8] To begin with, each of these studies is staked upon a relatively uncomplicated opposition between Beckett and the implicitly repressive Catholic sexual culture that the Censorship Act is taken to embody. In such readings, Beckett emerges as the defiant modernist par excellence, following proudly in the footsteps of Joyce in scandalizing all those who sought to place aesthetic or moral constraints on his work. On the one hand, such an account risks replicating the 'enlightened Irish artist transcends benighted Erin to join the liberal European avant-garde' narrative which studies of Irish modernism have been keen to problematize in recent years. On the other hand, it overlooks moments in which Beckett remained silent on the question of censorship (particularly the Irish suppression of *More Pricks Than Kicks*), or expressed active anxiety over projects which he felt might tarnish his reputation with the economically and culturally ghettoizing label of 'obscenity', an impulse most visible in his deliberations over a commission from Jack Kahane's Obelisk Press to translate the Marquis de Sade's *Les 120 journées de Sodome* [The 120 days of Sodom] (written 1785, published 1904, and not translated into English until 1938).[9] Perhaps most significantly, given the Foucauldian account of sexuality upon which the majority of these readings are staked, in presenting Beckett's obscenity, anti-natalism, and the often grisly tone of his depictions of sex as intrinsically valiant repudiations of the conservative sexual culture

---

[7] Seán Kennedy, 'First Love: Abortion and Infanticide in Beckett and Yeats,' *Samuel Beckett Today/Aujourd'hui* 22 (2010), 79–91; Paul Stewart, *Sex and Aesthetics in Samuel Beckett's Work* (New York: Palgrave Macmillan, 2011).

[8] I derive this useful formulation from Emilie Morin's reading of Beckett's engagement with his homeland in Morin, *Samuel Beckett and the Problem of Irishness.*

[9] Beckett confided to George Reavey his concerns over the effect this project would have on his 'situation in England' and how it 'might prejudice future publications' of his own work there. While Beckett did not 'mind the obloquy', he did not wish to be 'spiked as a writer', nor was he prepared to publish the translation pseudonymously. Samuel Beckett, *The Letters of Samuel Beckett*, ed. Martha Dow Fehsenfeld et al., vol. I: 1929–1940 (Cambridge: Cambridge University Press, 2009), 604.

of Ireland, such analyses risk conforming to the logic of precisely the 'repressive hypothesis' that Foucault's account of the history and deployment of sexuality was intended to problematize.[10] At the very least, these charitable accounts of Beckett's sexual politics have a tendency to downplay the most troubling features of his engagement with sex, offering a paradoxically sanitized image of Beckettian obscenity.

Where previous criticism has presented Beckett's response to censorship and pro-natalism in Ireland as an ethically valorous and politically subversive rejection of state-mandated fertility and confessional identity politics, in this chapter I stress the complexities of Beckett's engagement with eugenics and its fraught relationship to a strand of Irish sectarian agon which both contributed to and was intensified by the drafting and passage of the Censorship Act. To do so, I explore the ways in which, through the Act, discourses of sexual health, eugenics, and population control became bound up with a broader competition for political influence and cultural capital between different intellectual, governmental, and confessional factions within the Free State, and trace how Beckett continued to grapple with these debates, and his own position within them, long after his departure for France. In doing so, I wish to argue that, as an artist whose oeuvre has been held up as the 'only fitting reaction to the situation of the concentration camps' and the racial science through which they were justified, Beckett's interrogation of his own engagement with eugenicist discourses merits close and sensitive scrutiny, and should not be overlooked in an effort to position him as an uncomplicated champion of free speech and reproductive rights.[11] To offer such an account, it is first necessary to examine the ways in which the Censorship Act has been interpreted in Irish historiography and to identify the implications of such accounts for an analysis of Beckett's response to censorship in Ireland.

A 'rhetoric of shock, horror, and outrage': The Censorship Act in Irish Historiography

Due in large part to its notorious prohibition of all printed matter relating to birth control, the 1929 Censorship of Publications Act has become both a

---

[10] Michel Foucault, *The History of Sexuality, 1: The Will to Knowledge* (New York: Pantheon Books, 1978), pts. 2–4.
[11] Theodor W. Adorno, *Negative Dialectics*, trans. E. B. Ashton (New York, 1973), 380.

by-word for the sexual 'repression' of the Irish, and a focal point for critical efforts to interrogate and problematize this popular stereotype. This has resulted in the emergence of two relatively well-defined positions with regards to the Act and its broader significance as a reflection of Irish cultural attitudes to sex in the early twentieth century. The first, exemplified by the work of Tom Inglis (but a feature of responses to the Act from its inception), emphasizes its status as an archetypal legislative manifestation of the influence of the Catholic Hierarchy in the administration of the Free State and the shaping of Irish sexual identity. For Inglis, measures like the Censorship Act constitute one facet of the 'Catholic Church's monopoly on morality' in the emergent nation, establishing a social atmosphere in which 'even the mildest suggestion of or allusion to sexual transgression encountered a rhetoric of shock, horror, and outrage'.[12] In Inglis's reading, this censorious climate becomes one of a range of social, cultural, and institutional forces which, from the late nineteenth century onwards, shaped the 'Irish body' into a template established by a 'normative, particularly sexual, Catholic social order'.[13] The second position, articulated in the work of Diarmaid Ferriter and Senia Pašeta, downplays the centrality of Catholic doctrine to the Act by situating its proscriptions in the wider field of contemporary European nationalism and the discourses of pro-natalism with which France, Italy, and others responded to a period of diminishing birth-rates and demographic decline.[14] They argue that, when viewed in light of anti-Malthusian censorship policies such as the French *Loi du 31 juillet 1920* [law of 31 July 1920], which prohibited all perceived 'provocation à l'avortement' [provocation to abortion] and 'propagande anticonceptionnelle' [contraceptive propaganda] or the national battle for fertility declared by Mussolini in his 1927 'Ascension Day' speech, the Act seems less a uniquely Irish phenomenon than an idiosyncratic manifestation of a broader European

---

[12] Tom Inglis, 'Foucault, Bourdieu and the Field of Irish Sexuality,' *Irish Journal of Sociology* 7, no. 1 (1997), 5–28, 27. For the role of Catholic Action groups in generating this atmosphere and lobbying for the outright prohibition of contraception in Ireland, see Sandra McAvoy, ' "Its effect on public morality is vicious in the extreme": Defining Birth Control as Obscene and Unethical, 1926–32,' in *'She said she was in the family way': Pregnancy and Infancy in Modern Ireland*, ed. Elaine Farrell (London: Institute of Historical Research, 2012), 35–52.

[13] Tom Inglis, 'The Irish Body,' in *Are the Irish Different?*, ed. Tom Inglis (Manchester: Manchester University Press, 2014), 88–98, 90.

[14] Diarmaid Ferriter, *The Transformation of Ireland, 1900–2000* (London: Profile, 2005), 335–42; Diarmaid Ferriter, *Occasions of Sin: Sex and Society in Modern Ireland* (London: Profile Books, 2009), 185–91; Senia Pašeta, 'Censorship and Its Critics in the Irish Free State, 1922–1932,' *Past & Present* 232, no. (1) (2003), 193–218; Peter Martin, *Censorship in the Two Irelands, 1922–1939* (Dublin: Irish Academic Press, 2006), chap. 3.

trend.[15] Furthermore, Ferriter cautions against reading the Act in narrowly sectarian terms, noting that, despite being presented as 'promoted exclusively by the Catholic Church against the spirit of Anglo-Ireland', the Act was supported by representatives of all churches.[16]

Elements of both positions can be detected in 'Censorship in the Saorstat', Samuel Beckett's essay-length response to the Act. Commissioned in 1934 by the soon-to-be-defunct *Bookman* and revised in 1936 to note Beckett's own inclusion on the Irish Register of Prohibited Publications, Beckett would eventually disparage the essay as a piece of hack-work ground out in response to an unwelcome deadline.[17] However, read in its intended context as a publisher's guide to the logic and inner-workings of the Censorship Act, it offers a valuable opportunity to politicize and historicize the rejection of reproductive sexuality which Stewart and others identify as a hallmark of Beckett's work, and to test the applicability of Inglis and Ferrtier's accounts of the model of Irish sexuality the debates over censorship reflect. Analysing the Act section by section, Beckett identifies Part IV—its proscription of birth control literature—as the 'essence of the Bill and its exciting cause'.[18] He argues that under the conditions of the Act 'to waive the off chance of a reasonable creature is no longer a mere mortal sin, but a slapup social malfeasance'.[19] Like Inglis, Beckett perceives in the Act an effort to enshrine the 'mortal sin[s]' of Catholic fertility doctrine as the basis of the Free State's independent national identity. In a pastiche of the rhetoric of the Act's exponents, Beckett emphasizes the ways in which its

---

[15] 'Loi du 31 juillet 1920 réprimant la provocation à l'avortement et à la propagande anticonceptionnelle,' *Journal officiel de la République française*, 1 August 1920, 3666; Michael S. Teitelbaum and J. M. Winter, *The Fear of Population Decline* (Orlando: Academic Press, 1985); Maria Sophia Quine, *Population Politics in Twentieth-Century Europe: Fascist Dictatorships and Liberal Democracies*, Historical Connections (London: Routledge, 1996); Angus McLaren, *Twentieth-Century Sexuality: A History* (Oxford: Blackwell, 1999), chap. 4; Franz Eder, Lesley Hall, and Gert Hekma, eds., *Sexual Cultures in Europe: National Histories* (Manchester: Manchester Univ. Press, 1999); Richard A. Soloway, *Demography and Degeneration: Eugenics and the Declining Birthrate in Twentieth-Century Britain*, 3rd ed. (Chapel Hill: University of North Carolina Press, 2001), chaps 7–12; Marius Turda, *Modernism and Eugenics* (Basingstoke: Palgrave Macmillan, 2010), chaps 2–3.

[16] Ferriter, *The Transformation of Ireland*, 340. A middle ground is struck by Pašeta, who uses the broader European context outlined by Ferriter and Martin to analyze the ways in which the Act and the debates surrounding its passage allowed the Catholic Church to secure a substantial measure of cultural and administrative hegemony in the Free State. Pašeta, 'Censorship and Its Critics in the Irish Free State, 1922–1932.'

[17] Samuel Beckett to Thomas McGreevy, 28 August [*for* 27], 1934, TCD, MS 10402/62, quoted in Beckett, *The Letters of Samuel Beckett*, I: 1929–1940:224, n. 9.

[18] Samuel Beckett, *Disjecta: Miscellaneous Writings and a Dramatic Fragment*, ed. Ruby Cohn (London: J. Calder, 1983), 86.

[19] Ibid., 87.

restrictions on prophylaxis were justified under the rubric of a strained cultural nationalism: 'France may commit race suicide. Erin will never. And should she be found at any time deficient in Cuchulains, at least it shall never be said that they were contraceived.'[20] Beckett derived both the phrase 'race suicide' and the example of France from remarks made by Deputy J. J. Byrne, one of the Act's most vocal parliamentary supporters (and Beckett's most consistent target for derision), during the Second Stage Dáil debate on the Censorship Bill:

> To the vast majority of the people the limitation, the control of births, or the infliction of race suicide upon this nation is one that is bitterly resented [...] If one might refer with all respect to the great French nation, what has happened there? The French population actually exceeded the German population in 1850. To-day the German population stands at 69 millions and the French population at 39½ millions. Is that for the benefit of France? [...] Does it make for the production of a better race, and what is the effect upon a people from whom all moral responsibility, as far as the marriage tie is concerned, is removed?[21]

Beckett's parodic appropriation of Byrne's oratory mimics its histrionic tone to foreground the quasi-eugenicist fixation on producing 'a better race' which he feels underpins the Act's prohibition of birth control literature. Like Ferriter and Pašeta, Beckett thus situates the Act in a wider European context of anti-Malthusian fertility policies, in which the Act's blurring of public health and public morality in an effort to administer and direct sexuality becomes legible as one of the 'techniques' for the 'subjugation of bodies and the control of populations' which Foucault identifies as the basis of 'bio-power'.[22] However, where Ferriter treats the confessional and

---

[20] Ibid., 87–8.
[21] 'Censorship of Publications Bill, 1928—Second Stage (Resumed),' Pub. L. No. 26.6 (1928), http://oireachtasdebates.oireachtas.ie/debates%20authoring/debateswebpack.nsf/takes/dail1928101900003?opendocument. As Byrne's remarks reflect, the phrase 'race suicide' was used synonymously with 'birth control' in Irish debates over censorship. However, in European eugenics the term had a broader significance, denoting what alarmists such as R. R. Rentoul took to be the eschatological threat unchecked degeneration posed to humanity: 'Day by day, hour by hour, and year after year we add [to] diseased humanity—the children begotten by the diseased, idiots, imbeciles, epileptics, the insane, deformed, and those contaminated by venereal and other diseases. [...] Does anyone contend that such a scheme of pollution works for race culture? Rather, I contend, that it works for race suicide.' Robert Reid Rentoul, *Race Culture; Or, Race Suicide? A Plea for the Unborn* (London: Walter Scott, 1906), 7–8.
[22] Foucault, *The History of Sexuality, 1: The Will to Knowledge*: 140.

nationalist impulses which motivated Catholic action groups such as the Catholic Truth Association of Ireland (CTSI) to militate for censorship as coincidental to its drafting and operation, Beckett's reference to 'Cuchulains' positions the Act's implied pro-natal bio-power agenda as the logical correlative of the well-worn nationalist cult of Gaelic hypermasculinity and cultural de-Anglicization traced in Chapter 2.

As Beckett's remarks suggest, the synonymy of 'evil literature' and imported English papers and periodicals was, by the 1930s, a rather exhausted trope of Irish cultural nationalism. In the mid-nineteenth century Thomas Davis and Young Ireland lamented what they perceived to be an Irish popular mind 'contaminated' by an English press in the thrall of Jeremy Bentham.[23] Douglas Hyde, in his famous 1892 address on the 'The Necessity for De-Anglicizing Ireland', called upon the Irish to 'set [their] faces sternly against penny dreadfuls, shilling shockers, and still more, the garbage of vulgar English weeklies' in favour of 'everything that is most racial, most smacking of the soil' in Irish-language culture.[24] In the wake of Pope Pius X's 1907 encyclical *Pascendi Dominici Gregis* [feeding of the flock]—a polemic against Catholic 'Modernism' and the secular rationalism it was held to reflect—Hyde's imperative was taken up in increasingly sectarian form in Catholic periodicals such as the *Irish Ecclesiastical Record*, the *Catholic Pictorial*, and the *Irish Rosary*.[25] In his inaugural address to the 1911 CTSI annual conference, Rev. Robert Kane, SJ outlined the political and theological 'Vocation of the Celt' with regards to imported literature:

The modern infidel world has declared war against Christ. That war is intellectual [...] its triumph has been so far so complete that of all nations there is not now left one single nation thoroughly, profoundly and emphatically Catholic except one. That one true Catholic nation is Ireland [...] As the war is intellectual, so the chief weapon of the modern infidel is his literature [...] Our chief weapon must therefore be our Catholic literature.

---

[23] *Nation*, 13 April 1844, quoted in David Dwan, *The Great Community: Culture and Nationalism in Ireland* (Dublin: Field Day, 2008), 40.

[24] Douglas Hyde, 'The Necessity for De-Anglicizing Ireland,' in *The Revival of Irish Literature*, ed. Charles Gavan Duffy (London: T. Fisher Unwin, 1894), 117–61, 159.

[25] For an account of the role of this encyclical in catalysing the 'combative censoriousness' of the CTSI and its allies, see Ben Levitas, 'Reading and the Irish Revival, 1891–1922,' in *The Irish Book in English, 1891–2000*, ed. Clare Hutton and Patrick Walsh, vol. 5, Oxford History of the Irish Book (Oxford: Oxford University Press, 2011), 64–5.

But first we must hurl back from our shore the inroads of atheistic and immoral books. We must take all lawful means to resist the invasion of these satellites of Satan.[26]

This intensely combative rhetoric, with its martial imagery and fusion of confessional and national identity, had long been popular among the exponents of Irish Ireland. Outlining the grounds for conflict in what he termed 'The Battle of Two Civilisations' over a decade before, D. P. Moran had noted that, in an economically depressed Ireland, the ready availability of 'the cheapest class of periodicals' had left the Irish population 'feeding on a questionable type of British reading matter' to the continued detriment of the nation's moral and intellectual life.[27] Following the founding of the Irish Vigilance Association in 1911, the campaign against 'English dirties' became a regular feature of Moran's daily, the *Leader*, and served as a vehicle for attacks on a range of the editor's political and cultural bugbears. In a satirical verse intended to spur the lax Vigilance Committees of Waterford and Kilkenny to action, the *Leader* presented 'The Demon of Dirty Papers' as a flood of sewage surging into the country from across the Channel in 'ill-odoured streams'.[28] This corruption, which 'still fester[ed] unchecked' in the two cities, was presented as an 'alien decadence', whose fettering of the minds of the Irish population was made possible through the 'green toleration' of 'shoneens'.[29] As these remarks suggest, the threat of 'evil literature' was regularly metaphorized through images of bodily effluent, infection, and degeneration, in which the revival of the Irish language was presented as the

[26] *Catholic Truth Society of Ireland Annual and Record of Conferences* (Dublin: Catholic Truth Society, 1912) quoted in Levitas, 'Reading and the Irish Revival, 1891–1922,' 65.

[27] David Patrick Moran, *The Philosophy of Irish Ireland*, ed. Patrick Maume (Dublin: University College Dublin Press, 2006), 102. Philip O'Leary rightly counsels against treating Moran's opinions as representative of the attitude of the majority of language revivalists, many of whom regarded the issue of 'English dirties' as, at best, a trivial distraction, and, at worst, an effort on the part of the Irish Vigilance Association to seize control of the Gaelic League. Nevertheless, they merit citation in the present context as particularly extreme examples of the tradition which Beckett felt himself to be resisting. Philip O'Leary, *The Prose Literature of the Gaelic Revival, 1881–1921: Ideology and Innovation* (University Park, Pa: Pennsylvania State University Press, 1994), 42–5.

[28] 'A.M.W.,' 'The Demon of Dirty Papers,' *The Leader*, 18 January 1913, 572.

[29] Such campaigning also made good business sense, providing valuable opportunities for self-promotion on the part of Moran and other Catholic and nationalist publications. The typically caustic *Leader* was uncharacteristically fulsome in its praise of the activities of 'Good Literature Barrows' in Limerick and Queenstown, which stocked the paper as a sanitary alternative to 'English periodical filth'. 'A.M.W.,' 572; 'Current Affairs,' *The Leader*, 1 February 1913, 614; 'The Vigilance Committee,' *The Leader*, 8 February, 1913, 643; 'The War on Dirty Papers,' *The Leader*, 15 February 1913, 68.

best 'antidote' for the 'microbe' of the English popular press.[30] In a manner reminiscent of Healy's rhetoric in the Parnell Split, sexual and social hygiene thus came to be framed as key means by which the Irish could vouchsafe both their personal and national autonomy. The social upheavals of the First World War, the Easter Rising, the War of Independence, and the Civil War lent to this push for cultural autarchy many of the characteristics of the climate of 'moral panic' which predominated in European nations throughout the 1920s.[31] As Maria Luddy asserts, in the absence of an English garrison to blame for the nation's moral and physical corruption, state and ecclesiastical discourse increasingly came to focus on the 'redemption of chaste reproductive sexuality' as a panacea for the nation's social problems.[32] These problems were outlined in a range of published and unpublished official documents including the 'Report of the Interdepartmental Committee of Inquiry Regarding Venereal Disease' (1926), the *Report of the Commission on the Relief of the Sick and Destitute Poor* (1927), and the 'Report of the Committee on the Criminal Law Amendment Acts (1880–1885) and Juvenile Prostitution (1931)'—the infamously suppressed 'Carrigan report'.[33] In the context of the Committee on Evil Literature, whose 1926 findings provided the Censorship Bill's initial template, this resulted in a narrowing of focus from the broader concerns with cultural and physical purity which had animated the campaign for censorship to an explicit emphasis on issues of birth control and fertility. While partly a reflection of the doctrinaire Catholicism of the CTSI and the Vigilance Association, this shift was at least as much a by-product of the European and international legislation the Committee consulted in compiling their report, most of which prohibited material advocating contraception or

[30] 'The War on Dirty Papers,' 668; 'Carrigadrohid,' 'Waterford and Pernicious Literature,' *The Leader*, 18 January 1913, 571.

[31] For accounts of this 'moral panic' and its legislative outcomes in Europe and the Free State, see McLaren, *Twentieth-Century Sexuality*, 1999, chap. 1; Finola Kennedy, 'The Suppression of the Carrigan Report: A Historical Perspective on Child Abuse,' *Studies: An Irish Quarterly Review* 89, no. 356 (2000), 354–63; Mark Finnane, 'The Carrigan Committee of 1930-31 and the "Moral Condition of the Saorstát,"' *Irish Historical Studies* 32, no. 128 (2001), 519–36; James M. Smith, 'The Politics of Sexual Knowledge: The Origins of Ireland's Sexual Containment Culture and the Carrigan Report (1931),' *Journal of the History of Sexuality* 13, no. 2 (April 2004), 208–33; Ferriter, *The Transformation of Ireland*, 2005, 321; Ferriter, *Occasions of Sin*, chap. 2; Maria Luddy, 'Sex and the Single Girl in 1920s and 1930s Ireland,' *The Irish Review*, no. 35 (2007), 79–91.

[32] Luddy, 'Sex and the Single Girl', 81.   [33] Ibid., 79.

abortion.[34] This shift was also reflected in the evidence submitted to the Committee by ecclesiastical groups and social workers, with only one of the twelve witnesses and associations it consulted (the Protestant 'Dublin Christian Citizenship Council') expressing anything less than clear condemnation of the practice.[35] In a pamphlet prepared specifically for the Committee, the CTSI devoted one of six chapters to the dangers of 'Neo-Malthusian Birth Control Propaganda', while the Committee ultimately gave over a quarter of its final Report to condemning 'Propaganda Advocating the Prevention of Conception'.[36] What Beckett's remarks suggest, and this evidence highlights, are the ways in which, under the rubric of an apparent drive to de-Anglicize the Free State, but largely in response to a European and international climate of pro-natal nationalism, birth control increasingly came to be presented as antithetical to both Irish cultural identity, and to the physical, mental, and socio-economic well-being of the nation.

As these examples indicate, neither Ferriter nor Inglis can offer a holistic picture of the social and political issues with which the Act was implicated. On the one hand, a mono-causal account of the Act in which the Catholic Church's influence in a range of fields renders it omnipotent in its capacity to shape Irish sexual attitudes exaggerates the degree of Catholic hegemony in the Free State, and overlooks the ways in which legislation justified through a pietistic rhetoric could still participate in the operation of biopower. On the other hand, a revisionist reading which reduces the Act to a parochial manifestation of European pro-natalism occludes the range of cultural, denominational, and ethno-national tensions which manifested themselves in its drafting and operation, detaching it from the broader history of Irish cultural nationalism. As Beckett's critique of the Act suggests, only by establishing a dialectic between these positions does it become possible to appreciate the range of debates which the Act crystallized. One starting point for such a synthesis is a consideration of the ways in which the Act and the controversy its passage generated reflect and

---

[34] Michael Adams, *Censorship: The Irish Experience* (Dublin: Scepter Books, 1968), 33–4; Ferriter, *The Transformation of Ireland*, 2005, 341; Ferriter, *Occasions of Sin*, 185; Peter Martin, 'Irish Censorship in Context,' *Studies: An Irish Quarterly Review* 95, no. 379 (2006), 261–8; Martin, *Censorship in the Two Irelands, 1922–1939.*

[35] Adams, *Censorship: The Irish Experience*, 1968, 32.

[36] Catholic Truth Society of Ireland, *The Problem of Undesirable Printed Matter: Suggested Remedies* (Dublin: Catholic Truth Society, 1926), chap. ii; *Report of the Committee on Evil Literature* (Dublin: Stationery Office, 1926), 13–16.

participate in contemporary disputes over the role of the state within liberal political philosophy.

A 'depraved taste for equality': Censorship, Democracy, and the End of the State

In their efforts to position Beckett as a champion of reproductive rights, accounts of his response to censorship have tended to downplay the extent to which Beckett's horror of fertility was bound up with an anti-democratic animus shared by many of his contemporaries. As I suggested in my Introduction, this hostility reflected a wider uncertainty concerning the appropriate telos for an increasingly democratized state. Throughout the 1920s and 30s, the emergence of the institutional and intellectual apparatus of the welfare state placed classical liberal theories of government, in which the state remained neutral with regard to the physical and moral well-being of its citizens, under increasing pressure. In contrast to the laissez-faire state envisaged in various forms by Locke, Smith, and de Tocqueville, and manifested in the policies of successive Gladstone administrations, British new liberals such as L. T. Hobhouse and Lloyd George drew upon the work of Mill and Bentham to argue that true liberty could only be guaranteed if the state intervened to release its citizens from the burdens of poverty, hunger, ignorance, and disease.[37] In so doing, they sponsored a model of government in which physical and spiritual welfare of the population were regarded as both coextensive and within the purview of the state. This outlook took legislative form in a tranche of welfare reforms, exemplified by the 1907 Education (Administrative Provisions) Act, the 1908 Old-Age Pensions Act, and the 1911 National Insurance Act, which established the contours of the modern British welfare state.[38] In the midst of such an identity crisis, the vocation of the state, and the role of democracy in

[37] For major discussions of the ideological stakes of state intervention and welfare provision in new liberal thought, see Freeden, *The New Liberalism*; Michael Freeden, *Liberalism Divided: A Study in British Political Thought, 1914–1939* (Oxford: Clarendon Press, 1986); David Weinstein, *Utilitarianism and the New Liberalism* (Cambridge: Cambridge University Press, 2007).

[38] Geoffrey BAM Finlayson, *Citizen, State, and Social Welfare in Britain 1830–1990* (Oxford: Oxford University Press, 1994), chap. 1; John Brown, *The British Welfare State: A Critical History* (Oxford: Blackwell, 1995), chap. 1; Martin Pugh, *State and Society: A Social and Political History of Britain Since 1870*, Fifth edition (London: Bloomsbury Academic, 2017), pt. 2; Derek Fraser, *The Evolution of the British Welfare State: A History of Social Policy Since the Industrial Revolution*, Fifth Edition (London: Palgrave Macmillan Education, 2017), chaps 7 and 8. For a

its pursuit became unclear. Was the state's duty to recognize and foster excellence, or was it to reflect the will of the masses? The question itself was far from a political novelty. De Tocqueville sensed in democracy 'un goût dépravé pour l'égalité, qui porte les faibles à vouloir attirer les forts à leur niveau, et qui réduit les hommes à préférer l'égalité dans la servitude à l'inégalité dans la liberté' [a depraved taste for equality that leads the weak to want to bring the strong down to their level and that reduces men to preferring equality in servitude to inequality in liberty].[39] For Mill, nowhere was this 'tyranny of the majority' in democratic states more insidiously manifested than in the coercive and censorious influence of 'prevailing opinion' and its capacity to 'fetter the development' of independent thought.[40] These concerns found influential expression in Ireland in the writings of W. E. H. Lecky, who echoed de Tocqueville in highlighting the apparent irreconcilability of democratic principle and meaningful notions of cultural excellence. For Lecky, modern democracy 'level[led] down quite as much as it level[led] up' and was unfavourable to the 'higher forms of intellectual life', offering only the 'apotheosis of the average judgement'.[41] As David Dwan has noted, in Lecky's account, culture and democracy were 'implacably opposed' in so far as democracy was incapable of 'producing or even recognizing intellectual authority'.[42] It was to this apotheosis that George Russell (AE) was to object in his critique of the Bill in the *Irish Statesmen* for August 1928. Russell agreed with the advocates of censorship in their denunciation of the reading matter available to the majority of the Irish population, which, he noted, comprised 'little else than newspapers,' as books were 'too heavy reading for the quarter-educated mind'.[43] However, for Russell, the answer was not to homogenize the experience of readers through a lowest-common-denominator model of state-approved reading matter: 'Irish people read the cheapest journals. Instead of providing better reading, our moralists wish to bring about a national censorship, so that cultivated and uncultivated alike will be permitted to read only such

discussion of the emergence of the welfare state in Ireland, see Fred Powell, *The Political Economy of the Irish Welfare State: Church, State and Capital* (Bristol: Policy Press, 2017), chaps 1–3.

[39] Alexis de Tocqueville, *De la Démocratie en Amérique*, vol. 1 (Paris: Pagnerre, 1848), 85.

[40] John Stuart Mill, *On Liberty; with The Subjection of Women; and Chapters on Socialism*, ed. Stefan Collini (Cambridge: Cambridge University Press, 1989), 8.

[41] William Edward Hartpole Lecky, *Democracy and Liberty*, vol. 1 (London: Longmans, Green, and Co, 1896), 108.

[42] Dwan, *The Great Community*, 2008, 6.

[43] George Russell, 'The Censorship Bill,' *Irish Statesman* 10 (25 August 1928), 486.

books or papers as the State thinks are harmless.'[44] This paradoxically undemocratic one-size-fits-all mediocrity was exemplified for Russell by the composition of the 'recognized associations', whose task it was to present obscene works to the Censorship Board in early drafts of the Bill. Russell argued that, rather than 'associations of intelligent or cultivated men', the Bill would recognize those 'fanatics' who had most vocally advocated for censorship, and whose fervour had manifested itself in a spate of armed raids on trains transporting English papers.[45] Yeats concurred, decrying the 'incredible ignorance' and 'lawless vulgarity' of this 'Society of Angelic Warfare'.[46] For Pádraic Colum, the question was clear: if Ireland was to be made 'powerful, prosperous, and respected' it would have to set itself the task of 'training an elite' in a philosophy rooted in 'the traditions of the country', but open to 'the ideas of the modern world'.[47] In contrast, he argued, the CTSI seemed 'bent on giving outsiders the impression that the mental age of Catholic Irish people [was] about seven and a half'.[48]

In Beckett's view, the anti-intellectual populism for which Russell, Yeats, and Colum excoriated the Act was inseparable from its prudery and pro-natalism. For Beckett, the failure to recognize cultural excellence or aesthetic value in the stipulations of the Act, and the push to appoint a non-academic Censorship Board, paradoxically resulted in a group of censors equipped only to read texts through the prism of sex. Yeats, in his *Irish Statesman* response to the Bill, had taken the 'Catholic lawyers' and 'ecclesiastics' he believed to be its sponsors to task for betraying the Thomist principle that 'anima [...] est tota in toto corpore et tota in qualibet parte corporis' [the soul is in every part of the body, and whole in every part of the body] through a definition of indecency which demonized 'sexual passion'.[49] George Bernard Shaw had likewise castigated the framers of the Bill (an unholy alliance of 'morbid Catholics, mad with heresyphobia' and 'Calvinists mad with sexphobia') for enforcing through the proscriptions of the Act an intrinsically perverted mode of aesthetic perception that would teach the young 'to associate loveliness' not with 'blessedness', but 'with

[44] Ibid.   [45] Ibid., 487.
[46] W. B. Yeats, 'The Irish Censorship,' *Spectator*, 28 September 1928, 391; 392.
[47] M. Lyster, 'Padraic Colum on the Censorship,' *Irish Statesman* 11 (13 October 1928) : 107.
[48] Ibid.
[49] W. B. Yeats, 'The Censorship and St Thomas Aquinas,' *Irish Statesman* 11 (22 September 1928), 48; Saint Thomas Aquinas, *Summa Theologica*, vol. 1 (Paris: Bloud, 1880), 56; Dáil Éireann, 'Censorship of Publications Act,' pt. 1.2.

debauchery, like all censors'.[50] In 'Censorship in the Saorstat,' Beckett highlights and critiques this blend of philistinism and erotomania through a sexualized burlesque of the censorious reading process in which the Board's engagement with texts is rendered in bodily terms. In Beckett's parodic account, the Act 'emits [its] definitions' of indecency and obscenity as the 'cuttle squirts ooze from its cod', transforming its proscriptions against material 'inciting of sexual immorality or unnatural vice' into an ejaculatory discharge from a metonymically evoked cod-piece.[51] For Beckett, the debauched pleasure which he imagines the 'excited' TDs and Senators to have taken in rendering this definition 'orduretight' has led them to oblige the Censorship Board to disregard authorial intention and, by extension, considerations of literary value, in their assessment of texts.[52] Beckett notes that a plea to distinguish between indecency 'obiter' [in passing] and indecency 'ex professo' [as an expressed intention] was disregarded by 'a caucus that ha[d] bigger and better things to split than hairs, the pubic not excepted'.[53] Through a deliberately tired pun on bureaucratic hair-splitting, Beckett pastiches the 'down-to-earth' tone of the Bill's supporters to link their anti-intellectual disregard for literary value to what he perceives to be their equally cavalier desire to regulate the sexual practices of the Irish population. This somaticized rendering of the reading process continues when Beckett disparagingly quotes the Minister for Justice, James FitzGerald-Kenney's justification for disregarding authorial intention when considering the indecency of a book: 'it is the effect which [the author's] thought will have as expressed in the particular words into which he has *flung* (eyetalics mine) his thought that the censor has to consider'.[54] Through the corporeal *caveat lector* of his disdainful 'eyetalics', Beckett draws attention to FitzGerald-Kenney's visible disregard for authorial craft and offers a punning reminder that, like Job, and the Irish citizens whose sexual conduct so concerns them, the Censorship Board must encounter a text through 'eyes of flesh' (Job, 10:4). In doing so, Beckett emphasizes the well-worn paradox at the heart of censorship as an intellectual project: that the censor must read and pass judgement on texts that they believe will 'corrupt and deprave' others, without themselves being corrupted or depraved.[55] More damningly, Beckett also implies that the censor's

---

[50] George Bernard Shaw, 'The Censorship,' *Irish Statesman* 11 (17 November 1928), 208; 207.
[51] Beckett, *Disjecta*, 84.   [52] Ibid.   [53] Ibid.   [54] Ibid.
[55] The Act defines the word 'indecent' as 'likely [...] to corrupt or deprave' (I:2).

perversely sensuous optic is in fact a by-product of the philistinism FitzGerald-Kenney's remarks seem to flaunt.

Beckett's use of this somaticizing rhetoric to critique the Board's rejection of cultural merit in its deliberations reaches an obscene climax when Beckett addresses Deputy J. J. Byrne's ideal Board, and the level of textual engagement expected of them. Byrne discounted the 'literary crank' in favour of the more 'common sense' figure of the 'man broad minded and fair'.[56] As far as Byrne was concerned, it was 'not necessary' for such a 'sensible individual' to read the 'whole of a book' to be able to reach a conclusion as to its moral and aesthetic worth.[57] The Minister for Justice concurred, citing the example of *Ulysses* as a work 'so blatantly indecent' and infamously obscene that it would be unnecessary for the members of the Board to read every line.[58] Beckett's response to such anti-intellectualism is at once lurid and learned. Imagining the deputy's 'selection' to the Board confronted with the '*Secret Life* [sic] of Procopius'—an uncompromising account of the debauchery of the Emperor Justinian's court—Beckett contends that '[h]is position would be as invidious as that of Jerome reading Cicero [. . .] were it not that the man broad-minded and fair is at liberty to withdraw his purities from the pollution before they are entirely spent, that is to say almost at once'.[59] Through a series of pointedly ineffective euphemisms Beckett renders the censor's engagement with Procopius's text in sexual terms, linking it to the anti-contraceptive 'essence' of the Bill. In so doing, Beckett turns the Act's logic against itself, figuring the process of censorious reading as an example of exactly the modes of non-reproductive sexual activity which the Act circumscribed. The Board's ideal censorious reader (the 'man broad-minded and fair') must necessarily fail as the nation's ideal self-censoring lover through the liberty he enjoys to 'withdraw his purities' from the polluting

---

[56] 'Financial Resolutions—Censorship of Publications Bill, 1928—Committee,' Pub. L. No. 28.1, § Committee on Finance (1929), http://oireachtasdebates.oireachtas.ie/debates%20author ing/debateswebpack.nsf/takes/dail1929022000039?opendocument.

[57] Ibid.

[58] 'Financial Resolutions—Censorship of Publications Bill, 1928—Committee (Resumed),' Pub. L. No. 28.2, § sec. Committee on Finance (1929), sec. Committee on Finance, http://oireachtasdebates.oireachtas.ie/debates%20authoring/debateswebpack.nsf/takes/dail1929022100025? opendocument, quoted in Beckett, *Disjecta*, 85.

[59] Beckett, *Disjecta*, 85. In his letter to Eustochium, St Jerome describes a vision he experienced during a period of fasting and illness in which he is brought before the Seat of Judgement and scourged for preferring pagan reading matter to scripture: 'Interrogatus condicionem Christianum me esse respondi: et ille, qui residebat, "Mentiris," ait, "Ciceronianus es, non Christianus; "ubi thesaurus tuus, ibi et cor tuum".' ' [Asked to state my condition, I replied I was a Christian: and he, who presided, said 'You lie; you are a Ciceronian, not a Christian; "for where your treasure is, there your heart will also be".'] (Letter XXII, para. 30).

text 'before they are entirely spent'. Beckett thus accuses the Censorship Board of encouraging its members to engage in the intellectual equivalent of *coitus interruptus*, a form of contraception prohibited by the Catholic dogma to which Beckett attributed the Act's pro-natalist bent.[60] Beckett implies that the anti-intellectual disregard for literary expertise which the remarks of Byrne betray will lead to the appointment of censors whose ignorance will leave them capable only of viewing Procopius' text in pornographic terms, an anti-populist stance underscored by Beckett's recherché frame of literary reference. In Beckett's rendering, Byrne's demotic fetishization of the 'average judgement' lends legal backing to a reading process based on a partial and eroticized engagement with literature, that results in the premature intellectual ejaculation of a censorious judgement in which, as Beckett mischievously notes, the Board member finds his purities 'spent [. . .] *almost at once*'.[61] In doing so, Beckett performatively undermines both the intellectual and moral authority of the architects of the Act and the Board they constructed, by showing how their democratizing fetish for 'common sense' and their disregard for literary excellence would result in a hypocritical and sex-obsessed mode of reading to the detriment of the nation.

'Sterilization of the mind': The Censorship Act and Eugenics

In highlighting the negative impact of the Act's interimplicated cultural and sexual proscriptions, Beckett's caustic critique strongly resonates with debates over fertility politics, the role of the state, and questions of cultural capital which were taking place in the contemporary eugenics movement. Coined by the English statistician and polymath Francis Galton in his 1883 study *Inquiries into Human Faculty and Its Development*, 'eugenics'— derived from the Greek εὐγενής [well-born]—came to denote a diverse field of scientific (and pseudo-scientific) activity in which evolutionary biology, sociology, and public policy were combined in an effort to facilitate

---

[60] The Church's position on contraception in this period was outlined in the 1930 encyclical, *Casti Connubii* [of chaste marriage], which stated that those who frustrated the 'natural power and purpose' of the 'conjugal act' sinned against nature. Pope Pius XI, '*Casti Connubii*, Encyclical of Pope Pius XI on Christian Marriage to the Venerable Brethren, Patriarchs, Primates, Archbishops, Bishops, and Other Local Ordinaries Enjoying Peace and Communion with the Apostolic See,' The Holy See, February 2016, https://w2.vatican.va/content/pius-xi/en/encyclicals/documents/hf_p-xi_enc_19301231_casti-connubii.html.

[61] Emphasis mine.

the 'cultivation' of the human race through selective breeding.[62] The first decades of the twentieth century witnessed the proliferation of eugenics societies across Europe and the United States—including the establishment in 1911 of the short-lived Belfast Eugenics Society, which dissolved in 1915—with followers undertaking research into genetics and genealogy, organizing conferences and symposia, lobbying for changes to public health and education policy, and publishing treatises on a wide array of social issues.[63] While this 'science of improving stock' found a range of nationally specific expressions, advocates of eugenics shared an investment in the physical and mental improvement of humanity, a desire to regulate who reproduced with whom, and a set of 'positive' and 'negative' eugenic strategies for doing so.[64] 'Positive' eugenics sought to engender what Yeats, in his infamous 1938 polemic *On the Boiler*, envisaged as 'the best bred from the best', by encouraging exemplary individuals to reproduce under optimal conditions for the welfare of the resulting offspring.[65] Through positive eugenics, it was hoped the human race could be rendered 'intrinsically better, higher, stronger, healthier, [and] more capable' by cultivating features such as intelligence, creativity, and strength.[66] 'Negative' eugenics, conversely, sought to arrest the perceived 'deterioration' of humanity, by eliminating hereditary illnesses and checking the proliferation of what the Oxford philosopher F. C. S. Schiller dubbed 'human weeds'.[67] As Schiller's remarks suggest, the anxieties which animated eugenics had their roots in

---

[62] Francis Galton, *Inquiries into Human Faculty and Its Development* (London: Macmillan, 1883), 24. The goal of identifying the source of human intellectual ability and finding means by which to improve it was first explored in Galton's popular and highly influential *Hereditary Genius: An Inquiry into Its Laws and Consequences*, published in 1869 and updated in an equally successful second edition in 1891.

[63] For major historical overviews of the movement and its development in a range of national and trans-national contexts, see G. R. Searle, *Eugenics and Politics in Britain, 1900–1914* (Leyden: Noordhoff International Pub, 1976); Daniel J. Kevles, *In the Name of Eugenics: Genetics and the Uses of Human Heredity* (New York: Knopf, 1985); Mark B. Adams, ed., *The Wellborn Science: Eugenics in Germany, France, Brazil, and Russia* (New York: Oxford University Press, 1990); Richard A. Soloway, *Demography and Degeneration: Eugenics and the Declining Birthrate in Twentieth-Century Britain*, 3rd ed. (Chapel Hill: University of North Carolina Press, 2001); Marius Turda, *Modernism and Eugenics* (Basingstoke: Palgrave Macmillan, 2010); Alison Bashford and Philippa Levine, eds., *The Oxford Handbook of the History of Eugenics* (Oxford: Oxford University Press, 2010). For an account of Irish eugenics, see Greta Jones, 'Eugenics in Ireland: The Belfast Eugenics Society, 1911–1915,' *Irish Historical Studies* 28, no. 109 (May 1992), 81–95.

[64] Galton, *Inquiries into Human Faculty and Its Development*, 24–5.

[65] W. B. Yeats, *Later Essays. The Collected Works of W.B. Yeats, Vol. V*, ed. William H. O'Donnell (New York: Scribner, 1994), 238.

[66] F. C. S. Schiller, *Social Decay and Eugenical Reform* (London: Constable, 1932), 25.

[67] Ibid.

nineteenth-century theories of physical and cultural degeneration charted in Parts I and II. In its efforts to prevent 'dysgenic' individuals such as the mentally ill, the physically and mentally disabled, and those deemed to be of 'inferior' racial stock from procreating, negative eugenics could encompass not only relatively benign techniques such as sex education and birth control but more repressive measures such as voluntary and forced sterilization, restrictive marriage laws, institutionalization and segregation, and, in extreme cases, extermination.[68] As this overview suggests, eugenics came to bear an almost circular, if not tautologous relationship to notions of sexual health. In the logic of eugenics, healthy offspring are offspring who have healthy sex; in order to have healthy offspring who will have healthy sex, one must oneself have healthy sex; in order to breed those who will breed well, one must oneself have been well-bred. And so on. In such a system, sex becomes both the object of a regulatory scheme premised upon an ideal of 'health', and the mechanism through which that regulation is itself to be undertaken. As I suggested in my Introduction, in such a context a perceived lack of sexual continence or an incapacity for family planning could be taken as evidence of a lack of 'reason' or 'competence' on the basis of which individuals or groups could be disqualified from full membership of the liberal-democratic *polis* and the rights and protections it afforded in order to vouchsafe the 'health' and well-being of the body politic.[69]

Both Ferriter and Pašeta have claimed that what gave the Irish debate over censorship and birth control its idiosyncratic character with regard to its European counterparts was the absence of a visible engagement with theories of eugenics and anxieties over population decline which marked similar

---

[68] For an overview of these policies and their impact, see Stefan Kühl, *The Nazi Connection: Eugenics, American Racism, and German National Socialism* (Oxford: Oxford University Press, 1994); Stefan Kühl, *For the Betterment of the Race: The Rise and Fall of the International Movement for Eugenics and Racial Hygiene*, trans. Lawrence Schofer (London: Palgrave Macmillan, 2013), chaps. 5 and 6; King, *In the Name of Liberalism: Illiberal Social Policy in the USA and Britain*, pt. 2; Robert N Proctor, *Racial Hygiene: Medicine under the Nazis* (Cambridge, Mass: Harvard University Press, 2000); Eric Ehrenreich, *The Nazi Ancestral Proof: Genealogy, Racial Science, and the Final Solution* (Bloomington: Indiana University Press, 2007); Marius Turda and Paul Weindling, eds., *'Blood and Homeland': Eugenics and Racial Nationalism in Central and Southeast Europe, 1900–1940* (Budapest: Central European University Press, 2007); Turda, *Modernism and Eugenics*, chaps. 3 and 4; Marius Turda, 'Race, Science, and Eugenics in the Twentieth Century,' in *The Oxford Handbook of the History of Eugenics*, ed. Alison Bashford and Philippa Levine (Oxford: Oxford University Press, 2010), 62–79; A. Dirk Moses, and Dan Stone, 'Eugenics and Genocide,' in *The Oxford Handbook of the History of Eugenics*, ed. Alison Bashford and Philippa Levine, 192–209 (Oxford: Oxford University Press, 2010); Melvyn Conroy, *Nazi Eugenics: Precursors, Policy, Aftermath* (Stuttgart: Ibidem-Verlag, 2017).

[69] King, *In the Name of Liberalism: Illiberal Social Policy in the USA and Britain*, 52–64.

debates in France or Italy.[70] However, an examination of both literary and non-literary responses to the Censorship Bill suggests that such concerns were not absent from Ireland, but instead became part of an overdetermined competition for cultural capital and legislative authority among the confessional, intellectual, and political factions of the Free State. Although the multidenominational composition of the Committee on Evil Literature (composed of three Catholics and two Protestants) and the generally ecumenical tone of the Dáil debates caution against reading the Bill itself in narrowly sectarian terms, it is undeniable that such tensions did manifest themselves in the press coverage and public debate surrounding its drafting and passage, and that eugenic discourses were regularly deployed in their articulation.[71] Catholic advocacy for the Bill in the periodical press and in the statements of members of the Hierarchy at vigilance society conferences in the late 1920s manifest a clear tendency to exploit the Censorship Bill's proscriptions concerning birth control, and the anti-Malthusian discourses of 'race suicide' with which they were enmeshed, to stake a claim for a guiding role in the young nation. Addressing the CTSI annual conference in 1928, John Harty, the Archbishop of Cashel, endorsed the Bill unreservedly, asserting that there should be 'no compromise with the promoters of the empty cradle'.[72] His remarks were followed by a paper by T. A. Finlay on 'A Catholic Nation: Its Laws and Its Citizens', in which he deemed it the state's duty to 'remove by legislation [opportunities] for indulgence in immorality or vice' and to adopt 'measures to prevent the spread of physical disease'.[73] Finlay praised the Censorship Bill as just such a measure, a reflection of the extent to which organizations such as the CTSI viewed the legislation as an opportunity to cement the centrality of the Catholic Church to Irish government through policies which presented the moral and physical well-being of the nation as inextricably linked. While Pašeta is correct to assert

---

[70] These reflections are made on the basis that Ireland was not experiencing an abnormal decline in population in this period, and that the Free State did not engage in the same legal drive to incentivize reproductive sexual activity that was undertaken in France or Italy. Pašeta, 'Censorship and Its Critics in the Irish Free State, 1922–1932,' 217; Ferriter, *Occasions of Sin*, 191.

[71] The members of the Committee on Evil Literature were: Reverend James Dempsey; Robert Donovan, professor of English at University College, Dublin; Thomas O'Connell, Labour TD for Galway and General Secretary of the Irish National Teachers' Organization; Reverend T. Sinclair Stevenson (Church of Ireland); and William Edward Thrift, an independent unionist TD and professor at Trinity College, Dublin. Adams, *Censorship: The Irish Experience*, 1968, 24.

[72] 'Catholic Truth Society. Message from the Pope. Archbishop and Evil Literature,' *Irish Times*, 18 October 1928, 11.

[73] Ibid.

that ethical and doctrinal issues were the primary and most often discussed catalysts for Catholic opposition to birth control literature, that certainly did not prevent the *Irish Rosary* from adopting a decidedly triumphalist tone when foregrounding the demographic decline of the Protestant population in the new state. Writing in response to a discussion of birth control in the *Irish Times*, one contributor notes with a mixture of relief and pride that 'the crime of race suicide has gained no footing among the plain people of Ireland, that is, among the Catholic people'—a fact attested to by the healthy birth-rate of the 'peasant classes in rural areas' and 'the proletariat of Dublin'.[74] By contrast, the commentator asserts that Irish Protestants, 'tainted with the modern mania of race suicide', are 'heading for [an] extinction' which they are desperately seeking to avert by means of 'Souperism'.[75] This emotive evocation of the Famine and the image of a decadent and predatory Ascendancy it invokes serve to emphasize the ways in which the Catholic action groups who had sponsored the Bill sought to harness the issue of birth control to cement the Church's authority in the Free State.

The Anglo-Irish literati, whom Yeats was pleased to report the Bill had succeeded in bringing into a rare and revivifying moment of political accord, were equally alive to such questions.[76] For Shaw, the eugenic implications of the Bill were both obvious and disturbing. In his view, through its definition of indecency (which included any material 'calculated to excite sexual passion') and its prohibition of birth control manuals, the Bill sought to establish a 'Censorship extending in general terms to all human actions'.[77] More specifically, he argued that it was targeted to curtail 'any attempt to cultivate the vital passion of the Irish people' or 'to instruct it in any function which is concerned with that passion'.[78] As these remarks suggest, more

---

[74] 'Delta,' 'Race Suicide and Souperism,' *Irish Rosary* XXXII, no. 4 (April 1928) : 305–7, 305.

[75] Ibid., 306. The demographic decline of Ireland's Protestant community had been an ongoing phenomenon since the late nineteenth century, reaching its peak between 1911 and 1926, when the Protestant population fell by nearly 34 per cent. This process was still ongoing but had begun to slow by the time of the Act's passage. The role of birth control in precipitating such a decline was almost certainly negligible, with Kurt Derek Bowen citing heavy emigration, the withdrawal of British troops, and the disbanding of Irish regiments in the wake of the Treaty as its primary catalysts. Kurt Derek Bowen, *Protestants in a Catholic State: Ireland's Privileged Minority* (Kingston: McGill-Queen's University Press, 1983), 20–1.

[76] In his *Spectator* response to the Bill, Yeats records having awoken in the middle of the night with a suggestively eugenic 'sense of wellbeing, of recovered health and strength' which he attributes to the realization that Ireland's 'men and women of intellect, long separated by polities, have in the last month found a common enemy and drawn together'. Yeats, 'The Irish Censorship,' 391.

[77] Shaw, 'The Censorship,' 207.   [78] Ibid.

than an intellectual or aesthetic denunciation of the draft Bill's definition of indecency, Shaw's opposition to its proscriptions was rooted in an instrumental image of sexual activity, in which 'passion' possessed a range of 'functions' beyond the merely reproductive, and could be 'cultivated' in a carefully determined fashion. The Censorship Bill, by depriving the Irish population of the necessary 'instruction' in such matters, was thus predicated upon a fundamental 'terror of life' and 'aimed at the extermination of the Irish people'.[79] The obvious (and infamous) source for such 'instruction' was Dr Marie Carmichael Stopes, whose 1918 study *Married Love* and leading role in the Society for Constructive Birth Control and Racial Progress had made her name synonymous with family planning. In her best-selling manual, Stopes presented contraception as a eugenic and feminist adjunct to a healthy marriage, liberating women from the physically and emotionally exhausting ordeal of multiple consecutive pregnancies in which '[a] man swayed by archaic dogma will allow, even coerce, his wife to bear and bring forth an infant annually'.[80] In Stopes's view, only a well-informed approach to family planning, rooted in the use of contraceptives, could obviate this necessity. For Stopes and her fellow eugenicists, the unchecked reproduction that would otherwise result was not merely a matter of individual well-being, but a question of racial vitality. Such a flurry of fertility would 'sap and divide the vital strength which is available for the making of the offspring', resulting in a pattern of diminishing biological returns and progressively weaker children.[81] Parenthood, properly conceived, Stopes asserted, was thus no longer an 'individual right', but 'the concern of the whole community', whose 'urgent duty' it was to prevent the 'introduction of weakened, diseased, or debased future citizens'.[82]

Discussing what she framed as the 'Imperial and Racial Aspects' of birth control, Stopes offered a vision of 'Utopia' brought about the through the 'conscious elimination of all diseased and over-crowded lives *before* their

---

[79] Ibid.

[80] Marie Carmichael Stopes, *Married Love: A New Contribution to the Solution of Sex Difficulties* (London: A.C. Fifield, 1918), 88. For overviews of Stopes' life, work, and contribution to the birth control movement, see June Rose, *Marie Stopes and the Sexual Revolution* (London: Faber and Faber, 1992); Clare Debenham, *Marie Stopes' Sexual Revolution and the Birth Control Movement* (Cham, Switzerland): Palgrave Macmillan, 2018).

[81] Stopes, *Married Love*, 89.

[82] Marie Carmichael Stopes, *Radiant Motherhood: A Book for Those Who Are Creating the Future* (New York: G.P. Putnam's Sons, 1920), 211–12.

conception'.[83] In a foretaste of the positions he was to expound at greater length in *On the Boiler*, Yeats echoed Stopes in his *Spectator* article on the Bill, wryly noting that, if neo-Malthusian prophecies of apocalyptic over-population were accurate, the Catholic Church would be obliged either to ask married couples to live in celibacy or to rely upon Swift's 'Modest Proposal' to make 'love self-supporting'.[84] As the (admittedly tongue-in-cheek) reference to Swift's essay and its images of improvident over-breeders starving as a result of their ill-managed fertility makes clear, for Yeats and many other Protestant commentators, Ireland had already offered a chilling testament to the Malthusian thesis through the catastrophic events of the Great Famine.[85] Only by shouldering the burden of intellectual responsibility their free-thinking religious background entailed, Yeats implied, could the minority dissuade Ireland's Catholic population from conspiring in their own extinction.

Such eugenically inflected Famine imagery was not merely confined to responses to the Bill from within Protestant literary circles but became a feature of the editorial and correspondence pages of the Unionist press. In one particularly idiosyncratic example, Dudley Fletcher, a prominent Church of Ireland Rector and a regular *Irish Times* correspondent, deployed a surreal blend of economic theory and speculative science fiction to criticize the Bill's restrictions on information concerning family planning. Advancing the Malthusian premise that throughout 'nature' there occurs 'the strictest limitation of living creatures to economic conditions', Fletcher invited his readers to imagine a hypothetical future (the year 2198) in which

---

[83] Marie Carmichael Stopes, 'Imperial and Racial Aspects, II,' in *The Control of Parenthood*, ed. James Marchant (New York: G.P. Putnam's Sons, 1920), 221. Stopes's writings combine a romantic investment in the centrality of sexual compatibility to happy marital union with an intense commitment to a negative eugenics founded on hierarchies of class and race in which it should be made 'impossible for those whose mental and physical condition is such that there is well-nigh a certainty that their offspring should be physically and mentally tainted' to reproduce. This blend of feminism and eugenics will be explored in greater detail in Chapter 5. Marie Carmichael Stopes, *Radiant Motherhood: A Book for Those Who Are Creating the Future* (New York: G.P. Putnam's Sons, 1920), 237.

[84] Yeats, 'The Irish Censorship,' 391. For an account of Yeats's engagement with eugenicism and the difficulties it has posed for critics of his work, see David Bradshaw, 'The Eugenics Movement in the 1930s and the Emergence of *On the Boiler*,' in *Yeats Annual No. 9*, 189–215 (London: Macmillan, 1992) and Childs, *Modernism and Eugenics*, chap. 7.

[85] In his famous 1798 *Essay on the Principle of Population*, Malthus presented 'gigantic inevitable famine' as the ultimate corrective for the imbalance between the earth's material resources and the size of the human population. Thomas Robert Malthus, *An Essay on the Principle of Population, as It Affects the Future Improvement of Society. With Remarks on the Speculations of Mr Godwin, M. Condorcet and Other Writers*, 1st ed. (London: J. Johnson, 1798), 139.

a 'Peace Pact' and advances in medical science have rendered birth control the only means to avert apocalyptic overpopulation.[86] For Fletcher, Protestants held a position of particular moral and political responsibility to confront such possibilities, as the majority of the Irish population were 'not allowed to hold an independent opinion' on the subject out of deference to (Catholic) 'ecclesiastical authority'.[87] Yeats concurred, invoking the freedom of religion clauses of the Free State Constitution to call upon those unaffiliated to the Catholic Church to 'compel the fullest discussion' on the issue of birth control.[88] In the eyes of these critics, the Catholic members of the proposed Censorship Board had been denied the capacity to participate independently in such a discussion by the proscriptions of the Vatican's *Index Librorum Prohibitorum* [index of prohibited books], which effectively rubber-stamped Catholic clerical control over the intellectual life of Ireland.[89] The ramifications of this limited perspective were often quantified in terms of their dysgenic public health impact. In the words of one correspondent, the Bill's restrictions would shroud 'the diseases consequent upon ignorance of sex hygiene [...] in a prurient pall', leaving them free to multiply unchecked.[90] Another urged the government, in the absence of a British garrison to blame for the presence of venereal disease in Ireland, not to confuse suppressing any mention of its existences with effectively combatting its spread.[91] As Seán Kennedy has noted, for figures such as John Gregg, Archbishop of Armagh, and W. B. Stanford, Professor of Classics at Trinity College, Dublin, the more pressing issue was the survival of the Irish Protestant population itself.[92] Gregg consistently and bitterly opposed the practice of mixed marriages and the threat the Catholic doctrine of *ne temere* [be not rash]—the obligation to raise the children of such exogamous unions as Catholics—posed to Irish Protestantism, while Stanford called on Protestant 'young people to have larger families and for experts in each sphere to devise methods of dealing with special problems of economics,

[86] Dudley Fletcher, 'Letters to the Editor: The Free State Censorship Bill,' *Irish Times*, 5 September 1928, 4.
[87] Ibid.   [88] Yeats, 'The Irish Censorship,' 391.
[89] J. W. Poynter, 'Letters to the Editor: The Free State Censorship Bill,' *Irish Times*, 16 August 1928, 4; G. W. Murray, 'Letters to the Editor: The Free State Censorship Bill,' *Irish Times*, 1 September 1928, 7; Yeats, 'The Irish Censorship,' 391.
[90] 'Lux,' 'Letters to the Editor: The Free State Censorship Bill,' *Irish Times*, 24 August 1928, 8.
[91] James B. Leslie, 'Letters to the Editor: The Free State Censorship Bill,' *Irish Times*, 18 August 1928, 9.
[92] Kennedy, 'First Love,' 2010, 83–5.

finance, social organization and education, to assure the Church's future'.[93] In mounting these arguments and suggesting these remedies, figures such as Gregg and Stanford transposed long-standing eugenic anxieties concerning the differential fertility of the middle and working classes into an Irish sectarian context.[94] For a certain strand of Protestant and Anglo-Irish opinion, the Bill thus simultaneously rendered it possible to offer a patho-logized image of the cultural and numerical ascendancy of a hyper-fertile Catholic majority over the soon-to-be-eclipsed minority, and to present that minority as bound to the recently formed state by an intellectualized form of *noblesse oblige* upon which their claim to continued cultural and political relevance could be staked.

Accounts of Beckett's sexual politics have tended to situate him in uncomplicated opposition to this sort of eugenic thinking. Kennedy presents 'the rich cluster of abortions, abandonments[, and] infanticidal urges' in Beckett's mature works as a rejection of both the 'coercive sexual mores' of the Free State, and the eugenicist drive to 'reinvigorate the Irish Protestant tradition' advocated by figures such as Yeats and Stanford.[95] In a discussion of Beckett's response in *En attendant Godot* [Waiting for Godot] (1953) to the eugenicist discourses which predominated in the health, education, and social policies of Vichy France, Andrew Gibson presents Lucky's speech as a 'defence of indigent forms of humanity' in the face of a 'noxious violation' of their rights and dignity.[96] Such a defence would appear to be adumbrated in Beckett's caustic précis of the aims and impact of the Irish Censorship Act at

[93] John A. F. Gregg, *The 'Ne Temere' Decree: A Lecture Delivered Before the Members of the Church of Ireland Cork Young Men's Association on March 17th, 1911* (Dublin: Association for Promoting Christian Knowledge, 1911); *Irish Times*, 24 April 1924; *Irish Times*, 10 November 1926; *Irish Times*, 13 November 1926; William Bedell Stanford, *A Recognised Church: The Church of Ireland in Éire* (Dublin: Association for Promoting Christian Knowledge, Dublin and Belfast, 1944), 23.

[94] Daniel J. Kevles, *In the Name of Eugenics: Genetics and the Uses of Human Heredity* (New York: Knopf, 1985), chap. 5; Richard A. Soloway, *Demography and Degeneration: Eugenics and the Declining Birthrate in Twentieth-Century Britain*, 3rd ed. (Chapel Hill: University of North Carolina Press, 2001), chaps. 1, 2, 4, and 9.

[95] Kennedy cites the pro-natalism of Yeats's 'A Prayer for My Daughter' and the sectarian infanticide which concludes early drafts of *Purgatory* (1938) as examples of the poet's aversion to mixed marriages and increasingly intense investment in the need for Ireland's Protestant communities to reproduce both 'sexually' and 'socially'. Kennedy links this strain in Yeats's work to an encounter with Gregg at a Church of Ireland Synod in 1934, and Stanford's controversial 1944 pamphlet *A Recognised Church*. Seán Kennedy, 'First Love: Abortion and Infanticide in Beckett and Yeats,' *Samuel Beckett Today/Aujourd'hui*, 22 (2010): 79–91: 89; 84–5; R. F. Foster, *W.B. Yeats: A Life, The Arch-Poet, 1915–1939*, vol. 2 (Oxford: Oxford University Press, 2003), 737.

[96] Gibson, *Samuel Beckett*, 105.

the rhetorical climax of 'Censorship in the Saorstat': 'Sterilization of the mind and apotheosis of the litter suit well together. Paradise peopled with virgins and earth with decorticated multiparas.'[97] Approached in the manner Kennedy and Gibson suggest, Beckett's remarks function as a pastiche of the pseudo-scientific register of J. J. Bryne's call for a 'better race'. The nationalist ideal of a populous and sexually pure Ireland is to be bought at the expense of turning its (female) citizens into an army of continually pregnant mothers, stripped of their prophylactic skin. In such an analysis, the privileging of an idealized image of a 'pure' Catholic citizenry—the 'virgins'—necessarily entails the inhuman treatment of the nation's fully realized population—the 'multiparas'—whose task it is to 'people' a Paradise they will never inhabit. The corollary and condition of this 'apotheosis of the litter' is the 'sterilization of the mind' through censorship, paralleling and contributing to the growth of the population beyond the limits of sustainability. Read in this light, Beckett's remarks appear to emphasize the ways in which the Censorship Act justifies the constraints it places on the Irish population by reference to the legal fiction of an ideal reader-citizen whom the censor in the act of protecting seeks to reify. The textual logic of censorship, which effaces or replaces 'obscene' passages in publications, is thus replicated at the level of the readership it constructs and the forms of citizenship it seeks to enforce.

While both Kennedy and Gibson are undoubtedly correct to highlight Beckett's opposition to such schemes of regulated fertility, the risk of such accounts is the presentist desire they manifest to place Beckett on the 'right side' of a history in which eugenics has become synonymous with the Holocaust. Thus, though many elements of the above critique ring true, it is worth noting what it occludes. For one thing, it ascribes to the essay a feminist outlook which neither it nor the early Beckettian oeuvre can be held to reflect.[98] For another, read in the light of the remarks of Yeats, Shaw, and other Protestant commentators on the Bill, it become far harder to ignore the contemptuous tone of Beckett's remarks and the sectarian perspective with which they resonate. A key phrase in this regard is 'Sterilization of the mind', a formula which seems deliberately intended to evoke the British

[97] Beckett, *Disjecta*, 87.
[98] For an analysis of misogyny and its implications for Beckett's work, see Linda Ben-Zvi, ed., *Women in Beckett: Performance and Critical Perspectives* (Urbana: University of Illinois Press, 1990); Mary Bryden, *Women in Samuel Beckett's Prose and Drama: Her Own Other* (Basingstoke: Macmillan, 1993); Jeffers, *Beckett's Masculinity*; Kim, *Women and Ireland as Beckett's Lost Others*.

Departmental Committee on Sterilization—the so-called 'Brock Committee'—whose divisive 1934 *Report*, published only months before Beckett began work on his essay, had called for the voluntary sterilization of 'mental defectives' and the 'feeble-minded'.[99] In contrast to the Brock Committee, Beckett implies, the Catholic architects of the Censorship Act have committed an act of mental self-laceration which will leave Ireland both intellectually impotent and increasingly overpopulated. In such a context, rather than pitiable victims of clerically sanctioned bio-politics, the 'multiparas' come closer to resembling the hyper-fertile Catholic hoard whom Yeats and Fletcher had disparaged. As such, while it would be a mischaracterization to claim that Beckett actively endorses eugenics in this moment, it is important to recognize that, like many other Protestant intellectuals, the young author found it expedient to appropriate the movement's vocabulary and underlying neo-Malthusian logic to critique the philistinism and pro-natalism of the Censorship Act and its perceived affront to an implicitly anti-democratic ideal of cultural excellence which the minority intelligentsia felt duty-bound to uphold. Where Kennedy and others would have Beckett seeking to topple Yeats from his 'old boiler' in his response to the Censorship Act, the ways in which 'Censorship in the Saorstat' resonates with both literary and popular Protestant attacks on the legislation make this opposition difficult to sustain.[100] However, if this difficulty is embraced rather than elided, and this exculpatory approach to Beckett is set aside, it becomes possible to offer a fresh and more nuanced account of the political stakes of his obscene anti-natal aesthetic and his desire to affront Ireland's 'filthy censors' in the 1930s.

'Quite exceptionally anthropoid': Beckett and Eugenics

An obvious starting point for such an account is *Murphy*. Composed between August 1935 and June 1936—only a year after Beckett's first collection of short fiction, *More Pricks than Kicks* (1934), had been placed

---

[99] For an overview of the Committee's research, findings, and strong eugenic sympathies, see John Macnicol, 'Eugenics and the Campaign for Voluntary Sterilization in Britain Between the Wars,' *Social History of Medicine* 2, no. 2 (1989): 147–69; John Macnicol, 'The Voluntary Sterilization Campaign in Britain, 1918–39,' *Journal of the History of Sexuality* 2, no. 3 (January 1992): 422–38; Desmond King, *In the Name of Liberalism: Illiberal Social Policy in the USA and Britain* (Oxford: Oxford University Press, 1999), chap. 3.
[100] Yeats, *Collected Works*, 5: 220.

on the Irish 'Index of Forbidden Books'—and written with an uncharacteristic specificity of geographical and historical reference, Beckett's first novel has long been considered his most explicit literary response to the Ireland of the Censorship Act. Paul Stewart, among others, has highlighted the ways in which Murphy's euphemistic 'music, MUSIC, MUSIC' is used to highlight the commoditized forms of sexual exchange which animate much of the novel's plot, while at the same time positioning the 'filthy synecdoche' of censorship as a prominent effort by the state to regulate sexual activity.[101] Wylie's amorous encounter with Miss Counihan in (or, for legal reasons, '*not* in') Wynn's hotel in Dublin is evinced as one such example of this trend, in which musical terminology, an avowed desire to deprave the reader, and a eugenicist narratorial perspective coincide:

> A kiss from Wylie was like a breve tied, in a long slow amorous phrase, over bars' times its equivalent in demi-semiquavers. Miss Counihan had never enjoyed anything quite so much as this slowmotion osmosis of love's spittle.
>
> The above passage is carefully calculated to deprave the cultivated reader.
>
> For an Irish girl Miss Counihan was quite exceptionally anthropoid. Wylie was not sure he cared altogether for her mouth, which was a large one. The kissing surface was greater than the rosebud's, but less highly toned. Otherwise she did. It is superfluous to describe her, she was just like any other beautiful Irish girl, except, as noted, more markedly anthropoid. How far this constitutes an advantage is what every man must decide for himself.[102]

As Stewart highlights, the passage is deliberately overladen with implicit and direct sexual references, from the juxtaposition of the elevated music of Wylie's kiss with the grotesque exchange of 'love's spittle', to the suggestive image of the 'highly toned' rosebud (slang for both the anus and the vagina) Wylie would rather have been kissing. Even Miss Counihan's name, which collapses the non-sexual idealization of Cathleen ni Houlihan into a French pun on 'cunt', seems to throw down a nationally specific gauntlet to the Irish censor. However, what Stewart's account overlooks are the ways in which this censor-baiting relates to the 'markedly anthropoid' character of Miss

---

[101] Paul Stewart, *Sex and Aesthetics in Samuel Beckett's Work* (New York: Palgrave Macmillan, 2011); Beckett, *Murphy*, 147; 50.
[102] Beckett, *Murphy*, 75.

Counihan. In contrast to the ideal reader-citizen of the Censorship of Publications Act, obliged to remain an intellectually innocent 'Virgin' or a reproductively over-active 'multipara' in the name of producing a 'better race', Beckett plays upon a long-standing tradition of Irish simianization to present Miss Counihan (and, by extension, 'any other beautiful Irish girl') as an evolutionary hang-over whose most attractive feature (her 'toned' rose-bud) is identified with non-reproductive sexual activity.[103] Being generous to Beckett in this moment, one might argue that by collocating this anachronistic racialized slander with the implied presence of the 'filthy censor' Beckett seeks to remind Irish readers of the toxic political tradition to which eugenically inflected moral hygiene policies such as the Censorship Act belong. Being less charitable, one might link this moment to the recurrent flashes of sectarian disdain for the institutional authority of the Catholic 'Gael' which occur throughout the early prose to reflect on the ways in which Beckett, in his desire to affront the censorious Free State in this period, replicates not only the rhetoric but also the eugenicist logic of the Censorship Act's Protestant critics. More than simply a throwaway jibe at the expense of an economically underdeveloped and culturally insular Ireland, the opposition Murphy's horoscope posits between the *'Civilised World'* and the *'Irish Free State'* comes to take on the air of an unstated conviction on Beckett's part.[104]

Partly in recognition of this animus, Beckett's emigration to France in 1937 has been characterized by scholars as the moment in which the artist transcended his native 'prosodturfy' for the 'intellectual milieu' of a European avant-garde to which he had always belonged, 'despite his Irish roots'.[105] However, such a trajectory elides an important episode in Beckett's experience of Irish censorship and Irish sexual politics which necessitated his almost immediate return to Dublin—his involvement in Harry Sinclair's 1937 libel action against Oliver St John Gogarty and the crucial role that the suppression of *More Pricks* played in discrediting Beckett as a witness. Given

---

[103] Simianized depictions of the Irish were deployed throughout the nineteenth century by British political cartoonists to caricature Home Ruler agitators, physical force nationalists, and public figures such as Parnell, and by their American equivalents to characterize Irish immigrants. For an account of the fluctuating political ends to which these tropes were deployed, see Lewis Perry Curtis, *Apes and Angels: The Irishman in Victorian Caricature*, Rev. ed (Washington, DC: Smithsonian Institution Press, 1997); Michael Willem De Nie, *The Eternal Paddy: Irish Identity and the British Press, 1798–1882* (Madison: University of Wisconsin Press, 2004).

[104] Beckett, *Murphy*, 22.

[105] Chris Ackerley and S. E. Gontarski, *The Grove Companion to Samuel Beckett: A Reader's Guide to His Works, Life, and Thought* (New York: Grove Press, 2004), xv.

the embarrassment, anxiety, and shame the highly publicized Sinclair trial caused Beckett, it has traditionally been read in terms of its impact on his personal reputation in Dublin and its role in cementing his conviction to leave his homeland for good.[106] Yet, such readings occlude the extent to which the libellous passages of Gogarty's *As I Was Going Down Sackville Street* (1937) and the trial to which they gave rise reflect and extend the same bio-political debates over sexual conduct and the boundaries of Irish identity which the passage of the Censorship Act had catalysed. In particular, they overlook the ways in which these debates inscribe themselves in Gogarty's anti-Semitic portrait of Sinclair, his brother William (Beckett's uncle), and their grandfather, Morris Harris, in which ethnic alterity and sexual deviance are presented as synonymous.

'I can smell a Jew': Sex, Anti-Semitism, and the Sinclairs

As Emilie Morin has valuably outlined, the 'innuendos and rumours relayed in Gogarty's memoir and at the [libel] trial were far more pernicious and serious than they have been made out to be'.[107] In one particularly lurid passage, Gogarty describes Sinclair's grandfather, Morris Harris, and the habits he had allegedly bequeathed to his grandsons:

> Now, there was an old usurer who had eyes like a pair of periwinkles on which somebody had been experimenting with a pin, and a nose like a shrunken tomato, one side of which swung independently of the other. The older he grew, the more he pursued the immature and enticed little girls into his office. That was bad enough; but he had grandsons, and these directed the steps of their youth to follow in grandfather's footsteps, with more zeal than discrimination.[108]

[106] Deirdre Bair, *Samuel Beckett: A Biography* (London: Vintage, 1990), 281–5; James Knowlson, *Damned to Fame: The Life of Samuel Beckett* (London: Bloomsbury, 1997), 275–81; Anthony Cronin, *Samuel Beckett: The Last Modernist* (London: Harper Collins, 1996), 268–75; Ulick O'Connor, *Oliver St John Gogarty: A Poet and His Times* (Dublin: O'Brien Press, 2000), 276–85.
[107] Emilie Morin, *Beckett's Political Imagination* (Cambridge: Cambridge University Press, 2017), 73.
[108] Oliver St John Gogarty, *As I Was Going Down Sackville Street: A Fantasy in Fact* (London: Rich and Cowan, 1937), 70–1.

The passage's exaggeratedly grotesque style almost occludes the debts its blatant anti-Semitism and rhetorical structure owe to late nineteenth and early twentieth-century models of scientific racism. As has been show in Chapter 3, since the mid-nineteenth century, Jewishness and pathology (particularly mental illness) had been virtually synonymous in European medical and popular discourse.[109] This predisposition towards neurological illness was attributed (in often contradictory ways) to the sexual alterity of the Jewish, who were regarded by both popular opinion and the emerging field of sexology as simultaneously compulsively licentious and dangerously prone to endogamy.[110] This intellectual heritage is most visible in Gogarty's strategy of linking physical manifestations of what he views as the ethnic and cultural alterity of the Harris-Sinclairs (the grandfather's eyes and nose) with an itinerary of their allegedly rapacious, legally prohibited, and morally repugnant sexual appetites (child abuse and indiscriminate sexual preda-tion). Indeed, the very manner in which Gogarty introduces his description of Morris's continued line ('That was bad enough; but he had grandsons') seems intended to frame his abusive sexual preferences as an inevitable hereditary taint which would have been better left unpropagated. In an accompanying piece of doggerel Gogarty reiterates this caricature, and the model of mutually reinforcing sexual deviance and ethnic alterity on which it is predicated:

> Two Jews grew in Sackville Street
> And not in Piccadilly,
> One was gaitered on the feet,
> The other one was Willie.
> [...]
> They kept a shop for objects wrought
> By Masters famed of old,
> Where you, no matter what you bought
> Were genuinely sold.
> But Willie spent the sesterces
> And brought on strange disasters

[109] Sander L. Gilman, *Difference and Pathology: Stereotypes of Sexuality, Race, and Madness* (Ithaca: Cornell University Press, 1985), chaps. 6 and 8; Sander L. Gilman, *The Jew's Body* (New York: Routledge, 1991).

[110] Gilman, *Difference and Pathology*, 153–6; Otto Weininger, *Sex and Character: Authorised Translation from the Sixth German Edition* (London: William Heinemann, [German: 1903] 1906), chap. XIII.

> Because he sought new mistresses
> More keenly than old Masters.[111]

As in Gogarty's portrait of Harris, traditional anti-Semitic tropes (usury), markers of visible difference (Harry's gaiters—an apparently common piece of attire among Dublin's Jews), imputations of rapacious sexual misconduct (Willie's transparently phallic name and predilection for new and expensive 'mistresses'), and suggestions of sexual pathology ('strange disasters') combine to present the brothers as fundamentally alien to Irish culture.[112] Even the convoluted evocation of Piccadilly seems to offer a shrill testament to this perceived ethnic difference, implying through its redundant negation that the Jewish brothers would be more at home in the English metropolis than on a Dublin thoroughfare.[113]

Such rhetoric, of course, resonates strongly with the racial politics of Italian and German Fascism, however it also participates in the long-standing tradition of Irish anti-Semitism sketched in Chapter 3. In particular, as Morin has shown, this characterization of the Harris-Sinclairs had its roots in another, no less ethnically charged trial. In the final months of 1906, Harris's wife, Kathleen—an Irish Catholic by birth—sought to divorce him on grounds of adultery, cruelty, blasphemy, and paedophilia, and a variety of criminal activities which she alleged he had committed with the help of his grandsons.[114] Though the jury ultimately cleared Harris of every charge save cruelty (the minimum necessary for the divorce to proceed), the accusations were given a wide and eager airing in the press.[115] As the Harris divorce proceedings were reaching their apex, Gogarty began publishing his 'Ugly England' series in Arthur Griffith's Sinn Féin, in which he offered his diagnostic anthropology of the English and their corrupting influence in Ireland. As I noted in the previous chapter, in these exuberantly chauvinistic articles, the 'venereal excess' of the British Army, the 'gross materialism' of the English mercantile class, and the 'wormy' (which is to say 'syphilitic') blood of the Anglo-Irish Ascendancy are presented as linked manifestations of a decadent and degenerative Jewish influence to which all of Ireland's ills

---

[111] Gogarty, As I Was Going Down Sackville Street: A Fantasy in Fact, 65.

[112] For the Sinclairs' legal representative, Albert E Wood, the 'strange disasters' to which Willie was alleged to have fallen victim were plainly intended to insinuate 'venereal disease'. '£900 Damages Awarded in Libel Action,' The Irish Times, 24 November 1937, 5.

[113] '£900 Damages Awarded in Libel Action,' 5.

[114] Morin, Beckett's Political Imagination, 74.

[115] Morin cites coverage by the Freeman's Journal, Irish Independent, and Irish Times. Ibid., 74–5.

may be attributed: 'I can smell a Jew [...] and in Ireland there's something rotten.'[116] At times this whiff of Jewishness is largely analogical—a rhetorical means by which to identify and denigrate what Gogarty perceives to be the most reprehensible of England's many failings:

> England becoming Jewry...It explained how many things! [...] that shopkeeping, moneying instinct; that hatred of things generous or artistic: *-make ye no graven images*; that filthy sensuality, unrelieved even by gaiety; that furtive and narrow timidity, and that panic-stricken, cowardly way of taking revenge[...][117]

However, as noted in Chapter 3, at others it is presented in a pointedly anthropometric key, coded as a series of identifiable racial features whose pathological influence infuses itself into the blood of any nation to which it is introduced:

> If the race has really gained supremacy in the country, the race-type ought to be marked in the physiognomy or physique of the people. Yes; distinctly it was perceptible...when allowance was made for the blending of the races:– The shop-girl type with her anaemic face and aquiline nose, her eyes often brown and closely set; hair scanty. Her teeth are bad, for her palate is narrow, and she cannot breathe well through that long nasal cavity of hers. Yes; she lacks the better characteristics of either race, as is the case always in half-breeds...Oh Israel![118]

While it is impossible to say whether Gogarty was aware of the Harris divorce proceedings while writing these articles, his emphasis on the dysgenic character of 'half-breeds' is suggestive given how frequently the press emphasized the perceived incompatibility of Harris's Judaism and Kathleen's Irish-Catholic heritage.[119] Whatever their relation to the Harris divorce, as Gogarty's emphasis on 'race-type', 'physiognomy', and the various congenital defects with which the young shop-girl is afflicted suggests, his comments drew on and participated in a long-standing tradition of racial

---

[116] Oliver St John Gogarty, 'Ugly England (I),' *Sinn Féin,* 15 September 1906, 3; Oliver St John Gogarty, 'Ugly England (II),' *Sinn Féin,* 24 November 1906, 3; Oliver St John Gogarty, 'Ugly England (III),' *Sinn Féin,* 1 December 1906, 3; Gogarty, 4.
[117] Gogarty, 'Ugly England (II),' 3.   [118] Ibid. Ellipses Gogarty's.
[119] 'Her Life a Hell,' *Irish Independent,* 3 November 1906, 5; 'Humanity: Jew and Christian,' *Sunday Independent,* 4 November 1906, 7.

science and anti-Semitic discourse which figured Jews as a degenerate and degenerative sexual threat to a nation's physical and cultural integrity.

Further compounding the bio-political bite of Gogarty's anti-Semitic caricature was the immediate political context in which it was made. Damning under any circumstances, Gogarty's accusations of Harris's child abuse would have carried a particularly pointed charge in the wake of the Carrigan Committee. Established by the Cosgrave government in 1930 amid the same atmosphere of moral panic which had prompted the passage of the Censorship Act, the Committee had been tasked with gathering evidence of Irish sexual conduct as the basis for a more stringent Criminal Law Amendment Act. However, the Committee's Report, which detailed 'an alarming amount of sexual crime', 'increasing yearly' and frequently involving 'criminal interference with girls and children', was ultimately deemed unpublishable by the Fianna Fáil government which succeeded the Cosgrave administration.[120] The controversy surrounding the Report simmered until 1935, when a revised Criminal Law Amendment Act was passed. As a member of the Seanad, Gogarty would have been at least aware of the nature and general character of the Report, even if he did not personally have access to it. Such a familiarity is reflected in his remarks in a 1935 *Irish Times* article, in which he criticizes the Censorship Board for moving beyond their perceived remit of suppressing birth control literature: 'If this country had produced great sinners there would be something to censor but even the Carrigan report was not made public so we didn't know what is the enormity of our crimes.'[121] Diarmaid Ferriter has rightly warned against reading the Carrigan Report and the decisions which led to its suppression as the products of a univocal 'hegemonic discourse' of Irish purity or a unified 'containment culture' surrounding sexuality in the Free State.[122] Nevertheless, Beckett certainly appears to have perceived the Censorship Act and the Criminal Law Amendment Act as linked parts of a larger regulatory regime surrounding sexual conduct and Irish identity. His first act upon receiving the commission for 'Censorship in the Saorstat' from the

---

[120] William Carrigan (Chairman), *Report of the Committee on the Criminal Law Amendment Acts (1880–85), and Juvenile Prostitution* (Dublin: Stationery Office, 1931), 14; Kennedy, 'The Suppression of the Carrigan Report'; Mark Finnane, 'The Carrigan Committee of 1930-31 and the "Moral Condition of the Saorstát,"' *Irish Historical Studies* 32, no. 128 (2001): 519–36; Ferriter, *Occasions of Sin*, 134–45.

[121] 'Censorship of Books. Views of a Free State Senator. The Board's Great Fault,' *Irish Times*, 6 February 1935.

[122] Ferriter, *Occasions of Sin*, 136.

Bookman editors appears to have been to attempt to acquire a copy of the latter, as yet undrafted, Act:

> The <u>Bookman</u> writes, postponing all articles on Gide, Rimbaud & kindred dangers, in favour of one on the wicked Censorship in Ireland. By all means. I tried to get the Criminal Law Amendment Act, but it has not yet been issued in the form of a bill, or even taken shape as such according to Eason's expert.[123]

As such, Beckett would have been well placed to detect the ways in which Gogarty's portrait of Harris as an alien sexual threat to the vulnerable young women of Ireland was inflected both by the Report and by the climate which prompted its suppression, drawing on its image of an Ireland in which the sexual abuse of young girls was common, even as it displaces responsibility for such crimes away from the Irish (and Catholic) population and onto a perceived ethnic outsider. Called upon to defend his work, Gogarty contended that the 'usurer' was a 'composite photograph' intended 'to throw discredit on usury and moneylending' in general, tacitly acknowledging that, even if the specific libel against Harris and the Sinclairs had been unintentional, the characterization of Jews as a sexual threat to vulnerable Irish girls was wholly deliberate.[124] It is unimaginable that Beckett, freshly returned from a prolonged stay in a Germany increasingly vocal in its embrace of Nazi racial ideology, would have been deaf to the implications of Gogarty's remarks, and the rhetorics of sexual hygiene, eugenics, and racial science which underpinned them.[125] Nor, would he have missed the ways in which their influence was reflected in the efforts of Gogarty's representatives to discredit him in court.

A 'man who indulged in the psychology of sex': Beckett in the Dock

The ways in which Gogarty's barrister, J. M. Fitzgerald, KC, sought to undermine Beckett's credibility as a witness by emphasizing his continental

---

[123] Beckett, *The Letters of Samuel Beckett*, I: 1929–1940, 218.
[124] '£900 Damages Awarded in Libel Action,' 5.
[125] For an account of Beckett's awareness of and reaction to these discourses, see: Mark Nixon, *Samuel Beckett's German Diaries, 1936–1937* (London: Continuum, 2011).

connections, dubious scholarly interests, and obscene literary output are well established.[126] However, read in the light of the above analysis, it becomes clear that this line of attack was not only a piece of shrewd legal theatre but a strategically deployed reprisal of the logic and tone of Gogarty's text in which the Censorship Act would play a crucial role. Fitzgerald began his attack by ascertaining Beckett's present address ('Ah Paris [...] He lives in Paris'), and the nature of his academic output: 'Have you written a book about a man called Marcel Prowst?.'[127] The trap was an obvious one, with Beckett's impeccably pronounced correction, along with his Parisian lodgings, combining to position him from the outset in the minds of the jury as a morally suspect adherent of foreign decadence. This impression was compounded when Fitzgerald enquired if Proust was 'a man who indulged in the psychology of sex?'[128] The question was damning on a number of levels. For a lay-person, Fitzgerald's use of the verb 'indulge' framed the 'psychology of sex' as an obscene act which, the question implied, Beckett had sought to document and excuse. However, for those in the know, Fitzgerald's reference to Havelock Ellis' *Studies in the Psychology of Sex* (1897–1928, banned in Ireland in 1931) seems intended to invoke its most infamous volume, *Sexual Inversion* (published in 1897 and tried for obscenity in Britain in 1898), and the various modes of same-sex desire, queer experience, and gender-non-conformity it catalogued. Compounding these insinuations of sexual alterity, there was the question of Proust's ethnic background. The subject had been given a caustic public airing only a year before by the Abbé Ernest Dimnet in a widely reported address to the Royal Dublin Society in which he had attributed what he perceived to be the want of religious feeling in Proust's work to the influence of his Jewish mother.[129] Indeed, as Emilie Morin highlights, in an even-handed letter to the *Irish Times* Harry Sinclair had taken Dimnet to task for the 'race exceptionalism' which underpinned his dismissal of Proust and the critique of Zola which had preceded it.[130] In such a context, while it is impossible to ascertain how cognizant Fitzgerald was of Proust's Jewish heritage, it is hard not to read his comments on

[126] Bair, *Samuel Beckett*, 281–5; Knowlson, *Damned to Fame*, 275–81; Cronin, *Samuel Beckett*, 268–75; O'Connor, *Oliver St John Gogarty*, 276–85.
[127] Cronin, *Samuel Beckett*, 271.   [128] Ibid.
[129] 'Machiavelli of Statesmen: Abbe Dimnet on Mussolini: Gulf Between Nazism and Fascism,' *Irish Times*, 13 November 1936, 4; 'From a Paris Balcony: Lecture by Abbe Dimnet,' *Irish Times*, 14 November 1936, 10.
[130] Morin, *Beckett's Political Imagination*, 75; Henry M Sinclair, 'Letters to the Editor: Mehr Licht,' *The Irish Times*, 17 November 1936, 9; Henry M Sinclair, 'Letters to the Editor: Mehr Licht,' *The Irish Times*, 1 December 1936, 3.

'Prowst' in conversation with his cross-examination of Sinclair, in which he commented on the 'strange names' taken by Jews whose birth-names are 'unpronounceable'.[131] The question of ethnicity was further stressed when Fitzgerald emphasized Beckett's family connections to the Sinclairs and asked whether he 'called [himself] a Christian, Jew or Atheist' (Beckett characteristically declined all three labels).[132] Fitzgerald's opening salvo thus positioned Beckett as an ethnically ambiguous Parisian blasphemer who had appropriated sexually explicit scientific reading matter to sponsor the non-heteronormative and, by extension, anti-natal oeuvre of a foreign, Jewish author.[133]

When Beckett sensibly (if disingenuously) declared himself unaware of Proust's interest in the psychology of sex, Fitzgerald changed tack, deliberately eliding the *Proust* essay and *More Pricks Than Kicks* by asking how long it had been before his 'blasphemous and obscene' book had been 'banned by the Censorship Board of Ireland'.[134] He pressed his point by quoting a passage from the short story 'A Wet Night' in which the Polar Bear (a caricature of Beckett's French Professor at Trinity, Thomas Rudmose-Brown) discusses Christ with a no-nonsense Jesuit:

The *Lebensbahn* [...] of the Galilean is the tragi-comedy of the solipsism that will not capitulate. The humilities and *retro me*'s and quaffs of sirreverance are on a par with the hey presto's, arrogance and egoism. He is the first great self-contained playboy. The cryptic abasement before the woman taken red-handed is as great a piece of megalomaniacal impertinence as his interference in the affairs of his boy-friend Lazarus.[135]

---

[131] 'Dr. Oliver Gogarty Sued for Libel: Quotations from Book about Dublin: "Venomous Libels" Says Counsel: Dublin Divorce Case Recalled,' *Irish Times*, 23 November 1937, 5.
[132] 'Dr. Oliver Gogarty Sued for Libel,' *Irish Times*, 5.
[133] Echoes of Fitzgerald's innuendo-laden cross-examination may be caught in the long-suppressed early play *Eleutheria* (written in 1947, but not published until 1995), in which an inquisitorial and anti-Semitic Spectator takes to the stage to denounce the author of the play—whose name he mispronounces as 'Samuel Béquet'—as a 'juif groenlandais mâtiné d'Auvergnat' [a Jew from Greenland crossed with a peasant from the Auvergne] and call for his work to be pulped ('Au pilon'). Samuel Beckett, *Eleutheria* (Paris: Minuit, 1995), 136.
[134] Ibid.
[135] Samuel Beckett, *More Pricks Than Kicks*, ed. Cassandra Nelson (London: Faber and Faber, 2010), 50–1. The passage is transposed virtually unaltered from the conclusion of Beckett's abortive first novel, *Dream of Fair to Middling Women*, composed between May 1931 and July 1932. Samuel Beckett, *Dream of Fair to Middling Women*, ed. Eoin O'Brien and Edith Fournier (New York: Arcade Publishing, 1992), 199–241; John Pilling, *Samuel Beckett's 'More Pricks Than Kicks': In a Strait of Two Wills* (London: Bloomsbury, 2013), 1.

The features of this description which Fitzgerald intended to highlight in order to prejudice the jury against Beckett when he enquired whether this was not a 'blasphemous caricature of the Redeemer' are obvious enough.[136] However, without wishing to credit Fitzgerald with a subtler engagement with Beckett's work than might be expected of a working barrister, many features of the passage and its position within the story make it resonate strikingly with both Gogarty's remarks and with the proscriptions of the Censorship Act. As Andy Wimbush has noted, what animates the Polar Bear in this moment is the irreconcilability of two mutually contradictory images of Christ which have been central to Christian theology since the middle-ages: the *Ecce Homo* [behold the man] or suffering Christ, bowed and resigned to his fate, and the *Christus Victor* [Christ the victor], conquering death through his miraculous raising of Lazarus and his eventual resurrection.[137] Wimbush argues that, for Beckett, the *Christus Victor*'s triumphant failure to capitulate undermines the authenticity and appeal of the *Ecce Homo*'s solipsistic resignation. However, read in the context of the Censorship Act, what is striking are the ways in which the revivifying imperative the triumphant Christ apparently embodies is undermined throughout the passage through implicit and explicit references to non-reproductive sexual activity. The unrelenting 'solipsism' of Christ (which links him both to Belacqua and the, as-yet unconceived, Murphy) is given a distinctly, if paradoxically, sexual flavour through his figuration as 'the first great self-contained playboy'. This reference to the *Playboy* and the furore it generated transforms Christ's solipsism into an act of unrelenting onanistic self-love, comparable to Christy Mahon's narcissism and self-aggrandizing eroticism. Likewise, the Polar Bear's linking of Christ's abasement before an adulteress with his 'interference' with his 'boy-friend' Lazarus foregrounds the obvious sexual and homoerotic overtones of the latter jibe in a manner that collocates Christ at his most robustly triumphant with a range of non-reproductive and morally censured forms of sexual activity, all of which were deemed obscene under the terms of the Censorship Act.[138] The Catholic triumphalism which Beckett and others had detected in the Act's restrictions on birth control literature is thus subjected to an exuberant sexualized pastiche in a manner and tone comparable to that of the later

---

[136] 'Dr. Oliver Gogarty Sued for Libel,' *Irish Times*, 5.

[137] Andy Wimbush, 'Hey Prestos and Humilities: Two of Beckett's Christs,' *Journal of Beckett Studies* 25, no. 1 (April 2016), 78–95, 78.

[138] The Act's definition of indecency included all material 'inciting to sexual immorality or unnatural vice' (I.2), a long-standing euphemism for same-sex sexual activity.

Bookman essay. While, as John Pilling cautions, it is dangerous to present the Polar Bear's position as identical to Beckett's in this moment, (the Jesuit ultimately outwits the Polar Bear, obliging him to pay both their tram fares), it is clear that in court, Beckett was obliged to answer for these remarks as though he had made them *in propria person*.[139] By understanding the ways in which Beckett was publicly obliged to account for both the story and the collection in response to what he perceived to be a Church-sanctioned culture of philistinism, pro-natalism, and ethno-nationalism in the midst of his apparently decisive departure from Ireland, it is possible to arrive at a more nuanced consideration of his aesthetic practice in its aftermath. In particular, it sheds a telling light on one of the first substantial pieces of prose Beckett was to complete entirely in French after leaving Ireland, the 1946 novella *Premier amour/First Love*.

'Fibrome, or brone': Sectarianism, Eugenics, and Vichy France

As a range of critics have illustrated, *Premier amour/First Love* is firmly rooted in the Ireland of the Censorship Act.[140] The 'Elysium for the roofless' in which the story takes place is identified explicitly in terms of its 'scant population'—tellingly achieved 'without the help of the meanest contraceptive'—a comment which seems to gesture towards both the unprecedented death-toll of the Famine, and Ireland's uncommonly high rates of emigration.[141] Likewise, the narrator's meetings with 'Lulu', a sex worker and the eventual mother of what may be his child, regularly bring him back to a bench on the bank of one of the city's two (easily confused) canals, tacitly evoking Dublin's Liffey and Dodder. In this context, the narrator's abandonment of his child and its mother appears to constitute an effort towards independence comparable to Beckett's departure for France, or the obscene French idiom in which the novella is composed. However, as Kennedy emphasizes, though Beckett's narrator may 'leave' his new-born

---

[139] Pilling, *Samuel Beckett's 'More Pricks Than Kicks,'* 74.

[140] David Lloyd, 'Writing in the Shit: Beckett, Nationalism, and the Colonial Subject,' *Modern Fiction Studies* 35, no. 1 (1989): 69–85; David Lloyd, Anomalous States: *Irish Writing and the Post-Colonial Moment* (Dublin: Lilliput Press, 1993), chap. 2; Kennedy, 'First Love,' 2010; Ackerley and Gontarski, *The Grove Companion to Samuel Beckett*, 454.

[141] For ease of reference, all quotations are from Beckett's English translation. References to French diction will be made only where marked divergences occur. Samuel Beckett, *The Expelled/ The Calmative/The End & First Love*, ed. Christopher Ricks (London: Faber, 2009), 64.

child at the story's close, he cannot 'leave behind' the pro-natalist claims and Irish context its cries represent.[142] If Kennedy's insight is extended to the aesthetic of *Premier amour/First Love* as a whole, it becomes clear that the harder Beckett works to transgress the limitations of Irish censorship, the more they come to shape the text he produces. Following his father's death, Beckett's narrator finds himself evicted from his familial home during a period of troubled defecation: 'One day, on my return from stool, I found my room locked and my belongings in a heap before the door.'[143] His description of his faecal issues grows increasingly detailed and ultimately blasphemous: 'At such times I [. . .] just gazed dully at the almanac hanging from a nail before my eyes, with its chromo of a bearded stripling in the midst of sheep, Jesus no doubt, parted the cheeks with both hands and strained, heave! ho! heave! ho!, with the motions of one tugging at the oar.'[144] The narrator's Christological qualification, 'Jesus no doubt', nestles snugly between two longer descriptive clauses, which it serves to part like the narrator's 'cheeks'. The physical and syntactic proximity in which Beckett places 'Jesus' to the narrator's 'heaving' attempts at evacuation form part of a range of narratorial shock tactics that serve as provocations to censorship throughout the text. The narrator's exile status and this obscene aesthetic intensify in tandem throughout the story. The narrator's morbid preference for graveyards is explained with reference to the number of suitable locations they afford for a 'piss', and the relief they offer from the stench of the 'sticky foreskins' of the living.[145] When the narrator seeks refuge in a cowshed after attempting to break off his relationship with 'Lulu', he traces her name in the 'dry and hollow cowclaps' that surround him.[146] This act of faecal inscription prompts a reflection on his homeland, which the narrator presents as manured with 'history's ancient faeces', dropped in steaming piles to be 'sought after, stuffed and carried in procession' by the nation's 'patriots'.[147] Finding himself in Lulu's company one evening, the narrator considers 'kicking her in the cunt', but instead finds himself 'at the mercy of an erection' which she helps to relieve.[148] When 'Lulu' announces her pregnancy, the narrator advises her to '[a]bort, abort' so that her darkened nipples may 'blush like new'.[149] As this short summary deliberately empha-sizes, *Premier amour/First Love* seems to take the Censorship of Publications

---

[142]   Kennedy, 'First Love,' 2010, 89.
[143]   Beckett, *The Expelled/The Calmative/The End & First Love*, 64.   [144]   Ibid.
[145]   Ibid., 62; 61.   [146]   Ibid., 69.   [147]   Ibid., 69.   [148]   Ibid., 66; 67.
[149]   Ibid., 78.

Act as a schematic for its content, containing as it does obscenity, blasphemy, sex work, references to contraception, vocal advocacy of abortion, and a cloacal obsession fit to rival Joyce at his most eye-watering.

For Kennedy, this intense obscenity and the anti-natal outlook it reflects combine with the narrator's quietism and social isolation to register a dual rebuke to the Catholic-nationalist imaginary as encoded in the Censorship Act and the equally fertility-driven programme of Protestant rejuvenation advocated by Gregg, Yeats, and Stanford. In doing so, Kennedy mobilizes the conceptual armature of queer theory to present the narrator's abandonment of his new-born as politically, morally, and aesthetically preferable to the eugenicist and sectarian infanticide which conclude early drafts of Yeats's *Purgatory* (1938). In Kennedy's account, Beckett's narrator embodies the nay-saying ethical imperative of queerness by rejecting 'the child' as the heteronormative signifier of 'reproductive futurity' with reference to which Lee Edelman has argued all political discourse and activity is implicitly justified and regulated.[150] While Kennedy is correct to emphasize the rejection of fertility both in *Premier amour/First Love* and the Beckettian oeuvre at large, in positioning Beckett's as the ethically preferable response to the political and demographic twilight of Ireland's Protestant population, his analysis of the story elides the misogyny of the narrator, the ambivalence with which his calls for abortion and his departure from 'Lulu' are depicted, and the ways in which these features link the novella's Irish context to the immediate post-war French context of its composition.

As Emilie Morin has illustrated, the cluster of French-language texts which Beckett composed between 1946 and 1948—'La fin' [the end], 'L'expulsé' [the expelled], 'Le calmant' [the calmative] (collectively published as *Nouvelles* [novellas] in 1958), *Premier Amour, Mercier et Camier* (1970), *Eleutheria* (1995), *Molloy* (1951), *Malone Meurt* [Malone dies] (1951), and *En attendant Godot* (1952)—feature persistent, if deliberately obscured, references to the tensions, traumas, and political idioms of occupied France and the period of turmoil that followed its liberation, that have often been softened or excised in English translation.[151] In *Premier amour*, these resonances inscribe themselves most clearly in the relationship between the narrator's increasingly vocal rejection of reproductive sexuality

---

[150] Lee Edelman, *No Future: Queer Theory and the Death Drive* (Durham: Duke University Press, 2004), 2–3.

[151] For a detailed exploration of the various ways in which the ideological and cultural divisions of this period shape and inform Beckett's post-war French writing, see Morin, *Beckett's Political Imagination*, chap. 3.

and the increasingly eugenicist register he uses to describe 'Lulu' (whom he rechristens 'Anna') during his stay in her home. Despite his indifference to her appearance—she has a 'face like millions of others'—as she undresses for him for the first time he is struck by her 'squint'.[152] This realization, which occurs during a de facto strip-tease ('Anna' undresses with a 'slowness fit to enflame an elephant'), undermines the impression of normalcy which he had previously held of her face ('it *seemed* normal to me'), implicitly identifying 'Anna' as one of the 'human weeds' Schiller and his fellow eugenicists had been so anxious to eliminate.[153] The French rendering of this moment ('je vis qu'elle louchait') is even more suggestive.[154] Syntactically, it highlights the narrator's implicitly eugenicist perspective by juxtaposing his unimpaired vision ('je vis') with her straining sight ('elle louchait'). Semantically, it plays upon the varied senses of 'loucher'— the biological condition of 'squinting', the act of regarding someone in a deceptive manner, and the act of coveting something—to emphasize the hostility and suspicion with which the French narrator, the Vichy French government, and the eugenics movement more broadly regarded the sexual desires of those whom they perceived to deviate from the biological norm.[155]

The crucible for such ideas in occupied France was the *Fondation Française pour l'Étude des Problèmes Humains* [French foundation for the study of human problems], established by Vichy decree in 1941.[156] This institution, tasked with improving the French population by eugenic means, was overseen by the Nobel laureate, Alexis Carrel, whose best-selling 1935 popular scientific study *L'homme, cet inconnu* [man, this stranger], argued for the cultivation of 'une aristocratie biologique héréditaire' [a hereditary biological aristocracy] through a form of 'eugénisme volontaire' [voluntary eugenics], in which 'éducation appropriée' [appropriate education] would prevent the propagation of 'des fous' [the insane], 'des faible d'esprit' [the feeble-minded], and 'des individus inférieurs' [inferior individuals].[157]

---

[152] Beckett, *The Expelled/The Calmative/The End & First Love*, 73; 74.

[153] Ibid., 74; 73. Emphasis mine.

[154] Samuel Beckett, *Premier Amour* (Paris: Minuit, 1970), 40.

[155] 'Loucher (verbe transitif indirect): Regarder furtivement, de biais, à la dérobée: Loucher sur la copie du voisin. Convoiter quelque chose, quelqu'un, avoir des vues sur eux: Loucher sur l'héritage d'un vieil oncle.' ['To squint (transitive indirect verb): To look furtively, sideways, stealthily: To glance at a neighbour's copy. To covet something, someone, to have views on them: To eye up the inheritance of an old uncle.'] 'Loucher (v.t. Ind.)', Larousse dictionnaire de français, March 2017, https://www.larousse.fr/dictionnaires/francais/loucher/.

[156] Gibson, *Samuel Beckett*, 104–5.

[157] Alexis Carrel, *L'homme, cet inconnu* (Paris: Librarie Plon, 1935), 364; 367; 363. Carrel also sponsored a less 'voluntary' eugenics, in which 'un établissement euthanasique, pourvu de gaz

As Andrew Gibson has noted, such theories and their attendant rhetoric permeate Beckett's writing in this period, often lending an unsettling and authoritarian edge to its more explicitly anti-natal moments.[158] Their echo may be caught in the hyperbolic speeches of Dr Piouk in *Eleutheria*, who proposes a radical 'solution' to the 'problème [. . .] de l'humanité' [problem of humanity]:[159]

> J'interdirais la reproduction. Je perfectionnerais le condom et autres dispositifs et en generaliserais l'emploi. Je créerais des corps d'avorteurs sous le contrôle de l'État. Je frapperais de mort toute femme coupable d'enfantement. Je noyerais les nouveau-nés. Je militerais en faveur de l'homosexualite et en donnerais moi-même l'exemple. Et pour activer les choses, j'encouragerais par tous les moyens le recours à l'euthanasie, sans toutefois en faire une obligation.[160]

> [I would ban reproduction. I would perfect the condom and other devices and generalise their use. I would create a corps of abortionists under the control of the State. I would condemn to death all women guilty of childbirth. I would drown the newly-born. I would militate in favour of homosexuality and would, myself, set the example. And to speed things up, I would encourage the recourse by all available means to euthanasia, though without making it an obligation.]

While Piouk stops short of mandating euthanasia (a concession which recalls Carrell's 'eugénisme volontaire' and the 'voluntary sterilization' proposals of the British 'Brock Committee'), the militaristic terms ('corps', 'militerais') in which the deliberately absurd scheme is articulated betray the coercion and latent violence which haunt Piouk's desire to 'régler la situation du genre humain' through the apparatus of the State—a phrase that hovers between connoting a Galtonian desire to 'regulate' or 'arrange' the situation of the human species, and a Hitlerian desire to 'settle' or 'solve' the problem said species, or, at least, certain parts of it, are perceived to pose. The scheme is both literalized and further subverted later in the play, when Piouk seeks to persuade its protagonist, Victor Krap—whose contaminating stage presence encroaches on the domestic propriety of his parent's salon

---

appropriés' [a euthanasic institution supplied with appropriate gas] would permit society to dispose of 'des déficents et des criminels' [defectives and criminals] in a manner both 'humaine et économique' [humane and economical] (Carrel, 387–8).

[158] Gibson, *Samuel Beckett*, 104–5.   [159] Beckett, *Eleutheria*, 49.   [160] Ibid., 50.

'comme le sale au propre, le sordide au convenable' [like the dirty into the
clean, the sordid into the respectable]—to take his own life with a poison
capsule which Piouk briefly confuses with an aspirin.[161] Realizing his mis-
take, Piouk explains that while aspirin is suitable for '[l]es vieux, les laches,
les salauds, les pourris, les foutus' [the elderly, cowards, bastards, the
corrupted, the fucked], poison is better suited for 'the young, the pure, the
men of the future'—an assertion that both invokes and inverts the common
dichotomies of social hygiene through which eugenics policies were typically
justified.[162]

Confronted with Anna's squint, the narrator of *Premier amour/First Love*
engages in just such an act of Carrellian 'voluntary eugenics', deflecting her
sexual advances by refusing to undress and asking for a tour of the premises.
Having been shown the parlour, he proceeds to eject its furnishings, creating
a space of womb-like security in which only a single sofa remains. As he
removes the final item of furniture into the now obstructed corridor, the
narrator overhears the indeterminate word 'fibrome, or brone', which,
though he disavows recognizing it or understanding its meaning, he feels
compelled to record.[163] Phil Baker posits that the word the narrator most
likely overhears is *fibroma*, 'a benign tumour of the wall of the uterus', which
Paul Stewart reads as an analogue for the narrator, safely ensconced on his
sofa beside the vaginal (and now impassable) doorway, in implied contrast
with the 'malign growth' of the baby the narrator flees at the story's close.[164]
Like Kennedy, Stewart thus presents this moment as a queer rejection
of reproductive sexuality rooted in the Freudian death drive.[165] While
such resonances are available in the story, a solely anti-natal reading of
Premier amour/First Love elides several key narrative details. The first is
the relation the narrator's reference to uterine tumours and his reluctance
to consummate his relationship with 'Anna' bear to his reaction to her
'crooked' eyes.[166] Upon learning that 'Anna' is with child, the narrator
conducts a survey of her physical condition—a deliberate restaging of
the earlier strip-tease—in which the apparent obtrusiveness of her ocular
impairment and the evidence of her pregnancy increase in tandem:

---

[161] Ibid., 13.   [162] Ibid., 160.

[163] Beckett, *The Expelled/The Calmative/The End & First Love*, 75.

[164] '*fibroma*' may denote a benign growth on any part of the body. Both Baker and Stewart
identify the resonance as specifically uterine for the reasons outlined above. Phil Baker, *Beckett
and the Mythology of Psychoanalysis* (New York: St. Martin's Press, 1997), 95; Stewart, *Sex and
Aesthetics in Samuel Beckett's Work*, 65.

[165] Stewart, *Sex and Aesthetics in Samuel Beckett's Work*, 65–70.

[166] Beckett, *The Expelled/The Calmative/The End & First Love*, 73.

'The more naked she was, the more cross-eyed.'[167] The register adopted for the narrator's survey in the original French is equally eugenicist. The French narrator notes how 'Anna's nudity in this moment renders her 'strabique', a cognate of the diagnostic term *strabismus* and a reference to the congenital defect it denotes.[168] This clinical survey of 'Anna', in which the medical gaze and the male gaze operate in unison, follows hot on the heels of the revelation that she lives 'by prostitution'.[169] As discussed in the previous chapter, the female sex worker was a focal point for eugenicist social hygiene discourse and public health policy throughout the nineteenth and twentieth centuries. In Ireland, repressive state measures such as the Contagious Diseases Acts (1864, 1866, 1869) were infamously supplemented by an abusive network of ecclesiastically managed Magdalene Laundries and Mother-and-Baby Homes, in which 'fallen women' were ostensibly offered the opportunity to redeem their sexual transgressions through spiritually ennobling and financially rewarding labour, while at the same time being removed from a breeding pool and a public sphere it was feared they would contaminate.[170] In contrast to the rosy image Kennedy and Stewart offer of the narrator's advocacy of abortion and abandonment of 'Anna' in *Premier amour/First Love*, these actions, when read in such a context, take on a different complexion. Rather than reflecting a horror of reproduction qua reproduction, or an anti-eugenic strain of Protestant quietism, the narrator's insistence that 'Anna' should abort the impending infant may instead be taken to indicate a desire to ensure that the sexually compromised and physically inferior 'Anna' does not perpetuate a tainted line. The narrator's evacuation of the parlour, and symbolic obstruction of the corridor which leads to it, 'making egress impossible, and *a fortiori* ingress,' thus become acts not of thanatic self-annihilation, but of sterilization

---

[167] Ibid., 78.
[168] Beckett, *Premier Amour*, 52. 'Strabisme (nom masculin): Déviation permanente résultant du défaut de parallélisme des axes visuels des deux yeux. (Dans le strabisme convergent, la déviation se fait en dedans, par opposition au strabisme divergent.)' [Strabismus (masculine noun): Permanent deviation resulting from the lack of parallelism of the visual axes of the two eyes. (In convergent strabismus, the deviation is inward, as opposed to the divergent strabismus.)] 'Strabisme (n.m.),' Larousse dictionnaire de français, March 2017, http://www.larousse.fr/dictionnaires/francais/strabisme/74801.
[169] Beckett, *The Expelled/The Calmative/The End & First Love*, 78.
[170] Luddy, *Prostitution and Irish Society, 1800–1940*, chap. 3; James M. Smith, *Ireland's Magdalen Laundries and the Nation's Architecture of Containment* (Manchester: Manchester University Press, 2008), chaps. 1–2; Martin McAleese, 'Report of the Inter-Departmental Committee to Establish the Facts of State Involvement with the Magdalen Laundries' (Department of Justice and Equality, February 2013), http://www.justice.ie/en/JELR/Pages/MagdalenRpt2013.

intended to render birth (egress), and, indeed, penetrative sex of any kind (ingress), unfeasible.[171]

Beyond their eugenic resonances, these acts also possess a sectarian character, hinted at in the unattributed and deliberately ambiguous term 'fibrome, or brone'. While Baker's account offers a productive starting point for considering this moment of strategic obscurity, it does not engage with the specific national cues such a moment offers, nor the cultural resonances they engage. Thus, while Baker is justified in an Anglophone context to gloss 'fibrome', which has no direct parallel in English, with the medical Latin *fibroma*, he overlooks the fact that 'fibrome utérin' is the standard French term for a uterine tumour, disengaging the novella from the historical, political, and linguistic context in which it was composed. In doing so, he elides the ways in which the narrator's actions, and the depopulated and nationalistic landscape in which the story is set, evoke the eugenic logic of the government of Vichy France, through which Beckett had fled in 1942.[172] Moreover, while Baker accounts for the mysterious 'fibrome', he leaves the even more puzzling qualification 'or brone' unexamined. One suggestive homophonic resonance for this seemingly trivial syllable that presents itself in a Gaelic cultural context is the Irish word 'brón' ['sorrow' or 'regret'], a common piece of diction in Irish-language verse.[173] In contrast to the conventional expressions of sentimental Celtic heartache offered in *aislings* such as 'Mo Bhrón ar an Bhfarraige' [my grief is on the sea] or Pádraic Pearse's 'Bean Sléibhe Ag Caoineadh A Mhac' [a woman of the mountains keens her son], the only 'brón' Beckett's narrator appears to feel is that he may have conceived a child with a physically defective sex worker, whose unintelligible singing of 'old folk songs', association with a fragment of unattributed Irish, and unwillingness to abort the child, suggest a Gaelic cultural affiliation and a Catholic heritage the propagation of which the narrator is keen to prevent for eugenic reasons.[174]

---

[171] Beckett, *The Expelled/The Calmative/The End & First Love*, 74.

[172] Knowlson, *Damned to Fame*, 314–18.

[173] I am indebted to Alan Graham of University College, Dublin, for drawing this linguistic echo to my attention. For an account of Beckett's engagement with the Irish language, see Alan Graham, '"So much Gaelic to me": Beckett and the Irish Language,' *Journal of Beckett Studies* 24.2 (2015), 163–79. For a discussion of the Irish-language elements of *Premier amour/First Love*, see Alan Graham, '"The skull in Conemarra": Beckett, Joyce, and the Gaelic West,' in *Samuel Beckett and the 'State' of Ireland*, ed. Alan Graham and Scott Eric Hamilton (Newcastle upon Tyne: Cambridge Scholars Publishing, 2017), 173–93, 183–8.

[174] Beckett, *The Expelled/The Calmative/The End & First Love*, 66.

In contrast to the uncomplicatedly valorous and politically subversive rejection of the nativist fertility drive with which Kennedy and Stewart identify the story's anti-natalism, a sensitivity to these cultural resonances reveals that the enflamed elephant in the room in *Premier amour/First Love* is its deployment of a eugenically inflected and sectarian narratorial perspective far closer in logic and tone to the comments of Yeats, Gregg, and Stanford than has previously been acknowledged. This is not to suggest that Beckett's perspective is identical with that of the narrator—it most certainly is not. Instead, it is to highlight the self-indicting ways in which Beckett appears to construct the narrator as a parodic embodiment of his own earlier attitudes to the pro-natalism and cultural exceptionalism of the Irish Free State. At least as much as a rejection of the horrors of coerced fertility, it is the desire to highlight and subject this former sectarian agon to self-reflexive critique which animates *Premier amour/First Love* and its blurring of the geographical and political terrain of post-independence Ireland and Vichy France. Through the lexical and cultural slippages facilitated by strategically ambiguous terms such as 'fibrome' and the liaisons they forge between the positive eugenics of J. J. Byrne's drive for a 'better race' or Yeats and Stanford's push for a resurgent Protestant Ascendancy, and the negative eugenics of Nazism at its most monstrous, Beckett renders his own anti-natalism at best a questionable political good. In this regard the narrator's closing reflections are doubly fitting:

> [There] was no competing with those cries [. . .] As long as I kept walking I didn't hear them . . . But as soon as I halted I heard them again, a little fainter each time, admittedly, but what does it matter, cry is cry, all that matters is that it should cease. For years I thought they would cease. Now I don't think so any more.[175]

Just as the narrator can never fully escape the cries of his new-born, or the dysgenic, exogamous union to which they attest, so Beckett, in the first act of his apparent linguistic independence, revisits the Ireland of the Censorship Act to interrogate the ways in which its sectarian prejudices and cultural conflicts may have followed him across the Channel. In doing so, Beckett illustrates the potentially noxious social, political, and cultural outcomes of rooting a model of post-independence Irish national identity in a vexed

---

[175] Ibid., 79–80.

politics of sexual health, even as he advertises the ways in which his own responses to the (mis)birth of an independent Irish nation participated in precisely this dynamic. As Chapter 5 will suggest, Beckett was far from alone in discovering the politically troubling ramifications of using eugenicist discourse to critique censorship and pro-natalism in Ireland, or the ideological pitfalls into which it could lead apparently liberal and progressive authors.

5

'But perhaps this new child will be perfect!': Kate O'Brien's Eugenic Romances

> Unsuitable marriages, unhappy homes, ugly children are ter-
> ribly common; because the young woman who ought to have
> all the unmarried young men in the country open to her choice,
> […] finds that in fact she has to choose between two or three in
> her own class, and has to allow herself to be […] made desper-
> ate by neglect, before she can persuade herself that she really
> loves the one she dislikes least. Under such circumstances we
> shall never get a well-bred race[.]
>
> George Bernard Shaw, *The Intelligent Woman's Guide to
> Socialism and Capitalism* (1928)

> For, indeed, there is nothing to compare with the beauty of
> health.
>
> Caleb Saleeby, *The Eugenic Prospect* (1921)

In 1942 the actions of the Censorship of Publications Board became the object of sustained public scrutiny for the first time since its inception. Long-term opponent of the censorship, Senator Sir John Keane, brought a motion to the Seanad claiming that 'in the opinion of Seanad Eireann, the Censorship of Publications Board appointed by the Minister for Justice under the Censorship of Publications Act, 1929, has ceased to retain public confidence and that steps should be taken by the Minister to reconstitute the Board'.[1] Keane's motion had been prompted by an exchange of letters in the *Irish Times* between Frank O'Connor, Seán Ó Faoláin, and others concern-ing the banning of three books: *The Tailor and Ansty* (1942) by Eric Cross, a pseudo-ethnographic account of the relationship of an unmarried west Cork

---

[1] Seanad Éireann, 'Censorship of Publications—Motion,' Pub. L. No. 27 (1942), https://www.oireachtas.ie/en/debates/debate/seanad/1942-11-18/6/.

Irish Modernism and the Politics of Sexual Health. Lloyd (Meadhbh) Houston, Oxford University Press.

couple; *The Laws of Life* (1935), a guide to the 'safe period' method of birth control, published with the *permissu superiorium* [by permission of the superiors] of the Catholic Bishop of Westminster; and Kate O'Brien's *The Land of Spices* (1941), a *Bildungsroman* set in a French convent in rural Ireland.[2] The first had been suppressed for its sexual frankness and its depiction of pre-marital cohabitation, the second for its (albeit Church sanctioned) discussion of birth control—though, confusingly, the ban had been made on the basis of the text's 'indecency'—the third for a single explicit reference to male same-sex desire: 'She saw *Etienne* and her father, in the embrace of love.'[3] The debate crystallized a growing sense among Irish liberal intellectuals that the worst fears of the opponents of the 1929 Act had been realized.[4] Rather than targeting the British popular press as had been intended, the Board had centred its energies on Irish novelists, with notions of cultural value and a sensitivity to likely readership having apparently been disregarded in favour of pious philistinism. Moreover, in targeting even a text like Sutherland's—an ecclesiastically endorsed medical manual by a pro-natalist, Catholic doctor, which described in largely technical terms a non-barrier method of birth control intended to be used in situations where another pregnancy would threaten a mother's health—the Board had revealed itself to be out of step even with the Church whose doctrines it was widely believed to uphold.[5]

While it would be naïve to credit the over-worked and increasingly disgruntled censorship board with too detailed an awareness of Kate O'Brien's work and its implied sexual politics, the juxtaposition of O'Brien's novel and Sutherland's manual is instructive: in its attempts to balance a pragmatic approach to sexuality, a concern for women's

---

[2] For an account of the banning of the texts and their place in the debate, see respectively Caleb Richardson, '"They Are Not Worthy of Themselves": The Tailor and Ansty Debates of 1942,' *Éire-Ireland* 42, no. 3 (2007), 148–72; Michael Adams, *Censorship: The Irish Experience* (Dublin: Scepter Books, 1968), 88–92; Jana Fischerova, 'The Banning and Unbanning of Kate O'Brien's *The Land of Spices*,' *Irish University Review* 48, no. 1 (May 2018), 69–83.

[3] Kate O'Brien, *The Land of Spices*, Repr. (London: Virago, 2007), 165.

[4] For an exhaustive account of the debate see Adams, *Censorship: The Irish Experience*, 1968, chap. 4.

[5] A flavour of Sutherland's ardent pro-natalism may be caught in his alarmist 1922 polemic, *Birth Control: A Statement of Christian Doctrine Against the Neo-Malthusians*, in which he deems the 'declining birth-rate' to be the most serious issue ever to have 'confronted the British people', in comparison with which 'all other dangers, be they of war, of politics, or of disease, are of little moment': '"Where are my children?" was the question shouted yesterday from the cinemas. "Let us have children, children at any price," will be the cry of to-morrow.' Halliday Sutherland, *Birth Control: A Statement of Christian Doctrine Against the Neo-Malthusians* (London: Harding and More, 1922), 155.

reproductive health and general well-being, and a sincere regard for Catholic social teaching and medical ethics, *The Laws of Life* shares many of the key tensions of O'Brien's oeuvre and its handling of sex and fertility.[6] Keane's motion (which, following arduous discussion, was convincingly defeated) and the debates which precipitated it have been explored at length in a range of contexts, as have their implications for O'Brien's career.[7] However, what the debates suggest about the relationship between O'Brien's writing and the birth control movement in Ireland has received less attention. O'Brien is widely, and rightly, credited with bringing a liberal tolerance and candour to the discussion and representation of desire, pleasure, and their often physically and emotionally complicated consequences among the Irish Catholic bourgeoisie, that was often lacking in the literary and public discourse of her day.[8] Critical accounts of O'Brien's life and writing present her as an ardent advocate of 'aesthetic, emotional, and sexual freedom' for women, a queer dissenting voice who unsettles 'conventional views of femininity' and 'challenges the insularity of Free State Ireland', and 'an aesthete and a subversive'

[6] Jana Fischerova notes that between 1936 and 1953, five out of O'Brien's nine published novels were submitted to the Board for consideration (*Mary Lavelle, The Land of Spices, That Lady, Pray for the Wanderer*, and *The Flower of May*), with two (*Mary Lavelle* and *The Land of Spices*) being suppressed. Fischerova, 'The Banning and Unbanning of Kate O'Brien's *The Land of Spices*,' 69; 81 (n.4).

[7] The debate commenced on 18 November and was resumed on 2, 3, and 9 December, when the motion was defeated by thirty-four votes to two.
Seanad Éireann, 'Censorship of Publications—Motion (Resumed),' Pub. L. No. 27 (1942), https://www.oireachtas.ie/en/debates/debate/seanad/1942-12-02/8/;
Seanad Éireann, 'Censorship of Publications—Motion (Resumed),' Pub. L. No. 27 (1942), https://www.oireachtas.ie/en/debates/debate/seanad/1942-12-03/3/;
Seanad Éireann, 'Censorship of Publications—Motion (Resumed),' Pub. L. No. 27 (1942), https://www.oireachtas.ie/en/debates/debate/seanad/1942-12-09/3/.
For a discussion of the ways in which the ban and the debates it generated surface in O'Brien's work, see Michael Cronin, 'Kate O'Brien and the Erotics of Liberal Catholic Dissent,' *Field Day Review* 6 (2010): 28–51.

[8] Prominent examples include Adele M. Dalsimer, *Kate O'Brien: A Critical Study* (Dublin: Gill and Macmillan, 1990); Eibhear Walshe, ed., *Ordinary People Dancing: Essays on Kate O'Brien* (Cork: Cork University Press, 1993); Eibhear Walshe, *Kate O'Brien: A Writing Life* (Dublin: Irish Academic Press, 2006); Eibhear Walshe, 'Kate O'Brien,' in *A History of Modern Irish Women's Literature*, ed. Heather Ingman and Clíona Ó Gallchoir (Cambridge University Press, 2018), 227–43; Aintzane Legarreta Mentxaka, *Kate O'Brien and the Fiction of Identity: Sex, Art and Politics in* Mary Lavelle *and Other Writings* (Jefferson, NC: McFarland & Co, 2011); Heather Ingman, *Irish Women's Fiction: From Edgeworth to Enright* (Dublin: Irish Academic Press, 2013), 110–16; 123–30; Paige Reynolds, ed. 'Kate O'Brien,' special issue, *Irish University Review* 48, no. 1 (May 2018); Gerardine Meaney, 'A Disruptive Modernist: Kate O'Brien and Irish Women's Writing,' in *A History of Irish Modernism*, ed. Gregory Castle and Patrick Bixby (Cambridge: Cambridge University Press, 2019), 276–91.

who blends an 'engagement with the art of the novel on modernist terms' with an ongoing appreciation for 'nineteenth-century realism'.[9] However, as Michael G. Cronin has suggested, while all of the above is true, in the process of according O'Brien the recognition she is due as both a modernist and a liberalizing influence in Irish cultural life, it is important not to lose sight of the intellectual origins of her progressive outlook or the ideological investments that underpin it.[10] In particular, where O'Brien's sexual politics are concerned, it is necessary to acknowledge the extent to which O'Brien's model of an ideal relationship—one compacted between two intelligent, capable, and, above all, beautiful individuals, in which sex is the mutually fulfilling realization of shared desire, and where children are the products of active choice rather than unavoidable necessity—participates in and responds to ongoing debates concerning birth control and eugenics in European, British, and Irish culture.[11]

In what follows, I draw upon a range of recent scholarship on the cultural politics of twentieth-century eugenics to explore how issues of desire, fertility, and notions of 'fitness' are dramatized in O'Brien's writing in the 1930s and 40s.[12] In the process, I supplement the more conventional account of the sectarian, male-centred debate around censorship and fertility offered in the previous chapter, by exploring the ways in which O'Brien and a number of other Irish women and female modernists responded to the Censorship Act and its proscriptions, and illustrating the tensions and contradictions that could arise for those who sought to marry a eugenic conception of sex and sexuality with an investment in personal freedom, democracy, and equality. In order to place O'Brien's handling of birth control, eugenics, and sexual

[9] Dalsimer, *Kate O'Brien*, xvii; Anne Fogarty, 'Women and Modernism,' in *The Cambridge Companion to Irish Modernism*, ed. Joe Cleary (Cambridge: Cambridge University Press, 2014), 157; Meaney, 'A Disruptive Modernist: Kate O'Brien and Irish Women's Writing,' 277.

[10] Michael G. Cronin, *Impure Thoughts: Sexuality, Catholicism and Literature in Twentieth-Century Ireland* (Manchester: Manchester University Press, 2012), 86–87.

[11] For a probing account of O'Brien's fetishization of beauty and the challenges it poses for those who wish to stress the queer, feminist dimensions of her work, see Patricia Coughlan, 'Feminine Beauty, Feminist Writing, and Sexual Role in the Work of Kate O'Brien,' in *Ordinary People Dancing: Essays on Kate O'Brien*, ed. Eibhear Walshe (Cork: Cork University Press, 1993), 59–84. For a more exculpatory account of O'Brien's idealization of beauty, see Aintzane Legarreta Mentxaka, 'La Belle: Kate O'Brien and Female Beauty,' in *Women, Social, and Cultural Change in Twentieth-Century Ireland: Dissenting Voices?*, ed. Sarah O'Connor and Christopher C. Shepard (Newcastle: Cambridge Scholars Publishing, 2008), 183–98.

[12] Layne Parish Craig, 'Passion's Possibilities: Kate O'Brien's Sexological Discourse in *Without My Cloak*,' *Éire-Ireland* 44, no. 3–4 (2010), 118–39; Layne Parish Craig, *When Sex Changed: Birth Control Politics and Literature Between the World Wars*. (New Brunswick, New Jersey: Rutgers University Press, 2013), chap. 4.

health in its Irish cultural context, it is first necessary to explore the wider terrain of women's responses to the introduction of censorship to Ireland.

'Always to be legislated for by the other sex': Women's Responses to Irish Censorship

If Beckett's ambivalent vision of anti-natal independence in *Premier amour/ First Love* left little room for fellow-travelling, let alone feminist solidarity, it reflected a broader trend in early opposition to the Censorship Act. For all the voluminous commentary Irish censorship and reproductive rights have generated, women's responses to the Act and its restrictions on material relating to birth control and abortion in the decades immediately following its passage have proven harder to trace than the sectarian and neo-Malthusian arguments discussed in the previous chapter. That Irish people of all denominations practised birth control and abortion, albeit with regional and class variations, is clear enough.[13] The 1926 Committee on Evil Literature noted that all the major publications concerning birth control were 'on sale' in Ireland, and that 'cheaper pamphlets' were readily 'purchasable in the poorer districts of Dublin'.[14] The 1931 Carrigan Report described contraceptive use as 'extremely prevalent, not only in cities and larger towns, but also in villages and remote parts of the South and West of the country', with some vendors making 'no attempt to conceal the sale of them'.[15] Diarmaid Ferriter cites a 1933 letter in which Jesuit social reformer and censorship advocate, Father Richard Devane, informed the Minister for Justice that he was aware of 'four houses openly engaged in selling contraceptives' in Dublin alone, with 'several chemists' also engaged in the 'vile traffic'.[16] From 1936 to 1947, the Marie Stopes Society for Constructive Birth Control operated a Mother's Clinic in Belfast, which offered family planning advice and contraceptives—though not abortions—to married women,

---

[13] Cormac Ó Gráda and Niall Duffy, 'Fertility Control in Ireland and Scotland: C.1880–1930, Some New Findings,' *UCD Centre for Economic Research Working Paper Series; WP89/14*, December 1989; Mary E. Daly, *The Slow Failure: Population Decline and Independent Ireland, 1922–1973* (Madison, Wis: University of Wisconsin Press, 2006), 94–95; Diarmaid Ferriter, *Occasions of Sin: Sex and Society in Modern Ireland* (London: Profile Books, 2009), 193–99; Lindsey Earner-Byrne and Diane Urquhart, *The Irish Abortion Journey, 1920–2018* (London: Palgrave Macmillan, 2019).
[14] *Report of the Committee on Evil Literature* (Dublin: Stationery Office, 1926), 15.
[15] Carrigan (Chairman), *Report of the Committee on the Criminal Law Amendment Acts (1880-85), and Juvenile Prostitution*, 36–37.
[16] Ferriter, *Occasions of Sin*, 193–94.

while court records on both sides of the border in the decades following independence and partition reveal numerous cases in which young women sought to avoid both the stigma and practical difficulties of single motherhood through illegal terminations, with often calamitous results for their health and well-being.[17] However, Irish historiography has found evidence of the attitudes of women to the legislation which made such measures necessary harder to recover.[18]

Perhaps unsurprisingly for a parliamentary debate conducted almost exclusively by men—the Dáil had one female member and the Seanad only four at the time of the Act's passage—the voices of Irish women were conspicuous largely by their absence in public discourse surrounding censorship.[19] Notwithstanding the fact that senator Jane Wyse Power (Siobhán Bean an Phaoraigh), who had served as a member of the Irish Film Censorship Appeal Board since 1923, was one of the only parliamentarians directly qualified to speak to both the theory and practice of publications control, women made relatively few comments on the Bill as it moved through both houses of the Oireachtas.[20] Likewise, in both the literary and popular press, female-authored commentary on the proposed legislation was limited. A notable exception was respected feminist and anti-Treaty republican, Hanna Sheehy Skeffington, who addressed a meeting of the Women's Freedom League in Bloomsbury, London in November 1928

---

[17] Greta Jones, 'Marie Stopes in Ireland: The Mother's Clinic in Belfast, 1936–47,' *Social History of Medicine* 5, no. 2 (April 1992), 255–77; Cliona Rattigan, '"Crimes of Passion of the Worst Character": Abortion Cases and Gender in Ireland, 1925–50,' in *Gender and Power in Irish History*, ed. Maryann Gialanella Valiulis (Dublin: Irish Academic Press, 2009), 115–40.

[18] As Diarmaid Ferriter reminds commentators on 1930s Irish culture, one reason for this difficulty, particularly where working-class testimony is concerned, may simply be that '[e]lite debates about censorship and contraception were of little relevance to the majority, who carried on reading the westerns and romances they desired and having the children they felt duty-bound to.' Diarmaid Ferriter, *The Transformation of Ireland, 1900–2000* (London: Profile, 2005), 361.

[19] Mary Clancy, 'Aspects of Women's Contribution to the Oireachtas Debate in the Irish Free State, 1922-37,' in *Women Surviving: Studies in Irish Women's History in the 19th–20th Centuries*, ed. Maria Luddy and Clíona Murphy (Swords, Co. Dublin, Ireland: Poolbeg, 1989), 210–12; 231–32.

[20] Wyse Power's contributions to the drafting of the Bill were confined to practical reflections on the size of the proposed board, the necessity of anonymity for its members, and the need to recognize individual submissions from the public in its operation. Seanad Éireann, 'Censorship of Publications Bill, 1928 —Third Stage,' Pub. L. No. 12.5 (1929), https://www.oireachtas.ie/en/debates/debate/seanad/1929-04-25/2/; Seanad Éireann, 'Censorship of Publications Bill, 1928 —Third Stage (Resumed),' Pub. L. No. 12.10 (1929), https://www.oireachtas.ie/en/debates/debate/seanad/1929-05-15/4/; Seanad Éireann, 'Public Business. Censorship of Publications Bill, 1928 Recommittal Stage,' Pub. L. No. 12.12 (1929), https://www.oireachtas.ie/en/debates/debate/seanad/1929-06-05/8/.

on the subject of the 'ridiculous and impossible' legislation.[21] In remarks reproduced in the *Irish Times*, Sheehy Skeffington characterized the Bill as an exemplary manifestation of the Free State's patronising and paternalistic attitude towards women: 'We are not to be allowed to use the free will which we are all supposed to enjoy. But we are to have this grandmotherly, or rather, I should say, grandfatherly, legislation imposed on us; for it seems we are always to be legislated for by the other sex.'[22] To appreciative laughter from her audience, Sheehy Skeffington attributed the Bill to a 'monastic, celibate' mindset which viewed women as 'not only dangerous and explosive, but also rather an indecent quantity'.[23] As Shaw would do in his response to the Censorship Act, Sheehy Skeffington detected in such paternalism a fixation with women's dress and appearance often more perverse than the attitudes of those whose works they sought to suppress: 'They linger on the shortness of women's hair or her skirts, and seem to regard such things as just a little immoral (Laughter).'[24] While Sheehy Skeffington did not critique the Bill's prohibition of birth control literature in and of itself, she did express concern that it would inadvertently see 'some of the best papers' from Britain banned.[25] She also playfully foregrounded the issue of reproduction by presenting the 'grandmotherly' legislation as the mental offspring of its inherently suspect male authors: 'This bill, of course, was fathered by a lawyer, and anything that comes from a lawyer's brain we women have learnt to distrust.'[26] Sheehy Skeffington concluded her critique on a somewhat glib note of defiance, arguing that 'as far as we women are concerned, we may let them go ahead with the Censorship Bill; for we shall probably read in the end exactly what we want'.[27] That these remarks were made to a feminist society in liberal Bloomsbury, rather than an equivalent group in Dublin goes some way to undermine the blithe certainty of their conclusion. Returning to the topic almost a decade later for the New York *Saturday Review*, Sheehy Skeffington was more emphatic in highlighting and critiquing the Act's pro-natalism, and its broader impact on the capacity of Irish people to regulate their sexual lives:

The unusual, the daring, any criticism of the Catholic Church generally, or of individual clerics, indictments of marriage, sex, hygiene, medical views

---

[21] Hanna Sheehy Skeffington, 'A woman's view of censorship: "ridiculous and impossible"', *Irish Times*, 23 November 1928, reproduced in Margaret Ward, ed., *Hanna Sheehy Skeffington: Suffragette and Sinn Féiner Her Memoirs and Political Writings* (Dublin: University College Dublin Press, 2017), 254.
[22] Ibid.   [23] Ibid., 255.   [24] Ibid.   [25] Ibid.   [26] Ibid.   [27] Ibid.

of birth control, sex education for the young, all these are marked down, Marie Stopes, stock, lock and barrel, and writers like Bertrand Russell (*Marriage and Morals*) and Havelock Ellis (*Essays of Love and Virtue*) as well as Jules Romain's *Men of Good Will* are lumped together under the absurd formula 'in general tendency indecent'.[28]

Offering a taxonomy of recently banned books, Sheehy Skeffington high-lighted a range of titles in which birth control, abortion, or women's reproductive freedom and sexual self-knowledge feature prominently, including Ethel Mannin's *Common-Sense and the Child: A Plea for Freedom* (1931), Aldous Huxley's *Brave New World* (1932), Sinclair Lewis's *Ann Vickers* (1933), Vera Brittain's *Honourable Estate* (1936), and Signe Toksvig's *Eve's Doctor* (1937).[29] In many areas Sheehy Skeffington's criticisms overlap with those of the male, Protestant critics of the Act cited in the previous chapter—like Yeats, Beckett, and others she detects in the Act a blend of anti-intellectualism, prudery, and undue deference to ecclesiastical authority that threatens freedom of thought and expression and meaningful notions of cultural value. However, where the debates charted in the previous chapter largely framed birth control as a demographic and, implicitly, sectarian issue, Sheehy Skeffington appears more concerned with the realities of sex and fertility and their management in individual lives, particularly those of women.

This granular sensitivity to lived sexual experience is reflected in the texts Sheehy Skeffington singles out. Mannin's *Common-Sense and the Child*, a frank and polemical parenting manual heavily influenced by Freud and Adler, drew directly on her experiences in raising her daughter Jean (pictured in Mannin's author headshot) and featured chapters on 'Sex-Knowledge and the Child', 'The Sexual Life of the Child', and 'The "Sins" of the Child' (which included masturbation, sexual play, and 'fornicatory language').[30] In a moment which succinctly offends against multiple aspects of the 1929 Censorship Act, Mannin describes the

---

[28] Hanna Sheehy Skeffington, 'Censorship in Éire,' *The Saturday Review*, New York (18 March 1939), reproduced in Ward, 350.

[29] Ibid., 349.

[30] Mannin, a prolific author and ardent sex reformer, became a familiar figure to the Anglo-Irish literati through her relationship with the W. B. Yeats, who was introduced to Mannin by Norman Haire to test the efficacy of the Steinach rejuvenation operation he had just performed on the ageing poet. Ethel Mannin, *Common-Sense and the Child: A Plea for Freedom* (London: Jarrolds, 1931), chaps. 9, 10, and 18; Joseph M. Hassett, *W.B. Yeats and the Muses* (Oxford: Oxford University Press, 2010), 182.

questions the nine-year-old Jean had for her following a trip they took with a friend of Mannin's to a gynaecologist. When asked why the friend emerged from her consultation crying at the news that she was pregnant, Mannin proceeded to explain to Jean that 'people mated because they liked doing so, not always because they wanted to have children' and described 'a rubber pessary to her, as simply as possible'.[31] No less direct in its rendering of the physical realities of fertility and embodiment was Toksvig's *Eve's Doctor*, a novel set in an Irish maternity hospital closely modelled on the Rotunda, where Toksvig had undergone a hysterectomy and developed a close (most likely romantic) relationship with the Master, Bethel Solomons in 1931.[32] The novel is framed as a conflict between the 'materialist, cosmopolitan,' and studiously 'progressive' Michael Murrough—a sensitive and professional gynaecologist who 'did not go to mass, did not belong to a party, and openly scoffed at compulsory Irish'—and Frank Carrick, a loyal member of the government party (implicitly Fianna Fáil) and nephew of the local priest, who, through a combination of incompetence and deference to Catholic medical ethics has 'killed or maimed more women than Jack the Ripper'.[33] Throughout the novel, the spectre of clerically sanctioned pronatalism is evoked through the figure of the assistant surgeon, Shawn O'Rourke, who studiously observes Murrough in the hope of catching him performing an operation 'unlawful under the laws of both God and man', so that he can report it to the ultra-orthodox Father Cooley and see him dismissed.[34] In a dénouement that anticipates the fraught ethical dilemmas generated by the infamous Eighth Amendment to the 1937 constitution, Murrough is ultimately replaced by Carrick after privileging the life of a healthy mother over that of her hydrocephalic foetus during a protracted and meticulously described birth. That an appetite existed for the novel's

[31] Mannin, *Common-Sense and the Child: A Plea for Freedom*, 108.

[32] Toksvig's research for the novel and developing relationship with Solomons can be traced through her diaries from 1931 to 1937. Lis Pihl records that, preparing the diaries for possible future publication in 1967, Toksvig excised fifteen pages which detailed a crisis in her marriage precipitated by her involvement with Solomons. Lis Pihl, '"A Muzzle Made in Ireland": Irish Censorship and Signe Toksvig,' *Studies: An Irish Quarterly Review* 88, no. 352 (1999), 451–52; Sandra McAvoy, 'All About Eve: Signe Toksvig and the Intimate Lives of Irish Women, 1926–1937,' *Irish Review* 42 (Summer 2010): 47; Signe Toksvig, *Signe Toksvig's Irish Diaries, 1926–1937*, ed. Lis Pihl (Dublin: Lilliput Press, 1994); William Murphy, 'Solomons, Bethel Albert Herbert,' in *Dictionary of Irish Biography*, ed. James McGuire and James Quinn (Cambridge: Cambridge University Press, 2009), http://dib.cambridge.org/viewReadPage.do?articleId=a8187.

[33] Signe Toksvig, *Eve's Doctor* (London: Faber and Faber, 1937), 41; 77; 47.

[34] Ibid., 77–78.

candour and insistent concern with fertility politics is reflected in the weekly 'What Dublin Is Reading' feature of the *Irish Times*, in which *Eve's Doctor* appeared on multiple occasions during the month between its publication and suppression.[35]

While Sheehy Skeffington did not directly mention O'Brien in her 1938 article, she had singled out the author for praise the previous September in a talk on 'Irish Women Writers' chaired by O'Brien herself.[36] O'Brien's oeuvre undoubtedly shares a great deal with the work of Mannin and Toksvig in both outlook and subject matter. As a range of commentators have noted, physical, emotional, and sexual development are a recurrent concern in O'Brien's work, from the three generations of the Considine family traced from birth to maturity in *Without My Cloak*, to the *Bildungsroman* format of *The Land of Spices* and the queer, feminist rewriting of *A Portrait of the Artist* (1916) for which it provides the vehicle.[37] Likewise, as *Without My Cloak*'s title suggests through its simultaneous punning evocation of unprotected sex and the refusal of obfuscation, questions of fertility and free expression were central to O'Brien's writing from the outset. However, the tacit ideological implications of a eugenic conception of sex and sexuality meant that its utility as a means to make an intellectually consistent case for greater sexual liberty was often limited at best.

The 'weariness and pain of pregnancy': *Without My Cloak* and Birth Control

A useful starting point for getting to grips with this aspect of O'Brien's writing is the work of Layne Parish Craig, who has situated O'Brien's first

---

[35] 'What Dublin Is Reading,' *Irish Times*, 1 March 1937, 05; 'What Dublin Is Reading,' *Irish Times*, 6 March 1937, 07; 'What Dublin Is Reading,' *Irish Times*, 20 March 1937, 07.

[36] The talk was given to the Women's Freedom League in Minerva House, Bloomsbury and was reported in the group's October *Bulletin*. See Ward, *Hanna Sheehy Skeffington*, 342–43. The following month Sheehy Skeffington would contribute a favourable review of O'Brien's travelogue *Farewell Spain* (1937) to the *Irish Democrat*. Hanna Sheehy Skeffington, 'Frank, Warm-Hearted Irish Woman in Spain', *Irish Democrat* (16 October 1937), 2. Both women were active members, along with Mannin and Toksvig, of the Dublin-based Women Writers' Club, which operated from 1933 to 1958. For an account of the Club, its membership, and its response to the censorship of Mannin and others, see Deirdre F. Brady, *Literary Coteries and the Irish Women Writers' Club (1933–1958)* (Liverpool: Liverpool University Press, 2021), Chaps. 2 and 3.

[37] This queer, intertextual, Joycean reading of *The Land of Spices* is most fully articulated in Margot Backus and Joseph Valente, '*The Land of Spices*, the Enigmatic Signifier, and the Stylistic Invention of Lesbian (In)Visibility,' *Irish University Review* 43, no. 1 (May 2013), 55–73.

novel, *Without My Cloak*, within a wider tradition of 1930s 'family sagas' which respond to the Church of England's 1930 Lambeth Conference—which expressed qualified support for the use of contraceptives by married couples 'where there is a clearly-felt moral obligation to limit or avoid parenthood'—and the 1930 Papal encyclical, *Casti Connubii* [of chaste marriage], which denounced efforts to regulate fertility as a 'calamitous error' and 'intrinsically evil'.[38] Surveying the influence of the birth control movement on twentieth-century culture, Craig succinctly sketches the standard tropology of the 1930s birth control novel: 'the weakened mother, the overlarge family beset by economic and health problems, the sexually frustrated husband, and the dysgenic couple who bears sickly children'.[39] As Parish Craig notes, all are present in some form or another in *Without My Cloak*, a family saga which saw O'Brien dubbed the 'Irish Galsworthy'.[40] The novel charts the fortunes of three generations of the Considines—'Honest John and His Children: 1860–61', 'Molly, Caroline, Denis: 1861–70', and 'Denis: 1874–77'—as they rise from the status of runaway groomsmen to a position of comfort and prosperity amid the Catholic bourgeoisie of Mellick (O'Brien's fictional portrait of her native Limerick).[41] Through the various contortions of its multiple plots, a range of eugenic-, sexological-, and fertility-related issues are dramatized and debated, including, but not limited to: physical incompatibility and separation (Caroline and her sexually inept husband, Jim), a heavily implied queer romance (Eddy and his London associate, Richard Froud), incestuous flirtation (Eddy and Caroline), venereal disease (Teresa's son Reggie), an extra-marital affair with a foreign sex worker (Anthony), exhaustion through multiple pregnancies (Caroline and Molly), a fatal failure of family planning (Molly), and a forbidden romance across class lines (Anthony and Molly's son Denis and the illegitimate Christina Roche). In his discussion of the novel, Parish Craig focuses on three of the most substantial of these threads—Anthony and Molly's fatal romance, Caroline's unsatisfying marriage, and Eddy's queerness—with a particular emphasis on O'Brien's engagement with (and subversion of) the work of popular birth control advocates such as Marie Stopes and Margaret Sanger. Discussing the intense mutual attraction between Molly and her husband Anthony and its ultimately disastrous consequences for the

---

[38] 'Lambeth Conference: Resolutions Archive from 1930,' sec. 15; Pope Pius XI, '*Casti Connubii*,' sec. 61; Craig, *When Sex Changed*, chap. 4.
[39] Craig, *When Sex Changed*, 100.   [40] Ward, *Hanna Sheehy Skeffington*, 343.
[41] Kate O'Brien, *Without My Cloak*, Repr. (London: Virago, 2006), 8; 102; 230.

former's health, he notes the clear debt passages such as the following owe to the work of Stopes and her contemporaries:

> She [Molly] knew that he deplored for her the discomfort of incessant childbearing and would do much to lessen it, but saw no help within the social and religious code they both upheld. He knew that childbirth frightened her, wilted and crushed her and gave her in her babies only very slender compensation, for she was by nature far more wife than mother. But it was a problem which they could never thrash out, and it was heightened by the fact that they were both on the crest of life, and if not loving each other very perfectly at all times and in all the regions of love, yet doomed to find a terrible delight, again and again, each in the other's body.[42]

As Parish Craig notes, O'Brien's willingness to stress the equal intensity of Anthony and Molly's desire for one another, emphasize the shared satisfaction it affords them, and highlight the discomfort, fear, and harm the resultant pregnancies cause Molly all indicate a sympathy for and familiarity with contemporary sex manuals such as Stopes's best-selling *Married Love* (1918).[43] This sympathy is no less apparent in O'Brien's decision to attribute the fatal fecundity of the couple to the Roman Catholic 'social and religious code' to which they both subscribe and which, in the prefatory materials to *Married Love*, Stopes had presented as little more than a sanction for degeneration: 'Is then a Roman Catholic mother, the increases to whose large family get punier and punier, to be privileged to go deliberately with that host of puny children *at the expense of others*, not only through that part of Eternity called Time, but through all Eternity?'[44] As Parish Craig rightly highlights, this depiction of the late nineteenth-century Catholic middle classes as ignorant of and unwilling to engage in any form of family planning was, in fact, an expedient inaccuracy—in reality, by the 1870s, family size among the Irish Catholic bourgeoisie was in decline.[45] However, the polemical value of this anachronistic image of an over-populated Catholic Ireland in which innumerable women were sacrificed on the altar of uncontrolled

---

[42]   Ibid., 76.   [43]   Craig, *When Sex Changed*, 106–12.

[44]   Marie Carmichael Stopes, *Married Love: A New Contribution to the Solution of Sex Difficulties* (London: A.C. Fifield, 1918), xvii.

[45]   Layne Parish Craig, 'Passion's Possibilities,' 123; Timothy Guinnane, *The Vanishing Irish: Households, Migration, and the Rural Economy in Ireland, 1850–1914* (Princeton, N.J: Princeton University Press, 1997), 248–52.

fertility was too great to overlook, and both Stopes and O'Brien exploited it accordingly.[46]

While Parish Craig's account of the ways in which O'Brien's novel appropriates elements of contemporary birth control and sexological literature in order to offer a feminist critique of pro-natalism and a franker and more pleasure-centred engagement with sex and desire is well-supported and persuasively argued, his broader characterization of O'Brien's sexual politics invites a number of questions. Contrasting *Without My Cloak* with Charles Gilman Norris's *Seed: A Novel of Birth Control* (1930)—a similarly structured, but, as its title suggests, more orthodox and explicitly polemical endorsement of family planning—Craig argues that, where 'Norris's advocacy circumscribes his readers' contraceptive options within conventional— and eugenic—boundaries', O'Brien's 'undercover' birth control novel 'calls her readership towards a radically inclusive, woman-friendly approach to reproductive and sexual freedom'.[47] While undoubtedly more 'woman-friendly' and less orthodox or consistent in its sexual politics than *Seed* or some of the eugenicist tracts that inspired it, I would take issue with Craig's assertion that O'Brien's writing is 'radically inclusive' in its agenda or particularly forceful in its challenge to the 'conventional' boundaries of contemporary eugenics. Beyond the obvious paradox of a 'radically inclusive' eugenics—a difficult proposition for an ideological programme and reproductive system premised upon selection and exclusion—I would argue that such a reading risks eliding a central tension (and frequent source of contradiction) in O'Brien's work: the difficulty of squaring a eugenic approach to sex and sexuality with an aversion to authoritarianism and a passion for personal liberty.[48] The eugenics and birth control movements

<hr/>

[46] Stopes devotes a chapter of her 1933 broadside, *Roman Catholic Methods of Birth Control*, to 'Ireland, the Tail-Wagger', in which she offers an (unsurprisingly sectarian and tacitly Hibernophobic) account of the 'Roman Catholic intrigue' that introduced censorship to Ireland, and outlines its ramifications for the freedom of the British press. By obliging any British publication that wished to see the light of day in Ireland to exclude any material relating to birth control, Stopes argues, the 'Irish tail wagged the great English dog of the press'. In a succeeding chapter on 'Roman Catholic Defectives and the State', Stopes goes on to offer a Carlylean image of the Irish as degenerate over-breeders, who threaten to overwhelm a Protestant stronghold like Scotland with 'a race less moral and law-abiding than her own sons and daughters'. Marie Carmichael Stopes, *Roman Catholic Methods of Birth Control* (London: Peter Davies, 1933), 189; 191; 203.
[47] Craig, *When Sex Changed*, 103.
[48] For a succinct outline of the tensions and paradoxes confronting those who sought to advocate a more moderate and liberal 'reform eugenics' in the 1930s, see John Macnicol, 'The Voluntary Sterilization Campaign in Britain, 1918-39.' *Journal of the History of Sexuality* 2, no. 3 (January 1992), 422–38: 422–27.

undoubtedly provided a conceptual framework and vocabulary through which O'Brien could critique and confront what she perceived as the sexual conservatism, pro-natalism, and cultural isolationism of the Free State and its censorship regime. However, that framework and vocabulary came with an often noxious set of ideological presuppositions from which O'Brien would find it difficult and sometimes impossible to extricate her writing. A sense of the ways in which this tension informs O'Brien's work can be caught through an examination of what might be termed the cultural politics of O'Brien's candour regarding sex and sexuality in O'Brien's second novel, *The Ante-Room* (1934).

'She had better know the facts': *The Ante-Room* and the Cultural Politics of Candour

If much of the narrative tension and dramatic irony of the Anthony-Molly plot-line of *Without My Cloak* was premised upon an unstated and ana-chronistic readerly awareness that contemporary methods of birth control and family planning could have averted its tragic outcome, a similarly anachronistic perspective on questions of sexual health and fertility was to become an explicit, almost jarring feature of the novel's semi-sequel, *The Ante-Room*. Centred on the 'Eve of All Saints', the 'Feast of All Saints', and the 'Feast of All Souls'—the three days in the Catholic calendar most concerned with the boundary between life and death—the novel has rightly been discussed in terms of its juxtaposition of 'mortal and eternal' temporal perspectives.[49] However, this emphasis on the contrast between the dying Teresa Mulqueen's faith in a divinely vouchsafed afterlife and her daughter Agnes's more anxious awareness of the day-to-day personal cost of Catholic doctrine has occluded another significant temporal tension in the novel: the gulf between the historical moment of the plot—1880—and the socio-cultural moment of its narration—the early 1930s. This gap, which O'Brien repeatedly and deliberately highlights, manifests itself in a curious mode of narratorial anachronism that is consistently associated with dis-cussions of desire and sexual health. This is most apparent in O'Brien's presentation of the ardently anti-romantic young misogynist, Dr Curran. When Curran realizes himself to be both physically and emotionally in thrall

---

[49] Bridget English, *Laying Out the Bones: Death and Dying in the Modern Irish Novel* (Syracuse, New York: Syracuse University Press, 2017), 65.

to the novel's protagonist, Agnes Mulqueen, his response is introduced explicitly in terms of its historical and cultural situatedness:

> He was on fire, and for a space could do no more than suffer the unexpected flames.
>
> But he was not a poet. He was a Victorian bourgeois, rationalist in the idiom of his mind, Catholic in tradition and practice, a man eager to harness feeling into usefulness.[50]

Confronting his feelings again following the realization that Agnes was in love with her sister's husband, Vincent, Curran is again discussed explicitly in terms of his 'rationalism', 'flat prose', and status as a 'Victorian bourgeois in a temper'.[51] As the playfully self-aware reference to 'flat prose' suggests, sometimes this anachronistic perspective seems to trouble the borders of the novel's fictional world, granting a character like Curran a level of almost meta-narrative insight: 'He looked up again at the familiar furnishings of his solid, ugly study, and he laughed. This was 1880, and he was a small-town doctor. Where had his sense of humour gone?'[52] There is, undoubtedly, an element of under-examined, even self-congratulatory presentism to this anachronistic narratorial perspective. Where Curran makes a futile effort to restrain and channel his lust, O'Brien seems to imply, she and her worldly, Freud-literate readership know that such repression will only sublimate his desires. However, to read O'Brien's early novels as offering an unreflective Whig interpretation of Irish sexuality is to overlook the strategic political ends to which presentism is consciously being deployed in these texts and to ignore the multiple readerships they simultaneously address. There is a polemical, even coercive reasonableness to the candid and matter-of-fact tone in which so many of the more notionally salacious aspects of O'Brien's narratives are rendered that distinguishes her writing about sex and sexuality from her male contemporaries' more ribald, but often more squeamish handling of the topic.

As Parish Craig has suggested, when engaging with the topic of sexuality, O'Brien's historical novels had to navigate three separate contexts and corresponding levels of assumed sexual knowledge, experience, and possibility: the late nineteenth-century Ireland in which they were set, the post-Censorship-Act Ireland they implicitly addressed, and the British and

---

[50] Kate O'Brien, *The Ante-Room*, Repr. (London: Virago, 1997), 57.   [51] Ibid., 186.
[52] Ibid., 187.

American contexts in which they were published and circulated.[53] An examination of how the physical, emotional, and social impact of Reggie Mulqueen's syphilis are presented and discussed in *The Ante-Room* offers an opportunity to identify O'Brien's methods and motives in addressing these three contexts. In a novel peopled with medical professionals and insistently concerned with the practical, emotional, and spiritual challenges of chronic illness, it is telling that Teresa Mulqueen's cancer is handled with greater euphemistic circumspection than her son Reggie's syphilis. Despite catalysing *The Ante-Room*'s plot and determining its duration, Teresa's malady is not explicitly named until the novel's ante-penultimate chapter, with the reader otherwise left to infer the nature of her illness from descriptions of her pain, various surgeries, and passing references to the nature of the English cancer expert Sir Godfrey Bartlett-Crowe's specialism.[54] By contrast, Reggie's full medical history, including the name, nature, and debilitating physical and social implications of his illness, are matter-of-factly narrated early in chapter two:

> Reggie was now thirty-five. Ten years ago, in 1870, he had been infected with syphilis, and for three years had spent long periods in nursing homes, until sufficiently cured to live uninterruptedly at home. But marriage and love were forbidden him henceforward and seasonal doses of mercury, increased and decreased as considered necessary, and doing their specific work, also did harm. But a greater harm was wrought upon the mind and spirit by the sustained humiliations and fears of his state of health, so that a native invalidism became a justified habit, until he gave up all pretence of doing any work, or leading the life of a normal man.[55]

The forthright tone and medical lexicon which mark this passage, particularly in its punning use of the term 'specific', owe more to the case histories and medical treatises surveyed in Chapter 3 than they do to the romance genre within which the novel otherwise situates itself. This strategic infusion of late nineteenth-century syphological discourse into what is notionally framed as a popular romance setting serves to facilitate a franker handling of the topic of sexual health, even as the passage's somewhat archaic

---

phraseology and syntax ('wrought upon the mind', 'native invalidism') performatively suggest that such frankness is long overdue. Indeed, the novel even goes so far as to congratulate itself for its own forthrightness (and to praise its reader for what it assumes to be their want of squeamishness) when the narrator recounts how Dr Curran communicated the nature of Reggie's condition to Agnes:

> [As] he realised that Agnes was perplexed about her brother's ill-health without knowing anything definite to it, he decided that for everybody's sake she had better know the facts. Briefly and accurately, then, he gave them to her; but he was a conventional and puritanical young man, she was a young unmarried lady, and the year was 1880. They did not get through the conversation without some embarrassed pauses.[56]

As the pointed (and, by this point in the narration, superfluous) reference to the year in which the event takes place seems intended to make clear, unlike Agnes and Curran, neither O'Brien nor the reader has any excuse to be 'conventional', 'puritanical', or 'embarrassed' about the topic of sexual health or the details of Reggie's case. Indeed, O'Brien presents the 'sense of release and naturalness' this candour brings and the sense of 'ease and confidence' to which it gives rise as the basis for the couple's (albeit frustrated) intimacy and the grounds of possibility for Curran's growing attraction to Agnes.

As several critics have noted, this interplay between *Eros* and *Thanatos* is one of the primary structuring tensions of the novel, staged both in Teresa's refusal to die until the future of the syphilitic Reggie has been secured through marriage, and in Marie-Rose's husband Vincent's conviction that suicide is the only way to escape the impasse of his thwarted love for his sister-in-law, Agnes. For Bridget English, one of the more provocative formal features of O'Brien's novel in this regard is its pessimistic subversion of the traditional narrative telos of the romance genre. In English's view, by permanently sundering the novel's primary romantic pairing—the only union in the text governed wholly by mutual desire and sympathy—through a suicide framed in terms of Catholic martyrology, O'Brien presents the conflict between 'Catholicism and secular modernity' as fatally insoluble: 'The old world may be dying, but *The Ante-Room* offers no vision of a new world to come.'[57] English is right to emphasize the novel's failure to articulate an alternative to the Catholic social order it critiques, but, if anything, understates the thoroughgoing sterility of its conclusion and overlooks the centrality of sex and sexual health to its construction and articulation. In particular, what is missed in English's reading are the ways in which the novel's subversion of the traditional trajectory of the romance plot by extension serves to dramatize the frustration and failure of the model of heterosexual reproductive futurity upon which that plot is premised. In this sense, the novel pointedly resists what Patricia Dreschel Tobin has termed the 'genealogical imperative' of the nineteenth-century realist novel and the thematic and structural investments in families and filiation with which a range of critics have associated the form.[58] Nowhere is this more apparent than in the fact that the only relationship successfully compacted during the novel is one that has been consistently framed in terms of the impossibility of its safe consummation: the engagement of the syphilitic Reggie to the socially ambitious Nurse Cunningham. At multiple points throughout the novel the reader is reminded that Reggie is 'a man unfit to love, unfit to marry'; 'a 'wreck'; 'invalided and incapable'; a 'ruin'.[59] So apparent is Reggie's disqualification from the ranks of those deemed suitable for reproduction that both Curran and Bartlett-Crowe are able to diagnose him on sight, while his sister Agnes (the novel's most consistent voice of liberal Catholic dissent) is 'horrified' by his touch, and responds to news of his engagement with 'horror' and 'distaste' (while, admittedly, censuring herself for the 'folly' of such feelings).[60] One might argue that, in so ardently emphasizing the sterility of Reggie and Nurse Cunningham's anticipated union, O'Brien performs what Barry McCrea has presented as modernism's characteristic subversion of the realist novel's 'genealogical imperative', in the process queerly frustrating the implicit pro-natalism of both the nineteenth-century, middle-class Catholic culture she is dramatizing and the post-Censorship Act nation she is implicitly addressing.[61] However, as the consistently negative, often disgusted tone of these remarks suggest, in doing so, one must also concede that O'Brien's handling of Reggie and his

---

[57] English, *Laying Out the Bones*, 65.

[58] Patricia Drechsel Tobin, *Time and the Novel: The Genealogical Imperative* (Princeton: Princeton University Press, 1975); James Kilroy, *The Nineteenth-Century English Novel: Family Ideology and Narrative Form* (New York: Palgrave, 2007); Barry McCrea, *In the Company of Strangers: Family and Narrative in Dickens, Conan Doyle, Joyce, and Proust* (New York: Columbia University Press, 2011).

[59] O'Brien, *The Ante-Room*, 17; 22; 184; 288.   [60] Ibid., 280; 295; 296.

[61] McCrea, *In the Company of Strangers*, Introduction.

condition exposes an aspect of her much-celebrated progressive frankness concerning sex and sexuality that is less than comfortable for contemporary readers: the debts it owes not only to the discourses and vocabulary of the eugenics movement but also to its normative commitments and proscriptions.

'I'd be afraid to have a child': O'Brien's Eugenic Romances

Notwithstanding the debateable sympathy with which Reggie's inner life is handled—his refusal to confront his mother's impending death is presented as a psychologically coherent but nevertheless embarrassing failure of masculine self-possession—O'Brien's depiction of his physical appearance and fumbling efforts at seduction are consistently inflected with a tacit eugenicist disquiet, often verging on revulsion:

> He was a large wreck of a man, and although he had the habit of moving with caution, a non-adjustment between his big, virile bones and his increasing flaccidity kept him clumsy. His flesh, uniformly red, was dry and flaky about his mouth and bulging neck, and sweaty on his forehead and hands. His hair, which Teresa remembered thick and dark and wavy, had receded completely from his temples and the top of his head, and was only a dusty straggle about his ears and the back of his skull. His eyes, well set, and once quite fine with a spark of impudent virility, were lashless and bloodshot, and the black brows above them thinned away to untidy tufts. His teeth were discoloured and broken; his hands thick, hot and beautifully cared for. His whole appearance had an exaggerated, antiseptic immaculacy. He was a wreck, but still, in the tilt of his shoulders, and in the smile that now lit his face for Teresa, there were revealed the tatters of a commonplace charm, a departed power to please women.[62]

The passage is worth quoting at length not only for the tensions it reveals between O'Brien's liberal (or, at least, anti-censorious) candour and her eugenicist investments but for the ways in which it reveals these principles to be co-extensive. In its particulars—hair loss, skin irritation, tooth decay—the description offers an accurate, if somewhat sensationalized, depiction of

---

[62] O'Brien, *The Ante-Room*, 21–22.

the effects of mercury treatment, a remedy often more harmful than the infection it was intended to combat.[63] This graphic detail and unwillingness to euphemize the nature or ramifications of Reggie's condition clearly seem intended to affront the prudery and state-mandated culture of silence with which O'Brien appears to have associated the Censorship of Publications Act. However, in its emphasis on Reggie's flabby impotence, decayed virility, and implicitly feminine fastidiousness, the passage betrays an investment in a eugenic ideal of normative masculinity and physical ability reproduced through well-regulated generative sexual activity. While these features of the description may well form part of a performative evocation of the nexus of degenerationist anxieties and naturalist aesthetics the novel's 1880 setting evokes, they also seem to suggest that O'Brien's paradigm for determining the suitability or 'fitness' of a union was closely bound up with contemporary sexual science.

The Ante-Room's image of a childless union compacted for reasons of palliative care and financial gain stands in sharp contrast to *Without My Cloak*, which, as has been noted, presented the Considine family as an ever-expanding clan of hyper-fertile, middle-class Catholics sorely in need of a reliable method of contraception. While in *Without My Cloak* Teresa still possesses the same all-encompassing desire to see Reggie cured 'so that he might marry and she might see his sons before she died', in the earlier novel Teresa's syphilitic son is presented as the exception to an otherwise healthy and fertile generation of Catholic bourgeoisie, confident in its capacity to 'reproduce' itself both socially and sexually:

> She had grandchildren now. Her eldest daughter, Alice, married these four years to young Dr Condon of Galway, was about to have her third child this summer. Moreover, Daniel, Teresa's third son, who was on the Stock Exchange, was engaged to a nice, healthy girl, and would no doubt be quick to reproduce himself when wedded. And Marie-Rose had become engaged at Easter.[64]

No such quiet confidence bolsters *The Ante-Room*, whose cast is depicted as increasingly isolated from this familial network in a home which has 'grown

---

[63] Claude Quétel, *History of Syphilis* (Cambridge: Polity Press, 1990), 31–32; Kevin Brown, *The Pox: The Life and Near Death of a Very Social Disease* (Stroud: Sutton Publishing, 2006), 23–25. For nineteenth-century attitudes and approaches to syphilis as a medical and social issue, see Quétel, *History of Syphilis*, chap. 5.

[64] O'Brien, *Without My Cloak*, 422–23.

very quiet'.[65] There are shades of Ibsen in this narrative emphasis on a relationship which pointedly offends against a model of social reproduction rooted in generative (and eugenic) sexual activity. Like *Ghosts* (1881), the *Ante-Room* suggests that the social order it dramatizes is too constraining of desire, invested in propriety, and inimical to honest discussion of emotional and sexual matters to deserve or be capable of anything other than iterative decay. Likewise, in its image of an insular community in which Catholic social teaching conspires to frustrate the desires of the most 'virile', able, and attractive, while, at the same time, endorsing a dysgenic union such as Reggie's, there is more than a hint of Synge in *The Ante-Room*'s bleak outlook. Most obviously, Vincent—alongside Dr Curran, the most eligible and eugenically appealing male inhabitant of Mellick presented in the novel—dies without having fathered a child. There is no younger generation figured or suggested in the text to take up the narrative as the cast of *The Ante-Room* does from *Without My Cloak*. Likewise, while notionally undertaken so that Agnes and Marie-Rose may 'flower again', there is something pointedly backward-looking in the emotional and psychological framing of Vincent's suicide.[66] While undoubtedly presented in conversation with the tradition of Catholic martyrdom traced by English, Vincent's decision to take his own life is also pointedly framed in terms of the unresolved Oedipal imbroglio to which his relationship with Agnes presents the apparent solution. This is clearest in the novel's concluding sentences, which transcribe Vincent's final thoughts: 'Darling mother. He smiled. He could see every detail of her smile. Darling mother. He pulled the trigger, his thoughts far off in boyhood.'[67] This insistent Freudian transposition of Agnes and Vincent's mother, whose traumatic early death appears to have arrested Vincent's psycho-sexual development, is a recurrent motif of the novel, and is presented as central to Vincent's attraction to his wife's sister:

'When I'm tired the two of you get mixed in my head. But she wasn't ever, I should think, as beautiful as you. Only she had the trick you have—of somehow being perfection!'

She took his hands and kissed them.

'It seems to me,' she said, 'that she passed on that trick to you! Oh, I love you so much, so much!'

[...]

---

[65] O'Brien, *The Ante-Room*, 7.   [66] Ibid., 304.   [67] Ibid., 306.

'If you're ever the mother of a son,' he sobbed, 'oh, don't die until he's hardened to the idea!'

'I'd be afraid to have a child! There's too much in this business of attachment!'[68]

Read in the light of his remarks concerning the interchangeability of Agnes and his mother in his memory and affections, Vincent's insistence that Agnes should not die before her prospective son has sufficiently 'hardened' takes on a suggestively Freudian complexion. However, rather than resolve this Oedipal attachment through a primitivist escape to the idealized, neo-Hellenist landscape of 'Aegean hills', 'Adriatic rocks', and 'children with [Agnes] for mother' he envisages while trying to persuade Agnes to run away with him, Vincent ends his life with an act of fatal nostalgia.[69] Indeed, as Agnes's remarks suggest, not only does Vincent's sublimated incestuous desire root him in a past he is unable to transcend, but the attachment to which it gives rise likewise robs her of her willingness to reproduce, frustrating any apparent futurity that might be signalled by the respectable, if unsatisfying marriage the novel implies she will compact with Dr Curran. By having its most traditionally virile male character kill himself before having fathered a child, leaving behind a lover who has foresworn children and who concludes the novel wishing that she 'could only die', O'Brien's novel seems to augur no future for a society in which Catholic doctrine governs romantic and sexual behaviour.[70]

Yet, by staking the tragic character of its conclusion upon the frustration of this eugenic union and the flourishing of its dysgenic counterpart (Reggie's marriage), the novel reveals the tensions and contradictions that awaited those who employed eugenic thought as a mechanism to critique conservative and pro-natalist sexual cultures. The eugenicist perspective O'Brien adopts in *The Ante-Room* allows her to indict Irish Catholic doctrine and social teaching concerning sex and sexuality by implying that, in prohibiting divorce and disrupting the free and open acknowledgement of desire and the discussion of its consequences, Irish Catholic culture was obstructing its own most cherished reproductive ends and, in the process, compromising the physical and mental well-being of future generations of its adherents. The 'genealogical imperative' of the nineteenth-century novel is thus not, as a McCrea-inspired reading would have it, deconstructed or

---

[68] Ibid., 255.   [69] Ibid., 258.   [70] Ibid., 301.

queered, so much as suspended in order that its absence might be mourned. Likewise, in implying that candour regarding sexuality was valuable precisely because, without it, it would be impossible to determine who should or should not reproduce and under what circumstances, O'Brien unintentionally reveals the extent to which, for those who sought to wed a eugenic approach to sex and sexuality with a liberal political outlook, a commitment to freedom (particularly of expression and sexual activity) and an investment in equality could come into direct conflict. While it is clear that O'Brien believes the Catholic Church's opposition to divorce and its censorious proscriptions concerning the discussion of sex and reproduction are a dysgenic threat to the propagation of Irish society, it is less clear that she is certain that a figure such as Reggie should enjoy the same freedom to pursue relationships as his more biologically 'fit' siblings. O'Brien was not alone in confronting this difficulty, and the moments of strain it generates in her work reflect a tension at the heart of both the eugenics movement and the twentieth-century liberal-democratic state when confronted with the need to balance individual freedoms with the demands of public health.

'King Demos must be bred like all other kings': Liberty, Equality, and Eugenics

The question of whether a 'liberal eugenics' is possible, and, if so, desirable, remains a live one to this day.[71] As many commentators have noted, in a post-Holocaust world, the phrase can sound almost oxymoronic.[72] The term 'eugenics' has become so indelibly associated with state-mandated programmes of forced sterilization, mass extermination, and fantasies of 'racial purity', that it has come to function for many as a self-evident signifier of moral reprehensibility.[73] Even before the rise of Hitler, the eugenics

---

[71] For an influential recent attempt to outline a 'liberal eugenics', see Nicholas Agar, *Liberal Eugenics: In Defence of Human Enhancement* (Oxford: Blackwell, 2004).

[72] For commentators such as Jürgen Habermas and Michael J. Sandel, to attempt to accommodate the principles of eugenics within a liberal political framework is to arrive at a model of liberalism so far removed from traditional understandings of the term as to no longer merit the name. Jürgen Habermas, *The Future of Human Nature* (Cambridge: Polity Press, 2003), chap. 6; Michael J. Sandel, *The Case Against Perfection: Ethics in the Age of Genetic Engineering* (Cambridge, Mass: Belknap Press, 2007), chap. 4.

[73] The convolutions and solipsisms to which the debate has given rise are captured in the tongue-in-cheek title of a recent survey of the topic, 'How Liberal is (the Liberal Critique) of a Liberal Eugenics?' Nathan Van Camp, 'How Liberal Is (the Liberal Critique) of a Liberal Eugenics?,' *HUMANA.MENTE Journal of Philosophical Studies* 7, no. 26 (May 2014), 223–38.

movement was being critiqued for its apparent disregard for individual liberty and its failure to value all human life equally. In a detailed and even-handed discussion of 'The Catholic Church and Race Culture' featured in the *Dublin Review* in 1911, the English cleric Thomas J. Gerrard detected in the eugenic 'zeal for reform' the seeds of nascent 'oppression':

> Feeble-mindedness is so often a cause of poverty, and poverty so often a cause of feeble-mindedness, that there is a danger of confusing one with the other. Catholics, therefore, need to exercise a strong vigilance, lest, under pretence of eugenic reform, the rights of the poor are infringed. Poverty is no bar to the sacrament of marriage.[74]

Such objections were not confined to Catholic ecclesiastical circles. As early as 1901, G. K. Chesterton could be found arguing in a review of Karl Pearson's *National Life from the Standpoint of Science* (1901) that, in advocating the 'crushing and driving out' of 'weaker and more barbarous races', eugenics constituted little more than the 'principle of the survival of the nastiest' and the 'great biological morality of kicking a man when he's down'.[75] Returning to the topic in 1922, Chesterton presented eugenics as an exemplary manifestation of a 'modern craze for scientific officialism and strict social organization' which, in seeking to bring marriage and sex within the purview of modern medical bureaucracy, proposed 'to control some families [...] as if they were families of pagan slaves'.[76] For Chesterton, any positive liberty gained through the physical and mental improvements eugenics purported to offer were greatly outweighed by the compromise to negative liberty which institutionally administered eugenics would entail.[77] The influential new liberal, L. T. Hobhouse, concurred, arguing that if 'racial

---

[74] Rev Thomas J. Gerrard, 'The Catholic Church and Race Culture,' *Dublin Review* 149 (July 1911), 62. Gerrard argued that while Galton's overall aim was commendable, the movement he had inspired was hampered by both its materialism and its identification with figures such as Shaw and Nietzsche, who sponsored little more than 'a complete return to the life of the beast' (Gerrard, 53). Furthermore, insofar as eugenics was compatible with liberty, equality, and Christian ethics, Gerrard argued, its aims were already being met by the Catholic Church and its programmes of Catholic action (Gerrard, 61–68). Gerrard eventually extended this article and its arguments into a book-length discussion of the topic. Rev Thomas J. Gerrard, *The Church and Eugenics* (London: P.S. King & Son, 1917).

[75] G. K. Chesterton, 'Science and Patriotism,' *The Speaker: The Liberal Review*, 2 February 1901, 488.

[76] G. K. Chesterton, *Eugenics and Other Evils* (London: Cassell and Company, 1922), i; 10.

[77] For an influential outline of the distinction between 'positive' and 'negative' liberty, see Isiah Berlin, 'Two Concepts of Liberty,' in *Liberty*, ed. Henry Hardy (Oxford: Oxford University Press, 2002), 166–217.

progress' was to be sought, it was not through the homogenizing and coercive influence of state-administered programmes of selective breeding:

> [T]he most fundamental necessity from the point of view of racial progress is to maintain an environment in which any new mutation of promise socially considered may thrive and grow, and by this line of argument we arrive once more at the conclusion that liberty, equality of opportunity, and the social atmosphere of justice and considerateness are the most eugenic of agencies.[78]

Echoing Hobhouse, liberal historian W. L. Blease argued that, by ignoring the role of environment in human development, eugenics risked putting the cart before the horse: 'only when all have a chance of survival' would it be possible to 'distinguish the naturally inefficient from the accidentally inefficient'.[79] For figures such as Hobhouse and Blease, only when total equality of opportunity had been achieved could eugenics hope to address inequalities of ability effectively, let alone ethically. Until then, in the absence of a reliable and objective means by which to calculate human 'fitness' and ability, eugenics, through its tendency to conflate inequality of opportunity with inequality of ability, risked offering a biological sanction to a range of pre-existing prejudices. Confronted with poverty, the new liberal periodical the *Nation* argued, the 'eugenist tends to become an aristocrat, morbidly afraid of the 'uneducated'.[80] In the aftermath of the First World War, these arguments were taken up by many within the Labour movement, who viewed the Eugenics Society as a coterie of self-congratulatory elitists for whom poverty and mental disability were indistinguishable. When, in July

---

[78] In the lecture in which these remarks appear, Hobhouse offers an even-handed assessment of 'The Value and Limitations of Eugenics' in which he concludes that, while advocates of eugenics were right to argue that a rational form of artificial selection was preferable to unregulated natural selection, insufficient evidence and consensus existed to support their broader claims about human 'fitness' or licence the illiberal policies through which they sought to cultivate it. Leonard Trelawny Hobhouse, *Social Evolution and Political Theory* (New York: Columbia University Press, 1911), 71. Nevertheless, as Diane Paul notes, Hobhouse did concede that, in the case of the 'feeble-minded'—a group whom it was possible 'to identify with fair precision' and 'whose condition is asserted to be hereditary in a marked degree'—the eugenic case for institutionalization or sterilization was a valid one. Hobhouse, 45–46, quoted in Diane Paul, 'Eugenics and the Left,' *Journal of the History of Ideas* 45, no. 4 (October 1984), 571–72 n. 12.

[79] Walter Lyon Blease, *A Short History of English Liberalism* (London: T. Fisher Unwin, 1913), 340.

[80] 'Eugenics and Social Reform,' *The Nation*, 27 August 1910 quoted in Michael Freeden, *The New Liberalism: An Ideology of Social Reform* (Oxford: Oxford University Press, 1986), 189.

1931, the Labour MP, A. G. Church, sought leave to introduce a bill advocating voluntary sterilization for 'mental defectives', he was robustly denounced by his fellow party member, Hyacinth Morgan, who declared the proposal an ill-considered piece of 'anti-working-class legislation' founded on questionable science and reminded his colleague that society was 'not apical, with the Eugenist at the top and the hoi-polloi in the valley'.[81] In his 1932 primer, *Genetic Principles in Medicine and Social Science*, Lancelot Hogben, a professor in the newly formed Department of Social Biology at the London School of Economics and a vocal member of the Independent Labour Party, claimed that eugenics had become little more than a smoke-screen for 'ancestor worship, anti-Semitism, colour prejudice, anti-feminism, snobbery, and obstruction in educational progress'.[82] In a private letter to A. M. Carr-Saunders the same year, C. P. Blacker, the recently appointed head of the Eugenics Society, conceded that, when confronted with the old-guard of the organization, he struggled to disagree.[83]

Yet, as the example of A. G. Church suggests, a persistent (albeit fluctu-ating) 'ideological affinity' did exist between the eugenics movement and a range of 'progressive' social and political causes in the first decades of the twentieth century.[84] Of the new liberals, Hobhouse's contemporary and sometimes ally, J. A. Hobson, was the most eager to embrace eugenics and

---

[81] 'Sterilization,' *House of Commons Debates* 255 (21 July 1931), cols. 1249–56. John Macnicol emphasizes the fringe status of Church and his views within the party, noting his 'white-collar' union background and his repeated tendency to defy the party whip. John Macnicol, 'Eugenics and the Campaign for Voluntary Sterilization in Britain Between the Wars,' *Social History of Medicine* 2, no. 2 (1989), 162; Macnicol, 'The Voluntary Sterilization Campaign in Britain, 1918-39,' 429.

[82] Lancelot Hogben, *Genetic Principles in Medicine and Social Science* (London: Williams & Norgate, 1932), 210 quoted in Daniel J. Kevles, *In the Name of Eugenics: Genetics and the Uses of Human Heredity* (New York: Knopf, 1985), 123. Hogben was to develop these views further in Lancelot Hogben, 'Race and Prejudice,' in *Dangerous Thoughts* (London: George Allen & Unwin, 1939), 44–58. For an overview of Hogben and his contribution to a left-wing critique of eugenics, see Kevles, *In the Name of Eugenics*, chap. 8; Pauline M. H. Mazumdar, *Eugenics, Human Genetics and Human Failings: The Eugenics Society, Its Sources and Its Critics in Britain* (London: Routledge, 1992), chap. 4; Richard A. Soloway, *Demography and Degeneration: Eugenics and the Declining Birthrate in Twentieth-Century Britain*, 3rd ed. (Chapel Hill: University of North Carolina Press, 2001), chap. 9.

[83] Carlos Paton Blacker to Alexander Morris Carr-Saunders, 6 June 1932, quoted in Soloway, *Demography and Degeneration*, 196.

[84] Michael Freeden, 'Eugenics and Progressive Thought: A Study in Ideological Affinity,' *The Historical Journal* 22, no. 3 (September 1979), 645–71; Michael Freeden, 'Eugenics and Ideology,' *The Historical Journal* 26, no. 4 (December 1983), 959–62; Freeden, *The New Liberalism*, chap. 5. For a critical response to Freeden's account, see Greta Jones, 'Eugenics and Social Policy Between the Wars,' *The Historical Journal* 25, no. 3 (September 1982), 717–28.

what he saw as its potentially transformative contributions to 'national efficiency':

> Though 'stock' and 'race' are not everything in national life and the world struggle, they are most necessary starting-points of profitable study, especially for those who hold that the evolution of mind enables civilised man to economise energy by substituting rational for 'natural' selection and rejection as modes of progress.[85]

Fabians were particularly enthusiastic in their support for eugenics, finding in its model of biological meliorism an extra-moral normative framework through which to justify a variety of socio-economic interventions.[86] Figures such as Caleb Saleeby mobilized eugenic arguments to advocate for a range of social and political reforms, including 'no-fault' divorce, female suffrage, clean-air measures, socialized medicine, and nudism.[87] The latter he openly advocated in *Sunlight and Health* (1923) and tacitly sponsored through the work of the Sunlight League (1924–1940), an organization which promoted heliotherapy (sun-bathing), particularly for children in urban areas.[88] Following her 1924 divorce from the Dutch author-critic, Gustaaf Reiner, the young Kate O'Brien would spend two years serving as publications secretary for the organization and its journal, *Sunlight*, where some of her earliest writing appeared.[89] George Bernard Shaw went further still, arguing that true eugenics necessitated the suspension of a range of bourgeois institutions, particularly private property and marriage.[90] In the

---

[85] John Atkinson Hobson, 'New Books: Mr Wells' Utopia,' *Manchester Guardian*, 25 April 1905, 5; Freeden, *The New Liberalism*, 187.

[86] Freeden, 'Eugenics and Progressive Thought,' 664–65; Paul, 'Eugenics and the Left'; George Robb, 'The Way of All Flesh: Degeneration, Eugenics, and the Gospel of Free Love,' *Journal of the History of Sexuality* 6, no. 4 (April 1996), 589–603; Leo Lucassen, 'A Brave New World: The Left, Social Engineering, and Eugenics in Twentieth-Century Europe,' *International Review of Social History* 55, no. 2 (August 2010), 265–96.

[87] Caleb Williams Saleeby, *Woman and Womanhood: A Search for Principles* (London: Mitchell Kennerley, 1911), chaps. 1, 16, 17, 18, and 19; Caleb Williams Saleeby, *The Eugenic Prospect: National and Racial* (London: T. Fisher Unwin, 1921), pts. 2 and 4. For an overview of Saleeby's engagement with these issues and the potential limitations of his feminism and egalitarianism, see Soloway, *Demography and Degeneration*, 132–37 and 149–62.

[88] Caleb Williams Saleeby, *Sunlight and Health* (London: Nisbett & Co., 1923), 69–70; Philip Carr-Gomm, *A Brief History of Nakedness* (London: Reaktion Books, 2010), 159–60.

[89] Tellingly, O'Brien's biographer, Eibhear Walshe, downplays Saleeby's staunch advocacy of eugenics, euphemistically dubbing him a 'medical reformer' and philanthropist. Walshe, *Kate O'Brien*, 2006, 37–38.

[90] Freeden emphasizes both the relative idiosyncrasy of Shaw's views and the unease his support generated in eugenic circles. Freeden, 'Eugenics and Progressive Thought,' 648.

'Revolutionist's Handbook' which accompanied the published edition of *Man and Superman* (1903), Shaw has the play's protagonist, John Tanner, stress that equality is 'essential to good breeding; and equality, as all economists know, is incompatible with property'.[91] In Tanner's view, class divisions and socio-economic inequality, by 'cut[ting] humanity up into small cliques' and limiting the 'selection of the individual' to their 'own clique', would 'postpone the Superman for eons, if not forever'.[92] Marriage, by conflating 'domesticity' and 'conjugation', was no less dysgenic:

> There is no evidence that the best citizens are the offspring of congenial marriages, or that a conflict of temperament is not a highly important part of what breeders call crossing. On the contrary, it is quite sufficiently probable that good results may be obtained from parents who would be extremely unsuitable companions or partners [...] But mating such couples must clearly not involve marrying them.[93]

A similar argument is articulated in the play's supernatural third act by Don Juan (Tanner's avatar and alleged ancestor), who seeks to persuade Ana and the Devil that marriage is only valuable insofar as it furthers the interest of the 'Life Force'—the governing 'Will' and 'vital power' at the heart of Shaw's quasi-religion of 'Creative Evolution':[94]

> In the sex relation the universal creative energy, of which the parties are both the helpless agents, over-rides and sweeps away all personal considerations and dispenses with all personal relations [...] The pair may be utter strangers to one another, speaking different languages, differing in race and color [*sic*], in age and disposition, with no bond between them but

---

[91] George Bernard Shaw, *Man and Superman: A Comedy and a Philosophy* (Westminster: Archibald Constable & Co, 1903), 186.

[92] Ibid.   [93] Ibid., 186–87.

[94] Shaw himself noted what he presented as the coincidental but providential parallels between his theories of the 'Life Force' and 'Creative Evolution' and Henri Bergson's conception of 'élan vital' as outlined in *L'Évolution créatrice* (1907), which he attributed to the influence of Samuel Butler, whose *Luck, or Cunning, as the Main Means of Organic Modification?* (1886) Shaw had reviewed for the *Pall Mall Gazette* in 1887. George Bernard Shaw, *Bernard Shaw: Collected Letters, 1911–1925*, ed. Dan H. Laurence, vol. 3 (London: Max Reinhardt, 1985), 542–43. For an account of the 'Life Force' and 'Creative Evolution', particularly insofar as they pertain to eugenics, see Warren Sylvester Smith, *Bishop of Everywhere: Bernard Shaw and the Life Force* (University Park: Pennsylvania State University Press, 1982), chaps. 2, 8, 10, and 11; Stuart E. Baker, *Bernard Shaw's Remarkable Religion: A Faith That Fits the Facts* (Gainesville: University Press of Florida, 2002), chaps. 3,6, and 7; Matthew Yde, *Bernard Shaw and Totalitarianism: Longing for Utopia* (Houndmills: Palgrave Macmillan, 2013), chap. 3.

a possibility of that fecundity for the sake of which the Life Force throw them into one another's arms at the exchange of a glance.[95]

Addressing the topic in *propria person* in a published response to Galton's 'Eugenics: Its Definition, Scope, and Aims' (1904), Shaw argued that, in its present form, marriage militated against public health both in its successes and its failures: 'If the selection is eugenically erroneous, there is no remedy. If it is so brilliantly successful that it seems a national loss to limit the husband's progenitive capacity to the breeding capacity of one woman, or the wife's to an experiment with one father' then 'customs and norms' stood no less firmly in the way.[96]

Shaw's vision of how consent was to be gained for the measures necessary to supersede these norms was decidedly circular. In the 'Revolutionist's Handbook', Tanner argues that, since only the 'true Superman' could attain the lofty intellectual perspective necessary to 'snap his superfingers at all Man's present trumpery', only a 'Democracy of Supermen' could be trusted to introduce the measures a eugenic outlook on sex and health rendered necessary.[97] 'King Demos', he wryly notes, 'must be bred like all other kings.'[98] Thus, a 'State Department of Evolution' or 'some organization strong enough to impose respect upon the State' would have to enact eugenic reforms unilaterally in order to secure the consensus necessary to have justified them in the first place.[99] As these remarks imply, in Shaw's view, only eugenics could create the social conditions necessary to render eugenics palatable to the public:

The only fundamental and possible Socialism is the socialization of the selective breeding of Man: in other terms, of human evolution. We must eliminate the Yahoo, or his vote will wreck the commonwealth [...] [T]o hand the country over to riff-raff is national suicide, since riff-raff can neither govern nor will let anyone else govern except the highest bidder of bread and circuses.[100]

While pronouncements such as these were undoubtedly intended to be as playful as they were provocative—it is important to note that Tanner ends

---

[95] Shaw, *Man and Superman: A Comedy and a Philosophy*, 125.
[96] Sociological Society, ed., 'From Mr. G. Bernard Shaw,' in *Sociological Papers* (London: Macmillan, 1905), 74–75.
[97] Shaw, *Man and Superman: A Comedy and a Philosophy*, 194; 198.   [98] Ibid., 223.
[99] Ibid., 220; 222.   [100] Ibid., 219; 223.

Man and Superman a querulously married man—they reflected a commitment to a socialist eugenics premised upon the free operation of the 'Life
Force' that was to remain a mainstay of Shaw's literary and political writing.
Well into the 1930s Shaw could be found insisting that only by removing
'inequality of income' would it be possible for 'Nature' to bring about the
eugenic couplings necessary for a 'well-bred race', devoting a chapter to a
positive discussion of 'Eugenics' in both the 1928 and 1937 editions of *The
Intelligent Woman's Guide to Socialism*.[101] Though, publicly, he was ultimately to deem the possibility of a 'Government department' of eugenics
struggling to 'select our husbands and wives for us' more 'amusing' than
'practicable', in private, Shaw appeared to remain more sanguine on the
topic of state intervention on eugenic grounds, infamously commenting to
fellow Fabian Beatrice Webb in February 1938 that the 'Jewish question'
ought to be tackled 'by admitting the right of States to make eugenic
experiments by weeding out any strains that they think undesirable, but
insisting that they should do it as humanely as they can afford to, and not
shock civilization by such misdemeanors [*sic*] as the expulsion and robbery
of Einstein'.[102]

As her involvement with Saleeby's Sunshine League suggests, Kate
O'Brien's handling of eugenics bears the impress of these debates and
reflects many of their contradictions. On the one hand, she shares with
Chesterton a hostility to the homogenizing and centralizing tendencies of
socio-economic and political modernity, particularly in their illiberal intrusion into the realms of sex and health. In her 1937 travel-guide-cum-eulogy,
Farwell Spain, O'Brien positions herself in opposition to the 'forward
marchers' of contemporary Europe, celebrating what she presents as the
scandalous 'non-utilitarianism', 'individualist excitement', and 'intractable

---

[101] George Bernard Shaw, *The Intelligent Woman's Guide to Socialism and Capitalism* (New
York: Brentano's, 1928), 55. The 1928 edition's chapter on 'Eugenics' was reproduced verbatim
when the book was revised and expanded to form the first two volumes of Allan Lane's new
Pelican series. George Bernard Shaw, *The Intelligent Woman's Guide to Socialism, Capitalism,
Sovietism, and Fascism*, Pelican, vol. 1 (London: Penguin Books, 1937), chap. 16.
[102] Shaw, *The Intelligent Woman's Guide to Socialism and Capitalism*, 54; George Bernard
Shaw, *Bernard Shaw: Collected Letters, 1926–1950*, ed. Dan H. Laurence, vol. 4 (London: Max
Reinhardt, 1988), 493. For a largely charitable account and exculpatory account of Shaw's
engagement with eugenics in the context of his wider political thought, see Gareth Griffith,
Socialism and Superior Brains: The Political Thought of Bernard Shaw (London: Routledge,
1993), 118–20; 178–81; Baker, *Bernard Shaw's Remarkable Religion*, 169–72. For an excoriating
reading of Shaw's eugenic investments which stresses their totalitarian character, see Yde,
Bernard Shaw and Totalitarianism, chaps. 3–5.

beauty' of getting 'away from it all' in a world still sufficiently undeveloped to be variegated in its culture, heritage, and infrastructure:[103]

> Away from it all! That is a cliché of ours which for our great-grandchildren, in their uniformed world, will only have meaning when they die. One thing we can do and they will not find possible—get away from it all. That is a strength, that weakness of ours, which, unless they are indeed to be super-men, they are likely to feel the need of.
>
> […]
>
> Unless gland control can pull off such a monstrous miracle as poor old Christianity never even visualised, our descendants may, I fear, discover themselves to be—if they know the word—unhappy. A happy discovery, I venture incorrigibly to believe. Happy, even if bewildering, even if irredeemable—save by making ducks and drakes of the Home Counties. And someone may even take that retrogressive measure, since, whatever else their model citizens may be, their seed, controlled, conditioned, what-you-willed, may still be supposed to be Adam's. Or is such sentimental implication painfully outmoded?[104]

As the passage's well-advertised, albeit tongue-in-cheek references to endo-crinology ('gland control') and the pseudo-Nietzschean aspirations of both the Nazis and figures such as Shaw ('unless they are indeed to be supermen') make clear, in O'Brien's view, eugenics, in its efforts to 'control', 'condition', and 'what-you-will' human sexual conduct, offends against the 'sentimental individualism' with which she aligns herself throughout the text.[105] On the other hand, while she does not root her conception of sex and sexuality in anything as supernatural as the 'Life Force' or develop it into anything as systematized as 'Creative Evolution', O'Brien shares with Shaw and Saleeby a tendency to use an implicitly eugenic model of health and 'fitness' to naturalize her critique of the social and sexual mores of her contemporary culture.[106]

---

[103] Kate O'Brien, *Farewell Spain*, Repr. (London: Virago, 2006), 13; 17; 15.
[104] Ibid., 15–16.   [105] Ibid., 7.
[106] O'Brien's familiarity with *Man and Superman* is reflected in her 1943 novel, *The Last of Summer*, in which attending a production of the play at the Abbey while an undergraduate at UCD is presented (with a degree of self-indicting circumspection) as a transformative moment in the intellectual development of the protagonist's iconoclastic love interest, Martin Kernahan. Kate O'Brien, *The Last of Summer*, Reprint (London: Virago Press, 1990), 68.

222 IRISH MODERNISM AND THE POLITICS OF SEXUAL HEALTH

A paradox of O'Brien's depiction of sexuality, then, is that the most eugenic unions presented in her work are almost invariably spontaneous affairs, conducted in spite of the social institutions through which eugenic theory was typically envisaged as being administered, while the most dysgenic unions are those which are carefully overseen by concerned avatars of familial, religious, or state authority. In *Without My Cloak*, O'Brien follows Shaw in stressing the equal eugenic fitness of both Anthony Considine, whose 'peasant beauty' and 'bodily fineness' had been 'flung up accidentally' by 'nature's heedless work', and the horse he has stolen, whose 'inbred and high-bred quality' had been carefully cultivated 'through generations of great blood stock' in an 'aristocratic stable'.[107] Indeed, the major thesis of the novel, affirmed through the structural parallel between Anthony's theft of a thoroughbred and the illegitimate 'peasant girl' Christina's seduction of the now affluent Anthony's son, Denis, is that, only by breeding across class lines can 'beauty'—O'Brien's highest and most consistent term of eugenic approbation—be properly cultivated.[108] As this example and the reading of *The Ante-Room* offered above suggest, O'Brien presents desire as a fundamentally asocial force, with little regard for class distinction, Church doctrine, or institutions such as marriage. Terry Eagleton has noted the almost apocalyptic nature of desire in O'Brien's work, claiming that 'sexual love for her is a kind of delicious insanity, a wayward, unmanageable, implacable force which disrupts all settlement and involves an ecstatic casting loose of one's moorings'.[109] However, in stressing the 'wayward' and 'disruptive' quality, Eagleton downplays the ways in which desire operates in O'Brien's novels according to a largely consistent and uniform eugenic logic. As couples such as Agnes and Vincent in *The Ante-Room* indicate, O'Brien seems to believe that, without the interference of conservative social institutions and forces, desire will ultimately bring about unions that are beneficial to the social order and satisfying for all parties. Paradoxically, then, for O'Brien, it is a eugenic necessity and almost a prerequisite of social stability and cohesion that desire be unrestrained and unregulated. In this way, O'Brien seeks to square a Shavian investment in eugenics

---

[107] O'Brien, *Without My Cloak*, 3–4.

[108] Ibid., 290. O'Brien further underscores this point by revealing that Christina is the daughter of the 'second son of a great house in the west' where her mother had been a housemaid, and that this had secured her a claim to 'intellectual aristocracy' alongside her parents' equal 'beauty' (Ibid., 291).

[109] Terry Eagleton, *Crazy John and the Bishop and Other Essays on Irish Culture* (Cork: Cork University Press, 1998), 242.

as a mechanism through which to leverage, or, at least, justify greater socio-economic equality and sexual freedom, with a liberal, Catholic hostility to the coercive homogeneity of technical modernity and the compromises to physical and mental autonomy it was perceived to entail. As in the case of Shaw's 'Democracy of the Superman', undertaking this synthesis could generate moments of palpable strain in O'Brien's work, leading her to endorse a curiously unequal egalitarianism and a sometimes illiberal model of freedom. This strain is perhaps most visible in O'Brien's most explicitly polemical and self-avowedly 'contemporary' work, *Pray for the Wanderer* (1938).

'How they are to breed': Birth Control, Eugenics, and European Politics

Set only a year before its publication date and written as a clear riposte to the social, cultural, and political forces which O'Brien felt had conspired in the suppression of *Mary Lavelle*, *Pray for the Wanderer* is O'Brien's most direct indictment of what she presents as Éamon de Valera's growing political and cultural hegemony in the nascent Republic of Ireland.[110] This contemporary critique is reflected in the novel's setting, with the dénouement of its romantic plot keyed to coincide with the July plebiscite which would ratify the nation's new constitution and cement de Valera's influence on its culture.[111] The plot centres on Matt Costello, an Irish-born author and former IRA member whose books are regularly banned in Ireland and whose latest play, *The Heart of Stone*, is enjoying huge success on the West End. Costello returns to his childhood home in Mellick to stay with his brother, Will, sister-in-law, Una, and their children, to centre himself following the breakdown of his relationship with his lover and muse, Louise Lafleur, the married star of *The Heart of Stone*. During his stay, Matt meets and falls in love with Una's sister Nell, a de Valera devotee who 'teaches world history in Irish', and who was once engaged to Matt's friend and former comrade, Tom Mahoney, an urbane solicitor and sometime moral

[110] For an account of the novel's efforts to confront the perceived cultural politics of the censorship board, see Brad Kent, 'An *argument manqué*: Kate O'Brien's *Pray for the Wanderer*,' *Irish Studies Review* 18, no. 3 (August 2010), 285–98.

[111] Charles Travis, 'The 'Historical Poetics' of Kate O'Brien's Limerick: A Critical Literary Geography of Saorstát Éireann and the 1937 Bunreacht na hÉireann Plebiscite,' *Irish Geography* 42, no. 3 (November 2009), 323–41.

philosopher, but broke off the engagement and fled to Rome when she discovered Mahoney had fathered an illegitimate child in his paramilitary youth.[112] The novel is framed as a competition between Matt's commitment to Louise and the artistically vibrant and sexually liberated milieu with which she is associated and his growing attachment to the principled, but by no means naïve Nell, and the claims of history, tradition, and loyalty she represents. Underpinning Matt's choice between continuing his burgeoning career in cosmopolitan Bloomsbury and returning to Ireland to battle the rising tide of social conservatism and cultural isolation is the worsening political situation in Europe, which the majority of the novel's Irish characters are content to ignore or dismiss. Nell ultimately refuses Matt's proposal of marriage and returns to Tom Mahoney, who finally succeeds in articulating his long-standing feelings for her. The novel ends on a resigned note, with Costello steeling himself to return to London to 'write and in due course die' in that face of 'doom, panic, and despair'.[113]

As this dour ending suggests, notwithstanding its protagonist's impeccable liberal credentials, the novel is decidedly ambivalent in the model of individual liberty and intellectual and sexual freedom it articulates, especially when viewed in relation to the wider European context which O'Brien is so keen to evoke. For Matt (and, implicitly, O'Brien), the contemporary political moment is one in which liberal individualism ('freedom for everyone') is assailed on all sides by a bellicose and expansionist totalitarianism, intent on the management of every level of its citizens' private lives:[114]

> [G]rown men taking instructions from this little creature or that as to how they shall think; how, or if they shall pray; how they are to breed, what work they must do, how many rooms they may occupy; what salute they must give to what flag, and what songs they must sing. Abyssinia, China, Spain. Spain—one of Europe's eternal glories—tearing herself apart, not being hindered. The same doom awaiting every country in every other country's re-armament intentions. Man's courageous, individual heart undiscoverable everywhere.[115]

Such comparisons serve both to reinsert Ireland into a European intellectual and political milieu from which it had been complacently willing to insulate itself, and to align the 'curious anomalies' and 'alarming signposts' of the

---

[112] O'Brien, *Pray for the Wanderer*, 54.   [113] Ibid., 183.   [114] Ibid., 19.
[115] Ibid., 29.

proposed constitution with the worst authoritarian excesses of that milieu.[116] The novel abounds in indictments of Ireland under de Valera as a dictatorship in the making.[117] In several of Matt's extended reflections on his homeland, 'Dev' is presented as a thoroughly 'up-to-date' statesman, cut from the same authoritarian cloth as Franco, Mussolini, Hitler, and Stalin, though he deems him 'a more subtle dictator' than his Fascist and Communist counterparts.[118] However, when O'Brien comes to discuss the topic of sex and sexuality—one of the areas of 'personal liberty' she is most eager to defend—the novel's investments in reproductive freedom, freedom of conscience, and gender equality come into visible tension. While O'Brien may spend much of the novel eagerly decrying those who would tell the populations of Europe 'how they are to breed', in *Pray for the Wanderer* she nevertheless seems to maintain an equally well-developed sense of how they ought not to breed.

Both Matt's relationships and the narrative structure of the novel's romance plot are consistently shaped by an implied personal and narratorial investment in the teachings of eugenics and its sister discipline, sexology. As the preponderance of salmon imagery in the novel suggests, Matt's return to Ireland is, in part, framed as a migration to the place of his birth where he is expected to breed and ultimately extinguish himself. This narrative current is made most explicit when, confronted with an upsetting telegram from his former lover in London, Matt places the missive in his breast pocket and

---

[116] Ibid., 30.

[117] O'Brien was far from alone in viewing de Valera as an autocrat in the making in the mid–1930s. De Valera's decision, upon taking over as President of the Executive Council from Cosgrave in 1932, to dismiss Eoin O'Duffy as the Commissioner of the Garda Síochána was perceived by many in pro-Treaty circles as the beginnings of an anti-democratic Republican power-grab. The *Irish Times* remarked that, if a 'public servant' of O'Duffy's standing was 'liable to lose his office at the desire of a minority', then it was 'time that President de Valera should abandon his pretence of democracy.' For some, de Valera could not abandon this pretence quickly enough. In the eyes of W. B. Yeats, de Valera's greatest fault lay not in his authoritarian tendencies, but in his want of conviction in pursuing them. The poet initially identified de Valera's ascent to power with a 'heroic' turn in Irish politics in which 'any one' of 'half a dozen men' might become a new 'Caesar'. However, as 'Parnell's Funeral' (1934, rev. 1935) and its accompanying paratexts suggest, this optimism was relatively short-lived. *Irish Times*, 16 March 1933, quoted in Fearghal McGarry, *Eoin O'Duffy: A Self-Made Hero* (Oxford: Oxford University Press, 2007), 201; John Kelly et al., eds., *The Collected Letters of W.B. Yeats*, InteLex Electronic Edition (Oxford University Press, 2002), 5915. For a survey of recent scholarship putting pressure on traditional understandings of Ireland in the 1930s as an increasingly conservative monoculture fashioned in de Valera's image, see Ferriter, *The Transformation of Ireland*, chap. 5 and Diarmaid Ferriter, *Judging Dev: A Reassessment of the Life and Legacy of Eamon de Valera* (Dublin: Royal Irish Academy, 2007).

[118] O'Brien, *Pray for the Wanderer*, 30.

accompanies Nell and Una's son Liam to the river: 'Liam skipped and
shouted as the great fish hurled themselves at the leap. Matt held his left
arm tight against the pocket in his breast, and set himself resolutely to watch
for the heroic, up-going curves of the great salmon.'[119] As a result of this
moment and the conversation to which it gives rise, Matt decides to purchase a salmon-rod Nell has asked for ('The salmon of knowledge, Liam.
Aunt Nell's an Irish scholar and knows his noble place in Irish literature')
which will ultimately catalyse the novel's romantic plot by prompting him to
confess his attraction to her.[120] Prior to this point in the novel, Matt's lover
and muse, Louise, has been framed as the source of a creativity which
O'Brien makes synonymous with his sexual vitality. Discussing Stephen
Dedalus's characterization of Hamlet's return to Elsinore in the 'Scylla and
Charybdis' episode of *Ulysses* with his soon-to-be romantic rival, Tom
Mahoney, Matt reflects:

> Is it time to plant the mulberry tree? Oh, barrenness. Is it not enough to be
> in flight? The positive strength required for that makes it almost seem
> creative. But there whence he fled was the seed. There, in that face, where
> roses and soft lilies blow, he had found at his most emptied moment a
> personal answer to contemporary negation; found that which he had long
> ceased to look for. And found it good and durable. His seed, his potency.[121]

The seminal imagery with which the passage is laced and the juxtaposition
between 'barrenness' and fecundity upon which it is premised are so obvious
as to need almost no gloss: in the face of the 'contemporary negation' of
rising totalitarianism, philistinism, and censorship, Matt's pursuit of exile
and his attraction to Louise vouchsafe his generative intellectual and sexual
capacities.

What ultimately breaks this attachment and prompts Matt's return to the
streams of his youth is Louise's refusal to leave her 'kind, condoning, self-
centred, impotent' (and ironically named) husband, Adam Wolfe: 'You
won't be my lover, now the big, useless blond is home again?'[122] As these
remarks suggest, Costello's contempt for Wolfe is justified on almost entirely
sexological and eugenic grounds, indicting his lack of virility, his superficial
good looks (and the effeminate care with which he maintains them), and a
never explicitly articulated, but heavily queer-coded, sexual defect:

[119] Ibid., 82.   [120] Ibid., 99.   [121] Ibid., 43.   [122] Ibid., 89.

'Oh, my God! Divorce *him*, Louise!' 'I can't. There's no evidence. There never will be. Besides–' 'Besides, you don't want to!' 'No, perhaps I don't. For ordinary purposes our tame arrangement suits me.' '"Tame" is right. And within its tidiness there is no room for me.'

[...]

'He isn't *impotent*, Matt!' 'Oh no, not technically—but *impotent*, I say— returns at last from Hollywood, and refuses to have his domestic pattern broken up, his publicity spoilt, his fans disappointed, refuses to lose his façade as Louise Lafleur's magnificent and enviable husband—because he knows that he could never get another normally sexed woman of your fame to stay with him–'[123]

While Louise's sympathy for her husband's 'very touching' and 'alarming' plight is framed as a commendable index of her progressive credentials and emotional generosity, there is no doubt that Wolfe's queerness and aversion to physical intimacy are presented as pathological aberrations which render him a mediocre figure in comparison to the 'strange vitality' of Matt and an inappropriate partner for the 'normally sexed' Louise:[124]

But in the end I find his plight very touching—and alarming [...] I've seen him crying and humiliated and miserable. I've seen him at his very worst, and at his most unhappy [...] Before me there were women—who wouldn't stand things, and left him. He has told me. You see how grotesque it is. He looks like a natural ladies' man, doesn't he? Cut out for it, and he likes women. And they like him! Go to any of his films, any of his matinées. He has made an immense success on the suggestion of possessing immeas- urably the quality he hasn't got at all—sexual energy. He just hasn't got it. There's nothing wrong with him, and he *isn't* impotent, Matt—he's just unimaginative and inept in feeling—and infrequent. He likes what is called 'petting'—real feeling seams out of his range. And of course he has always devoted so much of his life to the sacred business of preserving his physical beauty that—oh, I suppose a lot of virility has escaped into that.[125]

In its presentation of Wolfe as a physically and emotionally immature figure, unable to progress beyond adolescent sexual fumbling ('he likes what is called "petting"—real feeling is out of his range') and an emasculating

---

[123] Ibid., 88–89. Emphasis O'Brien's.   [124] Ibid., 91; 90.   [125] Ibid., 91.

self-regard ('the sacred business of preserving his physical beauty'), this pseudo case history draws heavily on contemporary sexological and psycho-analytic understandings of bisexuality. In contrast to the present-day desig-nation of bisexuality as a sexual orientation and an identity category involving allosexual attraction to people of all genders, late nineteenth- and early twentieth-century sexology and evolutionary theory used the term to denote both embryonic hermaphroditism, sexual dimorphism, and the co-existence of male and female sex characteristics (male nipples, female facial hair, and a range of intersex traits) in human and animal bodies.[126] Extrapolating from this biological model, Freud conjectured a no less cap-acious conception of bisexuality as an infantile and atavistic psycho-sexual stage out of which a healthy individual would eventually develop along a stable heterosexual axis.[127] Alongside its ironic indictment of his deficient masculinity, the Edenic ring of Adam's name thus seems intended to convey a sense of this originary condition of sexual immaturity, against which Matt's much remarked 'sex appeal' is meant to bulk all the larger.[128] Thus, while sexology allows O'Brien to write with a measure of candour and sympathy about the gendered and sexual non-conformity of Wolfe, her eugenic investments generate a structural tension between such sympathy and the dictates of the romance plot upon which the novel is notionally premised: 'touching' though Wolfe's plight might be, there is little doubt that, in O'Brien's view, Matt is the more 'fit' and fitting partner for a woman of Louise's talent and beauty. O'Brien seems to foreground this point when she has a distressed Nell emphasize, following's Matt's profession of love for her, that if Matt had only 'stopped talking, and kissed her' he might have 'captured her love', despite her insistence that they could not marry.[129] Whatever the virtues of Nell's final reconciliation with Tom and the rap-prochement it is intended to signal between the conservative Republic and its revolutionary past, readers are undoubtedly invited to feel a pang of eugenic regret that the 'noble' and 'aristocratic' Nell, whose beauty appealed

[126] For an account of this development and its social, cultural, and epistemological implica-tions, see Steven Angelides, *A History of Bisexuality* (Chicago: University of Chicago Press, 2001), chap. 2.
[127] Freud most influentially expounded this theory in the *Drei Abhandlungen Zur Sexualtheorie* (1905) [three essays on sexuality], in which he stated that, without taking 'der Bisexualität' [bisexuality] into account as a starting-point for human psycho-sexual develop-ment, 'wird man kaum zum Verständnis der tatsächlich zu beobachtenden Sexualäußerungen von Mann und Weib gelangen können' [one will hardly be able to understand the actually observed sexual expressions of men and women.] Sigmund Freud, *Drei Abhandlungen Zur Sexualtheorie* (Leipzig und Wien: Franz Deuticke, 1905), 62.
[128] O'Brien, *Pray for the Wanderer*, 163.   [129] Ibid.

to 'sophisticated tastes', and the talented and dynamic Costello, a taller and more rugged 'Napoleon', will not raise a family together.[130]

Perhaps unsurprisingly, this eugenic tendency is perhaps most visible when the novel discusses the children of Will and Una, particularly their daughter, Maire. *Pray for the Wanderer* is positively exuberant in its disdain for Maire, who is made the butt of many jibes, both diegetic and narratorial. Matt deems Maire 'the dullest of the children', and, when Una jests that Nell is 'terrified' that any of Una's children 'may grow to have as good a figure as she has', Matt restrains himself from reflecting that 'it was clear that Maire would not'.[131] At multiple points in the novel the child is singled out for being intellectually unprepossessing, physically unassuming, and possessed of an unrestrained appetite—a fatal trifecta in O'Brien's scheme of values. Matt avoids inviting Maire on trips into town with him and her brother Liam ('that would have meant inviting Maire too, who bored him. Matt was never willing to suffer boredom') and salves her with 'presents and chocolates—a sop for which Maire forgave much'.[132] Crucially, this pattern of Maire-bashing culminates in a passage in which Matt confronts her parents, Una and Will, about their attitude to birth control, and implores Una not to compromise her vitality further through another pregnancy:

'We'll have another child before Christmas,' Una said.
[...]
'Six! My Heavens!'
'Don't be silly. Why not six? Why not twelve?'
'No, Una. Not one more than six. Do you hear?'
She laughed with deep amusement.
[...]
'But it isn't fair to them—to exhaust yourself, to grow ill and old—'[133]

To justify this Stopesian plea, Matt offers the example of his immediate family: of ten births, seven survived with '[n]o money' and 'no real love from the elders to direct' them, and, of those seven, only he and Will 'have got something worth living out of life'.[134] Adopting a well-worn Catholic counter-argument, Una ripostes that it is not Matt's place to determine that his sisters would 'have been better unborn' and chastises him for being so 'cocksure and materialistic'.[135] In Una's view, '[l]ife is worth living,

---

[130] Ibid., 77; 149.   [131] Ibid., 69.   [132] Ibid., 97.   [133] Ibid., 138.
[134] Ibid., 139.   [135] Ibid.

on most terms', and the Catholic Church is right to insist 'that man is a spirit' and that it is their 'duty to go on propagating him to the glory of God'.[136] Countering that Una is almost alone in that conviction now, Matt encourages Una to look around the other families in her social orbit:

> 'Yes, you're still Catholics—but in the middle class already with a difference. Look about you, Una. Count up any other young families of six that you know.'
>
> She smiled graciously in defeat.[137]

The exchange is a representative one in a novel often lamented for being self-congratulatory in its cosmopolitan liberalism and 'impotent' and 'self-defeating' in its critique of Catholic bourgeois hypocrisy.[138] More interesting, however, and less self-assured is the discussion that immediately follows this contretemps. Asked by Matt what kind of child she is hoping for this time, Una replies:

> 'I'd like to have a raving beauty of a daughter.'
>
> 'You have two already.'
>
> 'Don't be so correct. Una bán looks like being lovely—but Maire is plain. You know she is.'
>
> 'I know nothing of the kind.'
>
> 'Oh, Matt! The poor child *is* plain. It's most unfair—because look at these boys with their unnecessarily lovely faces! And she really is a nice kid—though I know she bores you. You know, Matt, when I consider the bland insolence of men, creatures like you and my cousin Tom, I could die of guilt towards Maire for having made her plain!'
>
> He laughed delightedly.
>
> 'Of all the nonsense!'
>
> 'It isn't nonsense. It's a fearful thing to be a downright plain woman—unless you're a saint or a genius. And I honestly see no hope of Maire's being either. But perhaps this new child will be perfect!'[139]

---

[136] Ibid.   [137] Ibid.   [138] Kent, 'An *argument manqué*,' 285.
[139] O'Brien, *Pray for the Wanderer*, 139–40.

On its surface, the passage offers a feminist critique of a beauty standard that denies 'downright plain' women such as Maire a meaningful position in a social order governed by the 'bland insolence of men'. However, the agency Una ascribes to herself in expressing her regrets over Maire ('I could die of guilt towards Maire for having made her plain!') and her, albeit tongue-in-cheek, desire to have a 'perfect' child, sit oddly with her earlier conviction that life is 'worth living on most terms' and that it is the duty of devout Catholics to 'go on propagating' it without regard to the difficulties it entails for those who would 'have been better unborn'. While it would be a gross over-statement to claim that O'Brien actively indicts Una for having allowed such an apparently mediocre specimen as Maire to have been conceived, like the Anthony-Molly plot in *Without My Cloak*, or the narratorial anachronism of *The Ante-Room*, this moment seems intended to prompt O'Brien's readers to recognize that a solution to Una's wishes for a 'perfect' child exists, if only she were prepared to look past her middle-class Catholic foibles: the strategies of artificial selection advocated by eugenics. As any good follower of Stopes or Galton would be able to tell Una, she might have avoided having 'made' Maire plain, if she had only better regulated her fertility. In *Pray for the Wanderer*, as in so much of O'Brien's writing, while eugenics discourse may allow her to offer a liberal critique of the unreflective pro-natalism of Irish Catholic culture and its casual disregard for women's well-being, the mode of sexual 'common sense' it allows her to sponsor in their place risks imposing serious limits on the scope of her egalitarian politics.

Conclusion

As the cross-section of O'Brien's work and the wider terrain of Irish feminist responses to pro-natalism offered here has demonstrated, the birth control and eugenics movements provided a set of decidedly double-edged political and rhetorical tools for those who sought to oppose the growing conservatism of the newly independent nation. On the one hand, the work of figures like Marie Stopes and Margaret Sanger provided a vocabulary through which to discuss female desire, sexual pleasure, and the physical and emotional costs of pregnancy and childbirth in an amoral register and offered a public health framework through which to justify doing so. It also provided a means by which to take a debate about censorship and fertility that was often conducted at the level of sectarian demography and in male-dominated environments and refocus it on the bodies of the women whom it was most likely to affect. On the other hand, as so much of O'Brien's fiction reflects, the difficulties of squaring the top-down, institutionally administered model of sexuality upon which much eugenic thought rested with the egalitarian liberalism that she and others cherished often led to writing which espoused a curiously etiolated, or, at the very least, inconsistent model of freedom and equality. Embracing the birth control movement's use of arguments from positive eugenics to critique the social policy and insular mindset of Irish Catholicism and de Valera's government made it difficult to avoid tacitly and sometimes explicitly embracing arguments from negative eugenics about who should be free to enjoy the social and sexual freedoms under discussion. O'Brien's oeuvre shows how, even in the work of a figure widely celebrated for her liberalizing influence, both positions could co-exist in apparently irresolvable tension.

PART IV
SEXUAL HEALTH AND EXHAUSTION

6

'Veni, V.D., Vici!': Flann O'Brien, Sexual Health, and the Exhaustion of Irish Modernism

In critical circles, Flann O'Brien's *The Hard Life* (1961) has more than lived up to its name. Despite enjoying positive reviews and relative commercial success on publication, the novel—a *Bildungsroman* set in turn-of-the-century Dublin, composed in the closest Brian O'Nolan ever came to a style of scrupulous meanness—is widely held to be among the author's weakest efforts.[1] What scholarly work *The Hard Life* has generated has tended to take its cue from the text's subtitle—'An Exegesis of Squalor'—to focus on its status as a failure or to interrogate its more onerous features. Tess Hurson and Neil Murphy contend that *The Hard Life* is most instructive as a guide to what is best about O'Nolan's other fiction, with Hurson suggesting that its 'conspicuous absences' are best taken as a template for better understanding the virtuoso efforts of *At Swim-Two-Birds* (1939) and *The Third Policeman* (written *c.* 1939–1940, published 1967).[2] Neil R. Davison and Maebh Long find in it an exemplary catalogue of O'Nolan's misogynistic tendencies, foregrounding his disgust over female corporeality, his minimizing of female intellect, and his consistent sidelining of women in general.[3] For Carol Taaffe, the novel reflects O'Nolan's implicit repudiation of the unmarketable experimentation of his early work in favour of a more 'commercial' style, while, for Hugh Kenner, its 'Joycean

---

[1] For an aggregate of the reviews, positive and negative, the novel enjoyed upon its release see Tess Hurson, 'Conspicuous Absences: *The Hard Life*', in *Conjuring Complexities: Essays on Flann O'Brien*, ed. Anne Clune and Tess Hurson (Belfast: Institute of Irish Studies, The Queen's University of Belfast, 1997), n. 3, p. 178.

[2] Hurson, 'Conspicuous Absences'; Neil Murphy, 'Flann O'Brien's The Hard Life & the Gaze of the Medusa', *Review of Contemporary Fiction* 31, no. 3 (Fall 2011), 148–61.

[3] Maebh Long, *Assembling Flann O'Brien* (London: Bloomsbury Academic, 2014), chap. 4; Neil R Davison, ' "We Are Not a Doctor for the Body": Catholicism, the Female Grotesque, and Flann O'Brien's *The Hard Life*', *Literature and Psychology: A Journal of Psychoanalytic and Cultural Criticism* 45, no. 4 (1999), 31–57.

Irish Modernism and the Politics of Sexual Health. Lloyd (Meadhbh) Houston, Oxford University Press.
© Lloyd (Meadhbh) Houston 2023. DOI: 10.1093/oso/9780192889492.003.0007

rescriptions' are manifestations of an impotent Oedipal *ressentiment*, in which 'mythic readings of Irish life' are revealed to be 'impossible and absurd'.[4] Even in the most charitable critical appraisals of the novel, a lexicon of weariness, fatigue and exhaustion predominates.[5] After a hard life, the consensus goes, Brian O'Nolan was spent.

In my concluding chapter, I want to take O'Nolan's final novel as the starting point for an examination of what might be at stake in this 'exhaustion', not only for O'Nolan but for Irish modernism more broadly, in relation to issues of sexual health. If, as Anthony Cronin reflects in a late issue of *The Bell*, the culturally and economically torpid Ireland of the 1950s had offered an exemplary 'climate for the death wish', by the 1960s conditions were looking less morbid.[6] While Diarmaid Ferriter rightly warns against the unqualified optimism of Fergal Tobin's 1984 study, *The Best of Decades*, the early 1960s nevertheless marked a period of liberalization, modernization, and relative prosperity for the Republic.[7] Though its 'seminal' status and uniformly beneficial impact have often been overstated, the First Programme for Economic Expansion (1959–1963), which signalled the Lemass government's increasing commitment to free trade policy, exceeded even the expectations of its instigators, yielding a 35 per cent rise in the value of the country's exports in little over a year.[8] By the Programme's end,

---

[4] Carol Taaffe, *Ireland Through the Looking-Glass: Flann O'Brien, Myles na gCopaleen and Irish Cultural Debate* (Cork: Cork University Press, 2008), 184; Hugh Kenner, *A Colder Eye: The Modern Irish Writers* (Baltimore: Johns Hopkins University Press, 1989), 260; Mary Power, 'Flann O'Brien and Classical Satire: An Exegesis of *The Hard Life*', *Éire-Ireland* XIII, no. 1 (Spring 1978), 89.

[5] Jonathan Bolton reads the novel as a travesty of the *Bildungsroman* that 'mimics the expectations of self-cultivation, but then subverts its own narrative trajectory' to generate a deliberate 'comedy of failure'. Jennika Baines reads the novel's themes of failure and exhaustion in the light of O'Nolan's late-modernist skepticism concerning the representational strategies of both realist and high modernist fiction, finding in it an 'insecure, imperfect' pastiche of the Joycean *Künstlerroman*. Jonathan Bolton, 'Comedies of Failure: O'Brien's *The Hard Life* and Moore's *The Emperor of Ice Cream*,' *New Hibernia Review* 12, no. 3 (2008), 118; Jennika Baines, 'A Portrait of the Artist as a Dubliner: Eroding the Künstlerroman in *The Hard Life*,' in *'Is It About a Bicycle?': Flann O'Brien in the Twenty-First Century*, ed. Jennika Baines (Dublin: Four Courts Press, 2011), 143.

[6] Anthony Cronin, 'This Time, This Place,' *The Bell* XIX, no. 8 (July 1954), 7.

[7] Diarmaid Ferriter, *The Transformation of Ireland, 1900–2000* (London: Profile, 2005), 537; Fergal Tobin, *The Best of Decades: Ireland in the Nineteen Sixties* (Dublin: Gill and Macmillan, 1984).

[8] Following Tom Garvan, Graham Brownlow argues against reading Secretary to the Department of Finance, T. K. Whitaker's *Economic Development* (1958) as a 'big bang' moment in Irish economics. Nevertheless, he acknowledges that the impact of the reforms it inaugurated should not be underestimated. Ferriter, *The Transformation of Ireland*, 2005, 542; Graham Brownlow, 'Fabricating *Economic Development*,' *Working Papers in British-Irish Studies*, no. 92 (2009), 1–21.

Lemass could be found on the cover of *Time* magazine, where he was lauded for 'Lifting the Green Curtain' of Ireland's protectionist tariff regime and opening the nation to direct foreign investment.[9] This rosier economic climate saw a substantial reduction in the rate of emigration, from 14 people per 1000 for the period 1951–1961, to just 5 per 1000 the following decade.[10] The 'arrival' of Ireland as a modern nation seemed to be cemented in the popular imagination by the 1963 visit of John F. Kennedy, the first by a serving US President, presented in the Irish media as an opportunity to celebrate 'one of their own' who had reached the highest political office in the West and returned to his ancestral home.[11] As Terence Brown has reflected, though the realities of economic and social modernization in the Republic were both less even and more pernicious than such a generalization allows, in the 'collective memory', 1958–1963 came to be seen as the 'period in which a new Ireland came to life'.[12]

While less uniform, explicit, or widely celebrated, the beginnings of a similar shift were also discernible in attitudes to sex and sexuality.[13] Edna O'Brien's debut novel, *The Country Girls* (1960), became a *succès de scandale* for its lyrical, forthright, and, above all, accessible rendering of the intellectual, emotional, and sexual development of a pair of young rural Irishwomen, initiating a pattern which would see O'Brien's first five novels banned in Ireland even as they were publicly praised by members of the censorship board and the clergy for their striking literary merit.[14] Less dramatic, but ultimately more representative evidence of this shift is visible in Irish women's publications of the period. As Caitríona Clear has illustrated, the letters and advice pages of magazines such as *Woman's Life* and *Woman's Way* register the uneven distribution of sexual knowledge in

[9] 'Ireland: Lifting the Green Curtain,' *Time Magazine* 82, no. 2 (12 July 1963), 28–40.
[10] Ferriter, *The Transformation of Ireland*, 2005, 542.
[11] Sylvia A. Ellis, 'The Historical Significance of President Kennedy's Visit to Ireland in June 1963,' *Irish Studies Review* 16, no. 2 (May 2008), 113–30.
[12] Terence Brown, *Ireland: A Social and Cultural History, 1922–2002*, Revised Edition (London: Harper Perennial, 2004), 229–30.
[13] Marjorie Elizabeth Howes, 'Public Discourse, Private Reflection: 1916–1970,' in *The Field Day Anthology of Irish Writing*, ed. Seamus Deane, Angela Bourke, and Andrew Carpenter, vol. 4 (Cork: Cork University Press, 2002), 929; Diarmaid Ferriter, *Occasions of Sin: Sex and Society in Modern Ireland* (London: Profile Books, 2009), 335–38.
[14] Donal Ó Drisceoil, '"The Best Banned in the Land": Censorship and Irish Writing Since 1950,' *The Yearbook of English Studies*, 2005, 154; Ferriter, *Occasions of Sin*, 381–88; John Horgan, 'Edna O'Brien Faces Limerick Audience: Priests Praise Her,' *Irish Times*, 23 April 1966, 7; 'What They Think About Her: Members of the Censorship Board and Prominent Literary Figures Give Their Assessment of Miss O'Brien's Work,' *Irish Times*, 14 December 1967, 8; Mary Maher, 'Who's Afraid of Edna O'Brien?,' *Irish Times*, 14 December 1967, 8.

Ireland, even as they signal a growing appetite among Irish women (or, at least, Irish editors) to approach questions of sex, sexual health, and fertility in a more frank and pragmatic manner.[15] On the one hand, letters from readers asking whether it was possible to get pregnant from 'heavy kissing and hugging' or from 'love-making in a car' suggest a profound (and, perhaps, playfully exaggerated) ignorance in matters of sex and fertility.[16] On the other hand, the regularity with which these topics were featured in such widely read publications suggests an editorial belief that an audience existed for such material.[17] As these examples suggest, though Larkin-esque assertions as to the 'watershed' status of the 1960s in Irish sexual life should be handled with due circumspection, a greater willingness to discuss and critique Irish sexual mores undoubtedly manifested itself in Irish public discourse and popular media.

Under such circumstances, it is intriguing to consider why, in 1961, returning to the novel form after a twenty-year hiatus, O'Nolan felt compelled to retreat from this increasingly confident present into what he constructs as the cultural and political paralysis of Dublin in the early 1900s. O'Nolan foregrounds precisely this deliberately backward-looking perspective in a 1961 letter to his literary agent, Mark Hamilton, in which he characterizes the novel as 'old, elegant, nostalgic piss'.[18] The formulation is suggestive in its fusion of wistful reminiscence and scatological disgust. Indeed, it is arguably this very disgust that serves as an object of and vehicle for that nostalgia. John McCourt highlights this dynamic in his discussion of the novel's 'Juvenalian emphasis on dirt and excremental humour' and the

---

[15] Caitríona Clear, *Women's Voices in Ireland: Women's Magazines in the 1950s and 60s* (London: Bloomsbury, 2016), chaps. 2, 5, and 6.

[16] *Woman's Way*, 19 May 1967, and *Woman's Way*, 26 April 1968, quoted in Clear, 82. Clear emphasizes the dangers of treating these letters and queries as unmediated forms of access to the sexual attitudes and knowledge of Irish women in this period, but, stresses their value as one of the only available sources of evidence of the ways in which women discussed what they identified as their most pressing 'problems' with other women in a secular context.

[17] Clear charts a shift in the explicitness with which questions of sex and sexual health were dealt across the two publications. Of the 477 problems submitted to *Woman's Life* between 1951 and 1959, 198 (41.6 per cent) concerned 'courtship' while 51 (10.5 per cent) were 'marital' in focus. Sexual and gynaecological questions were answered privately by 'Our Medical Advisor' or answered obliquely in the magazine without reproducing the original query. *Woman's Way*, by contrast, was more direct. Of the 1,186 problems submitted to the magazine between 1963 and 1969, Clear claims that 374 (31.5 per cent) concerned 'sex, pregnancy, and birth control'. Clear, *Women's Voices in Ireland*, 29 and 81.

[18] 'Flann O'Brien' (Brian O'Nolan), *The Collected Letters of Flann O'Brien*, ed. Maebh Long (Victoria, TX: Dalkey Archive, 2018), 264.

'clear connections with the Swiftian grotesque' it betrays.[19] Following Anne Clissmann and Taaffe, McCourt reads the novel's taxonomies of domestic squalor, 'alcohol and alcoholism, idleness, crime, illicit sex, sexual disease and vomit' as performative efforts to situate it within a canon of Irish cloacal obsessions in which Joyce and Sterne loom large.[20] As Taaffe notes, Collopy's characterization of Manus's literary wares as 'dirty books, lascivious peregrinations on the fringes of filthy indecency, cloacal spewings in the face of Providence' (CN, 541) deliberately echoes early critical characterizations of the Joycean oeuvre even as it seems to offer a script for the scandalized response O'Nolan was certain his own novel would provoke in Ireland ('I know that THE HARD LIFE will be banned here').[21] This curiously queasy nostalgia has its correlative in the novel's deliberately worse-for-wear aesthetic, which stands in sharp contrast with the ebullience of O'Nolan's early prose.

The O'Nolan oeuvre, particularly the early fiction, has often been read as exemplifying a postmodern aesthetic and outlook. In Keith Hopper's influential portrait, O'Nolan's 'dismemberment of Orpheus'—the overturning of Apollonian order by Dionysian chaos in a manner that is generative rather than destructive—is presented as a source of energy and abundance.[22] Hopper outlines the 'metonymic code' through which O'Nolan playfully evokes male same-sex intimacy (the 'impact between moving balls'; CN, 48), contraception (the 'advancement of French language'; CN, 45), and pregnancy (a 'very advanced state of sexuality'; CN, 269) even as he highlights the apparently repressed and repressive sexual culture which renders such circumlocutions necessary.[23] Such an account suits well with the virtuoso exuberance of At Swim-Two-Birds and The Third Policeman, in which bawdy puns and tongue-in-cheek allusions to prophylaxis, non-normative

[19] John McCourt, 'More "Gravid" than Gravitas: Collopy, Fahrt and the Pope in Rome,' in Flann O'Brien: Problems with Authority, ed. Ruben Borg, Paul Fagan, and John McCourt (Cork: Cork University Press, 2017), 176.
[20] McCourt, 'More "Gravid" than Gravitas,' 174.
[21] Carol Taaffe, Ireland Through the Looking-Glass: Flann O'Brien, Myles Na GCopaleen and Irish Cultural Debate (Cork: Cork University Press, 2008), 189; O'Brien, Collected Letters, 279.
[22] Keith Hopper, Flann O'Brien: A Portrait of the Artist as a Young Post-Modernist (Cork, Ireland: Cork University Press, 1995), chap. 1; Keith Hopper, 'The Dismemberment of Orpheus: Flann O'Brien and the Irish Censorship Code', in Literature and Ethics: Questions of Responsibility in Literary Studies, ed. Daniel K. Jernigan, Neil Murphy, Brendan Quigley, and Tamara S. Wagner, 221–42 (Amherst, N.Y: Cambria Press, 2009).
[23] Hopper, A Portrait of the Artist, chap. 2; Hopper, 'The Dismemberment of Orpheus'.

sexuality, and abortion (as well as darker and less palatably provocative themes such as rape and abuse) abound. However, it is a less comfortable fit with the aesthetically and ideologically fatigued character of the later fiction, which bears a closer relationship to another influential formulation of the so-called 'postmodern condition': 'the literature of exhaustion'.[24] The term was coined by the novelist and academic John Barth in a 1967 lecture at the University of Virginia. By it, Barth did not seek to diagnose a contemporary 'physical, moral, or intellectual decadence', or to presage the oft-heralded 'death of the novel', but instead to highlight 'the used-up-ness of certain forms or the felt exhaustion of certain possibilities'.[25] Leaving aside Barth's wider thesis (a defence of the virtuoso artist in the age of Warhol's Factory), this sense of exhausted possibility might nevertheless prompt us to regard O'Nolan's later work as more than simply a litany of failure, and to reflect on the political and cultural stakes of sexual health in the Ireland from which it emanates.

Without wishing to argue that *The Hard Life* is an under-rated classic of the O'Nolan oeuvre—it is not—or to suggest that the novel's sexual politics are anything other than problematic—a sleeveless errand—in what follows, I wish to interrogate why, in the midst of a tentative moment of social and cultural liberalization in Ireland, O'Nolan chose to revisit a high-water mark in the cultural revival and to examine why sexual health plays such a prominent role in this ambivalent homage. Put more bluntly, if the Irish had never had it so good, why did O'Nolan prefer the Dublin of *Dubliners* to the present-day metropolis, and why are the topics of venereal disease and sexual health so central to this shift in both form and content? To answer these questions, I explore how, in O'Nolan's late fiction, many of the key themes and debates from Irish modernism's engagement with sexual health which have been addressed in this book—the Parnell Split, the regulation of venereal disease, myths of Irish purity, eugenics, and censorship—re-emerge in a performatively 'exhausted' or 'used-up' manner. An early emanation of this performative exhaustion with the topic of sexual health can be detected in a series of *Cruiskeen Lawn* columns O'Nolan composed for the *Irish Times* in 1949.

---

[24] Throughout this chapter, 'exhaustion' is used in line with Barth's elaboration of the term, as distinct from Gilles Deleuze's influential formulation of 'The Exhausted'. John Barth, 'The Literature of Exhaustion,' in *The Friday Book: Essays and Other Nonfiction* (New York: Putnam, 1984), 62–76.

[25] Ibid., 64.

'Cesspools of infection': *Cruiskeen Lawn* and the Exhaustion of Purity

In late July 1949, the sexual (ill) health of the Irish population became front-page news. In response to an article on treatment default rates in the *Journal of the Medical Association for Eire*, the *Irish Times* published a four-part exposé on 'Venereal Disease in Ireland'.[26] Written by a 'special correspondent' following a week of statistical research and interviews with key health professionals and government officials, the series presented itself as an in-depth and clear-sighted analysis of the contentious topic.[27] In the *Medical Association* article, Dr Raymond Oliver had recorded that, of the 766 male syphilitic patients treated in the previous ten years at a clinic with which he was involved, 159 (20 per cent) had been 'cured', while 607 (80 per cent) had defaulted on treatment before its completion.[28] The articles sought to establish the veracity of Oliver's claims, interrogate the effectiveness of present measures to combat the spread of venereal disease, and canvass opinion on how the incidence of infection in the Republic might be lowered. Despite what the reporter described as the 'iron curtain' of secrecy which surrounded the topic of venereal disease in Ireland, the articles offered a detailed and even-handed account of (admittedly, well-worn) arguments for and against mandatory notification, compulsory treatment, and public awareness campaigns, framed in the context of British and European approaches to sexual health.[29]

The articles were the most thoroughgoing example of the sustained coverage the *Irish Times* gave to the regulation of sexual health in Ireland in the 1940s. Throughout 1943 and 1944, headline after headline attested to the increasing incidence of venereal disease in the country, with medical experts decrying the 'ignorance and apathy' of the general public concerning sexual health and the 'hush hush' policy of the Ministry of Health, which,

---

[26] 'A Special Correspondent,' 'Venereal Disease in Ireland – I,' *Irish Times*, 21 July 1949; 'A Special Correspondent,' 'Venereal Disease in Ireland – II,' *Irish Times*, 22 July 1949; 'A Special Correspondent,' 'Venereal Disease in Ireland – III,' *Irish Times*, 23 July 1949; 'A Special Correspondent,' 'Venereal Disease in Ireland – IV,' *Irish Times*, 25 July 1949.
[27] Interviewees included the Minister for Health, the Almoner of a Dublin hospital, a member of a Dublin hospital board, a Medical Officer of Health, a Dublin-based private practitioner, an 'Eminent Irish venerealogist', and a retired Army medical officer. 'A Special Correspondent,' 'Venereal Disease in Ireland – II,' 4; 'A Special Correspondent,' 'Venereal Disease in Ireland – IV,' 7.
[28] 'A Special Correspondent,' 'Venereal Disease in Ireland – I,' 4.   [29] Ibid.

they alleged, did nothing to remedy the problem.[30] The paper decried the 'complacency, and even smugness' of the Irish people concerning their sexual health, and the tendency to believe that 'the mere accident of birth in this little island endows the individual with moral and social virtues unknown, or, at any rate, exceedingly rare, elsewhere'.[31] The editor of a 'woman's paper' highlighted the volume of letters she had received in the last six months 'from young girls who are obviously suffering from venereal disease in one or other of its manifestations, but who simply [had] not the slightest notion of what [was] wrong with them'.[32] In October 1944, the paper covered the inaugural meeting of the TCD Philosophical Society, in which the society's president highlighted the 'absolute social, physical and psychological ruin' wrought by venereal disease, and the threat it posed to the future of the nation.[33] The speech, entitled 'The Diseased World', received a vote of thanks from the Church of Ireland Archbishop for Dublin, A. W. Barton, who complained of the barriers the Censorship Act erected to the circulation of effective educational material concerning sexual health and emphasized the minority episcopate's support for public health measures to prevent the spread of disease.[34]

Support for a more proactive approach to venereal disease was not confined to Protestant intellectual and ecclesiastical circles. In May 1944, the infamous John Charles McQuaid, Barton's Catholic opposite number, donated £3,000 for the establishment of 'a first-class modern unit' for the treatment of venereal disease at the Jervis Street Hospital, open to 'any person who may choose to visit', and for similar clinics to be established by the Sisters of Mercy at the Mater Misericordiae, Dublin and St. Michael's Hospital, Dun Laoghaire.[35] As part of the scheme, a young physician was sent to the Stopes Institute of the University of Philadelphia to receive postgraduate training in modern methods of diagnosis and treatment, a fact much trumpeted in the *Irish Times*.[36] The progress of the scheme was frustrated when the newly qualified physician drowned in a 'yachting mishap', but the clinic was eventually opened as per the Archbishop's

[30] 'Need for Women Police to Cope with V.D. Problem,' *Irish Times*, 20 May, 1944, 1; 'V.D. Should Be Notifiable,' *Irish Times*, 26 May 1944, 1.
[31] 'A Social Scourge,' *Irish Times*, 24 May 1944, 3.
[32] 'M.B.,' 'V.D.,' *Irish Times*, 23 May 1944, 3.
[33] 'Control of Venereal Disease Urged,' *Irish Times*, 27 October 1944, 3.
[34] 'T.C.D. Society Discussion,' *Irish Press*, 27 October, 1944, 4.
[35] 'Venereal Disease Clinics Founded,' *Irish Press*, 19 May, 1944, 3.
[36] 'Drive to Combat V.D. May Follow National Inquiry,' *Irish Times*, 19 May 1944, 1.

instructions.[37] Behind the scenes, McQuaid sought to harangue ecclesiastically maintained medical facilities such as St Vincent's Hospital, Dublin into providing outpatient clinics and gender-segregated inpatient sexual health wards, though these efforts were often met with resistance.[38] As Diarmaid Ferriter notes, while conservative in some particulars—sex education and public information campaigns were not to be countenanced—McQuaid's extensive correspondence on venereal disease is notable for 'its concern with medical treatment rather than casting moral or religious judgement'.[39]

Notwithstanding the increasingly pragmatic (if not uncomplicatedly 'progressive') nature of public discourse surrounding venereal disease in Ireland, the 1949 exposé ruffled feathers, particularly within medical circles. When, in the second article, the Minister for Health questioned the accuracy of Oliver's reported default rates, the doctor wrote to the *Irish Times* to excoriate the contemporary state of venereal disease treatment in Ireland: clinics were overcrowded, ill-equipped, and mismanaged, with one attempting to diagnose syphilis without even access to a microscope.[40] Oliver quoted a London-based venereal disease specialist and adviser to the British Ministry of Health, who claimed that 'nearly half of his patients contracted their disease in Ireland' and stated that he 'looked upon Dublin as being one of the greatest remaining cesspools of infection in Europe—a delightful reputation for our fair city, where, once, the girls were so pretty!'[41] The following day, Michael Ffrench O'Carroll, wrote to critique Oliver's letter for its 'cheap, destructive, and inaccurate approach' to the problem. In particular, Ffrench O'Carroll criticized Oliver for what he deemed his undergraduate assertions about infection rates in Dublin relative to those of other European cities, asking him to produce statistics to bear out his point:

I am ashamed of Irish doctors who refer to their native city as 'being one of the greatest remaining cess-pools of infection (V.D.) in Europe' without producing reliable European figures to verify these statements. However much they may wish to improve Irish medicine, such phraseology will not do credit to them or our country.[42]

---

[37] 'A Special Correspondent,' 'Venereal Disease in Ireland – I,' 4.
[38] Ferriter, *Occasions of Sin*, 265–67.   [39] Ibid., 266.
[40] 'A Special Correspondent,' 'Venereal Disease in Ireland – II,' 4; 'Letters to the Editor: "V.D." in Ireland,' *Irish Times*, 26 July 1949, 6.
[41] 'Letters to the Editor: "V.D." in Ireland,' 6.
[42] '"V.D." in Ireland,' *Irish Times*, 28 July 1949, 5.

G. L. M. McElligott, the authority whom Oliver had cited in making this claim, also contributed to the debate and adopted a similar tone of bruised national pride. McElligott emphasized that he had characterized Dublin not as a 'cesspool', but as a 'reservoir of infection', the source of which resided firmly in Great Britain.[43] Where Oliver had implied that McElligott's patients had carried infection from Ireland to Britain, McElligott claimed that the majority of his Irish patients contracted 'their infections from Irish consorts in London' and brought the infection back with them during their periodic trips home.[44] The contaminating influence, McElligott implied, was not that of the Irish on London, but of London on the Irish. Likewise, Dublin's status as a 'reservoir of infection' was not a reflection of native immorality, but the 'syphilitic legacy' of the Irish capital's time as 'the most heavily garrisoned city in the world', and the 'inordinately high' rates of infection experienced by the British Army.[45]

In the best traditions of the nationalist purity rhetoric outlined in Chapter 3, where McElligott could not ascribe responsibility for Ireland's venereally compromised condition to English 'syphilisation', he laid it at the door of Irish women. Thus, though 'the kaleidoscope of multicoloured uniforms' was no longer to be seen 'on a summer's evening on the Post Office side of O'Connell street', and the 'notorious houses in Tyrone and Mecklenburg streets' had been 'spiritually and physically exorcized', the 'promiscuous female population' could be relied upon to 'top up the reservoir of infection'.[46] Just as it had done in the pages of Sinn Féin and in the anti-enlistment campaigns of Inghinidhe na hÉireann in the first decade of the century, for McElligott, the presence of venereal disease in Ireland served as a pathological reification of British imperial rule. However, as McElligott's shift in register from medical pragmatism to almost literary reminiscence shows, the strain of plausibly sustaining such an argument in the twenty-second year of Irish independence was increasingly heavy. The pressing reality of British servicemen 'jostling', 'insulting', and soliciting Irish women which Maud Gonne had sought to address in her 1904 letter to the Freeman's Journal, gives place in McElligott's letter to something closer in manner to the 'phantasy in fact' of Oliver St John Gogarty's As I was Going Down Sackville Street.[47] Indeed, as McElligott's purple prose and almost

---

[43] '"V.D." in Ireland,' Irish Times, 3 August 1949, 5.
[44] Ibid.   [45] Ibid.   [46] Ibid.
[47] Maud Gonne-MacBride, 'To the Editor of the Freeman's Journal,' Freeman's Journal, 6 June 1904, 6.

nostalgic tone suggest, the effort to square the reality of an undeniably 'promiscuous' contemporary Ireland with an ideal of purity in which, for example, sex work could have no place, risked giving a rather appealing complexion to the balmy 'summer evenings' of British occupation.

It was precisely this florid style and somewhat wistful outlook that O'Nolan, through his Myles na gCopaleen persona, was to highlight and pastiche in his *Cruiskeen Lawn* column for 8 August the same year. Addressing the controversy between Oliver and McElligott, Myles reflects upon the pleasing 'delicacy and elegance' of the term venereal *'disease'*: 'It does not mean sickness, *morbus*, or deadly infection. It means just "non-ease," remote disquiet.'[48] On the grounds of a similarly 'dignified' linguistic performance, of the two combatants, Myles deems McElligott 'worthy to sit at [his] table in Santry':[49]

> Barring his reference to 'the kaleidoscope of multi-coloured uniforms on a summer's evening'—a rash prismic excursion by the good doctor—I find that he expresses himself coherently and temperately. I regret to record that Dr. Oliver is not yet old enough to dine with me.[50]

In line with his frequently professed relish for cliché and redundancy, Myles singles out for notice the most tautologous and banal assertions of the various participants in the debate, such as Ffrench O'Carroll's reflection that 'the Rotunda is a maternity hospital' or Oliver's wish that Shakespeare could serve as 'adviser in V.D. to the Ministry of Health' (Myles notes that his 'primitive experience of sanitation and hygiene' leave the Bard poorly qualified for such a role).[51] Chief among such banalities was McElligott's assertion that 'up to 1922, Dublin was probably the most heavily garrisoned city in the world'.[52] For Myles, the 'accretions of wisdom which come with age' precluded him from treating such an 'aphorism' as 'news'.[53] Noting that the diseases McElligott treats have 'ever been associated with crafts of Mars' (and, as such, form 'part of Marshall Aid'), Myles concludes the column by reflecting that Julius Caesar had made McElligott's point both 'quicker and better' through the immortal phrase *'Veni, V.D., Vici!'*.[54] As if to bear out his point, Myles frames these reflections on venereal disease by a discussion of a recent *Irish Times* headline—'BRITISH ARMY BEATEN BY LEPRECHAUNS'—which had trumpeted the success of the Irish Defence

[48] 'Myles na gCopaleen' (Brian O'Nolan), 'Cruiskeen Lawn,' *Irish Times*, 8 August, 1949, 4.
[49] Ibid.   [50] Ibid.   [51] Ibid.   [52] Ibid.   [53] Ibid.   [54] Ibid.

Force cricket team over their British counterparts.[55] Myles notes that 'there is nothing new' in such a headline, citing the Battle of Mag Tuired in the *Lebor Gabála Érenn* [book of the taking of Ireland], in which the invading *Tuatha Dé Danann* [tribes of Dana] triumphed over the *Fir Bolg* [men of bags] by disguising themselves beneath the smoke of their burning boats, as an example of Irish military prowess.[56]

While a general air of sardonic pedantry, often shading into crotchety ill-humour, was an increasing feature of the *Cruiskeen Lawn* from the mid–1940s, the exhaustion which Myles detects in McElligott's efforts to present sexual pathology and British occupation as synonymous is palpable. In part, this exhaustion is registered through the pseudo-historicism with which Myles frames both the martial history of venereal disease and Anglo-Irish relations. McElligott's invocation of the 'syphilitic legacy' of the British garrison in Dublin is shown to be as old as the Caesarean tag with which Myles concludes his column, and as tired as the pun for which it serves as the vehicle. More tellingly, if, as Myles contends, the dissemination of venereal disease has been the eternal prerogative of the invader, then, as his reference to the *Lebor Gabála Érenn* suggests, the true 'syphilitic legacy' of Ireland must not be English in origin, but born of the Irish themselves. In a manner evocative of the Finn McCool passages in *At Swim-Two-Birds*, in which the epic hero is figured as an elderly letch, this play upon Gaelic mythic history serves to implicate the *Tuatha Dé Danann* in the sexual pollution of Ireland through the very logic by which McElligott had sought to exculpate their successors.[57] The point is underscored in Myles's assertion that, like the smoke-screen deployed by the *Tuatha Dé Danann* in their conflict with the *Fir Bolg*, the 'Celtic twilight' was 'not a literary matter', but an 'ancient military phenomenon' which may yet serve as 'the spearhead of the approaching war with Russia'.[58] Notwithstanding the difficulty of extracting a consistent ideology or political orientation from the polyvocal and often deliberately contradictory *Cruiskeen Lawn*—the pun, gag, or leg-pull is apt to take precedence over a coherent thesis—this column offers a sustained critique of sexual health rhetoric as a 'used-up' tool in the

---

[55] Ibid.

[56] Ibid. Myles quotes the passage verbatim from Robert Alexander Stewart Macalister, trans., *Lebor Gabála Érenn: The Book of the Taking of Ireland*, vol. 4 (Dublin: Irish Texts Society, 1941), 141–43.

[57] 'Flann O'Brien' (Brian O'Nolan), *The Complete Novels* (New York: Alfred A. Knopf, 2007), 57–58. Hereafter cited parenthetically as *CN*.

[58] gCopaleen, 'Cruiskeen Lawn,' 4.

construction of Irish identity and the mediation of Anglo-Irish relations. In doing so, it strongly adumbrates the performative 'exhaustion' with which the topic is handled in *The Hard Life*, and the somewhat jaundiced realism through which it is dramatized.

'Old, elegant, nostalgic piss': *The Hard Life* and the Exhaustion of Realism

In an effort to account for what she presents as the novel's tonal and thematic deracination, Tess Hurson frames *The Hard Life* as a conflict between the 'marvellous'—exemplified by the literal, linguistic, and legal wire-walking of Manus—and 'realism'—exemplified by Finbarr's stolid moralism and Collopy's bathetic demise—in which O'Nolan is 'morally on the side of realism'.[59] Leaving aside the question of what the ethical investments of realism might constitute, it is worth asking how realistic the realism of *The Hard Life* actually is. This is not to attempt to quantify the 'success' or 'failure' of the novel as an act of mimesis, but, instead, to ask to what extent its deployment of the codes and tropes of turn-of-the-century realist fiction—most obviously the 'scrupulous meanness' of Joyce's *Dubliners*—function alongside an investment in the facticity of the social and political life of 1890s Ireland.

In John McCourt's view, to take the novel's realism at face value is to overlook the 'essential roguishness' of the novel and its efforts to 'both tender homage to and at the same time challenge the realist strain in Irish fiction'.[60] Yet, what is to be made of a novel that subverts the 'presumed cultural authority' of realism, even as it advertises the ways in which it is set 'rather precisely' in a specified cultural and historical moment?[61] An influential formulation of this question is offered by Frederic Jameson in his reflections on the features and function of the 'historical novel' in a postmodern milieu. For Jameson, a defining feature of postmodernism, and the intellectual correlative of its aesthetic 'depthlessness', is a 'weakening of historicity', in which both 'public History' and 'personal temporality' cease to be experienced as stable, linear phenomena.[62] In this dressing-up-box of

---

[59] Hurson, 'Conspicuous Absences,' 119; 122.
[60] McCourt, 'More "Gravid" than Gravitas,' 177.   [61] Ibid.
[62] Fredric Jameson, *Postmodernism, or, The Cultural Logic of Late Capitalism* (London: Verso, 1992), 6.

historical discourses and tropes, postmodern fiction foregoes any referential relationship with a 'past history which was once itself a present', offering only 'pop history' and simulacra: reproductions of ideas and stereotypes about the past for which no original has ever existed.[63] Just such a 'pop' historiography is foregrounded in O'Nolan's characterization of *The Hard Life* as 'old, elegant, nostalgic piss'. The concrete historicity suggested by the relatively value-neutral term 'old' jostles in O'Nolan's remark with the 'elegant'—which is to say posed, or, at least, poised—artificiality of 'nostalgic', and the playful vulgarity of 'piss' (and the 'piss-take' it metonymically evokes). As the sentence unfolds, a shift takes place from historical fact (that which is 'old') to a simulacrum of historicity ('nostalgic piss') in which wistful reminiscence and scatological disgust coalesce. In this sense, the novel's apparent 'realism' (the piss) in fact offers only an exhausted simulacrum (or piss-take) of the historical 'squalor' O'Nolan sets out to catalogue and critique.

This exhaustion is most immediately palpable in the novel's bathetic refiguring of the geographical and symbolic topography of *Ulysses* and *Finnegans Wake*—a pastiche firmly rooted in questions of sexuality and sexual health. As Mary Power has noted, in *The Hard Life*, O'Nolan offers readers not the Liffey, but the Grand Canal; not the vocal Ur-mother Anna Livia Plurabelle, but Annie, the almost silent servant-cum-sex-worker.[64] Nor, as Jennika Baines has suggested, is *A Portrait of the Artist as a Young Man* spared a Daedelian descent to earth.[65] Despite opening in 1890, barring one brief reference, the shade of Parnell is almost wholly absent from *The Hard Life* and its young narrator's cultural imaginary. The manner with which this date is introduced at the conclusion of the novel's first chapter seems deliberately intended to invite then frustrate the expectation of a figure of Parnell's stature, and the sea-change his sexual misconduct precipitated in Irish political and cultural life: 'Reckoning backward, I find I was about five years old. The year was 1890, and my young bones told me that a great change was coming in my life. Little did I know just then how big the change. I was about to meet Mr Collopy' (*CN*, 504). Where the young Stephen Dedalus experiences a sequence of febrile self-identification with the Uncrowned King of Ireland and witnesses his father reduced to tears at the Chief's fate, the transformative patriarch for O'Nolan's Finbarr is not

---

[63] Ibid., 25.   [64] Power, 'Flann O'Brien and Classical Satire,' 89.
[65] Baines, 'A Portrait of the Artist as a Dubliner: Eroding the Künstlerroman in *The Hard Life.*'

the betrayed figurehead of the Home Rule movement, but Mr Collopy, a thwarted advocate for female public lavatories. Where Stephen's entry into political awareness ('That was called politics. There were two sides in it:...') is precipitated by Parnell's fall from grace and influence, Finbarr's quietism is punctuated only by Collopy's literal fall through the stairs of a Roman opera house.[66] Even Collopy's uncertain living arrangements and the marital status of his bed-ridden spouse, Mrs Crotty, whom Finbarr speculates may be 'a kept-woman or resident prostitute' (CN, 508), seem intended as bathetic evocations of the more lurid revelations of the O'Shea affair, in which the question of Parnell's residency with Katharine ultimately proved central to the outcome of the trial.[67]

At one level, this consistent impulse to debase that which Joyce had elevated manifests an apparent commitment to the sort of blunt 'realism' Hurson regards as the novel's moral core and which O'Nolan strove to preserve as its aesthetic key-note. However, the novel's claims to 'realistic' historicity are strained by its stylistic proximity to early Joyce and the virtual absence of Parnell from the political and social life it depicts.[68] O'Nolan's intervention is thus not so much historical as it is intertextual, acting not to offer a more historically grounded image of turn-of-the-century Dublin life, but to replace one simulacrum with another. The operation and effects of this substitution are particularly visible in the positioning of Collopy as a kind of Chief-writ-small, and the implications this has, when read in the light of Chapter 1's discussion of rhetorics of sexual pathology in the Parnell Split, for how his Vespasian reform schemes are to be interpreted throughout the novel.

[66] James Joyce, A Portrait of the Artist as a Young Man: Authoritative Text, Backgrounds and Contexts, Criticism, ed. John Paul Riquelme, Hans Walter Gabler, and Walter Hettche (New York: W.W. Norton, 2007), 14.
[67] Parnell's co-habitation with Katharine O'Shea was consistently evinced by both critics and supporters during the Split to suggest the sexual impropriety or emphasize the domestic normalcy of their relationship. Perhaps most infamously, Parnell was reported to have regularly fled encounters with Katharine by means of 'a balcony' or 'fire escape' when disturbed by her husband, a farcical manoeuvre which, William O'Shea's representatives argued, would have been unnecessary if he had colluded in the affair. T. P. O'Connor, Charles Stewart Parnell: A Memory (London: Ward, Lock, Bowden & Co., 1891), 135–37; 19 November 1890; The O'Shea-Parnell Divorce Case: Full and Complete Proceedings (Boston: National Publishing Company, n.d.), 27.
[68] This whiff of spilled Joyce was recently confirmed by a computational stylometric analysis which identified statistically 'significant' similarities of style, vocabulary, and syntax between The Hard Life and Dubliners. James O'Sullivan et al., 'Measuring Joycean Influences on Flann O'Brien,' Digital Studies/Le Champ Numérique 8, no. 1 (27 March 2018), 7.

'What-you-know': *The Hard Life* and the Exhaustion of Venereal Disease

Maebh Long has elucidated the deluge of liquids (Mrs Crotty's urine, the rain, the gravid water) which eventually precipitate Collopy's tragi-comic downfall and their metonymic relationship to both menstruation and female desire.[69] To this list of resonances and the abjection they encode, I would add the suggestion of venereal disease and the efforts to regulate its spread. One of the structuring principles of the novel, and an intended source of much of its humour (however debatable), is the persistent deferral of certainty over the nature and focus of Collopy's project to improve the lives of Dublin's women. The comedy of Collopy's interview with Pope Pius X, in which Collopy's comments are consistently elided ('COLLOPY spoke'; 'COLLOPY spoke again'; 'COLLOPY mumbled something'; *CN*, 592), is staked upon the reader's efforts to infer what the zealous reformer has proposed from the remarks of the increasingly incensed pontiff:[70]

> *Dear Cardinal, I fear you have made a mistake in bringing this pious man to see us.* [...] *Can it be that he is in the wrong place? We are not a doctor for the body.*
>
> [...]
>
> *But this is monstrous. Nor should our office be confused with that of a city council.*
>
> [...]
>
> *It is a derogation of our presence. Does such an unheard-of suggestion lie within reason? We have never heard such a thing before.*   (*CN*, 592)

The revelation of Collopy's scheme in its entirety is withheld until the reading of his will and the elucidation of the groan-worthy epitaph Manus has chosen for him, '*Here lies one whose name / is writ in water*' (*CN*, 602):

---

[69] Long, *Assembling Flann O'Brien*, 167–68.

[70] Alana Gillespie has convincingly used this ambiguity to link *The Hard Life* to O'Nolan's response to the 1951 'mother and child affair'. See Alana Gillespie, 'The Soft Misogyny of Good Intentions: The Mother and Child Scheme, *Cruiskeen Lawn*, and *The Hard Life*,' in *Flann O'Brien: Gallows Humour*, eds. Ruben Borg and Paul Fagan (Cork: Cork University Press, 2021), 77–96.

– After all that has been done, Mr Sproule went on, we have to set up the Collopy Trust. [. . .] The Trust will erect and maintain three establishments which the testator calls rest rooms. There will be a rest room at Irishtown, Sandymount, at Harold's Cross and at Philsborough. Each will bear the word PEACE very prominently on the door and each will be under the patronage of a saint—Saint Patrick, Saint Jerome and Saint Ignatius.

(*CN*, 604)

The debts Collopy's scheme owes to Leopold Bloom's ruminations on the urinal below Sir Thomas Moore's statue on Westmoreland Street have been well-attested.[71] However, Collopy's scheme and the manner of its (non-)articulation also echo another moment of Bloomian reformism: his remarks to Stephen on the need to regulate commercial sex in 'Eumaeus'.

As was suggested in Chapter 3, Bloom's paterfamilial insistence that female sex workers should be 'licensed and medically inspected by the proper authorities' (*U* 16.743) evokes the Contagious Diseases Acts of 1864, 1866, and 1869, which legislated for the mandatory inspection, treatment, and incarceration of women suspected of engaging in sex work. The parallels between the rest rooms envisaged in Collopy's will and the Lock hospitals which these Acts mandated are clear enough. The ecclesiastical soubriquet ('Saint Patrick, Saint Jerome and Saint Ignatius') and pietistic tag ('PEACE') with which each rest room is to be emblazoned echo Ireland's landscape of Church-maintained hospitals and dispensaries, just as their fusion of physical and spiritual hygiene evoke the Magdalene laundries with which efforts to regulate venereal disease in Ireland were closely associated. O'Nolan draws attention to the link when, in one of the novel's less clumsy gestures towards a feminist critique of the hypocrisy inherent in Irish efforts to regulate female sexuality, Finbarr notes that Collopy 'had a horror of laundries and mass-washing' which he held were 'a certain way to get syphilis and painful skin diseases' (*CN*, 557). Collopy's solution is to insist that 'Annie had to wash his things' (*CN*, 557), a manifestation of patriarchal complacency which, if Manus is to be believed, leaves Collopy prey to precisely the infectious influences he wishes to hold at bay. Read in this light, Collopy's comic circumlocutions around the true nature of his reforms

---

[71] 'They did right to put him up over a urinal: meeting of the waters. Ought to be places for women. Running into cakeshops. Settle my hat straight.' (*U* 8.414–16). Myles alludes to the statue and the passage in Myles na gCopaleen, 'Cruiskeen Lawn: Oft in the Stilly,' *Irish Times*, 28 November 1961, 8.

seem partially intended to leave open the possibility that they are concerned with women's sexual health. Revealing the news of Mrs Crotty's death, Collopy refuses to confirm 'that what-you-know was the sole reason for the woman's demise [...] But by Christ it had plenty to do with it' (*CN*, 537). The 'what-you-know' in question is apparently Mrs Crotty's fatal incontinence, but the euphemistic refusal to specify the nature of the malady leaves room for speculation that her illness may be more severe and socially stigmatizing. This speculation is only intensified by Collopy's response to the suggestion that he should stand for election to the Corporation in two years: 'But two years, you said? Only the Almighty knows how many unfortunate women would be brought to an early grave in that time' (*CN*, 537). Both the fatal implications of this delay—comic in the context of public lavatories, but more plausible as an echo of public health discourse around venereal disease—and the tone of paternalistic concern in which it is evoked are of a piece with the rhetoric of both regulationists and moral hygiene advocates discussed in Chapter 3 and exemplified in Tumulty's concluding speeches in Oliver Gogarty's *Blight* (1917).[72]

The link between feminine (sexual) incontinence and venereal disease is made explicit when Annie, one of the three-and-a-half women in the novel, is discovered by Finbarr to be frequenting Wilton Place, which he knows 'from other experiences to be haunted by prostitutes of the very lowest cadres' (*CN*, 572). As has been noted by Long and others, these remarks fuse in Finbarr's mind with his reflections on his idealized love-interest Penelope (the most explicit and least developed of the novel's Joycean intertexts), to suggest that all women are corrupting sources of potential pollution:

> I had, in fact, been thinking of Penelope, and that one word ['*Seemingly*': Annie's catchphrase] threw my mind into a whirl. What was the meaning of this thing sex, what was the nature of sexual attraction? Was it all bad and dangerous? What was Annie doing late at night, standing in a dark place with young blackguards? Was I any better myself in my conduct, whispering sly things into the ear of lovely and innocent Penelope?
>
> (*CN*, 572)

---

[72] 'Alpha and Omega' (Oliver St John Gogarty), *Blight, the Tragedy of Dublin: An Exposition in Three Acts* (Dublin: Talbot Press, 1917), 62–74.

Less often remarked upon than this misogynistic horror of the monstrous feminine, and the general aversion to desire in all its forms which pervades the O'Nolan canon, is the reaction of Manus to the news of Annie's nocturnal activities.

'Diagnosis without examination': *The Hard Life* and the Exhaustion of Regulation

In a letter to Finbarr written in response to his Wilton Place revelations, Manus offers a voluminous clinical account of granuloma inguinale, lymphogranuloma venereum, gonorrhoea, and syphilis in its primary, secondary, and tertiary manifestations, which he presents as the 'inevitable' (*CN*, 575) infectious outcome of Annie's suspected (but never confirmed) profession. A number of critiques are coded in O'Nolan's rendering of this epistle. First, in its essentially groundless certainty that Annie must be infected and in the self-professed futility of its efforts toward 'diagnosis without examination at [. . .] distance', the letter absurdly performs precisely the kinds of paternalistic bio-political policing of female bodies endorsed by the Contagious Diseases Acts and satirized by Joyce in 'Eumaeus'. As in Bloom's indictment of a 'frowsy whore' (*U*11.1252) he has himself solicited, the irony of this moment resides in the dubious claims to purity of both the author and recipient of the letter. More even than his hand-wringing self-interrogation over the nature of his desire for Penelope, Finbarr's allusion to 'other experiences' in Wilton Place suggests a more compromised and compromising attitude to 'this thing sex' than the string of rhetorical reflections would appear to allow. Likewise, as Maebh Long has highlighted, the nature of Manus's relationship with Annie and the 'what-you-know' (*CN*, 557) for which he pays her is deliberately left open to readerly speculation:[73]

> In the last eighteen months or so, she was asked to undertake another duty to which she agreed willingly enough. The brother had given up the early-rising of his schooldays but would often hand Annie some money for 'what-you-know' from his bedside. He was in need of a cure, and the poor girl would slip out and bring him back a glass of whiskey. (*CN*, 557)

---

[73] Long, *Assembling Flann O'Brien*, 174–75.

The recurrence of the euphemistic 'what-you-know' serves to link Annie's more dubious domestic duties both to Mrs Crotty's possible status as a 'resident prostitute' and to Collopy's schemes for female health. Likewise, while the money Manus gives her is ultimately suggested to be for the purchase of whiskey, the strategic ambiguity of the 'need' Annie meets and the 'cure' Manus procures from her serve to undermine his later pretensions to medical objectivity at least as thoroughly as his fly-by-night scholarly approach to sexual pathology.

The second critique concerns the relationship between venereal disease and national identity which the letter seems to posit. In a novel from which O'Nolan boasted '[d]igression and expatiation' had been studiously excised, Manus's encyclopaedic account of the venereal consequences of Annie's apparent profession stands out in its sheer length (two pages in the novel's first edition) as both exhaustive and exhausting.[74] Particularly striking in their redundancy are the descriptions of granuloma inguinale and lympho-granuloma venereum, both of which Manus discounts on the basis of their being 'a near-monopoly of the negro' (CN, 575). While of a piece with both the haphazard scholarship of Manus's pseudo-academic correspondence courses, the invocation of these 'tropical' illnesses and the pointedly racial-ized grounds on which they are dismissed implicitly invokes the use of sexual health as a means to police the boundaries of ethnic, racial, or national identity. As Chapter 3 suggests, 'the "venereal excess" cry' and the 'racial hatred' which had so incensed Joyce in 1907 had long operated in tandem, both in the policies and discourses of British imperialism, and in the purity rhetoric of Irish Ireland and Sinn Féin.[75] In their deliberate over-elaboration, Manus's remarks draw upon both traditions to 'exhaust' this rhetoric, both in the aesthetically 'used-up' manner Barth suggests, and in a manner closer to the frustration betrayed by the young Joyce.

O'Nolan's interest in this rhetoric recurs in the unfinished novel frag-ment, Slattery's Sago Saga, which he was drafting in the months prior to his death in 1966. The eponymous Sago (a starch extracted from the spongy centre and pith of various tropical palm stems) is introduced to Ireland by Crawford MacPherson—a short-tempered Scots Presbyterian whom O'Nolan consistently presents as a grotesque termagant—as a part of a

[74] O'Brien, Collected Letters, 269.
[75] Richard Ellmann, ed., Letters of James Joyce, vol. 2 (London: Faber and Faber, 1966), 167. For the colonial politics of British sexual health policy, see Philippa Levine, Prostitution, Race, and Politics: Policing Venereal Disease in the British Empire (New York: Routledge, 2003).

megalomaniacal scheme to ensure that the Irish never again emigrate to America due to famine. MacPherson's motives in seeking to prevent Irish emigration centre on her belief that the Irish are a locus of venereal disease, sex work, over-population, and degeneration:

> They bred and multiplied and infested the whole continent, saturating it with crime, drunkenness, illegal corn liquor, bank robbery, murder, prostitution, syphilis, mob rule, crooked politics and Roman Catholic Popery [...] Adultery, salacious dancing, blackmail, drug peddling, pimping, organising brothels, consorting with niggers and getting absolution for their crimes from Roman Catholic Priests....[76]

The nineteenth-century origins of this litany of Hibernophobic clichés are not far to seek—an archaism underscored by the novel's repeated references to the Land League, 'agrarian kidnapping', and Fenianism—situating MacPherson and her scheme firmly in the debates over degeneration and emigration mapped in Chapter 2.[77] Likewise, its insistence on the unsustainable hyper-fecundity of the degenerate Irish strongly recalls the objections raised by Protestant opponents to the Censorship Act discussed in Chapter 4. However, as has been noted above, by 1966 Irish emigration was at an all-time low. For Synge, Griffith, and the agitated audiences of the Abbey, questions of emigration and its impact on Ireland's breeding stock had been a pressing matter of national socio-economic and sanitary concern. As the pointedly outdated nature of MacPherson's anti-emigration rhetoric, and the racial slur with which her invective culminates seem intended to suggest, by the time of the novel's drafting, they were little more than an anachronistic pretence for jingoistic racism. In the Ireland of the mid-60s, O'Nolan suggests, the use of sexual health as a rhetorical tool to police the boundaries of national identity was at once exhausted, and perniciously resilient.

The same logic underpins the extrusive culmination of *The Hard Life*—Finbarr's 'tidal surge of vomit' (*CN*, 607)—which is precipitated by Manus's suggestion that Annie might prove a suitable wife for him: 'Annie is an industrious, well-built quiet girl. There are not so many of them knocking about. And you don't see many of that decent type across in London. Over

---

[76] Flann O'Brien, *The Short Fiction of Flann O'Brien*, ed. Neil Murphy and Keith Hopper, trans. Jack Fennell (Champaign, Illinois: Dalkey Archive Press, 2013), 102.

[77] Ibid., 103; 122.

there they are nearly all prostitutes [...] Decent people are rare everywhere [...] And decent people who are well got are rarest of all' (*CN*, 606). Given what Finbarr has witnessed in Wilton Place, the ironies of this recommendation are not far to seek: the ill-concealed suggestion of sex work in the image of the 'industrious' Annie 'knocking about' Dublin rather puts the lie to Manus's efforts to characterize commercial sex as an exclusively English phenomenon. What is perhaps more telling is not that Manus commends Annie as a fit and fitting bride for Finbarr—an in-character reflection of his unscrupulous pragmatism—but that he does so on the grounds of ethnonational affiliation, wealth, and an implicitly eugenicist notion of good breeding. The claim that Annie is a 'decent type' is rendered ridiculous precisely because it is staked upon her apparent distinction from what Manus presents as the endemic sex work of London. Likewise, the assertion that she is 'well got'—a reference to the 'substantial house and three hundred pounds a year for life' (*CN*, 606) she has been willed by Collopy—also seems to suggest that she is well-gotten, a claim to eugenic fitness hardly borne out by the 'streel of a girl with long lank fair hair' (*CN*, 501), 'permanent bad temper' (*CN*, 501), and vocabulary composed almost exclusively of the word 'seemingly'. Like Synge in the *Playboy*, O'Nolan pastiches Irish pretensions to physical and moral purity by emphasizing the dysgenic character of the population and highlighting the spurious exceptionalism upon which such pretensions were predicated.

This frustration with the stymieing effect of pious narratives of Irish purity also registers itself in Collopy's invectives against the inertia of the Dublin Corporation—in which traces of *Blight* are again discernible—and in his refusal to enlist the support of the Gaelic League to his cause because he is convinced that they 'wouldn't understand this crisis in our national life' and might instead dub him 'a dirty old man' and 'send for the D.M.P'. (*CN* 523). However, as the bathetic revelation of Collopy's lavatorial life's work emphasizes, what Synge presented as an evolutionary threat to Ireland's future, Joyce broached as a serious question of self-determination and state regulation, and Beckett understood as one of the defining issues of sectarian relations and cultural identity in the Free State, O'Nolan ultimately deflates to an exhausted pun on Keats's epitaph. This is not to diminish the value of O'Nolan's treatment of venereal disease and eugenics in Ireland per se, but to highlight the ways in which O'Nolan's efforts to revisit the interrelationship of sexual health and Irish identity in Irish modernism ultimately serve only to emphasize and extend its 'used-up' character. Where the handling of venereal disease in the 'Eumaeus' episode of *Ulysses* was tired, *The Hard Life* is positively exhausted.

'Ignorant balloxes': *The Hard Life* and the Exhaustion of Censorship

One corollary of this sense of sexual health rhetoric as a vitiated tool of social critique in Ireland was its increasing failure to shock, a form of exhaustion clearly reflected in O'Nolan's struggles with the nation's censors. The problem posed by the Censorship of Publications Board to Brian O'Nolan was, if not unique among Irish authors, then certainly idiosyncratic: they consistently failed to ban his work. As has often been remarked, O'Nolan wrote *The Hard Life* with the deliberate intention of provoking its suppression under the Censorship Act and subsequently contesting the ban in court.[78] Keith Hopper sees in the novel a mode of censor-baiting 'textual manipulation', which goes 'well beyond scatological naming'—though he is less clear on its operation or effect.[79] Undoubtedly, as Anthony Cronin suggests, by 1961, O'Nolan, conscious of the cultural cachet conferred by inclusion on the Register of Prohibited Publications, was keen to 'join [a] club' which included almost every major Irish author of the last half-century.[80] A hint of this desire for notoriety can be caught as early as 1941, in a *Cruiskeen Lawn* column in which Myles disparages *The Bell* for its formulaic denunciations of the Censorship Act. Responding to an editorial in which Seán O'Faoláin had claimed that there was 'hardly an Irish writer of repute [...] who has not been banned', Myles derided the suggestion as 'bunkum of a dimension which is grandiose': 'I know many good Irish writers who have not been banned. Have we reached the stage when a writer is considered to be "of repute" because he has been banned?'[81] If these comments betray more than a hint of bruised ego—one cannot help but think that one of the 'good Irish writers' Myles has in mind is Flann O'Brien—they also convey a sense that, by the 1940s, the myth of the defiant modernist facing down the apparatus of a socially conservative state was wearing thin: 'The rule is that you must make a scathing reference to the Censorship at every possible opportunity. [...] Then you are made as an Irish intellectual and eligible for your first corduroys.'[82] Notwithstanding such protestations, however, it is clear that, by the mid-40s, O'Nolan was keen to expand his wardrobe.

---

[78] Anthony Cronin, *No Laughing Matter: The Life and Times of Flann O'Brien* (London: Grafton, 1990), 214–15.

[79] Hopper, 'The Dismemberment of Orpheus,' 224.

[80] Cronin, *No Laughing Matter*, 214.

[81] 'Myles na gCopaleen' (Brian O'Nolan), 'Cruiskeen Lawn: Bell-Idiocy,' *Irish Times*, 6 October 1941, 2.

[82] Ibid.

This desire to court controversy was to manifest itself in *Rhapsody in Stephen's Green: The Insect Play*, O'Nolan's 1943 adaptation of the Čapek brothers' 1921 play, *Ze života hmyzu* [the lives of the insects], commissioned by Hilton Edwards for the Gaiety Theatre. The play, advertised as the work of Myles na gCopaleen, was denounced by the actor and director Gabriel Fallon in the Catholic *Standard* as a 'Disgusting Performance' which bombarded its audience members 'with expletives until [their] ear-drums [...] burst under the detonated consonance of b–s'.[83] In Fallon's view, na gCopaleen's fetish for 'innuendo' and his willingness to make light of 'subjects like sex and maternity' reflected a failure to distinguish between 'honest dung of the farmyard' and the 'nasty dirt of the chicken run'.[84] Particularly objectionable for Fallon, in the light of this perceived profanity, was the Gaiety's use of the '20th Dublin Troop of the Catholic Boy Scouts of Ireland' as extras.[85] O'Nolan's response, published in the *Standard* the following week, was concerned less with refuting Fallon's accusations than with amplifying them. In a letter from Myles to the Editor of the *Standard*, O'Nolan showcased the same capacity for innuendo and disregard for propriety which Fallon had singled out for censure. In a pastiche of what he perceived to be the perverse and fetishistic perspective of the censorious critic, Myles attacks Fallon for his 'latrine erudition' and 'faecal reveries', refusing to speculate on the 'odd researches that led [the critic] to his great discovery', and expressing his concern that Fallon will seek to 'associat[e] Boy Scouts with dung'.[86] In doing so, Myles dwelt at length on Fallon's objections to the play's language, inflating references to 'expletives' and 'innuendo' into a claim that the play 'abounded in obscenity, filthy language, and gibes at sacred things'.[87] While the image such comments offer of the censorious critic as a monomaniac, more perverse than the supposedly obscene authors whose corrupting influence they seek to arrest, chimes with Beckett's critique of 'Censorship in the Saorstat', O'Nolan's attack on Fallon seems less a challenge to Irish censorship culture than an effort to exploit it for publicity.

Intriguing in this regard is the letter which featured alongside Myles's response, purporting to be from an audience member, 'S.M. Dunn', who seconds Fallon's attack on the play's explicit language and references to

---

[83] Gabriel Fallon, 'Disgusting Performance,' *The Standard*, 26 March 1943, 3.
[84] Ibid.   [85] Ibid.
[86] 'Myles na gCopaleen' (Brian O'Nolan), 'Our Theatre Critic Attacked and Defended: (Letter from Myles Na gCopaleen),' *The Standard*, 2 April 1943, 5.
[87] Ibid.

maternity in a heightened tone of pietistic outrage. Where Fallon had failed to cite specific examples of what he found most objectionable in the play, 'Dunn' quotes several exchanges from Act I, in which a pair of bees discuss their desire for 'the "Queen" up in the sky' and their intention to 'keep pure' until they are able to 'meet' her, to emphasize the scene's status as a burlesque of Catholic Mariology as a sexual lottery in which Holy Mother is the ultimate prize.[88] 'Dunn' likewise draws attention to what they coyly dub 'the "maternity" act' in the play's mid-section, which they decry as 'vile'.[89] In response to this perceived blasphemy from a 'Catholic (!)' playwright, 'Dunn' calls upon *The Standard* to form a 'league [...] to rouse public opinion against the "taking in vain" of God's name' modelled on the life and conduct of the working-class Dublin ascetic, Matt Talbot.[90] It is possible that these were indeed the comments and reflections of a more than usually zealous reader of the robustly Catholic publication. However, as Robert Tracy suggests, it is difficult to escape the suspicion that 'Dunn' was in fact another in a long line of O'Nolan pseudonyms, a suggestion borne out by 'Dunn's apparently detailed familiarity with the play-text.[91] Read as a strategic intervention by O'Nolan himself, 'Dunn's targeted objections to the play appear intended to draw readers' attention to the 'metonymic code' through which the play's sexualized blasphemy operates, exaggerating its apparent obscenity.[92] Meanwhile, the cumbrous euphemism of 'the "maternity" act' (by which is presumably meant the laying and hatching of the talking Egg in Act II) simultaneously derides the prudishness of Catholic moral alarmism and suggests something more shocking than the play itself delivers. More significantly, if a deliberate intervention by O'Nolan, 'Dunn's calls for a 'Matt Talbot League' bespeak a desire to incite a public controversy comparable to that of the *Playboy* riots or the opening night of O'Casey's *The Plough and the Stars* (1926). As Chapter 2 makes clear, it took more than a shift to incite the ire of the Abbey audience in 1907, and

---

[88] The passages which correspond to those complained of by 'Dunn' would appear to be Basil's expression of his desire to 'meet the Queen [...] Alone, I mean quite alone, you knaow [*sic*], in the sky' and Cyril's advocacy of '[c]ontrol of the passions and all that'. S.M. Dunn, 'Our Theatre Critic Attacked and Defended: (Letter from Member of Audience),' *The Standard*, 2 April 1943, 5; Flann O'Brien, *Plays and Teleplays*, ed. Daniel K. Jernigan (Champaign: Dalkey Archive Press, 2013), 173, 174.

[89] Dunn, 'Our Theatre Critic Attacked and Defended: (Letter from Member of Audience),' 5.

[90] Sir Joseph Aloysius Glynn, *Life of Matt Talbot* (Dublin: Catholic Truth Society of Ireland, 1928).

[91] Robert Tracy, 'Introduction,' in *Rhapsody in Stephen's Green: The Insect Play*, by Flann O'Brien, ed. Robert Tracy (Dublin: Lilliput Press, 1994), 15.

[92] Hopper, 'The Dismemberment of Orpheus,' 229–30.

the controversies surrounding the *Playboy* were at least as a much a product of its engagement with the social and biological implications of Irish autarchy as they were with perceived slanders on Irish womanhood. Unfortunately for O'Nolan (and the Gaiety's box office receipts), changing sensibilities and the *Rhapsody*'s lack of a comparably consistent and disquieting theme, meant that such a paroxysm of moral outrage was not forthcoming, and the play finished its short run unmolested, and with a tepid critical reception.[93] As the *Bell*'s theatre critic noted of the controversy, having only a 'normally healthy dirty-mind', he was inclined to find that the play's lack of 'proportion' and focus were more immediately objectionable than its double-entendres.[94]

By the time of *The Hard Life*, O'Nolan's censor-baiting had grown both less subtle and even further out of step with contemporary mores and the operation of the Censorship Act, which had been moderately reformed in 1946 to introduce an appeal process, and the censorship board, whose membership had been reconstituted in 1957 following an internal schism.[95] A sense of O'Nolan's rather tame desire to shock can be caught in a sequence of letters to his friend and editor Timothy O'Keefe, in which he outlined his plan to ensure that *The Hard Life* is suppressed in Ireland. O'Nolan informed O'Keefe of his certainty that the novel would be censored because the Board, 'composed exclusively of ignorant balloxes', ban 'any book they do not like'.[96] In particular, he explained, the flatulent epithet of Father Kurt Fahrt had been chosen to cause 'holy bloody ructions' and 'wirepulling behind the scenes [...] to have the book banned as obscene'.[97] 'Following the anticipated suppression, O'Nolan planned to mount a legal challenge 'in the High Court' to show that the book offended against neither of what he perceived to be the Censorship Act's key stipulations—'(a) plain obscenity, and (b) advocating the unnatural prevention of birth'—and to sue for not only a 'declaration that the book [was] one to be properly on sale' but also 'damages from those who imposed the ban'.[98] O'Nolan was confident that

---

[93] The *Irish Times* found the play 'rather more of an entertainment' than its source material, but concluded that this was not to its benefit, a position shared by the *Bell*, who felt O'Nolan had 'lost most of the point' of the play. The *Irish Independent* was more positive, dubbing the play an 'amusing satire' and praising its use of an Irish setting. The *Irish Press* echoed the *Standard*'s objections to the play's language, which it deemed 'a poor substitute for drama'. *Irish Times*, 22 March 1943, 3; 'C.C.,' 'The Theatre,' *The Bell* 6, no. 2 (May 1943), 156; *Irish Independent*, 22 March 1943, 6; 'T.W.,' 'The Insect Play at the Gaiety,' *Irish Press*, 23 March 1943, 3.

[94] 'C.C.,' 'The Theatre,' 157.

[95] For a detailed account of these reforms and shifts, see Adams, *Censorship: The Irish Experience*, 1968, chaps. 5–7.

[96] O'Brien, *Collected Letters*, 279.   [97] Ibid., 283.   [98] Ibid., 279; 280.

the 'quite intelligent' High Court would find in his favour—he was convinced that the Board would 'be shown in court to be incapable of quoting a line that contravenes' the Act—and feared only that the trial might be a 'jury case'.[99] As his scrotal soubriquet for the Censorship Board and his investment in the wisdom of the upper judiciary over the judgement of the general public suggest, like Beckett, O'Nolan perceived in the Censorship Act a form of state-endorsed philistinism. Likewise, as his characterization of the Act's proscriptions and the grounds upon which he anticipated that *The Hard Life* would be suppressed indicate, O'Nolan shared the Protestant intelligentsia's sense that this anti-intellectual populism served as the vehicle for a noxious blend of pro-natalism, Catholic cultural hegemony, and ignorant caprice. Above all, like the novel's cast, setting, and aesthetic, the plan seems intended to recall or recapture an earlier, Joycean moment of modernist controversy, hoping to replicate in Ireland what the elder author had achieved three decades before in his tussles with the United States' justice system.[100] Yet, the book remained obstinately uncontroversial, and the desired suppression and ensuing legal battle never occurred. This muted reception should not be taken to suggest that the Censorship Act had been defanged—the board banned almost four times as many books in 1961 as it did in 1946—or that the debates over sexual health which had attended its passage had been resolved—contraception would remain illegal (albeit increasingly available) in Ireland until 1978 and unmentionable in print until 1979.[101] Instead, it reflects the extent to which Irish modernism's approach to questions of sexual health had lost its iconoclastic charge.

---

[99] Ibid., 283; 280; 283.

[100] For an overview of the circumstances surrounding Judge John M. Woolsey's decision in *United States vs. One Book Called 'Ulysses'* (1933) and its impact for Joyce and modernism at large, see Paul Vanderham, *James Joyce and Censorship: The Trials of Ulysses* (Basingstoke: Macmillan, 2002), chaps. 4 and 5; Kevin Birmingham, *The Most Dangerous Book: The Battle for James Joyce's Ulysses* (London: Head of Zeus, 2014), chaps. 26 and 27.

[101] In 1973, the Irish Supreme Court ruled that section 17 of the Criminal Law (Amendment) Act—which prohibited the importation and sales of contraceptives—was unconstitutional, prompting an unsuccessful and contentious effort by the Fine Gael–Labour Party coalition government to legislate the issue in 1974. In 1976, the Supreme Court ruled that the Irish Family Planning Association's 1971 publication *Family Planning* should not be banned under the Censorship Act. The 1979 Health (Family Planning) Act addressed both issues (albeit in a relatively conservative fashion), by deleting references to 'the unnatural prevention of conception' from the Censorship Act, and by making contraceptives available to married couples by doctor's prescription. Michael Adams, *Censorship: The Irish Experience* (Dublin: Scepter Books, 1968), 119; Chrystel Hug, *The Politics of Sexual Morality in Ireland* (Basingstoke: Palgrave Macmillan, 1998), chaps. 4 and 5; Brian Girvin, 'Contraception, Moral Panic and Social Change in Ireland, 1969–79,' *Irish Political Studies* 23, no. 4 (December 2008), 555–76; Ferriter, *Occasions of Sin*, 407–30.

Where a previous generation of Irish modernists had been comfortably able to frame themselves as the virile traducers of conservative sexual norms, it was now the Edna O'Briens of the world, not the Flanns, who were facing 'wirepulling behind the scenes' for their engagement with debates over sex, health, and their fraught interrelation in Irish culture.[102] As O'Nolan's dashed hopes of having his Joycean day in court suggest, by 1961, Irish modernist provocations in the domain of sexual health had been surpassed by their context, even as the issues which animated them remained both socially divisive and culturally urgent. Like *The Hard Life* itself, O'Nolan's thwarted gesture of defiance was thus simultaneously belated and timely.

Conclusion

Returning to the question of *The Hard Life*'s 'realism' and O'Nolan's turn away from his contemporary socio-economic moment in the light of this discussion, it becomes clear that the novel offers not an exegesis of squalor, but of the simulacra that compose the appearance of such squalor, and, by extension, the virtue with which such squalor is contrasted. On the one hand, the novel exposes the moral alarmism and purity rhetoric of Irish modernism's ancestral bugbears—the Catholic hierarchy, the Gaelic revival, and their various socially conservative institutional and cultural metastases—as empty simulacra of virtue—kitsch, Plastic Paddy performances of Irishness as a condition of hypocritical piety, artificial shame, and a sexuality whose repression is honoured more in the breach than the observance. On the other, O'Nolan's text, in its squeamishness around directly depicting sex, its failure to goad the censors, and its paradoxically conservative critique of the plight of Irish women, offers a no less unconvincing simulacrum of the kinds of cultural and political rebellion for which Synge, Joyce, and Beckett had been both lauded and vilified. By the 1960s, the novel seems to suggest—for a certain strand of the nation's liberal intelligentsia at the very least—the relationship between Irishness, sexual health, and ideals of purity had become a register of language that had lost all reference in the real world. In its failure to incense the censors and its bathetic recapitulation of many of the key debates within Irish modernism over sexual health, *The Hard Life* seems to throw into sharp relief the famous refrain of John

---

[102] Discussing *Country Girls* with Dermot O'Flynn in 1962, Archbishop McQuaid would boast that he had 'had the book banned'. Ferriter, *Occasions of Sin*, 382.

Montague's 'The Siege of Mullingar, 1963': '*Puritan Ireland's dead and gone,* / *A myth of O'Connor and O'Faolain.*'[103] More than simply auguring the death of the 'myth' of Ireland as an exceptionally repressed and repressive environment—it was and is alive and well—*The Hard Life* seems to highlight, by accident and by design, that efforts to envisage and police models of Irish identity on the grounds of sexual health were both an exhausted hangover of turn-of-the-century cultural politics, and a pernicious presence in the novel's contemporary moment. More than this, it foregrounds the paradoxical conservatism of the iconoclast in a period of relative liberalization, resurrecting old taboos simply so as to have something to subvert. Much as Beckett's *First Love/Premier Amour* seems almost to depend upon the proscriptions of the Censorship Act for its tone and content, in *The Hard Life*, the conservative germ of iconoclasm blossoms into a mode of rebellion not merely parasitically reliant upon, but actively sustaining of the social and political conditions it apparently seeks to critique. In its jaundiced realism and self-defeating efforts to scandalize nineteenth-century social mores for the benefit of a mid-twentieth-century audience, the novel attests to the postmodern status of Irish sexual health rhetoric as a simultaneously exhausted literary trope and a seemingly inexhaustible political tool: a zombie rhetoric, unkillable, yet already long dead. In the process, *The Hard Life* may help to explain how, even in an increasingly liberal Ireland, the logic of '*Veni, V.D., Vici!*' could remain so exhaustingly unvanquished.

---

[103] John Montague, *Selected Poems* (Toronto: Exile Editions, 1991), 62.

Conclusion

In a 1904 diary entry quoted in Chapter 3, Stanislaus Joyce records that his brother 'talks much of the syphilitic contagion in Europe' and Ireland, 'tracing practically everything to it', and claiming it was 'useless to try to avoid it'.[1] While not every Irish modernist may have shared Joyce's conviction concerning the endemic nature of syphilis, as this book has shown, many shared his tendency to understand and respond to his political and cultural milieu through the prism of sexual health. For the authors, politicians, and activists whose work I have surveyed in the preceding chapters, the medicalized and politicized model of sex that emerged in Europe and North America in the nineteenth and twentieth centuries provided an extramoral normative framework through which to envisage and critique a range of (often conflicting) models of Irish identity, culture, and political community. In doing so, it informed the self-fashioning of many Irish modernists, both major and minor, and came to set the terms of debate between nationalists and anti-nationalists, and, in the wake of independence, between the competing social, cultural, and political factions of the emergent Free State. As a concept, sexual health allowed figures such as Yeats, Synge, and Joyce to present themselves as the potent opponents of a conservative sexual culture, even as it enabled them to espouse a model of hygienic autonomy in which sex was treated with deep suspicion. At the same time, it provided a discourse of sexual hygiene through which advanced nationalists such as Moran, Griffith, and Gonne could denounce British influence in Ireland as alien and contaminating—though, as the case of Gogarty suggests, in doing so, it also served to offer a notionally scientific sanction to a noxious strain of anti-Semitic jingoism. It dominated debates surrounding the Censorship of Publications Act, allowing figures such as Beckett and Kate O'Brien to denounce the populism and pro-natalism of what they perceived to be an increasingly conservative and Catholic Free State. However, as my analysis of the fraught relationship that both authors

---

[1] Stanislaus Joyce, *The Complete Dublin Diary of Stanislaus Joyce*, ed. George H. Healy (Ithaca: Cornell University Press, 1971), 51.

Irish Modernism and the Politics of Sexual Health. Lloyd (Meadhbh) Houston, Oxford University Press.
© Lloyd (Meadhbh) Houston 2023. DOI: 10.1093/oso/9780192889492.003.0008

maintained with eugenic thought has shown, it also consistently threatened to expose the conservativism and contradiction that haunted such iconoclasm. Ultimately, as the case of Flann O'Brien (Brian O'Nolan) reveals, it was to prove an issue whose evolving political significance and enduring cultural relevance were to outpace and outlast Irish modernism's capacity for provocation and subversion.

Reflecting on the increasingly robust body of scholarship on Irish modernism that has emerged in the last two decades, Paul Fagan has asserted that the time has come to cease trumpeting the 'arrival' of Irish Modernist Studies as a 'new field' and, instead, 'initiate a conversation that tests the field's borders, co-ordinates, and key texts for their blind-spots and as yet untapped possibilities'.[2] It is my belief that the politicized model of sexual health I have charted in this book provides a valuable lens through which to undertake such an audit. As my re-readings of well-canvassed events such as the Parnell Split, the *Playboy* riots, and the passage of the Censorship of Publications Act have demonstrated, attending to these late nineteenth- and early twentieth-century debates over the sexual health of the Irish reveals both a more 'modern' and scientifically literate nationalism than has hitherto been acknowledged, and a more conservative and sectarian modernism than has sometimes been conceded. As my discussion of Brian O'Nolan's late work suggests, it also raises questions about the period boundaries within which Irish modernism may be situated, and how the 'sexual revolution' of the 1960s should factor in to emerging critical theorizations of late modernism in Ireland (and elsewhere). In a recent discussion of the topic, for example, Andrew Kalaidjian argues that traditional exegeses of late modernism, which focus on British responses to the uncertainty generated by the Second World War and the unravelling of the Empire, do not fit the Irish case, because Irish neutrality in the 'Emergency' arguably meant that the Irish state had never been more drearily secure.[3] In Kalaidjian's account, the Irish late modernist 'turns to uncertainty not', as in the case of their high

---

[2] Paul Fagan, 'Opening Remarks' (Irish Modernisms: Gaps, Conjectures, Possibilities, University of Vienna, 2016). I am grateful to Paul for sharing the text of these remarks with me. Fagan, in collaboration with John Greaney and Tamara Radak, articulates this invitation and explores its implications for Irish Studies and Modernist Studies more fully in the introduction to *Irish Modernisms: Gaps, Conjectures, Possibilities* (London: Bloomsbury Academic, 2021), 1–7.

[3] Andrew Kalaidjian, 'The Uncertainty of Late Irish Modernism: Flann O'Brien and Erwin Schrödinger in Dublin,' in *Science, Technology, and Irish Modernism*, ed. Kathryn Conrad, Cóilín Parsons, and Julie McCormick Weng (Syracuse, New York: Syracuse University Press, 2019).

modernist predecessors, 'because Ireland itself is murky', but because 'Ireland—as a nation—is entirely too real.'[4] It is intriguing to speculate how the increasing normalization of sexual health as an aspect of public discourse and public health policy which I traced in Chapter 6 might figure in these dynamics. In raising such questions, the account I have offered of the role of sexual health in Irish cultural debate also puts substantial pressure on accounts of the history of medicine and sexuality in Ireland that seek to downplay the medicalization and politicization of sex in nineteenth- and twentieth-century Ireland or exceptionalize the Irish case in this regard. As this study has sought to demonstrate, while the specificities of Irish social, political, and cultural life necessarily served to distinguish the forms that 'sexual modernism' took in Ireland from its European and Anglo-American manifestations, these idiosyncrasies tended only to heighten its significance as a matter of public debate and a source of artistic inspiration. In this sense, as I have illustrated throughout *Irish Modernism and the Politics of Sexual Health*, to trace the history of modernism in Ireland is, almost unavoidably, to trace the history of the medicalization and politicization of sex in the emergent nation, and vice versa.

Nevertheless, while intended to be comprehensive in scope, this book cannot claim to have exhausted the topic of sexual health and its politicized role in Irish modernism, or modernism at large. Though focusing on major debates in late nineteenth- and early twentieth-century Irish cultural history has allowed me to offer a fresh and robustly contextualized reading of the emergence and development of modernism in Ireland, it has, with some exceptions, also confined my focus to a corpus of relatively well-established figures in the Irish modernist canon. If, as I have argued, a medicalized and politicized engagement with sex and its relationship to questions of hygiene, autonomy, fertility, and heredity constitutes a major feature of modernism in Ireland, it is intriguing to consider which underexamined figures in the nation's cultural and political history might take on new significance as contributors to Irish modernism when read in this light. For example, while the Abbey Theatre and its founders have loomed large in this study, the work produced by Micheál Mac Liammóir and Hilton Edwards at the Gate Theatre in the 1930s, 40s, and 50s, which consistently sought to queer and query Irish gendered and sexual norms, readily lends itself to being explored

---

[4] Ibid., 248.

through the prism of sexual health.[5] An examination of the ways in which Gate regulars such as Mary Manning and Maura Laverty registered and responded to issues of sexual hygiene or the regulation of fertility in mid-century Irish life would yield not only a fuller sense of the cultural stakes of sexual health in the newly independent nation but a clearer picture of the performance practices (casting, costume, physicality, blocking, etc) through which a medicalized and politicized model of sex was embodied and dramatized in this period. Moreover, though I have made a sustained effort to situate my account of the politics of sexual health in Irish modernism in a wider European and trans-Atlantic context, the inherently trans-national nature of the discourses which informed the concept of sexual health and the medical, legal, and cultural networks through which they were disseminated necessarily strains against a single-nation frame. Indeed, as this book has illustrated, it was this capacity for questions of sexual health to trouble the bodily, cultural, and national borders which the concept was often conscripted to reinforce that made it such a vexed, vibrant, and urgent topic for modernists. The history of modernism and the trans-national politics of sexual health has yet to be written. It is my hope that *Irish Modernism and the Politics of Sexual Health* provides future scholarship with both the framework and the impetus to do so.

Finally, it is my hope that this book will afford historians of culture, medicine, and sexuality in Ireland, and further afield, a firm base from which to explore the ramifications of the medicalization and politicization of sex for late nineteenth- and early twentieth-century culture at large, particularly in its 'popular' and 'middle-brow' manifestations. If, as Luke Seabar and Michael Shallcross asserted in a recent dialogue on 'The Trouble with Modernism', the time has come to interrogate, and, perhaps, even check the impulse towards 'expansion' which has characterized the New Modernist Studies and its deployment of the approbative label 'modernist', and instead resituate modernism as simply one among many aesthetically viable and culturally valuable responses to a broadly conceived modernity, then it may also behove scholars of late nineteenth- and early twentieth-century culture to look beyond the paradigm of 'sexual modernism' to identify the heterogenous ways in which sex and its perceived relationship to health were conceived, experienced, and discussed by those outside the

---

[5] For a recent collection which surveys these aspects of the Gate's programme and praxis, see Marguérite Corporaal and Ruud van den Beuken, eds., *A Stage of Emancipation: Change and Progress at the Dublin Gate Theatre* (Liverpool: Liverpool University Press, 2021).

modernism-sexology nexus in this period.[6] Here, too, as this study has demonstrated, late nineteenth- and early twentieth-century Irish culture, with its uneven socio-economic development, ambivalent relationship to modernity, and robust religious culture, might prove particularly illuminating, offering a valuable opportunity to study what Eve Sedgwick has identified as the 'unrationalized coexistence of different models' which characterizes the operation of conceptual paradigms such as 'sexual health' and 'sexuality' in a given cultural context, and the social relations and discursive practices to which they give rise.[7] In this sense, while *Irish Modernism and the Politics of Sexual Health* attests to the inextricable link between the development of modernism in Ireland and the medicalization of politicization of sex in Irish culture, it also lays the ground-work for scholarship that will look beyond this paradigm to identify alternative conceptions and articulations of sex, health, and their inter-relation in Irish thought and Irish life in the nineteenth and twentieth centuries.

[6] Luke Seaber and Michael Shallcross, 'The Trouble with Modernism: A Dialogue,' *The Modernist Review*, no. 10 (June 28, 2019), https://modernistreviewcouk.wordpress.com/2019/06/28/the-trouble-with-modernism/.

[7] Sedgwick offers this famous characterization in Axiom 5 of the hugely influential 'Introduction' to *Epistemology of the Closet* (1990), in which she challenges the model of 'supervention' which she argues has underpinned the mis-leading search for a singular 'Great Paradigm Shift' in histories of sexuality and, above all, homosexuality. Eve Kosofsky Sedgwick, *Epistemology of the Closet*, Updated with a New Preface (Berkeley: University of California press, 2008), 47; 44. Its implications for the study of the history of sexualities have been usefully elaborated by David Halperin in the essays which comprise *How to Do the History of Homosexuality* (2002), particularly the 'Introduction', 'Forgetting Foucault', and 'How to Do the History of Male Homosexuality', and in the increasingly self-interrogating work of those associated with the 'New British Queer History', particularly Laura Doan and Matt Houlbrook. David M. Halperin, *How to Do the History of Homosexuality* (Chicago: University of Chicago Press, 2002); Laura Doan, 'Forgetting Sedgwick,' *PMLA* 125, no. 2 (March 2010): 370–73; Laura L. Doan, *Disturbing Practices: History, Sexuality, and Women's Experience of Modern War* (Chicago: The University of Chicago Press, 2013); Matt Houlbrook, 'Thinking Queer: The Social and Sexual in Inter-War Britain,' in *British Queer History: New Approaches and Perspectives*, ed. Brian Lewis (Manchester: Manchester University Press, 2013), 134–64.

Bibliography

Primary Sources

Archival Material

'TF to TPC Kirkpatrick,' 6 February 1924. TPCK/3/5: Kirkpatrick Collection, Patient Letters (1 of 2). Royal College of Physicians of Ireland.

Reports, Legislation, and Parliamentary Records

Carrigan (Chairman), William. *Report of the Committee on the Criminal Law Amendment Acts (1880–85), and Juvenile Prostitution*. Dublin: Stationery Office, 1931.

Censorship of Publications Bill, 1928—Second Stage (Resumed), Pub. L. No. 26.6 (1928). http://oireachtasdebates.oireachtas.ie/debates%20authoring/debateswebpack.nsf/takes/dail1928101900003?opendocument.

'Census Bill—[Bill 211]—Second Reading.' *House of Commons Debates*, no. 203 (22 July 1870): cols 805–13.

Dáil Éireann. 'Censorship of Publications Act, 1929.' Irish Statute Book, July 2014. http://www.irishstatutebook.ie/1929/en/act/pub/0021/print.html.

'Dáil in Committee—Local Government Bill, 1924 (Third Stage) Resumed,' Pub. L. No. 9.13 (1924), https://www.oireachtas.ie/en/debates/debate/dail/1924-11-19/8/.

Financial Resolutions—Censorship of Publications Bill, 1928—Committee, Pub. L. No. 28.1, § Committee on Finance (1929). http://oireachtasdebates.oireachtas.ie/debates%20authoring/debateswebpack.nsf/takes/dail1929022000039?opendocument.

Financial Resolutions—Censorship of Publications Bill, 1928—Committee (Resumed), Pub. L. No. 28.2, § Committee on Finance (1929). http://oireachtasdebates.oireachtas.ie/debates%20authoring/debateswebpack.nsf/takes/dail1929022100025?opendocument.

Immigration Act of 1891, 26 Stat. 1084 (Chapter 551) https://govtrackus.s3.amazonaws.com/legislink/pdf/stat/26/STATUTE-26-Pg1084a.pdf.

'Loi du 31 juillet 1920 réprimant la provocation à l'avortement et à la propagande anticonceptionnelle.' *Journal officiel de la République française*, 1 August 1920, 3666.

McAleese, Martin. 'Report of the Inter-Departmental Committee to Establish the Facts of State Involvement with the Magdalen Laundries.' Department of Justice and Equality, February 2013. http://www.justice.ie/en/JELR/Pages/MagdalenRpt2013.

Report of the Committee on Evil Literature. Dublin: Stationery Office, 1926.

Report of the Select Committee on Dublin Hospitals, 1854.

Seanad Éireann. Censorship of Publications Bill, 1928—Third Stage, Pub. L. No. 12.5 (1929). https://www.oireachtas.ie/en/debates/debate/seanad/1929-04-25/2/.

Seanad Éireann. Censorship of Publications Bill, 1928—Third Stage (Resumed). Pub. L. No. 12.10 (1929). https://www.oireachtas.ie/en/debates/debate/seanad/1929-05-15/4/.

Seanad Éireann. Censorship of Publications—Motion. Pub. L. No. 27 (1942). https://www.oireachtas.ie/en/debates/debate/seanad/1942-11-18/6/.

Seanad Éireann. Censorship of Publications—Motion (Resumed). Pub. L. No. 27 (1942). https://www.oireachtas.ie/en/debates/debate/seanad/1942-12-02/8/.

Seanad Éireann. Censorship of Publications—Motion (Resumed). Pub. L. No. 27 (1942). https://www.oireachtas.ie/en/debates/debate/seanad/1942-12-03/3/.

Seanad Éireann. Censorship of Publications—Motion (Resumed). Pub. L. No. 27 (1942). https://www.oireachtas.ie/en/debates/debate/seanad/1942-12-09/3/.

Seanad Éireann. Public Business. Censorship of Publications Bill, 1928 Recommittal Stage. Pub. L. No. 12.12 (1929). https://www.oireachtas.ie/en/debates/debate/seanad/1929-06-05/8/.

'Sterilization.' *House of Commons Debates* 255 (21 July 1931): cols. 1249–56.

Contemporary Newspaper and Journal Articles

Freeman's Journal, 18 February 1881.

The Nation, 2 January 1886.

The Guardian, 19 November 1890.

National Press, 7 July 1891.

The Nation, 29 June 1891.

The Nation, 24 July 1891.

The Nation, 8 October 1891.

National Press, 13 October 1891.

The Times, 18 November 1891.

United Irishman, 20 May 1899.

The Leader, 2 November 1901.

The Leader, 16 November 1901.

United Irishman, 28 May 1904.

The Leader, 17 January 1905.

United Irishman, 18 February 1905.

Irish Times, 24 April 1924.

Irish Times, 10 November 1926.

Irish Times, 13 November 1926.

Irish Times, 22 March 1943.

Irish Independent, 22 March 1943.

'£900 DAMAGES AWARDED IN LIBEL ACTION.' *The Irish Times*, 24 November 1937.

'A Social Scourge.' *Irish Times*, 24 May 1944.

'A Special Correspondent.' 'Venereal Disease in Ireland – I.' *Irish Times*, 21 July 1949.

'A Special Correspondent.' 'Venereal Disease in Ireland – II.' *Irish Times*, 22 July 1949.

'A Special Correspondent.' 'Venereal Disease in Ireland – III.' *Irish Times*, 23 July 1949.

'A Special Correspondent.' 'Venereal Disease in Ireland – IV.' *Irish Times*, 25 July 1949.

'A.M.W.' 'The Demon of Dirty Papers.' *The Leader*, 18 January 1913.

Archer, William. 'Ghosts and Gibberings.' *Pall Mall Gazette*, no. 8127 (8 April 1891): 3.

'At the Outset.' *National Press*, 7 March 1891.

'Carrigadrohid.' 'Waterford and Pernicious Literature.' *The Leader*, 18 January 1913.

'Catholic Truth Society. Message from the Pope. Archbishop and Evil Literature.' *Irish Times*, 18 October 1928.

'C.C.' 'The Theatre.' *The Bell* 6, no. 2 (May 1943): 155–61.

'Censorship of Books. Views of a Free State Senator. The Board's Great Fault.' *Irish Times*, 6 February 1935.

'Control of Venereal Disease Urged.' *Irish Times*, 27 October 1944.

Creagh, Fr John. 'Jewish Trading, Its Growth in Limerick, Address to the Confraternity.' *Munster News*, 13 January 1904.

'Current Affairs.' *The Leader*, 1 February 1913.

Davis, Thomas. 'The Morality of War.' *The Nation*, 10 June 1843.

'Delta.' 'Race Suicide and Souperism.' *Irish Rosary* XXXII, no. 4 (April 1928): 305–7.

'Dr. Oliver Gogarty Sued for Libel: Quotations from Book about Dublin: "Venomous Libels" Says Counsel: Dublin Divorce Case Recalled.' *Irish Times*, 23 November 1937.

'Drive to Combat V.D. May Follow National Inquiry.' *Irish Times*, 19 May 1944.

Dunn, S. M. 'Our Theatre Critic Attacked and Defended: (Letter from Member of Audience).' *The Standard*, 2 April 1943.

'Eugenics and Social Reform.' *The Nation*, 27 August 1910.

Fallon, Gabriel. 'Disgusting Performance.' *The Standard*, 26 March 1943.

Fletcher, Dudley. 'Letters to the Editor: The Free State Censorship Bill.' *Irish Times*, 5 September 1928.

Frederic, Harold. 'Is Parnell a Crazy Man: His Foul Betrayal of the Cause of Ireland. Lunacy a Charitable Construction to Put Upon His Conduct—What His Colleagues Bear—Beginning of the O'Shea Scandal.' *New York Times*, 7 December 1890.

'From a Paris Balcony: Lecture by Abbe Dimnet.' *Irish Times*, 14 November 1936.

Garvin, J. L. 'Parnell and His Power.' *Fortnightly Review* 64 (1 December 1891).

gCopaleen, Myles na (Brian O'Nolan). 'Cruiskeen Lawn: Bell-Idiocy.' *Irish Times*, 6 October 1941.

gCopaleen, Myles na (Brian O'Nolan). 'Our Theatre Critic Attacked and Defended: (Letter from Myles na gCopaleen).' *The Standard*, 2 April 1943.

gCopaleen, Myles na (Brian O'Nolan). 'Cruiskeen Lawn.' *Irish Times*, 8 August 1949.

gCopaleen, Myles na (Brian O'Nolan). 'Cruiskeen Lawn: Oft in the Stilly.' *Irish Times*, 28 November 1961.

Gerrard, Rev Thomas J. 'The Catholic Church and Race Culture.' *Dublin Review* 149 (July 1911): 49–69.

Gogarty, Oliver St John. 'Ugly England (I).' *Sinn Féin*, 15 September 1906.

Gogarty, Oliver St John. 'Ugly England (II).' *Sinn Féin*, 24 November 1906.

Gogarty, Oliver St John. 'Ugly England (III).' *Sinn Féin*, 1 December 1906.

Gonne-MacBride, Maud. 'To the Editor of the Freeman's Journal.' *Freeman's Journal*, 6 June 1904.

Griffith, Arthur. 'The Economics of the Irish Famine.' *United Irishman*, 6 December 1902.

Healy, T. M. 'The Rise and Fall of Mr Parnell.' *New Review* IV, no. 22 (March 1891): 194–203.

'Her Life a Hell.' *Irish Independent*, 3 November 1906.

Hobson, John Atkinson. 'New Books: Mr Wells' Utopia.' *Manchester Guardian*, 25 April 1905.

Horgan, John. 'Edna O'Brien Faces Limerick Audience: Priests Praise Her.' *Irish Times*, 23 April 1966.

'Humanity: Jew and Christian.' *Sunday Independent*, 4 November 1906.

'Ireland: Lifting the Green Curtain.' *Time Magazine* 82, no. 2 (12 July 1963): 28–40.

'J.R.S. of Knocklong' (Oliver St John Gogarty). 'The Irish Yeoman's Return, or Love Is Lord of All.' *Irish Society*, June 1901.

Leslie, James B. 'Letters to the Editor: The Free State Censorship Bill.' *Irish Times*, 18 August 1928.

'Letters to the Editor: "V.D." in Ireland.' *Irish Times*, 26 July 1949.

'Lux.' 'Letters to the Editor: The Free State Censorship Bill.' *Irish Times*, 24 August 1928.

Lyster, M. 'Padraic Colum on the Censorship.' *Irish Statesman* 11 (13 October 1928): 107–8.

Mac Piarais, Pádraig. 'Fabhal-Scéalta: Sliocht Leabhair Bhuidhe Bhaile i bhFad Síos Annso: VII. An Fear Meatha.' *An Barr Buadh* I, no. 7 (April 1912): 2.

'Machiavelli of Statesmen: Abbe Dimnet on Mussolini: Gulf Between Nazism and Fascism.' *Irish Times*, 13 November 1936.

Maher, Mary. 'Who's Afraid of Edna O'Brien?' *Irish Times*, 14 December 1967.

'M.B.' 'V.D.' *Irish Times*, 23 May 1944.

'Míceál' (Michael Cusack). 'The Gaelic Athletic Association.' *United Irishman*, 25 March 1899.

'Míceál' (Michael Cusack). 'The Gaelic Athletic Association – What Does It Mean?' *United Irishman*, 18 March 1899.

Moty. 'Hystérie chez l'homme.' *Gazette des hôpitaux* 30 (12 March 1885): 235–6.

Murray, G. W. 'Letters to the Editor: The Free State Censorship Bill.' *Irish Times*, 1 September 1928.

'Nationalist.' 'The New Patriotism.' *United Irishman*, 11 March 1899.

'Need for Women Police to Cope with V.D. Problem.' *Irish Times*, 20 May 1944.

'Parnell and Our Policy.' *United Ireland*. 12 October 1895.

Poynter, J. W. 'Letters to the Editor: The Free State Censorship Bill.' *Irish Times*, 16 August 1928.

Renan, Ernest. 'La poésie des races celtiques.' *Revue des deux mondes* 5 (1854): 473–506.

Russell, George. 'The Censorship Bill.' *Irish Statesman* 10 (25 August 1928): 486–7.

Scott, Clement. 'Royalty Theatre.' *The Daily Telegraph*, 14 March 1891.

Shaw, George Bernard. 'The Censorship.' *Irish Statesman* 11 (17 November 1928): 206–8.

Sheehy Skeffington, Hanna. 'Frank, Warm-Hearted Irish Woman in Spain.' *Irish Democrat* (16 October 1937): 2.

Sinclair, Henry M. 'Letters to the Editor: Mehr Licht.' *The Irish Times,* 17 November 1936.

Sinclair, Henry M. 'Letters to the Editor: Mehr Licht.' *The Irish Times,* 1 December 1936.

Smith, S. Anderson. 'The Degeneration of Race.' *The Lancet* 77, no. 1956 (23 February 1861): 202–3.

Stewart, R. S. 'The Increase of General Paralysis in England and Wales: Its Causation and Significance.' *Journal of Medical Science* 42 (October 1896): 760–77.

'T.C.D. Society Discussion.' *Irish Press,* 27 October 1944.

'The British Army.' *Sinn Féin,* 6 May 1906.

'The British Army.' *Sinn Féin,* 7 July 1906.

'The Degeneration of Race.' *The Lancet* 76, no. 1947 (22 December 1860): 619–20.

The O'Shea-Parnell Divorce Case: Full and Complete Proceedings. Boston: National Publishing Company, n.d.

'The Third Oireachtas.' *An Claidheamh Soluis,* 10 June 1899.

'The Vigilance Committee.' *The Leader,* 8 February 1913.

'The War on Dirty Papers.' *The Leader,* 15 February, 1913.

'T.W.' 'The Insect Play at the Gaiety.' *Irish Press,* 23 March 1943.

'"V.D." in Ireland.' Irish Times, 28 July 1949.

'"V.D." in Ireland.' *Irish Times,* 3 August 1949.

'V.D. Should Be Notifiable.' *Irish Times,* 26 May 1944.

'Venereal Disease Clinics Founded.' *Irish Press,* 19 May 1944.

'What Dublin Is Reading.' *Irish Times,* 1 March 1937.

'What Dublin Is Reading.' *Irish Times,* 6 March 1937.

'What Dublin Is Reading.' *Irish Times,* 20 March 1937.

'What They Think About Her: Members of the Censorship Board and Prominent Literary Figures Give Their Assessment of Miss O'Brien's Work.' *Irish Times,* 14 December 1967.

Yeats, W. B. 'The Censorship and St Thomas Aquinas.' *Irish Statesman* 11 (22 September 1928): 47–8.

Yeats, W. B. 'The Irish Censorship.' *Spectator,* 28 September 1928: 391–2.

Contemporary Books and Essays

'Alpha and Omega' (Oliver St John Gogarty). *Blight, the Tragedy of Dublin: An Exposition in Three Acts.* Dublin: Talbot Press, 1917.

Anglican Community Document Library. 'Lambeth Conference: Resolutions Archive from 1930,' 2019. https://www.anglicancommunion.org/media/127734/1930.pdf.

Aquinas, St, Thomas. *Summa Theologica.* Vol. 1. 8 vols. Paris: Bloud, 1880.

Arnold, Matthew. *On the Study of Celtic Literature.* London: Smith, Elder, & Co. 1867.

Beckett, Samuel. *Premier Amour.* Paris: Minuit, 1970.

Beckett, Samuel. 'Censorship in the Saorstat.' In *Disjecta: Miscellaneous Writings and a Dramatic Fragment,* edited by Ruby Cohn, 84–8. London: J. Calder, 1983.

Beckett, Samuel. *Disjecta: Miscellaneous Writings and a Dramatic Fragment*. Edited by Ruby Cohn. London: J. Calder, 1983.

Beckett, Samuel. *Dream of Fair to Middling Women*. Edited by Eoin O'Brien and Edith Fournier. New York: Arcade Publishing, 1992.

Beckett, Samuel. *Eleutheria*. Paris: Minuit, 1995.

Beckett, Samuel. *Murphy*. Edited by J. C. C. Mays. London: Faber, 2009.

Beckett, Samuel. *The Expelled/The Calmative/The End & First Love*. Edited by Christopher Ricks. London: Faber, 2009.

Beckett, Samuel. *The Letters of Samuel Beckett*. Edited by Martha Dow Fehsenfeld, Lois More Overbeck, George Craig, and Dan Gunn. Vol. I: 1929–1940. 4 vols. Cambridge: Cambridge University Press, 2009.

Beckett, Samuel. *More Pricks Than Kicks*. Edited by Cassandra Nelson. London: Faber and Faber, 2010.

Burstel, R. 'Consanguinity (in Canon Law).' In *The Catholic Encyclopaedia*. Vol. 4. New York: Robert Appleton Company, 1908. http://www.newadvent.org/cathen/04264a.htm.

Carrel, Alexis. *L'homme, cet inconnu*. Paris: Librarie Plon, 1935.

Catholic Truth Society of Ireland. *The Problem of Undesirable Printed Matter: Suggested Remedies*. Dublin: Catholic Truth Society, 1926.

Catholic Truth Society of Ireland Annual and Record of Conferences. Dublin: Catholic Truth Society, 1912.

Charcot, Jean Martin. *Leçons du Mardi à la Salpêtrière: Policliniques, 1888–1889*. Paris: Progrés Médical, 1889.

Charcot, Jean Martin. *Lectures on the Diseases of the Nervous System*, translated by George Sigerson. London: New Sydenham Society, 1881.

Chesterton, G. K. *Eugenics and Other Evils*. London: Cassell and Company, 1922.

Chesterton, G. K. 'Science and Patriotism.' *The Speaker: The Liberal Review*, 2 February 1901: 488–9.

Clery, Arthur. *Dublin Essays*. Dublin: Maunsel, 1919.

Connellan, J. *Life of Charles Stewart Parnell, Esq. M.P. Reprinted from the Leader*. London, 1888.

Crawley, Alfred Ernest. *The Mystic Rose: A Study of Primitive Marriage*. London: Macmillan, 1902.

Darwin, Charles. *On the Various Contrivances by Which British and Foreign Orchids Are Fertilised, and on the Good Effects of Intercrossing*. London: John Murray, 1862.

Ellis, Havelock. *Studies in the Psychology of Sex*. Vol. 1. New York: Random House, 1897.

Ellis, Havelock. *Sexual Selection in Man: Touch. Smell. Hearing. Vision*. Philadelphia: FA Davis Company, 1905.

Ellmann, Richard, ed. *Letters of James Joyce*. Vol. 2. 3 vols. London: Faber and Faber, 1966.

Ellmann, Richard, ed. *Selected Letters of James Joyce*. London: Faber and Faber, 1975.

Fournier, Alfred. *Prophylaxie de la Syphilis*. Paris: J. Rueff, 1903.

Freud, Sigmund. *Drei Abhandlungen Zur Sexualtheorie*. Leipzig und Wien: Franz Deuticke, 1905.

Gabler, Hans Walter, A Walton Litz, David Hayman, and Danis Rose, eds. *The James Joyce Archive*. Vol. 4. 63 vols. New York: Garland, 1977.

Galton, Francis. *Inquiries into Human Faculty and Its Development*. London: Macmillan, 1883.

Gerrard, Rev Thomas J. *The Church and Eugenics*. London: P.S. King & Son, 1917.

Gilbert, Stuart, ed. *Letters of James Joyce*. Vol. 1. 3 vols. London: Faber and Faber, 1957.

Gladstone, Mary. *Her Diaries and Letters*. Edited by Lucy Masterman. London: E.P. Dutton, 1930.

Glynn, Sir Joseph Aloysius. *Life of Matt Talbot*. Dublin: Catholic Truth Society of Ireland, 1928.

Gogarty, Oliver St John. *As I Was Going Down Sackville Street: A Fantasy in Fact*. London: Rich and Cowan, 1937.

Gogarty, Oliver St John. *Tumbling in the Hay*. London: Constable and Company, 1939.

Gogarty, Oliver St John. *The Poems & Plays of Oliver St John Gogarty*. Edited by A Norman Jeffares. Gerrards Cross: Colin Smythe, 2001.

Grasset, Joseph, and Sidoine Jeannet. *Quelques cas d'hystérie mâle et de neurasthénie*. Montpellier: C Coulet, 1892.

Gregg, John A. F. *The 'Ne Temere' Decree: A Lecture Delivered Before the Members of the Church of Ireland Cork Young Men's Association on March 17th, 1911*. Dublin: Association for Promoting Christian Knowledge, 1911.

Gregory, Isabella Augusta Persse. *Our Irish Theatre: A Chapter of Autobiography*. New York: Capricorn Books, 1965.

Hobhouse, Leonard Trelawny. *Social Evolution and Political Theory*. New York: Columbia University Press, 1911.

Hogan, Robert Goode, and Michael J. O'Neill, eds. *Joseph Holloway's Abbey Theatre: A Selection from His Unpublished Journal: Impressions of a Dublin Playgoer*. Carbondale: Southern Illinois University Press, 2009.

Hogben, Lancelot. *Genetic Principles in Medicine and Social Science*. London: Williams & Norgate, 1932.

Hogben, Lancelot. 'Race and Prejudice.' In *Dangerous Thoughts*, 44–58. London: George Allen & Unwin, 1939.

Huth, Alfred Henry. *The Marriage of Near Kin Considered with Respect to the Laws of Nations: The Results of Experience and the Teachings of Biology*. Longmans, Green, and Company, 1887.

Hyde, Douglas. 'The Necessity for De-Anglicizing Ireland.' In *The Revival of Irish Literature*, edited by Charles Gavan Duffy, 117–61. London: T. Fisher Unwin, 1894.

Ibsen, Henrik. *Henrik Ibsen, Ghosts; An Enemy of the People; The Wild Duck*, Authorized English Edition, trans. William Archer (London: Walter Scott, 1904).

Inghinidhe na hÉireann. Irish Girls! Dublin: *Inghinidhe na hÉireann*, 1914.

Joyce, James. *Ulysses*. Edited by Hans Gabler. New York: Vintage, 1986.

Joyce, James. *Poems and Shorter Writings: Including Epiphanies, Giacomo Joyce, and 'A Portrait of the Artist.'* Edited by Richard Ellmann, A. Walton Litz, and John Whittier-Ferguson. London: Faber and Faber, 1991.

Joyce, James. *Dubliners: A Norton Critical Edition*. Edited by Margot Norris, Hans Walter Gabler, and Walter Hettche. New York: W.W. Norton, 2006.

Joyce, James. *A Portrait of the Artist as a Young Man: Authoritative Text, Backgrounds and Contexts, Criticism*. Edited by John Paul Riquelme, Hans Walter Gabler, and Walter Hettche. New York: W.W. Norton, 2007.

Joyce, James. *Occasional, Critical, and Political Writing*. Edited by Kevin Barry. Translated by Conor Deane. Oxford: Oxford University Press, 2008.

Joyce, Stanislaus. *The Complete Dublin Diary of Stanislaus Joyce*. Edited by George H. Healy. Ithaca: Cornell University Press, 1971.

Kaan, Heinrich. *Psychopathia Sexualis*. Leipzig: Leopold Voss, 1844.

Kant, Immanuel. *Lectures on Ethics*. Translated by Louis Infield. New York: Harper and Row, 1963.

Kelly, John, Eric Domville, Warwick Gould, Ronald Schuchard, and Deirdre Toomey, eds. *The Collected Letters of W. B. Yeats*. InteLex Electronic Edition. Oxford University Press, 2002.

Keynes, John Maynard, and Alexander Carr-Saunders. 'The Galton Lecture, 1946: Presentation of the Society's Gold Medal.' *Eugenics Review* 38, no. 1 (1946): 39–42.

Kilroy, James. *The 'Playboy' Riots*. Dublin: Dolmen Press, 1971.

Krafft-Ebing, Richard von. *Psychopathia Sexualis: Eine klinisch-forensische Studie*. Stuttgart: Verlag von Ferdinand Enke, 1886.

Krafft-Ebing, Richard von. *Psychopathia Sexualis: Mit besonderer Berucksichtigung der kontraren Sexualempfindung: Eine medizinisch-gerichtliche Studie fur Arzte und Juriste*. 12. Ausgabe. Stuttgart: Verlag von Ferdinand Enke, 1902.

Krafft-Ebing, Richard von. *Psychopathia Sexualis: Mit besonderer Berucksichtigung der kontraren Sexualempfindung: Eine medizinisch-gerichtliche Studie fur Arzte und Juriste*. 13. Ausgabe. Stuttgart: Verlag von Ferdinand Enke, 1907.

Lecky, William Edward Hartpole. *Democracy and Liberty*. Vol. 1. 2 vols. London: Longmans, Green, and Co, 1896.

Luby, T. C. R. F. Walsh, and J. C. Curtin. *The Story of Ireland's Struggle for Self-Government*. New York: Gay Brothers & Company, 1893.

Lynn, Kathleen, and Richard Hayes. 'Public Health Circulars, No. 1.' Sinn Féin Public Health Department, Dublin, February 1918.

Macalister, Robert Alexander Stewart, trans. *Lebor Gabála Érenn: The Book of the Taking of Ireland*. Vol. 4. 5 vols. Dublin: Irish Texts Society, 1941.

MacCabe, Frederick F. *War with Disease*. 2nd ed. London: Baillière, Tindall, and Cox, 1907.

Malthus, Thomas Robert. *An Essay on the Principle of Population, as It Affects the Future Improvement of Society. With Remarks on the Speculations of Mr. Godwin, M. Condorcet and Other Writers*. 1st ed. London: J. Johnson, 1798.

Mangan, James Clarence. *The Collected Works of James Clarence Mangan. Vol. 3. Poems, 1845–1847*. Edited by Jacques Chuto. 4 vols. Blackrock: Irish Academic Press, 1996.

Mannin, Ethel. *Common-Sense and the Child: A Plea for Freedom*. London: Jarrolds, 1931.

Maricourt, Elisé-Samuel. *Contribution à l'étude de l'hystérie Chez l'homme*. Paris: Medical Dissertation, 1877.

Maudsley, Henry. *The Physiology and Pathology of the Mind*. London: Macmillan, 1867.

Mickle, William Julius. *General Paralysis of the Insane*. London: H.K. Lewis, 1880.

Mill, John Stuart. *On Liberty; with The Subjection of Women; and Chapters on Socialism*. Edited by Stefan Collini. Cambridge: Cambridge University Press, 1989.

Mitchel, John. *Jail Journal*. New York: Press of the Citizen, 1854.

Montague, John. *Selected Poems*. Toronto: Exile Editions, 1991.

Moore, George. *A Mere Accident*. London: Vizetelly & Co, 1887.

Moore, George. *A Drama in Muslin: A Realistic Novel*. Edited by Alexander Norman Jeffares. Gerrards Cross: Colin Smythe, 1981.

Moore, George. *The Untilled Field*. Edited by Richard Allen Cave. Gerrards Cross: Colin Smythe, 2000.

Moran, David Patrick. *The Philosophy of Irish Ireland*. Edited by Patrick Maume. Dublin: University College Dublin Press, 2006.

Morel, Bénédict Augustin. *Traité des Dégénérescences Physiques, Intellectuelles et Morales de l'Espèce Humaine et des Causes qui Produisent ces Variétés Maladives*. Paris: J.B. Ballière, 1857.

Nietzsche, Friedrich Wilhelm. *Human, All Too Human: A Book for Free Spirits*. Translated by R. J. Hollingdale. Cambridge: Cambridge University Press, 1996.

Nietzsche, Friedrich Wilhelm. *The Birth of Tragedy and Other Writings*. Edited by Raymond Geuss and Ronald Speirs. Translated by Ronald Speirs. Cambridge: Cambridge University Press, 1999.

Nietzsche, Friedrich Wilhelm. *The Gay Science: With a Prelude in German Rhymes and an Appendix of Songs*. Edited by Bernard Williams. Translated by Josefine Nauckhoff and Adrian Del Caro. Cambridge: Cambridge University Press, 2001.

Nietzsche, Friedrich Wilhelm. *Writings from the Late Notebooks*. Edited by Rüdiger Bittner. Translated by Kate Sturge. Cambridge: Cambridge University Press, 2003.

Nietzsche, Friedrich Wilhelm. *The Anti-Christ, Ecce Homo, Twilight of the Idols, and Other Writings*. Edited by Aaron Ridley and Judith Norman. Translated by Judith Norman. Cambridge: Cambridge University Press, 2005.

Nietzsche, Friedrich Wilhelm. *On the Genealogy of Morality*. Edited by Keith Ansell-Pearson. Translated by Carol Diethe. Rev. student ed. Cambridge: Cambridge University Press, 2007.

Nordau, Max. *Entartung*. Vol. 1. 2 vols. Berlin: Carl Dunder, 1893.

Nordau, Max. *Entartung*. Vol. 2. 2 vols. Berlin: Carl Dunder, 1893.

O'Brien, Flann (Brian O'Nolan). *The Complete Novels*. New York: Alfred A. Knopf, 2007.

O'Brien, Flann (Brian O'Nolan). *Plays and Teleplays*. Edited by Daniel K. Jernigan. Champaign: Dalkey Archive Press, 2013.

O'Brien, Flann (Brian O'Nolan). *The Short Fiction of Flann O'Brien*. Edited by Neil Murphy and Keith Hopper. Translated by Jack Fennell. Champaign, Illinois: Dalkey Archive Press, 2013.

O'Brien, Flann (Brian O'Nolan. *The Collected Letters of Flann O'Brien*. Edited by Maebh Long. Victoria, TX: Dalkey Archive, 2018.

O'Brien, Kate. *Pray for the Wanderer*. London: Penguin, 1951.

O'Brien, Kate. *The Last of Summer*. Repr. London: Virago Press, 1990.

O'Brien, Kate. *The Ante-Room*. Repr. London: Virago, 1997.

O'Brien, Kate. *Farewell Spain*. Repr. London: Virago, 2006.

O'Brien, Kate. *Without My Cloak*. Repr. London: Virago, 2006.

O'Brien, Kate. *The Land of Spices*. Repr. London: Virago, 2007.

O'Brien, R. Barry. *The Life of Charles Stewart Parnell, 1846–1891*. Vol. 1. 2 vols. London: Smith, Elder, 1898.

O'Connor, T. P. *Charles Stewart Parnell: A Memory*. London: Ward, Lock, Bowden & Co. 1891.

O'Grady, Standish. *The Story of Ireland*. London: Methuen & Co, 1894.

Oxford, Margot. *More Memories*. London: Cassell, 1933.

Parnell, John Howard. *Charles Stewart Parnell: A Memoir*. New York: Henry Holt, 1914.

Parnell, Katharine. *Charles Stewart Parnell, His Love Story and Political Life*. Vol. 2. 2 vols. London: London & Co, 1914.

Plato. *The Dialogues of Plato Translated into English with Analyses and Introductions*. Translated by Benjamin Jowett. 3rd ed. Revised and updated. Oxford: Oxford University Press, 1892.

Plato. *Republic*. Translated by Robin Waterfield. Reissued [1993]. Oxford: Oxford University Press, 1998.

Pope Pius XI. 'Casti Connubii, Encyclical of Pope Pius XI on Christian Marriage to the Venerable Brethren, Patriarchs, Primates, Archbishops, Bishops, and Other Local Ordinaries Enjoying Peace and Communion with the Apostolic See.' The Holy See, February 2016. https://w2.vatican.va/content/pius-xi/en/encyclicals/documents/hf_p-xi_enc_19301231_casti-connubii.html.

Power, D'Arcy, and J. Keogh Murphy, eds. *A System of Syphilis, with an Introduction by Sir Jonathan Hutchinson*. 6 vols. London: Frowde, 1908.

Rentoul, Robert Reid. *Race Culture; or, Race Suicide? A Plea for the Unborn*. London: Walter Scott, 1906.

Rousseau, Jean Jacques. *Œuvres complètes de J.-J. Rousseau*. Vol. tome II : *La nouvelle Héloïse. Émile. Lettre à M. de Beaumont*. Paris: Alexandre Houssiaux, 1852.

Russell, G. W. E. *Portraits of the Seventies*. London: T. Fisher Unwin, 1916.

Saleeby, Caleb Williams. *Woman and Womanhood: A Search for Principles*. London: Mitchell Kennerley, 1911.

Saleeby, Caleb Williams. *The Eugenic Prospect: National and Racial*. London: T. Fisher Unwin, 1921.

Saleeby, Caleb Williams. *Sunlight and Health*. London: Nisbett & Co, 1923.

Schiller, F. C. S. *Social Decay and Eugenical Reform*. London: Constable, 1932.

Searle, G. R. *Eugenics and Politics in Britain, 1900–1914*. Leyden: Noordhoff International Pub, 1976.

Shaw, George Bernard. *Bernard Shaw: Collected Letters, 1911–1925*. Edited by Dan H. Laurence. Vol. 3. 4 vols. London: Max Reinhardt, 1985.

Shaw, George Bernard. *Bernard Shaw: Collected Letters, 1926–1950*. Edited by Dan H. Laurence. Vol. 4. 4 vols. London: Max Reinhardt, 1988.

Shaw, George Bernard. *Man and Superman: A Comedy and a Philosophy*. Westminster: Archibald Constable & Co, 1903.

Shaw, George Bernard. *The Intelligent Woman's Guide to Socialism and Capitalism.* New York: Brentano's, 1928.

Shaw, George Bernard. *The Intelligent Woman's Guide to Socialism, Capitalism, Sovietism, and Fascism.* Pelican. Vol. 1. 2 vols. London: Penguin Books, 1937.

Shaw, George Bernard. 'The Other Side. Bernard Shaw Repeats His Sticking Tight Advice.' In *The Matter with Ireland*, edited by Dan H. Laurence and David H. Greene, 2nd ed. 31–4. Gainesville: University Press of Florida, 2001.

Shaw, George Bernard. *The Quintessence of Ibsenism.* London: Walter Scott, 1891.

Shaw, George Bernard. 'Shall Parnell Go?' In *The Matter with Ireland*, edited by Dan H. Laurence and David H. Greene, 2nd ed. 30–1. Gainesville: University Press of Florida, 2001.

Sociological Society, ed. 'From Mr. G. Bernard Shaw.' In *Sociological Papers*, 74–5. London: Macmillan, 1905.

Spencer, Herbert. 'Progress: Its Law and Cause.' In *Essays: Scientific, Political, and Speculative*, Library. 1:8–62. London: Williams & Norgate, 1891.

Spencer, Herbert. *The Principles of Biology.* Revised and enlarged. Vol. 1. 2 vols. London: Williams & Norgate, 1898.

Stanford, William Bedell. *A Recognised Church: The Church of Ireland in Éire.* Dublin: Association for Promoting Christian Knowledge, Dublin and Belfast, 1944.

Stopes, Marie Carmichael. *Married Love: A New Contribution to the Solution of Sex Difficulties.* London: A.C. Fifield, 1918.

Stopes, Marie Carmichael. 'Imperial and Racial Aspects, II.' In *The Control of Parenthood*, edited by James Marchant, 207–22. New York: G.P. Putnam's Sons, 1920.

Stopes, Marie Carmichael. *Radiant Motherhood: A Book for Those Who Are Creating the Future.* New York: G.P. Putnam's Sons, 1920.

Stopes, Marie Carmichael. *Roman Catholic Methods of Birth Control.* London: Peter Davies, 1933.

Sutherland, Halliday. *Birth Control: A Statement of Christian Doctrine Against the Neo-Malthusians.* London: Harding and More, 1922.

Synge, J. M. *Collected Works, 2: Prose.* Edited by Alan Price. Gerrards Cross: Colin Smythe, 1982.

Synge, J. M. *Collected Works, 4: Plays, Book 2.* Edited by Ann Saddlemyer. Gerrards Cross: Colin Smythe, 1982.

Synge, J. M. *The Collected Letters of John Millington Synge*, edited by Ann Saddlemyer. Vol. 1. Oxford: Clarendon Press, 1983.

Synge, J. M. 'The Last Fortress of the Celt.' In *Travelling Ireland: Essays, 1898–1908*, edited by Nicholas Grene, 10–21. Dublin: Lilliput Press, 2009.

Tocqueville, Alexis de. *De la Démocratie en Amérique.* Vol. 1. 4 vols. Paris: Pagnerre, 1848.

Toksvig, Signe. *Eve's Doctor.* London: Faber and Faber, 1937.

Toksvig, Signe. *Signe Toksvig's Irish Diaries, 1926–1937.* Edited by Lis Pihl. Dublin: Lilliput Press, 1994.

Weininger, Otto. *Sex and Character: Authorised Translation from the Sixth German Edition.* London: William Heinemann, 1903.

Westermarck, Edward. *The History of Human Marriage*. London: Macmillan, 1891.

Wilde, Oscar. *The Picture of Dorian Gray: A Norton Critical Edition*. Edited by Michael Patrick Gillespie. 2nd ed. New York: W.W. Norton & Co, 2007.

Yeats, W. B. *The Variorum Edition of the Plays of W.B. Yeats*. Edited by Russell K. Alspach and Catherine C. Alspach. London: Macmillan, 1966.

Yeats, W. B. *Uncollected Prose*. Edited by John P. Frayne. Vol. 1. London: Macmillan, 1970.

Yeats, W. B. *Memoirs*. Edited by Denis Donoghue. London: Papermac, 1988.

Yeats, W. B. *Later Essays. The Collected Works of W.B. Yeats. Vol. V*. Edited by William H. O'Donnell. New York: Scribner, 1994.

Yeats, W. B. *Autobiographies. The Collected Works of W.B. Yeats. Vol. III*. Edited by William H. O'Donnell and Douglas N. Archibald. New York: Scribner, 1999.

Yeats, W. B. *The Poems*. Edited by Daniel Albright. London: Everyman, 2000.

Yeats, W. B. *Later Articles and Reviews: Uncollected Articles, Reviews, and Radio Broadcasts Written After 1900*. Edited by Colton Johnson. Vol. X. The Collected Works of W. B. Yeats. New York: Scribner, 2000.

Yeats, W. B. *The Plays. The Collected Works of W.B. Yeats. Vol. II*. Edited by David R Clark and Rosalind E Clark. Houndmills: Palgrave Macmillan, 2001.

Yeats, W. B. *The Irish Dramatic Movement. The Collected Works of W.B. Yeats. Vol. VIII*. Edited by Mary Fitzgerald and Richard J. Finneran. Houndmills: Palgrave Macmillan, 2003.

Yeats, W. B.. *Early Essays. The Collected Works of W.B. Yeats. Vol. IV*. Edited by Richard J. Finneran and George Mills Harper. New York: Scribner, 2007.

Secondary Criticism

Ackerley, Chris, and S. E. Gontarski. *The Grove Companion to Samuel Beckett: A Reader's Guide to His Works, Life, and Thought*. New York: Grove Press, 2004.

Adams, Mark B., ed. *The Wellborn Science: Eugenics in Germany, France, Brazil, and Russia*. New York: Oxford University Press, 1990.

Adams, Michael. *Censorship: The Irish Experience*. Dublin: Scepter Books, 1968.

Adorno, Theodor W. *Negative Dialectics*. Translated by E. B. Ashton. New York: Continuum, 1973.

Agar, Nicholas. *Liberal Eugenics: In Defence of Human Enhancement*. Oxford: Blackwell, 2004.

Alexander, Sally. 'The Mysteries and Secrets of Women's Bodies: Sexual Knowledge in the First Half of the Twentieth Century.' In *Modern Times: Reflections On a Century of English Modernity*, edited by Mica Nava and Alan O'Shea, 161–75. London: Routledge, 1996.

Anderson, Nancy Fix. 'Cousin Marriage in Victorian England.' *Journal of Family History* 11, no. 3 (1986): 285–301.

Anderson, Perry. 'Modernity and Revolution.' *New Left Review* 144 (April 1984): 96–113.

Angelides, Steven. *A History of Bisexuality*. Chicago: University of Chicago Press, 2001.

Armstrong, Tim. *Modernism, Technology, and the Body: A Cultural Study*. Cambridge: Cambridge University Press, 1998.

Arrington, Lauren. *W.B. Yeats, the Abbey Theatre, Censorship, and the Irish State: Adding the Half-Pence to the Pence*. Oxford: Oxford University Press, 2010.

Arrington, Lauren. 'Irish Modernism and Its Legacies.' In *The Princeton History of Modern Ireland*, edited by Richard Bourke and Ian McBride, 236–52. Princeton: Princeton University Press, 2016.

Arrington, Lauren. 'Irish Modernism.' Oxford Research Encyclopaedia of Literature, February 2017. http://literature.oxfordre.com/view/10.1093/acrefore/9780190201098. 001.0001/acrefore-9780190201098-e-237.

Backus, Margot, and Joseph Valente. 'The Land of Spices , the Enigmatic Signifier, and the Stylistic Invention of Lesbian (In)Visibility.' *Irish University Review* 43, no. 1 (May 2013): 55–73.

Baines, Jennika. 'A Portrait of the Artist as a Dubliner: Eroding the Künstlerroman in *The Hard Life*.' In *'Is It About a Bicycle?': Flann O'Brien in the Twenty-First Century*, edited by Jennika Baines, 142–56. Dublin: Four Courts Press, 2011.

Bair, Deirdre. *Samuel Beckett: A Biography*. London: Vintage, 1990.

Baker, Phil. *Beckett and the Mythology of Psychoanalysis*. New York: St. Martin's Press, 1997.

Baker, Stuart E. *Bernard Shaw's Remarkable Religion: A Faith That Fits the Facts*. Gainesville: University Press of Florida, 2002.

Baldwin, Peter. *Contagion and the State in Europe, 1830–1930*. Cambridge: Cambridge University Press, 1999.

Barkan, Elazar, and Ronald Bush, eds. *Prehistories of the Future: The Primitivist Project and the Culture of Modernism*. Stanford: Stanford University Press, 1995.

Bashford, Alison, and Philippa Levine, eds. *The Oxford Handbook of the History of Eugenics*. Oxford: Oxford University Press, 2010.

Bateman-House, Alison, and Amy L. Fairchild. 'Medical Examination of Immigrants at Ellis Island.' *AMA Journal of Ethics* 10, no. 4 (April 2008): 235–41.

Bauer, Heike. *English Literary Sexology: Translations of Inversion, 1860–1930*. Basingstoke: Palgrave Macmillan, 2009.

Bauer, Heike, ed. *Sexology and Translation: Cultural and Scientific Encounters Across the Modern World*. Philadelphia: Temple University Press, 2015.

Beccalossi, Chiara. 'Sex, Medicine, Disease: From Reproduction to Sexuality.' In *A Cultural History of Sexuality in the Age of Empire*, edited by Chiara Beccalossi and Ivan Crozier, 101–22. Oxford: Berg, 2011.

Beer, Gillian. *Darwin's Plots: Evolutionary Narrative in Darwin, George Eliot and Nineteenth-Century Fiction*. 3rd ed. Cambridge: Cambridge University Press, 2009.

Beier, Lucinda McCray. '"We Were Green as Grass": Learning about Sex and Reproduction in Three Working-Class Lancashire Communities, 1900–1970.' *Social History of Medicine* 16, no. 3 (1 December 2003): 461–80.

Beier, Lucinda McCray. *For Their Own Good: The Transformation of English Working-Class Health Culture, 1880–1970*. Columbus: Ohio State University Press, 2008.

Ben-Zvi, Linda, ed. *Women in Beckett: Performance and Critical Perspectives*. Urbana: University of Illinois Press, 1990.

Berlin, Isiah. 'Two Concepts of Liberty.' In *Liberty*, edited by Henry Hardy, 166–217. Oxford: Oxford University Press, 2002.

Bew, Paul. *Enigma: A New Life of Charles Stewart Parnell*. Dublin: Gill & Macmillan, 2012.

Birmingham, Kevin. *The Most Dangerous Book: The Battle for James Joyce's Ulysses*. London: Head of Zeus, 2014.

Bixby, Patrick. *Samuel Beckett and the Postcolonial Novel*. Cambridge: Cambridge University Press, 2009.

Bland, Lucy, and Laura L. Doan, eds. *Sexology in Culture: Labelling Bodies and Desires*. Cambridge: Polity Press, 1998.

Blease, Walter Lyon. *A Short History of English Liberalism*. London: T. Fisher Unwin, 1913.

The Abbey Archive. 'Blight—The Tragedy of Dublin by Oliver St John Gogarty as Gideon Ousley,' 2017. https://www.abbeytheatre.ie/archives/play_detail/10218/.

Bohlmann, Otto. *Yeats and Nietzsche: An Exploration of Major Nietzschean Echoes in the Writings of William Butler Yeats*. London: Macmillan, 1982.

Bolton, Jonathan. 'Comedies of Failure: O'Brien's *The Hard Life* and Moore's *The Emperor of Ice Cream*.' *New Hibernia Review* 12, no. 3 (2008): 118–33.

Bourke, Angela, Siobhán Kilfeather, Maria Luddy, Margaret Mac Curtain, Gerardine Meaney, Máirín Ní Dhonnchadha, Mary O'Dowd, and Clair Wills, eds. *The Field Day Anthology of Irish Writing, Volume IV: Irish Women's Writings and Traditions*. Cork University Press, 2002.

Bourke, Angela, Siobhán Kilfeather, Maria Luddy, Margaret Mac Curtain, Gerardine Meaney, Máirín Ní Dhonnchadha, Mary O'Dowd, and Clair Wills, eds. *The Field Day Anthology of Irish Writing, Volume V: Irish Women's Writings and Traditions*. Cork University Press, 2002.

Bourke, Richard. 'Introduction.' In *The Princeton History of Modern Ireland*, edited by Richard Bourke and Ian McBride, 1–18. Princeton: Princeton University Press, 2016.

Bowen, Kurt Derek. *Protestants in a Catholic State: Ireland's Privileged Minority*. Kingston: McGill-Queen's University Press, 1983.

Boyce, David George, and Alan O'Day, eds. *Parnell in Perspective*. London: Routledge, 1991.

Bradbury, Malcolm, and James Walter McFarlane, eds.*Modernism, 1890–1930: A Guide to European Literature*. Repr. London: Penguin Books, 1991.

Bradshaw, David. 'The Eugenics Movement in the 1930s and the Emergence of *On the Boiler*.' In *Yeats Annual No. 9*, 189–215. London: Macmillan, 1992.

Brady, Deirdre F. *Literary Coteries and the Irish Women Writers' Club (1933–1958)*. Liverpool: Liverpool University Press, 2021.

Brandt, Allan M. *No Magic Bullet: A Social History of Venereal Disease in the United States Since 1880*, 35th Anniversary Edition. Oxford: Oxford University Press, 2020.

Broberg, Gunnar, and Nils Roll-Hansen, eds. *Eugenics and the Welfare State: Sterilization Policy in Denmark, Sweden, Norway, and Finland*. East Lansing: Michigan State University Press, 1996.

Brooker, Peter, Andrzej Gąsiorek, Deborah Longworth, and Andrew Thacker, eds. *The Oxford Handbook of Modernisms*. Oxford: Oxford University Press, 2010.

Brown, John. *The British Welfare State: A Critical History*. Oxford: Blackwell, 1995.

Brown, Kevin. *The Pox: The Life and Near Death of a Very Social Disease*. Stroud: Sutton Publishing, 2006.

Brown, Terence. *Ireland: A Social and Cultural History, 1922–2002*. Rev. ed. London: Harper Perennial, 2004.

Brown, Terence. *The Literature of Ireland: Culture and Criticism*. Cambridge: Cambridge University Press, 2010.

Brownlow, Graham. 'Fabricating *Economic Development*.' *Working Papers in British-Irish Studies*, no. 92 (2009): 1–21.

Bryden, Mary. *Women in Samuel Beckett's Prose and Drama: Her Own Other*. Basingstoke: Macmillan, 1993.

Burdett, Carolyn. 'The Hidden Romance of Sexual Science: Eugenics, the Nation and the Making of Modern Feminism.' In *Sexology in Culture: Labelling Bodies and Desires*, edited by Lucy Bland and Laura L. Doan, 44–59. Cambridge: Polity Press, 1998.

Burke, Mary. 'Evolutionary Theory and the Search for Lost Innocence in the Writings of J. M. Synge.' *The Canadian Journal of Irish Studies* 30, no. 1 (2004): 48.

Callanan, Frank. *The Parnell Split: 1890–91*. Cork: Cork University Press, 1992.

Callanan, Frank. *T.M. Healy*. Cork: Cork University Press, 1996.

Carr-Gomm, Philip. *A Brief History of Nakedness*. London: Reaktion Books, 2010.

Caslin, Samantha. 'Transience, Class and Gender in Interwar Sexual Health Policy: The Case of the Liverpool VD Scheme.' Social History of Medicine, 23 September, 2017.

Castle, Gregory. *Modernism and the Celtic Revival*. Cambridge: Cambridge University Press, 2001.

Castle, Gregory, and Patrick Bixby, eds. *A History of Irish Modernism*. Cambridge: Cambridge University Press, 2019.

Castle, Gregory, and Patrick Bixby, eds. 'Introduction: Irish Modernism, from Emergence to Emergency.' In *A History of Irish Modernism*, edited by Gregory Castle and Patrick Bixby, 1–22. Cambridge: Cambridge University Press, 2019.

Center for Disease Control. 'STD Surveillance Case Definitions.' STD Surveillance Case Definitions, 10 December 2013. https://www.cdc.gov/std/stats/Case Definitions-2014.pdf.

Chamberlin, J. Edward and Sander L. Gilman, eds. *Degeneration: The Dark Side of Progress*. New York: Columbia University Press, 1985.

Childs, Donald J. *Modernism and Eugenics: Woolf, Eliot, Yeats, and the Culture of Degeneration*. Cambridge: Cambridge University Press, 2001.

Clancy, Mary. 'Aspects of Women's Contribution to the Oireachtas Debate in the Irish Free State, 1922–37.' In *Women Surviving: Studies in Irish Women's History in the 19th–20th Centuries*, edited by Maria Luddy and Clíona Murphy, 206–32. Swords, Co. Dublin, Ireland: Poolbeg, 1989.

Clark, Anna. *Desire: A History of European Sexuality*, 2nd ed. Abingdon: Routledge, 2019.

Clear, Caitríona. *Women's Voices in Ireland: Women's Magazines in the 1950s and 60s*. London: Bloomsbury, 2016.

Cleary, Joe. 'Toward a Materialist-Formalist History of Twentieth-Century Irish Literature.' *Boundary 2* 31, no. 1 (1 March 2004): 207–41.

Cleary, Joe. 'Introduction: Ireland and Modernity.' In *The Cambridge Companion to Modern Irish Culture*, edited by Joe Cleary and Claire Connolly, 1–21. Cambridge: Cambridge University Press, 2005.

Cleary, Joe. 'Introduction.' In *The Cambridge Companion to Irish Modernism*, edited by Joe Cleary, 1–18. Cambridge: Cambridge University Press, 2014.

Cleary, Joe, ed. *The Cambridge Companion to Irish Modernism*. Cambridge: Cambridge University Press, 2014.

Conolly, Leonard W. '*Mrs Warren's Profession* and the Lord Chamberlain.' *Shaw* 24, no. 1 (2004): 46–95.

Connolly, Linda. *The Irish Women's Movement: From Revolution to Devolution*. Basingstoke: Palgrave, 2002.

Connolly, Linda. 'The Limits of "Irish Studies": Historicism, Culturalism, Paternalism.' In *Enemies of Empire: New Perspectives on Imperialism, Literature, and Historiography*, edited by Eóin Flannery and Angus Mitchell, 189–210. Dublin: Four Courts Press, 2007.

Conrad, Peter. *The Medicalization of Society: On the Transformation of Human Conditions into Treatable Disorders*. Baltimore: Johns Hopkins University Press, 2007.

Conrad, Peter, and Joseph W. Schneider. *Deviance and Medicalization: From Badness to Sickness*. Expanded ed. Philadelphia: Temple University Press, 1992.

Conroy, Melvyn. *Nazi Eugenics: Precursors, Policy, Aftermath*. Stuttgart: Ibidem-Verlag, 2017.

Cook, Hera. *The Long Sexual Revolution: English Women, Sex, and Contraception, 1800–1975*. Oxford: Oxford University Press, 2004.

Corporaal Marguérite, and Ruud van den Beuken, eds. *A Stage of Emancipation: Change and Progress at the Dublin Gate Theatre*. Liverpool: Liverpool University Press, 2021.

Coughlan, Patricia. 'Feminine Beauty, Feminist Writing, and Sexual Role in the Work of Kate O'Brien.' In *Ordinary People Dancing: Essays on Kate O'Brien*, edited by Eibhear Walshe, 59–84. Cork: Cork University Press, 1993.

Cox, Pamela. 'Compulsion, Voluntarism, and Venereal Disease: Governing Sexual Health in England after the Contagious Diseases Acts.' *The Journal of British Studies* 46, no. 01 (January 2007): 91–115.

Craig, Layne Parish. *When Sex Changed: Birth Control Politics and Literature Between the World Wars*. New Brunswick, New Jersey: Rutgers University Press, 2013.

Cronin, Anthony. 'This Time, This Place.' *The Bell* XIX, no. 8 (July 1954).

Cronin, Anthony. *No Laughing Matter: The Life and Times of Flann O'Brien*. London: Grafton, 1990.

Cronin, Anthony. *Samuel Beckett: The Last Modernist*. London: Harper Collins, 1996.

Cronin, Michael G. 'Kate O'Brien and the Erotics of Liberal Catholic Dissent.' *Field Day Review* 6 (2010): 28–51.

Cronin, Michael G. *Impure Thoughts: Sexuality, Catholicism and Literature in Twentieth-Century Ireland.* Manchester: Manchester University Press, 2012.

Curtis, Lewis Perry. *Apes and Angels: The Irishman in Victorian Caricature.* Rev. ed. Washington, DC: Smithsonian Institution Press, 1997.

Dalsimer, Adele M. *Kate O'Brien: A Critical Study.* Dublin: Gill and Macmillan, 1990.

Daly, Mary E. *The Slow Failure: Population Decline and Independent Ireland, 1922–1973.* Madison, Wis: University of Wisconsin Press, 2006.

Darby, Robert. 'Pathologizing Male Sexuality: Lallemand, Spermatorrhea, and the Rise of Circumcision.' *Journal of the History of Medicine and Allied Sciences* 60, no. 3 (1 July 2005): 283–319.

Davidson, Arnold I. *The Emergence of Sexuality: Historical Epistemology and the Formation of Concepts.* Cambridge, Mass: Harvard University Press, 2001.

Davidson, Roger. *Dangerous Liaisons: A Social History of Venereal Diseases in Twentieth-Century Scotland.* Amsterdam: Brill|Rodopi, 2000.

Davis, Tracy C. 'The Independent Theatre Society's Revolutionary Scheme for an Uncommercial Theater.' *Theatre Journal* 42, no. 4 (December 1990): 447.

Davison, Neil R. '"We Are Not a Doctor for the Body": Catholicism, the Female Grotesque, and Flann O'Brien's *The Hard Life.*' *Literature and Psychology: A Journal of Psychoanalytic and Cultural Criticism* 45, no. 4 (1999): 31–57.

De Nie, Michael Willem. *The Eternal Paddy: Irish Identity and the British Press, 1798–1882.* Madison: University of Wisconsin Press, 2004.

Dean, Joan Fitzpatrick. *Riot and Great Anger: Stage Censorship in Twentieth-Century Ireland.* Madison: University of Wisconsin Press, 2004.

Deane, Seamus. *Strange Country: Modernity and Nationhood in Irish Writing Since 1790.* 1995. Oxford: Oxford University Press, 1997.

Deane, Seamus. 'Dead Ends: Joyce's Finest Moments.' In *Semicolonial Joyce,* edited by Derek Attridge and Marjorie Elizabeth Howes, 21–36. Cambridge: Cambridge University Press, 2000.

Debenham, Clare. *Marie Stopes' Sexual Revolution and the Birth Control Movement.* Cham, Switzerland: Palgrave Macmillan, 2018.

Doan, Laura L. 'Forgetting Sedgwick.' *PMLA* 125, no. 2 (March 2010): 370–3.

Doan, Laura L. *Disturbing Practices: History, Sexuality, and Women's Experience of Modern War.* Chicago: The University of Chicago Press, 2013.

Doyle, Laura, and Laura A. Winkiel, eds. *Geomodernisms: Race, Modernism, Modernity.* Bloomington: Indiana University Press, 2005.

Dukore, Bernard Frank. *Bernard Shaw and the Censors: Fights and Failures, Stage and Screen.* Cham, Switzerland: Palgrave Macmillan, 2020.

Dwan, David. *The Great Community: Culture and Nationalism in Ireland.* Dublin: Field Day, 2008.

Dwan, David. 'Cultural Development: Young Ireland to Yeats.' In *The Princeton History of Modern Ireland,* edited by Ian McBride and Richard Bourke, 217–35. Princeton, NJ: Princeton University Press, 2016.

Eagleton, Terry. *Heathcliff and the Great Hunger: Studies in Irish Culture.* London: Verso, 1995.

Eagleton, Terry. *Crazy John and the Bishop and Other Essays on Irish Culture.* Cork: Cork University Press, 1998.

Earner-Byrne, Lindsey, and Diane Urquhart. *The Irish Abortion Journey, 1920–2018.* London: Palgrave Macmillan, 2019.

Edelman, Lee. *No Future: Queer Theory and the Death Drive.* Durham: Duke University Press, 2004.

Eder, Franz, Lesley Hall, and Gert Hekma, eds. *Sexual Cultures in Europe: National Histories.* Manchester: Manchester University Press, 1999.

Ehrenreich, Eric. *The Nazi Ancestral Proof: Genealogy, Racial Science, and the Final Solution.* Bloomington: Indiana University Press, 2007.

Ellenberger, Henri F. *The Discovery of the Unconscious: The History and Evolution of Dynamic Psychiatry.* New York: Basic Books, 1970.

Ellis, Sylvia A. 'The Historical Significance of President Kennedy's Visit to Ireland in June 1963.' *Irish Studies Review* 16, no. 2 (May 2008): 113–30.

Ellmann, Maud. *The Nets of Modernism: Henry James, Virginia Woolf, James Joyce, and Sigmund Freud.* Cambridge: Cambridge University Press, 2010.

Ellmann, Richard. *The Consciousness of Joyce.* London: Faber and Faber, 1977.

Ellmann, Richard. *James Joyce.* Rev. ed. Oxford: Oxford University Press, 1984.

Ellmann, Richard. *W.B. Yeats's Second Puberty: A Lecture Delivered at the Library of Congress on April 2, 1984.* Washington: Library of Congress, 1985.

English, Bridget. *Laying Out the Bones: Death and Dying in the Modern Irish Novel.* Syracuse, New York: Syracuse University Press, 2017.

English, Daylanne K. *Unnatural Selections: Eugenics in American Modernism and the Harlem Renaissance.* Chapel Hill: University of North Carolina Press, 2004.

Evans, David. 'Tackling the "Hideous Scourge": The Creation of the Venereal Disease Treatment Centres in Early Twentieth-Century Britain.' *Social History of Medicine* 5, no. 3 (1992): 413–33.

Fagan, Paul. 'Opening Remarks.' Irish Modernisms: Gaps, Conjectures, Possibilities, University of Vienna, 2016.

Fagan, Paul, John Greaney, and Tamara Radak. 'Introduction: Irish Modernisms in the Plural.' In *Irish Modernisms: Gaps, Conjectures, Possibilities*, edited by Paul Fagan, John Greaney, and Tamara Radak, 1–7. London: Bloomsbury Academic, 2021.

Fairchild, Amy L. *Science at the Borders: Immigrant Medical Inspection and the Shaping of the Modern Industrial Labor Force.* Baltimore: Johns Hopkins University Press, 2003.

Felski, Rita. *The Gender of Modernity.* Cambridge, Mass: Harvard University Press, 1995.

Ferris, Kathleen. *James Joyce and the Burden of Disease.* Lexington: University Press of Kentucky, 1995.

Ferriter, Diarmaid. *The Transformation of Ireland, 1900–2000.* London: Profile, 2005.

Ferriter, Diarmaid. *Judging Dev: A Reassessment of the Life and Legacy of Eamon de Valera.* Dublin: Royal Irish Academy, 2007.

Ferriter, Diarmaid. *Occasions of Sin: Sex and Society in Modern Ireland*. London: Profile Books, 2009.

Finlayson, Geoffrey B. A. M. *Citizen, State, and Social Welfare in Britain 1830–1990*. Oxford: Oxford University Press, 1994.

Finnane, Mark. 'The Carrigan Committee of 1930–31 and the "Moral Condition of the Saorstát."' *Irish Historical Studies* 32, no. 128 (2001): 519–36.

Fischerova, Jana. 'The Banning and Unbanning of Kate O'Brien's *The Land of Spices*.' *Irish University Review* 48, no. 1 (May 2018): 69–83.

Fisher, Kate. *Birth Control, Sex and Marriage in Britain, 1918–1960*. Oxford: Oxford University Press, 2006.

Fogarty, Anne. 'Women and Modernism.' In *The Cambridge Companion to Irish Modernism*, edited by Joe Cleary, 147–60. Cambridge: Cambridge University Press, 2014.

Foster, R. F. *W.B. Yeats: A Life, The Apprentice Mage, 1865–1914*. Vol. 1. 2 vols. Oxford: Oxford University Press, 1997.

Foster, R. F. *W.B. Yeats: A Life, The Arch-Poet, 1915–1939*. Vol. 2. 2 vols. Oxford: Oxford University Press, 2003.

Foster, R. F. *Modern Ireland: 1600–1972*. Repr. London: Penguin Books, 2011.

Foucault, Michel. *The History of Sexuality. Vol. 1: The Will to Knowledge*. 3 vols. New York: Pantheon Books, 1978.

Foucault, Michel. *The Birth of the Clinic: An Archaeology of Medical Perception*. Translated by A. M. Sheridan. London: Routledge, 2003.

Foucault, Michel. *Madness and Civilization: A History of Insanity in the Age of Reason*. Edited by David Cooper. Translated by Richard Howard. London: Routledge, 2007.

Foucault, Michel, Mauro Bertani, Alessandro Fontana, François Ewald, and David Macey. *Society Must Be Defended: Lectures at the Collège de France, 1975–1976*. 1st ed. New York: Picador, 2003.

Foucault, Michel, Valerio Marchetti, and Graham Burchell. *Abnormal: Lectures at the Collège de France, 1974–1975*. Lectures at the Collège de France. London: Verso, 2003.

Fraser, Derek. *The Evolution of the British Welfare State: A History of Social Policy Since the Industrial Revolution*. 5th ed. London: Palgrave Macmillan Education, 2017.

Fraser, James Alexander. *Joyce & Betrayal*. London: Routledge, 2016.

Frazier, Adrian. *Behind the Scenes: Yeats, Horniman, and the Struggle for the Abbey Theatre*. Berkeley: University of California Press, 1990.

Freeden, Michael. 'Eugenics and Progressive Thought: A Study in Ideological Affinity.' *The Historical Journal* 22, no. 3 (September 1979): 645–71.

Freeden, Michael. 'Eugenics and Ideology.' *The Historical Journal* 26, no. 4 (December 1983): 959–62.

Freeden, Michael. *Liberalism Divided: A Study in British Political Thought, 1914–1939*. Oxford: Clarendon Press, 1986.

Freeden, Michael. *The New Liberalism: An Ideology of Social Reform*. Oxford: Oxford University Press, 1986.

Friedman, Susan Stanford. 'Definitional Excursions: The Meanings of Modern/ Modernity/Modernism.' *Modernism/Modernity* 8, no. 3 (2001): 493–513.

Funke, Jana. 'Modernism, Sexuality, and Gender.' In *The Bloomsbury Companion to Modernist Literature*, edited by Ulrika Maude and Mark Nixon, 249–66. London: Bloomsbury Publishing, 2018.

Garrigan Mattar, Sinéad. *Primitivism, Science, and the Irish Revival.* Oxford: Oxford University Press, 2004.

Geary, Laurence M. '"The Wages of Sin Is Death": Lock Hospitals, Venereal Disease, and Gender in Pre-Famine Ireland.' In *Gender and Medicine in Ireland, 1700–1950*, edited by Margaret H. Preston and Margaret Ó hÓgartaigh, 154–68. Syracuse, New York: Syracuse University Press, 2012.

Giami, Alain. 'Sexual Health: The Emergence, Development, and Diversity of a Concept.' *Annual Review of Sex Research* 13, no. 1 (2002): 1–35.

Giami, Alain. 'Sex, Medicine, and Disease.' In *A Cultural History of Sexuality in the Modern Age*, edited by Gert Hekma, 127–48. Oxford: Berg, 2011.

Gibson, Andrew. *James Joyce.* London: Reaktion Books, 2006.

Gibson, Andrew. *Samuel Beckett.* Critical Lives. London: Reaktion Books, 2010.

Gillespie, Alana. 'The Soft Misogyny of Good Intentions: The Mother and Child Scheme, *Cruiskeen Lawn*, and *The Hard Life*.' In *Flann O'Brien: Gallows Humour*, edited by Ruben Borg and Paul Fagan, 77–96. Cork: Cork University Press, 2021.

Gilman, Sander L. *Difference and Pathology: Stereotypes of Sexuality, Race, and Madness.* Ithaca: Cornell University Press, 1985.

Gilman, Sander L. 'Sexology, Psychoanalysis, and Degeneration: From a Theory of Race to a Race to Theory.' In *Degeneration: The Dark Side of Progress*, edited by J. Edward Chamberlin and Sander L. Gilman, 72–96. New York: Columbia University Press, 1985.

Gilman, Sander L. *The Jew's Body.* New York: Routledge, 1991.

Gilman, Sander L. '"The skull in Conemarra": Beckett, Joyce, and the Gaelic West.' In *Samuel Beckett and the 'State' of Ireland*, edited by Alan Graham and Scott Eric Hamilton, 173–93. Newcastle upon Tyne: Cambridge Scholars Publishing, 2017.

Gilman, Sander L. 'Sassenachs and Their Syphilization: The Irish Revival, Deanglicization, and Eugenics.' In *Science, Technology, and Irish Modernism*, edited by Kathryn Conrad, Cóilín Parsons, and Julie McCormick Weng, 203–14. Syracuse, New York: Syracuse University Press, 2019.

Girvin, Brian. 'Contraception, Moral Panic and Social Change in Ireland, 1969–79.' *Irish Political Studies* 23, no. 4 (December 2008): 555–76.

Goodall, Jane R. *Performance and Evolution in the Age of Darwin: Out of the Natural Order.* London: Routledge, 2002.

Graham, Alan. '"So much Gaelic to me": Beckett and the Irish Language.' *Journal of Beckett Studies.* 24, no. 2 (2015): 163–79.

Graham, Alan, and Scott Eric Hamilton, eds. *Samuel Beckett and the 'State' of Ireland.* Newcastle upon Tyne: Cambridge Scholars Publishing, 2017.

Gray, Fred D. *The Tuskegee Syphilis Study: The Real Story and Beyond.* Montgomery: New South Books, 1998.

Greenslade, William. *Degeneration, Culture, and the Novel, 1880–1940*. Cambridge: Cambridge University Press, 1994.

Griffith, Gareth. *Socialism and Superior Brains: The Political Thought of Bernard Shaw*. London: Routledge, 1993.

Guinnane, Timothy. *The Vanishing Irish: Households, Migration, and the Rural Economy in Ireland, 1850–1914*. Princeton, N.J: Princeton University Press, 1997.

Habermas, Jürgen. *The Future of Human Nature*. Cambridge: Polity Press, 2003.

Halperin, David M. *How to Do the History of Homosexuality*. Chicago: University of Chicago Press, 2002.

Hanley, Anne R. *Medicine, Knowledge and Venereal Diseases in England, 1886–1916*. Basingstoke: Palgrave Macmillan, 2017.

Hanley, Anne R. 'Histories of "a loathsome disease": Sexual Health in Modern Britain.' *History Compass* 20 no.3 (March 2022): 1–16.

Hare, E. H. 'Masturbatory Insanity: The History of an Idea.' *Journal of Mental Science* 108, no. 452 (January 1962): 1–25.

Harrington, John P. *The Irish Beckett*. Syracuse, New York: Syracuse University Press, 1991.

Harris, Susan Cannon. *Gender and Modern Irish Drama*. Bloomington: Indiana University Press, 2002.

Hassett, Joseph M. *W.B. Yeats and the Muses*. Oxford: Oxford University Press, 2010.

Hatch, David A. 'Samuel Beckett's "Che Sciagura" and the Subversion of Irish Moral Convention.' *Samuel Beckett Today/Aujourd'hui* 18 (2007): 241–55.

Hewitt, Seán. *J.M. Synge: Nature, Politics, Modernism*. Oxford: Oxford University Press, 2021.

Hopper, Keith. *Flann O'Brien: A Portrait of the Artist as a Young Post-Modernist*. Cork, Ireland: Cork University Press, 1995.

Hopper, Keith. 'The Dismemberment of Orpheus: Flann O'Brien and the Irish Censorship Code.' In *Literature and Ethics: Questions of Responsibility in Literary Studies*, edited by Daniel K. Jernigan, Neil Murphy, Brendan Quigley, and Tamara S. Wagner, 221–42. Amherst, N.Y: Cambria Press, 2009.

Horgan, John. 'Saving Us from Ourselves: Contraception, Censorship and the "Evil Literature" Controversy of 1926.' *Irish Communications Review* 5 (1995): 61–7.

Horrocks, Roger, and Jo Campling. *Masculinity in Crisis: Myths, Fantasies, and Realities*. New York: St. Martin's Press, 1994.

Houlbrook, Matt. 'Thinking Queer: The Social and Sexual in Inter-War Britain.' In *British Queer History: New Approaches and Perspectives*, edited by Brian Lewis, 134–64. Manchester: Manchester University Press, 2013.

Houston, Lloyd (Meadhbh). '"Dear Dr Kirkpatrick": Recovering Irish Experiences of Venereal Diseases, 1924–1947.' In *Patient Voices in Modern Britain*, edited by Anne R. Hanley and Jessica Meyer, 255–98. Manchester: Manchester University Press, 2021.

Howarth, Herbert. *The Irish Writers, 1880–1940: Literature Under Parnell's Star*. London: Rockcliff, 1958.

Howe, Stephen. *Ireland and Empire: Colonial Legacies in Irish History and Culture*. Oxford: Oxford University Press, 2000.

Howe, Stephen. 'Questioning the (Bad) Question: "Was Ireland a Colony?"' *Irish Historical Studies* 36, no. 142 (November 2008): 138–52.

Howell, Philip. 'The Politics of Prostitution and the Politics of Public Health in the Irish Free State: A Response to Susannah Riordan.' *Irish Historical Studies* 35, no. 140 (November 2007): 541–52.

Howes, Marjorie Elizabeth. *Yeats's Nations: Gender, Class, and Irishness*. Cambridge: Cambridge University Press, 1996.

Howes, Marjorie Elizabeth. 'Public Discourse, Private Reflection: 1916–1970.' In *The Field Day Anthology of Irish Writing*, edited by Seamus Deane, Angela Bourke, and Andrew Carpenter, 4:923–1035. Cork: Cork University Press, 2002.

Hug, Chrystel. *The Politics of Sexual Morality in Ireland*. Basingstoke: Palgrave Macmillan, 1998.

Hurley, Kelly. 'Hereditary Taint and Cultural Contagion: The Social Etiology of Fin-de-siècle Degeneration Theory.' *Nineteenth-Century Contexts* 14, no. 2 (January 1990): 193–214.

Hurson, Tess. 'Conspicuous Absences: *The Hard Life*.' In *Conjuring Complexities: Essays on Flann O'Brien*, edited by Anne Clune and Tess Hurson. Belfast: Institute of Irish Studies, The Queen's University of Belfast, 1997.

Inglis, Tom, ed. 'Foucault, Bourdieu and the Field of Irish Sexuality.' *Irish Journal of Sociology* 7, no. 1 (1997): 5–28.

Inglis, Tom. *Moral Monopoly: The Rise and Fall of the Catholic Church in Modern Ireland*. 2nd ed. Dublin: University College Dublin Press, 1998.

Inglis, Tom. 'Origins and Legacies of Irish Prudery: Sexuality and Social Control in Modern Ireland.' *Éire-Ireland* 40, no. 3 (2005): 9–37.

Inglis, Tom. *Are the Irish Different?* Manchester: Manchester University Press, 2014.

Inglis, Tom. 'The Irish Body.' In *Are the Irish Different?*, edited by Tom Inglis, 88–98. Manchester: Manchester University Press, 2014.

Ingman, Heather. *Irish Women's Fiction: From Edgeworth to Enright*. Dublin: Irish Academic Press, 2013.

Jacobsen, Rockney. 'Desire, Sexual.' In *Sex from Plato to Paglia: A Philosophical Encyclopedia*, edited by Alan Soble, 1:222–8. Westport, Conn: Greenwood Press, 2006.

Jameson, Fredric. *Postmodernism, or, The Cultural Logic of Late Capitalism*. London: Verso, 1992.

Jeffers, Jennifer M. *Beckett's Masculinity*. New York: Palgrave Macmillan, 2009.

Jennifer Wallis. '"Atrophied", "Engorged", "Debauched": Muscle Wastage, Degenerate Mass and Moral Worth in the General Paralytic Patient.' In *Insanity and the Lunatic Asylum in the Nineteenth Century*, edited by Thomas Knowles and Serena Trowbridge, 99–114. London: Pickering & Chatto, 2015.

Jensen, Robin E. *Dirty Words: The Rhetoric of Public Sex Education, 1870–1924*. Urbana: University of Illinois Press, 2010.

Jones, Greta. 'Eugenics and Social Policy Between the Wars.' *The Historical Journal* 25, no. 3 (September 1982): 717–28.

Jones, Greta. 'Eugenics in Ireland: The Belfast Eugenics Society, 1911–1915.' *Irish Historical Studies* 28, no. 109 (May 1992): 81–95.

Jones, Greta. 'Marie Stopes in Ireland: The Mother's Clinic in Belfast, 1936-47.' *Social History of Medicine* 5, no. 2 (April 1992): 255–77.

Jones, Greta, and Elizabeth Malcolm, eds. *Medicine, Disease, and the State in Ireland, 1650–1940*. Cork: Cork University Press, 1999.

Jones, James H. 'The Tuskegee Syphilis Experiment.' In *The Oxford Textbook of Clinical Research Ethics*, edited by Ezekiel J. Emanuel, Christine Grady, Robert A. Crouch, Reidar K. Lie, Franklin G. Miller, and David Wendler, 86–96. Oxford: Oxford University Press, 2010.

Jones, James H. *Bad Blood: The Tuskegee Syphilis Experiment*. New and Expanded. New York: Free Press, 1993.

Junker, Mary. *Beckett: The Irish Dimension*. Dublin: Wolfhound Press, 1995.

Kahan, Benjamin. *Celibacies: American Modernism and Sexual Life*. Durham: Duke University Press, 2013.

Kalaidjian, Andrew. 'The Uncertainty of Late Irish Modernism: Flann O'Brien and Erwin Schrödinger in Dublin.' In *Science, Technology, and Irish Modernism*, edited by Kathryn Conrad, Cóilín Parsons, and Julie McCormick Weng, 248–63. Syracuse, New York: Syracuse University Press, 2019.

Kelly, John. 'Parnell in Irish Literature.' In *Parnell in Perspective*, edited by David George Boyce and Alan O'Day, 242–83. London: Routledge, 1991.

Kelly, Katherine E. 'Pandemic and Performance: Ibsen and the Outbreak of Modernism.' *South Central Review* 25, no. 1 (2008): 12–35.

Kennedy, Finola. 'The Suppression of the Carrigan Report: A Historical Perspective on Child Abuse.' *Studies: An Irish Quarterly Review* 89, no. 356 (2000): 354–63.

Kennedy, Robert E. *The Irish: Emigration, Marriage, and Fertility*. Berkeley: University of California Press, 1973.

Kennedy, Seán, ed. *Beckett and Ireland*. Cambridge: Cambridge University Press, 2010.

Kennedy, Seán. 'First Love: Abortion and Infanticide in Beckett and Yeats.' *Samuel Beckett Today/Aujourd'hui* 22 (2010): 79–91.

Kenner, Hugh. *A Colder Eye: The Modern Irish Writers*. London: Allen Lane, 1983.

Kent, Brad. 'Zealots, Censors and Perverts: Irish Censorship and Liam O'Flaherty's *The Puritan*.' *Irish Studies Review* 14, no. 3 (August 2006): 343–58.

Kent, Brad. 'An *Argument Manqué*: Kate O'Brien's *Pray for the Wanderer*.' *Irish Studies Review* 18, no. 3 (August 2010): 285–98.

Keogh, Dermot, and Andrew McCarthy. *Limerick Boycott 1904: Anti-Semitism in Ireland*. Douglas Village, Cork: Mercier Press, 2005.

Keown, Edwina, and Carol Taaffe. 'Introduction: Ireland and Modernism.' In *Irish Modernism: Origins, Contexts, Publics*, edited by Edwina Keown and Carol Taaffe, 1–6. Oxford: Peter Lang, 2010.

Keown, Edwina, and Carol Taaffe, eds. *Irish Modernism: Origins, Contexts, Publics*. Oxford: Peter Lang, 2010.

Kevles, Daniel J. *In the Name of Eugenics: Genetics and the Uses of Human Heredity*. New York: Knopf, 1985.

Kilfeather, Siobhán. 'General Introduction: Sexuality, 1685–2001.' In *The Field Day Anthology of Irish Writing, Volume IV: Irish Women's Writings and Traditions*. Edited by Angela Bourke, Siobhán Kilfeather, Maria Luddy, Margaret Mac Curtain, Gerardine Meaney, Máirín Ní Dhonnchadha, Mary O'Dowd, and Clair Wills, 755–60. Cork: Cork University Press, 2002.

Kilroy, James. *The Nineteenth-Century English Novel: Family Ideology and Narrative Form*. New York: Palgrave, 2007.

Kim, Rina. *Women and Ireland as Beckett's Lost Others: Beyond Mourning and Melancholia*. Basingstoke: Palgrave Macmillan, 2010.

King, Desmond. *In the Name of Liberalism: Illiberal Social Policy in the USA and Britain*. Oxford: Oxford University Press, 1999.

Knowlson, James. *Damned to Fame: The Life of Samuel Beckett*. London: Bloomsbury, 1997.

Kraut, Alan M. *Silent Travelers: Germs, Genes, and the 'Immigrant Menace.'* Baltimore: Johns Hopkins University Press, 1995.

Kühl, Stefan. *For the Betterment of the Race: The Rise and Fall of the International Movement for Eugenics and Racial Hygiene*. Translated by Lawrence Schofer. London: Palgrave Macmillan, 2013.

Kühl, Stefan. *The Nazi Connection: Eugenics, American Racism, and German National Socialism*. Oxford: Oxford University Press, 1994.

Lantéri-Laura, Georges. *Lecture des Perversions: Histoire de leur appropriation médicale*. Edited by Markos Zafiropoulos. Paris: Economica-Anthropos, 2012.

Larousse dictionnaire de français. 'Loucher (v.t. Ind.),' March 2017. https://www.larousse.fr/dictionnaires/francais/loucher/47869.

Larousse dictionnaire de français. '"Strabisme (n.m.),"' March 2017. http://www.larousse.fr/dictionnaires/francais/strabisme/74801.

Latham, Sean, and Gayle Rogers. *Modernism: Evolution of an Idea*. London: Bloomsbury Academic, 2015.

Layne Parish Craig. 'Passion's Possibilities: Kate O'Brien's Sexological Discourse in *Without My Cloak*.' *Éire-Ireland* 44, no. 3–4 (2010): 118–39.

Lemar, Susan. '"The Liberty to Spread Disaster": Campaigning for Compulsion in the Control of Venereal Diseases in Edinburgh in the 1920s.' *Social History of Medicine* 19, no. 1 (1 April 2006): 73–86.

Leonard, Thomas C. 'Retrospectives: Eugenics and Economics in the Progressive Era.' *Journal of Economic Perspectives* 19, no. 4 (November 2005): 207–24.

Levine, Philippa. *Prostitution, Race, and Politics: Policing Venereal Disease in the British Empire*. New York: Routledge, 2003.

Levitas, Ben. *The Theatre of Nation*. Oxford University Press, 2002.

Levitas, Ben. 'Reading and the Irish Revival, 1891–1922.' In *The Irish Book in English, 1891–2000*, edited by Clare Hutton and Patrick Walsh, 5:43–69. Oxford History of the Irish Book. Oxford: Oxford University Press, 2011.

Lloyd, David. 'Writing in the Shit: Beckett, Nationalism, and the Colonial Subject.' *Modern Fiction Studies* 35, no. 1 (1989): 69–85.

Lloyd, David. *Anomalous States: Irish Writing and the Post-Colonial Moment*. Dublin: Lilliput Press, 1993.

Long, Maebh. *Assembling Flann O'Brien*. London: Bloomsbury Academic, 2014.

Longley, Edna. '"The Rhythm of Beauty": Joyce, Yeats, and the 1890s.' In *Parnell and His Times*, edited by Joep Leerssen, 185–98. Cambridge: Cambridge University Press, 2020.

Lowe-Evans, Mary. *Crimes Against Fecundity: Joyce and Population Control*. Syracuse, New York: Syracuse University Press, 1989.

Lucassen, Leo. 'A Brave New World: The Left, Social Engineering, and Eugenics in Twentieth-Century Europe.' *International Review of Social History* 55, no. 2 (August 2010): 265–96.

Luddy, Maria. *Prostitution and Irish Society, 1800–1940*. Cambridge: Cambridge University Press, 2007.

Luddy, Maria. 'Sex and the Single Girl in 1920s and 1930s Ireland.' *The Irish Review*, no. 35 (2007): 79–91.

Lyons, J. B. *James Joyce and Medicine*. Dublin: Dolmen Press, 1973.

Lyons, J. B. 'Sigerson, George.' In *Dictionary of Irish Biography*, edited by James McGuire and James Quinn. Cambridge: Cambridge University Press, 2009. https://doi.org/10.3318/dib.008072.v1.

Lyons, F. S. L. 'The Parnell Theme in Literature.' In *Place, Personality, and the Irish Writer*, edited by Andrew Carpenter, 69–96. Gerrards Cross: Colin Smythe, 1977.

Lyons, F. S. L. *Ireland Since the Famine*. Repr. London: Fontana Press, 1992.

Lyons, F. S. L. *Charles Stewart Parnell*. New ed. Dublin: Gill & Macmillan, 2005.

Macnicol, John. 'Eugenics and the Campaign for Voluntary Sterilization in Britain Between the Wars.' *Social History of Medicine* 2, no. 2 (1989): 147–69.

Macnicol, John. 'The Voluntary Sterilization Campaign in Britain, 1918–39.' *Journal of the History of Sexuality* 2, no. 3 (January 1992): 422–38.

Maglen, Krista. *The English System: Quarantine, Immigration and the Making of a Port Sanitary Zone*. Manchester: Manchester University Press, 2014.

Magness, Phillip W, and Sean J Hernandez. 'The Economic Eugenicism of John Maynard Keynes.' *Journal of Markets and Morality* 20, no. 1 (Spring 2017): 79–100.

Malone, Irina Ruppo. *Ibsen and the Irish Revival*. Basingstoke: Palgrave Macmillan, 2010.

Manganaro, Marc, ed. *Modernist Anthropology: From Fieldwork to Text*. Princeton: Princeton University Press, 1990.

Manganiello, Dominic. *Joyce's Politics*. London: Routledge, 1980.

Mannion, Elizabeth. 'Staging Parnell: Biodrama at the Early Abbey Theatre.' *New Hibernia Review* 22, no. 2 (2018): 146–58.

Mao, Douglas, and Rebecca L. Walkowitz. 'The New Modernist Studies.' *PMLA* 123, no. 3 (May 2008): 737–48.

Marcus, Laura. *Dreams of Modernity: Psychoanalysis, Literature, Cinema*. Cambridge: Cambridge University Press, 2014.

Martin, Elizabeth A., ed. *Concise Medical Dictionary*. 8th ed. Oxford: Oxford University Press, 2010.

Martin, Peter. *Censorship in the Two Irelands, 1922–1939*. Dublin: Irish Academic Press, 2006.

Martin, Peter. 'Irish Censorship in Context.' *Studies: An Irish Quarterly Review* 95, no. 379 (2006): 261–8.

Mathews, P. J. *Revival: The Abbey Theatre, Sinn Féin, the Gaelic League and the Co-Operative Movement*. Cork: Cork University Press in Association with Field Day, 2004.

Mazumdar, Pauline M. H. *Eugenics, Human Genetics and Human Failings: The Eugenics Society, Its Sources and Its Critics in Britain*. London: Routledge, 1992.

Mc Cormack, W. J. *Fool of the Family: A Life of J.M. Synge*. London: Weidenfeld & Nicolson, 2000.

McAvoy, Sandra. 'All About Eve: Signe Toksvig and the Intimate Lives of Irish Women, 1926–1937.' *Irish Review* 42 (Summer 2010): 43–57.

McAvoy, Sandra. '"Its effect on public morality is vicious in the extreme": Defining Birth Control as Obscene and Unethical, 1926–32.' In *'She said she was in the family way': Pregnancy and Infancy in Modern Ireland*, edited by Elaine Farrell), 35–52. London: Institute of Historical Research, 2012.

McCarthy, Conor. *Modernisation, Crisis and Culture in Ireland, 1969–1992*. Dublin: Four Courts Press, 2000.

McCormick, Leanne. 'Prophylactics and Prejudice: Venereal Diseases in Northern Ireland During the Second World War.' In *Gender and Medicine in Ireland, 1700–1950*, edited by Margaret H. Preston and Margaret Ó hÓgartaigh, 221–34. Syracuse, New York: Syracuse University Press, 2012.

McCourt, John. 'More "Gravid" than Gravitas: Collopy, Fahrt and the Pope in Rome.' In *Flann O'Brien: Problems with Authority*, edited by Ruben Borg, Paul Fagan, and John McCourt, 169–85. Cork: Cork University Press, 2017.

McCracken, Donal P. *Forgotten Protest: Ireland and the Anglo-Boer War*. Updated and revised. Belfast: Ulster Historical Foundation, 2003.

McCrea, Barry. *In the Company of Strangers: Family and Narrative in Dickens, Conan Doyle, Joyce, and Proust*. New York: Columbia University Press, 2011.

McDiarmid, Lucy. *The Irish Art of Controversy*. Ithaca: Cornell University Press, 2005.

McDonald, Rónán. '"Accidental Variations": Darwinian Traces in Yeats's Poetry.' In *Science and Modern Poetry: New Approaches*, edited by John Holmes, 152–67. Liverpool: Liverpool University Press, 2012.

McDonald, Rónán. 'The "Fascination of What I Loathed": Science and Self in W.B. Yeats's *Autobiographies*.' In *Modernism and Autobiography*, edited by Maria DiBattista and Emily O. Wittman, 18–30. Cambridge: Cambridge University Press, 2014.

McDonald, Rónán. 'The Irish Revival and Modernism.' In *The Cambridge Companion to Irish Modernism*, edited by Joe Cleary, 51–62. Cambridge: Cambridge University Press, 2014.

McGarry, Fearghal. *Eoin O'Duffy: A Self-Made Hero*. Oxford: Oxford University Press, 2007.

McLaren, Angus. *Sexuality and Social Order: The Debate over the Fertility of Women and Workers in France, 1770–1920*. New York: Holmes & Meier, 1983.

McLaren, Angus. *A History of Contraception: From Antiquity to the Present Day*. Oxford: Blackwell, 1990.

McLaren, Angus. *Twentieth-Century Sexuality: A History*. Oxford: Blackwell, 1999.

McLaren, Angus. *Impotence: A Cultural History*. Chicago: University of Chicago Press, 2007.

McLaren, Angus. *Our Own Master Race: Eugenics in Canada, 1885–1945*. Repr. Toronto: University of Toronto Press, 2014.

Meaney, Gerardine. *Gender, Ireland and Cultural Change: Race, Sex and Nation*. New York: Routledge, 2010.

Meaney, Gerardine. 'A Disruptive Modernist: Kate O'Brien and Irish Women's Writing.' In *A History of Irish Modernism*, edited by Gregory Castle and Patrick Bixby, 276–91. Cambridge: Cambridge University Press, 2019.

Mentxaka, Aintzane Legarreta. 'La Belle: Kate O'Brien and Female Beauty.' In *Women, Social, and Cultural Change in Twentieth-Century Ireland: Dissenting Voices?*, edited by Sarah O'Connor and Christopher C. Shepard, 183–98. Newcastle: Cambridge Scholars Publishing, 2008.

Mentxaka, Aintzane Legarreta. *Kate O'Brien and the Fiction of Identity: Sex, Art and Politics in Mary Lavelle and Other Writings.* Jefferson, NC: McFarland & Co, 2011.

Micale, Mark S. *Hysterical Men: The Hidden History of Male Nervous Illness.* Cambridge, Mass: Harvard University Press, 2008.

Micale, Mark S., ed. *The Mind of Modernism: Medicine, Psychology, and the Cultural Arts in Europe and America, 1880–1940.* Stanford: Stanford University Press, 2004.

Moore, Gregory. *Nietzsche, Biology, and Metaphor.* Cambridge: Cambridge University Press, 2002.

Morash, Chris. *A History of Irish Theatre: 1601–2000.* Cambridge: Cambridge University Press, 2004.

Morin, Emilie. *Samuel Beckett and the Problem of Irishness.* Basingstoke: Palgrave Macmillan, 2009.

Morin, Emilie. *Beckett's Political Imagination.* Cambridge: Cambridge University Press, 2017.

Morin, Emilie. 'Theatres and Pathologies of Silence: Symbolism and Irish Drama from Maeterlinck to Beckett.' In *Silence in Modern Irish Literature*, edited by Michael McAteer, 35–48. Leiden: Brill Rodopi, 2017.

Morrisson, Mark S. 'Why Modernist Studies and Science Studies Need Each Other.' *Modernism/Modernity* 9, no. 4 (2002): 675–82.

Morrisson, Mark S. *Modernism, Science, and Technology.* London: Bloomsbury Academic, 2017.

Mort, Frank. *Dangerous Sexualities: Medico-Moral Politics in England Since 1830.* Rev. ed. London: Routledge, 2002.

Moses, A. Dirk, and Dan Stone. 'Eugenics and Genocide.' In *The Oxford Handbook of the History of Eugenics*, edited by Alison Bashford and Philippa Levine, 192–209. Oxford: Oxford University Press, 2010.

Moses, Michael Valdez. 'The Rebirth of Tragedy: Yeats, Nietzsche, the Irish National Theatre, and the Anti-Modern Cult of Cuchulain.' *Modernism/Modernity* 11, no. 3 (2004): 561–79.

Murphy, Neil. 'Flann O'Brien's The Hard Life & the Gaze of the Medusa.' *Review of Contemporary Fiction* 31, no. 3 (Fall 2011): 148–61.

Murphy, William. 'Solomons, Bethel Albert Herbert.' In *Dictionary of Irish Biography*, edited by James McGuire and James Quinn. Cambridge: Cambridge University Press, 2009. http://dib.cambridge.org/viewReadPage.do?articleId=a8187.

Murphy, William Michael. *The Parnell Myth and Irish Politics, 1891–1956.* New York: Peter Lang, 1986.

Nixon, Mark. *Samuel Beckett's German Diaries, 1936–1937.* London: Continuum, 2011.

Nolan, Emer. 'Modernism and the Irish Revival.' In *The Cambridge Companion to Modern Irish Culture*, edited by Joe Cleary and Claire Connolly, 157–72. Cambridge: Cambridge University Press, 2005.

Ó Drisceoil, Donal. *Censorship in Ireland, 1939–1945: Neutrality, Politics, and Society.* Cork: Cork University Press, 1996.

Ó Drisceoil, Donal. '"The Best Banned in the Land": Censorship and Irish Writing Since 1950.' *The Yearbook of English Studies*, 2005, 146–60.

Ó Gráda, Cormac. *Jewish Ireland in the Age of Joyce: A Socioeconomic History*. Princeton: Princeton University Press, 2006.

Ó Gráda, Cormac, and Niall Duffy. 'Fertility Control in Ireland and Scotland: C.1880–1930, Some New Findings.' *UCD Centre for Economic Research Working Paper Series; WP89/14*, December 1989.

O'Brien, Conor Cruise. *Parnell and His Party, 1880–90*. Corrected Impression. Oxford: Oxford University Press, 1978.

O'Brien, Conor Cruise. *Ancestral Voices: Religion and Nationalism in Ireland*. Chicago: University of Chicago Press, 1995.

O'Connor, Ulick. *Oliver St John Gogarty: A Poet and His Times*. Dublin: O'Brien Press, 2000.

O'Leary, Philip. *The Prose Literature of the Gaelic Revival, 1881–1921: Ideology and Innovation*. University Park, Pa: Pennsylvania State University Press, 1994.

Oppel, Frances Nesbitt. *Mask and Tragedy: Yeats and Nietzsche, 1902–10*. Charlottesville: University Press of Virginia, 1987.

Oppel, Frances Nesbitt. *Mask and Tragedy: Yeats and Nietzsche, 1902–10*. Charlottesville: University Press of Virginia, 1987.

O'Sullivan, James, Katarzyna Bazarnik, Maciej Eder, and Jan Rybicki. 'Measuring Joycean Influences on Flann O'Brien.' *Digital Studies/Le Champ Numérique* 8, no. 1 (27 March 2018).

Paris, Václav. *The Evolutions of Modernist Epic*. Oxford: Oxford University Press, 2021.

Pašeta, Senia. 'Censorship and Its Critics in the Irish Free State, 1922–1932.' *Past & Present* 232, no. (1) (2003): 193–218.

Paul, Diane. 'Eugenics and the Left.' *Journal of the History of Ideas* 45, no. 4 (October 1984): 567–90.

Peppis, Paul. *Sciences of Modernism: Ethnography, Sexology, and Psychology*. Cambridge: Cambridge University Press, 2014.

Pick, Daniel. *Faces of Degeneration: A European Disorder, c.1848–c.1918*. Cambridge: Cambridge University Press, 1989.

Pihl, Lis. '"A Muzzle Made in Ireland": Irish Censorship and Signe Toksvig.' *Studies: An Irish Quarterly Review* 88, no. 352 (1999): 448–57.

Pilling, John. *Samuel Beckett's 'More Pricks Than Kicks': In a Strait of Two Wills*. London: Bloomsbury, 2013.

Porter, Roy, and Lesley A. Hall. *The Facts of Life: The Creation of Sexual Knowledge in Britain, 1650–1950*. New Haven: Yale University Press, 1995.

Powell, Fred. *The Political Economy of the Irish Welfare State: Church, State and Capital*. Bristol: Policy Press, 2017.

Preston, Margaret H., and Margaret Ó hÓgartaigh, eds. *Gender and Medicine in Ireland, 1700–1950*. Syracuse, New York: Syracuse University Press, 2012.

Proctor, Robert N. *Racial Hygiene: Medicine under the Nazis*. Cambridge, Mass: Harvard University Press, 2000.

Pruitt, Virginia D. 'Yeats and the Steinach Operation.' *American Imago* 34, no. 3 (Fall 1977): 287–96.

Pugh, Martin. *State and Society: A Social and Political History of Britain Since 1870*. 5th ed. London: Bloomsbury Academic, 2017.

Quétel, Claude. *History of Syphilis*. Cambridge: Polity Press, 1990.

Quine, Maria Sophia. *Population Politics in Twentieth-Century Europe: Fascist Dictatorships and Liberal Democracies*. Historical Connections. London: Routledge, 1996.

Rabaté, Jean-Michel, ed. *A Handbook of Modernism Studies*. Oxford: Wiley-Blackwell, 2013.

Rabaté, Jean-Michel. 'Intellectual and Aesthetic Influences.' In *The Cambridge Companion to Irish Modernism*, edited by Joe Cleary, 21–34. Cambridge: Cambridge University Press, 2014.

Rattigan, Cliona. '"Crimes of Passion of the Worst Character": Abortion Cases and Gender in Ireland, 1925–50.' In *Gender and Power in Irish History*, edited by Maryann Gialanella Valiulis, 115–40. Dublin: Irish Academic Press, 2009.

Reverby, Susan, ed. *Tuskegee's Truths: Rethinking the Tuskegee Syphilis Study*. Chapel Hill: University of North Carolina Press, 2000.

Reverby, Susan. *Examining Tuskegee: The Infamous Syphilis Study and Its Legacy*. Chapel Hill: University of North Carolina Press, 2013.

Reynolds, Paige, ed. *Modernism, Drama, and the Audience for Irish Spectacle*. Cambridge: Cambridge University Press, 2007.

Reynolds, Paige. 'Kate O'Brien.' Special issue, *Irish University Review* 48, no. 1 (May 2018).

Richardson, Caleb. '"They Are Not Worthy of Themselves": The Tailor and Ansty Debates of 1942.' *Éire-Ireland* 42, no. 3 (2007): 148–72.

Ritschel, Nelson O'Ceallaigh. 'Shaw and the Dublin Repertory Theatre.' *Shaw* 35, no. 2 (2015): 168–84.

Riordan, Susannah. 'Venereal Disease in the Irish Free State: The Politics of Public Health.' *Irish Historical Studies* 35, no. 139 (2007): 345–64.

Riordan, Susannah. '"A Probable Source of Infection": The Limitations of Venereal Disease Policy, 1943–1951.' In *Gender and Medicine in Ireland, 1700–1950*, edited by Margaret H. Preston and Margaret Ó hÓgartaigh, 203–20. Syracuse, New York: Syracuse University Press, 2012.

Riordan, Susannah. 'In Search of a Broadminded Saint: The Westmorland Lock Hospital in the Twentieth Century.' *Irish Economic and Social History* 39, no. 1 (1 December 2012): 73–93.

Ritschel, Nelson O'Ceallaigh. *Bernard Shaw, W.T. Stead, and the New Journalism: Whitechapel, Parnell, Titanic, and the Great War*. Cham, Switzerland: Palgrave Macmillan, 2018.

Robb, George. 'The Way of All Flesh: Degeneration, Eugenics, and the Gospel of Free Love.' *Journal of the History of Sexuality* 6, no. 4 (April 1996): 589–603.

Rose, June. *Marie Stopes and the Sexual Revolution*. London: Faber and Faber, 1992.

Sandel, Michael J. *The Case Against Perfection: Ethics in the Age of Genetic Engineering*. Cambridge, Mass: Belknap Press, 2007.

Schaffner, Anna Katharina. 'Fiction as Evidence: On the Uses of Literature in Nineteenth-Century Sexological Discourse.' *Comparative Literature Studies* 48, no. 2 (2011): 165–99.

Schaffner, Anna Katharina. *Modernism and Perversion*. Houndmills: Palgrave Macmillan, 2012.

Schotten, C. Heike. *Nietzsche's Revolution: Décadence, Politics, and Sexuality.* New York: Palgrave Macmillan, 2009.

Scull, Andrew. *Hysteria: The Disturbing History.* Oxford: Oxford University Press, 2011.

Schneider, Erik Holmes. *Zois in Nighttown: Prostitution and Syphilis in the Trieste of James Joyce and Italo Svevo (1880–1920).* London: Ashgrove Publishing, 2014.

Seaber, Luke, and Michael Shallcross. 'The Trouble with Modernism: A Dialogue.' *The Modernist Review*, no. 10 (28 June 2019). https://modernistreviewcouk. wordpress.com/2019/06/28/the-trouble-with-modernism/.

Sedgwick, Eve Kosofsky. *Epistemology of the Closet.* Updated with a New Preface. Berkeley: University of California Press, 2008.

Shepherd-Barr, Kirsten. *Theatre and Evolution from Ibsen to Beckett.* New York: Columbia University Press, 2015.

Showalter, Elaine. 'Syphilis, Sexuality, and the Fiction of the Fin de Siècle.' In *Sex, Politics, and Science in the Nineteenth-Century Novel*, edited by Ruth Bernard Yeazell, 88–115. Baltimore: Johns Hopkins University Press, 1990.

Showalter, Elaine. *Sexual Anarchy: Gender and Culture at the Fin de Siècle.* London: Virago, 1992.

Showalter, Elaine. *The Female Malady: Women, Madness, and English Culture, 1830–1980.* Reprinted. London: Virago, 2009.

Siedler, Victor J. 'Reason, Desire, and Male Sexuality.' In *The Cultural Construction of Sexuality*, edited by Pat Caplan, Repr. [1987], 82–112. London: Routledge, 1996.

Singerman, David Roth. 'Keynesian Eugenics and the Goodness of the World.' *Journal of British Studies* 55, no. 3 (July 2016): 538–65.

Smith, James M. 'The Politics of Sexual Knowledge: The Origins of Ireland's Sexual Containment Culture and the Carrigan Report (1931).' *Journal of the History of Sexuality* 13, no. 2 (April 2004): 208–33.

Smith, James M. *Ireland's Magdalen Laundries and the Nation's Architecture of Containment.* Manchester: Manchester University Press, 2008.

Smith, Virginia Sarah. *Clean: A History of Personal Hygiene and Purity.* Oxford: Oxford University Press, 2007.

Smith, Warren Sylvester. *Bishop of Everywhere: Bernard Shaw and the Life Force.* University Park: Pennsylvania State University Press, 1982.

Söder, Hans-Peter. 'Disease and Health as Contexts of Modernity: Max Nordau as a Critic of Fin-de-Siècle Modernism.' *German Studies Review* 14, no. 3 (October 1991): 473.

Soloski, Alexis. '"The Great Imitator": Staging Syphilis in *A Doll's House* and *Ghosts*.' *Modern Drama* 56, no. 3 (2013): 287–305.

Soloway, Richard A. *Birth Control and the Population Question in England, 1877–1930.* Chapel Hill: University of North Carolina Press, 1982.

Soloway, Richard A. *Demography and Degeneration: Eugenics and the Declining Birthrate in Twentieth-Century Britain.* 3rd ed. Chapel Hill: University of North Carolina Press, 2001.

Steinman, Michael. *Yeats's Heroic Figures: Wilde, Parnell, Swift, Casement.* Albany: State University of New York Press, 1983.

Stewart, Paul. *Sex and Aesthetics in Samuel Beckett's Work*. New York: Palgrave Macmillan, 2011.

Stonebridge, Lyndsey. *The Destructive Element: British Psychoanalysis and Modernism*. New York: Routledge, 1998.

Szasz, Thomas. *The Manufacture of Madness: A Comparative Study of the Inquisition and the Mental Health Movement*. New ed. Syracuse, New York: Syracuse University Press, 1997.

Szasz, Thomas. *The Medicalization of Everyday Life: Selected Essays*. Syracuse, New York: Syracuse University Press, 2007.

Szreter, Simon, and Kate Fisher. *Sex Before the Sexual Revolution: Intimate Life in England, 1918-1963*. Cambridge: Cambridge University Press, 2010.

Taaffe, Carol. *Ireland Through the Looking-Glass: Flann O'Brien, Myles na gCopaleen and Irish Cultural Debate*. Cork: Cork University Press, 2008.

Taaffe, Carol. 'Irish Modernism.' In *The Oxford Handbook of Modernisms*, edited by Peter Brooker, Andrzej Gąsiorek, Deborah Longworth, and Andrew Thacker, 782–96. Oxford: Oxford University Press, 2010.

Taylor, Becky. 'Immigration, Statecraft and Public Health: The 1920 Aliens Order, Medical Examinations and the Limitations of the State in England.' *Social History of Medicine* 29, no. 3 (August 2016): 512–33.

Teitelbaum, Michael S., and J. M. Winter. *The Fear of Population Decline*. Orlando: Academic Press, 1985.

Tobin, Fergal. *The Best of Decades: Ireland in the Nineteen Sixties*. Dublin: Gill and Macmillan, 1984.

Tobin, Patricia Drechsel. *Time and the Novel: The Genealogical Imperative*. Princeton: Princeton University Press, 1975.

Toomey, Deirdre. 'Moran's Collar: Yeats and Irish Ireland.' In *Yeats Annual No. 12*, edited by Warwick Gould and Edna Longley, 45–83. London: Macmillan, 1996.

Tosh, John. 'What Should Historians Do with Masculinity? Reflections on Nineteenth-Century Britain.' *History Workshop* 38 (1994): 179–202.

Tracy, Robert. 'Introduction.' In *Rhapsody in Stephen's Green: The Insect Play*, by Flann O'Brien, edited by Robert Tracy, 1–17. Dublin: Lilliput Press, 1994.

Travis, Charles. 'The "Historical Poetics" of Kate O'Brien's Limerick: A Critical Literary Geography of Saorstát Éireann and the 1937 Bunreacht Na HÉireann Plebiscite.' *Irish Geography* 42, no. 3 (November 2009): 323–41.

Turda, Marius. *Modernism and Eugenics*. Basingstoke: Palgrave Macmillan, 2010.

Turda, Marius. 'Race, Science, and Eugenics in the Twentieth Century.' In *The Oxford Handbook of the History of Eugenics*, edited by Alison Bashford and Philippa Levine, 62–79. Oxford: Oxford University Press, 2010.

Turda, Marius, and Paul Weindling, eds. *'Blood and Homeland': Eugenics and Racial Nationalism in Central and Southeast Europe, 1900-1940*. Budapest: Central European University Press, 2007.

Valente, Joseph, ed. *Quare Joyce*. Ann Arbor: University of Michigan Press, 1998.

Valente, Joseph. *The Myth of Manliness in Irish National Culture, 1880-1922*. Urbana, Ill: University of Illinois Press, 2011.

Valentine, Kylie. *Psychoanalysis, Psychiatry, and Modernist Literature*. Houndmills: Palgrave Macmillan, 2003.

Van Camp, Nathan. 'How Liberal Is (the Liberal Critique) of a Liberal Eugenics?' *HUMANA.MENTE Journal of Philosophical Studies* 7, no. 26 (May 2014): 223–38.

Vanderham, Paul. *James Joyce and Censorship: The Trials of Ulysses*. Basingstoke: Macmillan, 2002.

Waisbren, Burton A., and Florence L. Walzl. 'Paresis and the Priest: James Joyce's Symbolic Use of Syphilis in "The Sisters."' *Annals of Internal Medicine* 80, no. 6 (1 June 1974): 758.

Walkowitz, Judith R. *Prostitution and Victorian Society: Women, Class, and the State*. Cambridge: Cambridge University Press, 1980.

Walshe, Eibhear. *Kate O'Brien: A Writing Life*. Dublin: Irish Academic Press, 2006.

Walshe, Eibhear. 'Kate O'Brien.' In *A History of Modern Irish Women's Literature*, edited by Heather Ingman and Clíona Ó Gallchoir, 227–43. Cambridge University Press, 2018.

Walshe, Eibhear, ed. *Ordinary People Dancing: Essays on Kate O'Brien*. Cork: Cork University Press, 1993.

Walzl, Florence L. 'Joyce's' The Sisters': A Development.' *James Joyce Quarterly* 10, no. 4 (1973): 375–421.

Ward, Margaret, ed. *Hanna Sheehy Skeffington: Suffragette and Sinn Féiner Her Memoirs and Political Writings*. Dublin: University College Dublin Press, 2017.

Weeks, Jeffrey. *Sexuality and Its Discontents: Meanings, Myths, and Modern Sexualities*. Reprinted. London: Routledge, 1985.

Weeks, Jeffrey. *Sex, Politics, and Society: The Regulation of Sexuality Since 1800*. Third Edition [1981]. London: Pearson, 2012.

Weindling, Paul. 'Ernst Haeckel, *Darwinismus*, and the Secularization of Nature.' In *History, Humanity, and Evolution: Essays for John C. Greene*, edited by John C. Greene and James R. Moore, 311–27. Cambridge: Cambridge University Press, 1989.

Weinstein, David. *Utilitarianism and the New Liberalism*. Cambridge: Cambridge University Press, 2007.

Weir, David. 'A Womb of His Own: Joyce's Sexual Aesthetics.' *James Joyce Quarterly* 31, no. 3 (Spring 1994): 207–31.

Whitworth, Michael H., ed. 'Introduction.' In *Modernism: A Guide to Criticism*, 3–60. Oxford: Wiley-Blackwell, 2007.

Whitworth, Michael H., ed. *Modernism: A Guide to Criticism*. Oxford: Wiley-Blackwell, 2007.

Williams, Raymond. *Politics of Modernism: Against the New Conformists*. Edited by Tony Pinkney. London: Verso, 1989.

Wilson, Aimee Armande. *Conceived in Modernism: The Aesthetics and Politics of Birth Control*. New York: Bloomsbury Academic, 2016.

Wimbush, Andy. 'Hey Prestos and Humilities: Two of Beckett's Christs.' *Journal of Beckett Studies* 25, no. 1 (April 2016): 78–95.

Wollaeger, Mark A., and Matt Eatough, eds. *The Oxford Handbook of Global Modernisms*. Oxford: Oxford University Press, 2012.

Wolff, Tamsen. *Mendel's Theatre: Heredity, Eugenics, and Early Twentieth-Century American Drama*. Houndmills: Palgrave Macmillan, 2009.

Worboys, Michael. 'Unsexing Gonorrhoea: Bacteriologists, Gynaecologists, and Suffragists in Britain, 1860–1920.' *Social History of Medicine* 17, no. 1 (April 2004): 41–59.

Worboys, Michael. 'Chlamydia: A Disease without a History.' In *The Hidden Affliction: Sexually Transmitted Infections and Infertility in History*, edited by Simon Szreter, 153–83. Rochester: University of Rochester Press, 2019.

Yde, Matthew. *Bernard Shaw and Totalitarianism: Longing for Utopia*. Houndmills: Palgrave Macmillan, 2013.

Zimmerman, Jonathan. *Too Hot to Handle: A Global History of Sex Education*. Princeton: Princeton University Press, 2015.

Zweiniger-Bargielowska, Ina. *Managing the Body*. Oxford: Oxford University Press, 2010.

Index

For the benefit of digital users, indexed terms that span two pages (e.g., 52–53) may, on occasion, appear on only one of those pages.

and Irish marriage patterns 92–7
and masculine virility 56–61, 77–8, 93–7,
    100–2
and primitive sexuality 82–92
and psychiatry 59–60, 59n.81
and the rhetoric of health 70–1, 77–8, 81,
    85, 90–2, 94–5, 98
and sexual precocity 82–4
autobiography fragments 82–5
childhood relationship with Florence
    Ross 82–5
evolutionary theory and the Aran
    islanders 87–92
Yeats's posthumous construction
    of 97–101
The Aran Islands 86–92, 98–9
'Can We Go Back into Our Mother's
    Womb?' 59–61, 77–8
'The Curse' 69–71
'Étude Morbide' 59n.81, 81n.46, 98–9
In the Shadow of the Glen 59n.81, 99–100
'The Oppression of the Hills' 59n.81
'The People of the Glens' 59n.81
The Playboy of the Western World 1–2,
    21–3, 56–62, 69–71, 77–8, 92–7, 99,
    101–2, 179–81, 258–60, 265–6
'Vita Vecchia' 98
The Well of the Saints 97
syphilis (*see also*, Contagious Diseases Acts;
    venereal disease)
and anti-enlistment campaigns 115–17,
    130, 244–5, 254
and anti-Semitism 123–32
and Bloom's potato 129–32
and degeneration 49–56, 134–6
and the Gaelic League 128–9
and Parnell 49–56
and sex work 13–14, 69–71, 70n.3,
    105–7, 120–3, 128–32, 134–9,
    244–5, 251–2, 254–5
and social hygiene 13–14
and stigma 13–14, 20–1, 69–71, 105–7,
    119n.36, 251–2
and the Tuskegee Syphilis
    Experiment 7n.21
as source of concern for British colonial
    administrators 23–5, 134–8
congenital syphilis 49–51, 53, 133–6
general paralysis of the insane
    (GPI) 49–56, 107–8, 110–15

in O'Brien's *The Ante-Room* 205–13
in Joyce's writing 107–17, 123–4, 126–39
locomotor ataxia 128
medical and social significance 12n.46
rates of infection in the British
    military 117, 119–20, 122, 244–7

Taaffe, Carol 235–6, 238–9
Talbot, Matt 258–60
testicular anaesthesia 44–5
Tobin, Fergal 69
Toksvig, Signe
    diaries 199n.32
    Eve's Doctor 198–200
    gynaecology in *Eve's Doctor* 198–200
    large audience for *Eve's Doctor* 198–200
Tracy, Robert 258–60
Trinity College, Dublin Philosophical
    Society 241–2
tuberculosis 96–7, 118

United States vs One Book Entitled
    Ulysses 261n.100

Valente, Joseph 46–7, 63n.89
Van Camp, Nathan 213n.73
venereal disease
    and anti-enlistment campaigns 115–17,
        130, 244–5, 254
    and anti-Semitism 123–32
    and British immigration policy 7n.20
    and hygiene 12–14
    and Sinn Féin 115–20, 122–6, 129–30,
        132–6, 189, 244–5, 254
    and the Censorship Act 165–7
    and the *Playboy* riots 1–2, 69–71
    and United States immigration policy 5–9
    gonorrhoea (*see* gonorrhoea)
    in the *Irish Times* 241–7
    in Joyce's writing 107–17, 123–4, 126–39
    in O'Brien's *The Ante-Room* 205–13
    in O'Brien's *Without My Cloak* 200–2
    in O'Nolan's *Cruiskeen Lawn*
        columns 245–7
    in O'Nolan's *The Hard Life* 250–7
    in O'Nolan's *Slattery's Sago Saga* 254–5
    Interdepartmental Committee of
        Inquiry Regarding Venereal
        Disease 151–3
    Joyce's brush with 118–19, 118n.35

venereal disease (*cont.*)
  Local Government Board Venereal Disease
      Regulations and Service 5–9, 18–20
  Royal Commission on Venereal
      Diseases 5–9
  syphilis (*see* syphilis)
Vichy France (*see also*, Beckett, Samuel)
  Alexis Carrel 184–5, 185n.158
  and eugenics 184–6
  Fondation Française pour l'Étude des
      Problèmes Humains 184–5

Waisbren, Burton A. 107–8
Walzl, Florence L. 107–8, 108n.5
War of Independence, the
  and sex work 105–7
  climate of moral panic 151–3
Waterford Vigilance Committee 151–3
Webb, Beatrice 219–20
Weir, David 65–6
Westermarck, Edward 80–1, 87
Westmoreland Lock Hospital, the 120–1
Wilde, Oscar 54n.61, 113–15
Women's Freedom League, the 196–7, 200,
      200n.36
Woman's Life 237–8, 238n.17
Woman's Way 237–8, 238n.17
Wyse Power, Jane (Siobhán Bean an
      Phaoraigh) 196–7, 196n.20

Yeats, W.B.
  and celibacy 100–1, 164–5
  and censorship 155–8, 163n.76, 164–7
  and Darwin 84–5
  and de Valera 225n.117
  and D.P. Moran 72–6
  and eugenics 97–101, 159–61, 164–5,
      168–9, 183, 189
  and hygienic autonomy 36–8, 46, 62–4, 66
  and hysteria 46, 46n.33, 59n.81
  and Irish Ireland *ressentiment* 98, 100–1

and Malthusianism 164–5
and Mannin 198n.30
and Nietzsche 100–1
and Parnell 36–8, 56–7, 62–4, 66,
      78n.34
and the *Playboy* riots 1–2, 14–15, 18–20,
      46, 46n.33, 69–71, 70n.3, 95–7,
      99–101
and reproduction 36–8, 62–4, 66
and Spencer 89–90
and Steinach rejuvenation operation 37–8,
      198n.30
and Swift's *Modest Proposal* 164–5
and Synge 1–2, 46, 46n.33, 89–92, 96–102
'A Prayer for My Daughter' 167n.96
'The Blood and the Moon' 78n.34
Cathleen ni Houlihan 75
'The Celtic Element in Literature' 89–90
'The Censorship and St Thomas
      Aquinas' 156–8
The Countess Cathleen 56–7
Diarmuid and Grania 74
'The Irish Censorship' 163n.76, 164–7
The King's Threshold 120
'Leda and the Swan' 64
Memoirs 69–71, 70n.3, 91–2, 98–101
'Nationality and Literature' 89–90
On Baile's Strand 62–4, 66
On the Boiler 159–61, 168–9
'On Those That Hated *The Playboy of
      the Western World*, 1907' 46,
      46n.33, 101
'Parnell's Funeral' 36–7, 225n.117
'Preface' to *The Well of the Saints* 97–9
Purgatory 167n.96, 183
Synge and the Ireland of His Time 1–2,
      23n.80, 69, 98–9
The Trembling of the Veil 71–2
Young Ireland 72–4, 76–7, 129–30, 150

Zola, Emile 177–9